Praise for *Standing on the Shoulders*

One of the year's most **inspiring** books

– Holly Willoughby, *This Morning*

Extraordinary

– Julia Kuttner, *Sunday Express*

Such an **incredible** read

– Zoe Ball, *BBC Radio 2*

An **extraordinary** book

– Nihal Arthanayake, *BBC Radio 5 Live*

Dan Walker was born in Crawley in West Sussex in 1977. He is a TV presenter and journalist who recently moved to become one of the faces of Channel 5. Previously he presented BBC1's *Breakfast* for six years and *Football Focus* for twelve years. His other books are *Remarkable People: Extraordinary Stories of Everyday Lives, Dan Walker's Football Thronkersaurus: Football's Finest Tales* and *Dan Walker's Magic, Mud & Maradona: Cup Football's Finest Tales*. He lives in Sheffield with his wife, three children and Winne the dog.

Also by Dan Walker and available from Headline

Remarkable People: Extraordinary Stories of Everyday Lives

DAN WALKER

Standing on the Shoulders

Incredible heroes and how they inspire us

HEADLINE

First published in 2022 by
HEADLINE PUBLISHING GROUP

First published in paperback in 2023 by
HEADLINE PUBLISHING GROUP

1

Cataloguing in Publication Data is available from the British Library

ISBN 978 1 4722 9128 8

Typeset by CC Book Production

Printed and bound in Great Britain by Clays Ltd, Elcograf S.p.A.

HEADLINE PUBLISHING GROUP
An Hachette UK Company
Carmelite House
50 Victoria Embankment
London EC4Y 0DZ

www.headline.co.uk
www.hachette.co.uk

CONTENTS

Foreword by Rose Ayling-Ellis   vii

Introduction   ix

'Every day I climb a mountain'   1

A Rose in Bloom   32

Three Dads, Three Daughters   69

Four Notes   112

The Man with the Narwhal Tusk   143

Jimi   174

Strictly Nadiya   201

Beyond the Pandemic   239

Still Remarkable   272

The Truth About Monsters   299

Acknowledgements   331

Index   339

FOREWORD

By Rose Ayling-Ellis

I first met Dan back in 2021 when *Strictly Come Dancing* started and we gathered to do our very first dance, the group dance. We were put in a room full of celebrities, and we were all extremely nervy. I was the most nervous I had ever been. I didn't see myself as a 'celebrity' as I had only been on *EastEnders* for a year and no one knew me, and yet here I was surrounded by these famous personalities. I couldn't believe I was in the same room as all of them!

Dan was one of the people that I recognised from his years of regular appearances on my morning TV screen. He was chatting away to someone else and, after a bit of hesitation, I finally picked up the courage to approach him and introduce myself. I immediately felt the warmness and kindness radiate from him. Our very first conversation stood out and made a huge impression on me. We talked about me being deaf, appearing on the biggest show ever and how terrified we both were; we even joked about our terrible dance moves! He told me about his dad being deaf, some of the frustration he had experienced and about what he learned from his dad. As I got to know Dan better, I came to realise that was one of his standout qualities: it was always about other people's experiences, never about him.

This is what the book is all about. It's never about Dan, it's about the people Dan meets in his life. It's an important lesson for all of us. It is what we can learn from other people's experiences that shapes us into who we are and how we could do better for others. It is what makes us all so beautiful: the imperfect, ugly, unimaginable experience that life throws at us, and finding a way to come out on the brighter side. However, one important thing that I noticed throughout the book is that all these people never did it alone. They always had someone reaching out or wanting to reach out. No one can do it alone. In the chapter that Dan wrote about me, it was my mother who stayed by my side, she was that person to me, and I am honoured that she is a part of this book.

In these crazy times, especially with what's going on around the world, we all need that someone by our side. Whether it is our friends, family, a stranger or even our pets. The act of kindness, no matter how small, can change everything for others. Sometimes we forget that. But most importantly, sometimes we forget to reach out for help when we need to. I love the fact that Dan has called this *Standing on the Shoulders*. It is all about what is important in life: that we are who we are because of the people around us. The title perfectly encapsulates the book and I have really enjoyed reading about the people in it. I hope you do too.

INTRODUCTION

It's never a good idea to make assumptions, so I am just going to remind you that the book you are about to read is a sort of follow-up to one that I wrote a few years ago called *Remarkable People*.

It was lovely that so many people read and enjoyed the last one but, if you know nothing about it, fear not . . . you don't have to have read a single page of that to enjoy this one. The themes are the same but you don't need to have any previous knowledge of the characters involved and you can always read it later. I suppose the one benefit of reading *Remarkable People* before *Standing on the Shoulders* is that you probably have an expectation of what you are going to get.

In music, they talk about a 'tricky second album'; in football it's 'second season syndrome'. After the success of *Remarkable People*, I was really keen to write about a fresh bunch of humble heroes and follow the same simple pattern as before. Here are some amazing people I have had the privilege of meeting: let's see what makes them tick and try and learn something along the way.

The last book came out in the middle of a global pandemic and things have changed a lot in the world since then. The cost-of-living crisis is biting hard at millions of people across the UK, and the conflict in Ukraine dominated the international headlines in the first half of 2022. In my own little world, I finally gave in and agreed to go on *Strictly Come Dancing* and, to my great surprise, it will go down as one of my best ever experiences on TV – as you will find out when you get to the chapter about my 'professional partner'.

Over the last few years, particularly since I started presenting *BBC Breakfast* and definitely since I went on *Strictly*, I have noticed that people are taking more of an interest in my opinion on certain issues. I did a lot of interviews about my recent move from the breakfast sofa to Channel 5 and I had to spend quite a bit of my time gently dodging questions about my thoughts on big topics of the day. Of course I have opinions, but my broadcasting has never been centred or dependent on them. I love to bring the best out of those around me.

When I interview a politician, I don't want you to watch that interview and think 'Well, I now know what Dan thinks about that'. I want you to be able to listen to them and make your mind up about whether they are someone you can trust, believe in and vote for. I firmly believe you can still do that and ask the tough, pertinent and thoughtful questions.

As a journalist, I am far more interested in what other people feel than what I think. I love talking to others and finding out what motivates them, what drives them on, what inspires them, how they respond to the highs and lows of life and how those varying emotions translate into action.

In a world where you are often told what to think or, perhaps more truthfully, what you are not allowed to think, I am not laying out an ideology in this book. I really hope that it never comes across as preachy or unnecessarily argumentative. The whole plan here is to simply show you some people who have incredible stories to tell.

You will hopefully find a huge range of voices. I conducted hours of interviews with the people in here and, in some cases, have spent large portions of my life with them. Some you will have heard of, some you will know quite well and others will be new to you. Some I met first on the *BBC Breakfast* sofa and others have wandered into my life in different ways, but one thing unites them all . . . they are all eye-openers. What I mean by that is they all allow us to see a little further than we would on our own.

Our middle daughter is disappointed by the book title. After *Remarkable People*, she told me this book should have been called *Remark at the Remarkable People* and she thought I had missed a trick. Jessica was not particularly impressed when I told her the title of this one. *Standing on the Shoulders* is half a quote from a letter written by Isaac Newton in 1675. The great physician and mathematician wrote that 'If I have seen further it is by standing on the shoulders of giants' and that's what I feel I have been able to do by speaking to the people in this book.

You will find doctors in here, three normal dads, a communications officer, a Hollywood superstar, a convicted murderer, a bomb survivor, a knight of the realm, bereaved parents, heroic friends, migrants, a couple of musical geniuses, a two-time world champion, a double amputee, a *Strictly* winner and many many more.

There is tragedy and triumph, there are heroes and villains and themes like forgiveness, rehabilitation, loss, love, grief, pain, trust, truth, faith and friendship regularly rise to the surface. We often talk about post-traumatic stress but, as one of our contributors comments, there is such a thing as post-traumatic growth and you'll hopefully see much of that too.

It is lovely that so many people have been waiting patiently for the publication of this book and I look forward to conversations about it on social media, in the street, on train platforms, in the frozen-food aisle of the supermarket, or maybe even at a book-signing somewhere. I couldn't do any of them last time because of Covid. I still receive so many beautiful messages about *Remarkable People* and I really hope this book has a similar impact. When I first mentioned that I was writing again, I received the most beautiful message from someone who wishes to remain anonymous but was happy for me to put it in the introduction.

Dear Dan
The fact that you are writing a new book is the best news I've heard in a while. I read your last one in the middle of the global pandemic and, I have to say, the people in there got me through. They taught me so much from their experiences and, through the tears and the laughter of each chapter, I continue to learn. It was exactly the book I needed at exactly the right time. I was inspired and encouraged in equal measure and I hope the next one does the same.

My ultimate aim for this book is that you are inspired and encouraged by the people in these pages, as I have been. I hope through their testimony, they are able to challenge your preconceptions and your way of thinking as they did mine. Researching and writing *Standing on the Shoulders* has enabled me to understand a lot more about the world around me, and I trust it does the same for you.

'EVERY DAY I CLIMB A MOUNTAIN'

Monday 22 May 2017 was a dad-and-daughter date night for Martin and Eve Hibbert. Growing up in Bolton, music had always been a huge part of Martin's life. His mum loved The Beatles, The Carpenters and Motown, which was always on in the house somewhere. Martin was desperate to make sure his own children shared that same love of music, so he used to love taking Eve to concerts.

Martin was a dutiful dad. 'Eve was always going on about Ariana Grande, so I got all her CDs and started listening to them in the car to get into her music too. I've always been able to pick up the words pretty quickly. For Christmas that year (2016) I got Eve tickets for us to go and see her in concert in Manchester the following May. She was so excited when she opened the present. I was wearing this T-shirt which said 'Ariana Grande Is My Wife' which I think she saw the funny side of. The whole first part of 2017 was basically a build-up to that night at the MEN Arena.'

Finally, the day came. It was a Monday night and Eve had her mock exams starting in just a few weeks so Martin had promised Eve's mum that he wouldn't let her stay up too late. They had their tickets for the show and, even before they arrived at the arena, the plan was to leave during the encore to make sure they avoided the legendary arena traffic jams.

'It's impossible to get away if you all leave at the same time as everyone else,' says Martin with a smile on his face that tells you he's been stuck in that traffic before. 'It can take ninety minutes to get out and I didn't want to be sat in a queue for ages fielding calls from her mum telling me she needed to be in bed.'

The night had gone perfectly. They had been to one of their favourite Manchester restaurants – San Carlo – and arrived at the venue in good time.

'The one thing that really sticks in my mind,' remembers Martin, 'was the scream when Ariana Grande came out on stage. I've been to the biggest nights at Old Trafford, but it was nothing compared to the noise at the MEN that night. She put on an amazing show and Eve was so happy. Our cut-off was 10.30 and when the time came, I told Eve we had to go, but she was desperate to stay. I knew that would be the case, but I dragged her away and we started the walk back to our car.'

Martin and Eve walked down from their seats to the ground floor level and then, like many of the other early leavers, made their way out into the vestibule of the arena. Eve was just in front of Martin as they were heading towards the main doors. They walked past the terrorist but never saw him.

'I had my head down and I was running, or at least the fastest walk that I could do,' remembers Martin. 'There were loads of people there either trying to get out or waiting to pick up children who were coming out of the concert.' Martin pauses as he thinks over the night in his head. 'It's hard to say for certain, but I reckon there must have been a couple of hundred people around us.'

When the bomb was detonated, it's estimated that Martin and Eve were somewhere between five and seven metres from the terrorist. Everyone around them died instantly. Pieces of shrapnel were travelling at speeds of around 100 mph. Some people died forty metres away from the centre of the explosion having been hit by a single piece of metal. Martin's body was covered in it and his daughter had been hit in the head.

'I remember it as an almighty bang,' says Martin, taking his time to recall the events clearly. 'There was a really high-pitched noise. I've never been hit by a ten-tonne truck but I imagine that is what it felt like. This might sound a bit stupid, but I wasn't worried or scared at the time. I remember feeling very tranquil and surreal. I was just concerned about Eve.'

What Martin didn't know was that one of the bolts from the blast had completely severed his spinal cord. Eve had been knocked unconscious instantly by the blow to her head.

'I don't know how long it was after the explosion but the first thing I saw was an arm on the floor and I thought it was mine. I checked and thankfully I still had both of them. There was this strange, eerie silence for a couple seconds before people started screaming in pain.'

The situation was incredibly serious for many of the people in the arena that night and Martin was one of them. One of the bolts had struck him in the neck and severed two of his main arteries. The blood was pouring out of his body. A security guard called Chris was one of the first to come and see if he was ok.

'I could feel my body was shutting down,' recalls Martin. 'I knew it wasn't good and at that moment it was hard to have any hope of leaving the arena alive. I looked up at Chris and asked him to tell my wife that I loved her, but I wasn't giving up. I knew that if I closed my eyes that would be it. I could feel the strength going out of me, but I also knew that I was the only one who could make a difference for Eve. I had to try and stay awake, stay active for her sake. She needed just as much help as me.'

The 'help' that Martin and many others needed that night wasn't fast in coming. The subsequent inquiry into the emergency response highlighted a number of failings in communication and leadership which led to Martin, and many other people, being left untreated for far too long. Martin was determined that he was going to stay awake until the paramedics arrived.

'I remember that, in all the chaos and the screaming, I had a little laugh to myself. I had so many plans about what I wanted to do with my life and yet, here I was, about to die on a freezing cold concrete floor. The only thing driving me on was the knowledge that Eve needed me. Chris, the security guard, kept asking me my name and my address and I just kept saying it back to him over and over again. All the time my body was closing down, but I managed to fight it for an hour.'

Eve was lying unconscious next to her dad. The fourteen-year-old was going blue. She desperately needed help and Martin was doing everything he could.

'At one point they put a cover over her face to say that she had died. I begged them to take it off because I could still see her lips quivering. I could see she was still there. I could see she was gasping for air. That drove me on and gave me the strength I needed to stay awake. I knew that if I went under, they'd cover Eve's face again and we'd both be goners. I just had to keep going until the help arrived.'

Paul Harvey was on shift that night. He and his colleague were waiting in an ambulance outside Manchester Royal Infirmary. 'The first thing we heard was that there was a potential fire at the arena,' remembers Paul. His account tallies with the official inquiry which showed how information was both confused and inaccurate. 'Initially we got told to stand by, and then we were told to head to the arena as quickly as possible. We were the second or third vehicle to arrive, but one of the things we were told was that there might be an active gunman still inside, so all the emergency help was held back from the venue.'

When Paul and his colleague were eventually given the all-clear to enter the site, their job was initially to assess the walking wounded. That thirty-minute job continues to have a profound impact on Paul. 'I'd been doing the job for twenty years, but that was the first major incident I'd been involved in. We all take part in training exercises, but nothing prepares you for the real thing. I went into autopilot. We were dealing with a constant stream of people,' says Paul. 'I remember there were a couple who couldn't find their daughter and a young girl with burst eardrums. She couldn't hear a thing. People were just wandering around with empty heads. They were all in a daze and, it might sound silly, but that affected me so much.'

When I spoke to Paul, his wife Louise was sat next to him at the kitchen table. You could instantly tell the bond between the two of them when they started speaking. Paul has been through a lot and his wife has been there every step of the way.

'I could tell it was serious when our daughter called me to tell me I had to come home straightaway,' says Louise. 'She said that Paul was at the bottom of the garden crying.'

This was the night after the bomb at the arena. Paul was trying to get through a shift like normal, but it just wasn't happening. The shock and trauma of the previous evening was beginning to kick in. Louise remembers it well.

'He was silently struggling. He was there but he wasn't there, if you know what I mean? I could tell he wasn't sleeping. He was wide awake, and he was absolutely shattered at the same time. For weeks it was hard to see a way out of things. Every time the bomb was on the news, every time there was an Ariana Grande song on the radio, he was in pieces. It's still hard for him to listen to "One Last Time" even now. That was the last song she played at the concert that night. It was hard for me to see him crying, but I was so proud of him for being able to accept that he needed help.'

Counselling has really helped Paul to deal with what he saw that night. He has also taken great strength from his friendship with Martin. The first time they met, Paul was lifting him into the back of his ambulance on a 'stretcher' made from a security hoarding.

'We had been dealing with the walking wounded for about half an hour,' says Paul, 'when we were asked to move a patient.' That patient was Martin Hibbert.

Martin had stayed awake long enough to be seen by the trained medical staff. Eve was still unconscious, but alive, and had been taken to Manchester Children's Hospital.

'The last thing I remember from the night,' says a tearful Martin, 'was Eve being taken away on a security hoarding. I was thankful that she was being looked after and I just felt that at least I had done my job as a dad. I don't mean for this to sound morbid because I still wanted to live, but I thought, I can close my eyes now . . . I can die now. I had seen the way that people were looking at me and I had accepted that death was the most likely outcome.'

While Eve was on her way to the specialist children's hospital, Paul was told to take Martin to Wythenshawe Hospital, a thirty-minute drive from the arena. Paul quickly assessed his new patient and decided that there was no way he would survive that journey. He defied the order and went instead to the major trauma unit at the Salford Royal. That decision saved Martin's life.

Paul has clear memories of that journey and recalls it with classic medical understatement. 'You could tell Martin was poorly. He was going in and out of consciousness and I was constantly trying to rouse him. The neck injury was obvious, and we knew he was bad internally because he kept bringing up blood and his observations were all over the place. I talked to him about his family and his work. He told me about his daughter, but I think he thought that trip in the back of my ambulance was going to be the final journey of his life. Over the years I have seen lots of people deteriorate on me, but I was determined we weren't going to lose him. I assured him that he was going to be ok and, in my head, I said, "You're not going anywhere, mate. I am going to get you to the hospital alive.'"

The first time I met Martin was on the *BBC Breakfast* sofa – four years after the blast. Martin had come in to talk about his work with the Spinal Injuries Association and his desire to raise money for others in the same situation by attempting to climb Mount Kilimanjaro.

You get to meet all sorts on that sofa, and I'm fascinated by how people respond to trials in their lives. You get to see the full spectrum of human reaction. Some people struggle to talk about it, some break down as soon as they sit down, some worry about whether they are doing the right thing, and there are also some who carry that sense of responsibility to others. Martin was one of those.

'Hello, Dan! Hi, Louise!' he shouted as he wheeled himself across the studio floor and up the ramp to the raised area before shuffling across to the far side of the sofa. There was something about him from minute one. There was a huge smile across his face but also a sense of pride and just the right amount of nervousness about being on live television. As per usual, we had read all about Martin's story before he arrived on *BBC Breakfast*, but it was only when he started talking that what he had been through really hit home.

Martin had a real gift. He was able to explain what the night was like without being too graphic, explain how he felt without a trace of self-pity and describe his hopes for the future without allowing one iota of doubt to enter into the conversation. He told us all about his desire to raise funds and awareness for those with spinal injuries. He spoke passionately about disabled rights and also declared his plan to raise £1 million by becoming the first person in history with a complete spinal cord injury to climb Mount Kilimanjaro.

His enthusiasm for helping others and lust for life was infectious. As he left the sofa after the interview, I thanked him for being so honest and for lifting the spirits of everyone watching. 'When you've been as close to death as I have, Dan, every single day is a blessing,' he said as he wheeled himself back towards the green room. I knew, from that moment, that I wanted to include Martin in this book. I knew it had been a real privilege to meet him.

One of the people climbing Kilimanjaro with Martin is Stuart Wildman, a consultant nurse at Salford Royal. On the night of the blast, Stuart wasn't on shift. He was in bed but, like many people, he got a call at 4 a.m. to come in.

'You just get told there is a "major incident" and that you are needed in the hospital. I've been working for twenty-two years, seventeen of those as a nurse, and like an awful lot of people that night I had never been called to a major incident. I remember that everyone was focused.'

On the night Martin was admitted, no one thought he was going to survive. The neurosurgeon, Mr Saxena, had just finished a twelve-hour shift when he heard about the bomb and returned to Salford Royal. He operated on Martin for fourteen hours.

Martin has very little memory of the next few weeks of his life. He kept asking questions about how he was and how Eve was but was struggling to get to the truth about how serious things were.

'I knew why they were doing it,' he says. 'My wife Gabby was telling me what the doctors told her to tell me about my legs because no one wants to talk about stuff like that. The medical team had advised her not to mention my injuries in those early days. My first clear memory is of my wife and my mum standing next to a bunch of doctors in white coats. Eventually, we got to the brutal truth: they told me I had a complete spinal injury and that I would never walk again.'

The first thing that went through Martin's head was that he wouldn't be able to walk the family dog – Alfie – ever again. 'I know it sounds daft,' says Martin with a little smile, 'but Alfie was suffering from separation anxiety. He had stopped eating for weeks because I wasn't around. Then I thought I would never be able to kick a football again. I think the doctors expected me to erupt; for the air to be filled with expletives and for me to start throwing things around. But, for some reason, I stayed calm.'

'How did you manage to stay so controlled in those circumstances?' I asked.

'I thought about where I had been, Dan,' says Martin. You can almost see the determination in his face as he engages. 'I genuinely thought I was dead, and the game was over. I was lying on the floor, choking on my own blood, thinking "this is it" I had the overwhelming joy of knowing that I was alive. I knew that Eve was in a bad way, but I also knew she was alive. I was so thankful that I still had a life to live.'

Martin spent just over two weeks in intensive care before being moved to the major trauma ward. That's where he came under the care of Stuart Wildman. 'I knew about Martin before I met him. We were all amazed he had survived and, you can imagine, there was huge media interest in all the survivors, so Martin was put in a side room off the main ward for his own protection. I remember him being so incredibly calm. He was processing a lot of information and was quiet. In those early days he wasn't bright or joyful. I often think that, at times like that, it's best to talk about things that aren't clinical. It's so important to do something normal, something that feels like an everyday thing that you'd do if you were at home. I offered to give him a shave.'

I asked Martin if he can remember that offer from Stuart. 'It was amazing,' says Martin, rubbing his chin, as if he can remember the straggly beard that had grown during his weeks in intensive care. 'It was just a simple thing but it meant so much at the time to me. It's strange how something so normal can turn into something so emotional, and how one tiny act of kindness can make such a difference.'

Stuart's overwhelming memory of that time spent with Martin was his desire to see his daughter, Eve. In the same way that keeping her alive on the night of the blast had kept him alive, now it was the thought of seeing her again that was driving his recovery.

'He was so early on in coming to terms with what had

happened to him. He had gone from being busy, active and able bodied to paralysed in a heartbeat. He had hardly any upper body strength and it takes time for your core to adjust to be able to hold yourself up. You can't rush these things but I knew how much Martin wanted to see his daughter and I knew it would be important for his recovery. It was a logistical nightmare. We didn't really know how his body would cope with being sat down for a long time after being on his back for weeks, and there were also all sorts of blood pressure issues and pain medication concerns which had to be really carefully managed. But, despite all that, we managed to make it happen and I know how much that meant to Martin. It was a real privilege to be there with him on the day.'

Seeing Eve had become everything to Martin because he was well aware how close he had come to losing her. He gathers himself before telling me about the day he saw her again for the first time since the bomb went off. It was 11 July 2017, his birthday.

'The coroner had been ringing the ward she was on every day at the start because they were convinced she was going to be victim number twenty-three,' explains Martin. 'In total, Eve was in intensive care for nearly four months but I simply had to see her. I knew she was alive and I just wanted to be with her.'

Just before Martin went into the room where Eve was being looked after, the senior doctor took him to one side and let him know what he was about to see. It was all about managing expectation and it was a body-blow to an already battered dad.

'He was as kind as it's possible to be for someone in that situation. He explained to me that, what I was about to see, wasn't really Eve. She'd been hit by a bolt in the temple and it had passed into her brain and taken out the vast majority of her frontal lobe. I remember watching his lips as he told me that he didn't know if she would ever wake up and, even if she did, whether she would ever regain any memory or have the ability to communicate. He told me there was a good chance she would remain in a permanently vegetative state.'

Understandably, Martin stops as he remembers how hard those words hit him at the time. 'Are you ok to carry on?' I ask tentatively. 'It helps to talk about it,' says Martin. 'Every time it gets easier.'

'How do you respond when someone tells you that about your daughter?' I ask.

'I completely broke down at that moment,' he says with tears in his eyes. 'I was opposite this doctor and I just couldn't stop crying. I thought to myself that if she's not here then I don't want to be here either. I was glad that he told me. I needed to know the truth. I needed to know how bad things were. Eve was, and is, the whole reason that I do everything in life. She was the biggest and best part of my life. The heart-breaking thing for me, being stood outside that door, was that I had always promised her that I would keep her safe and I felt like I had failed. I still give myself a hard time about it. I used to tell her a lot that, as long as she was with me, nothing would ever happen to her. She used to smile when I told her that I would protect her from anything bad and yet, there she was, unable to breathe on her own after a night out with me. My superhero cape had been ripped off and we were both fighting to rebuild our lives.'

Martin is incredibly strong. He rarely talks about Eve because it hurts too much and yet it's clear that she is a big driving force behind his relentless positivity and desire to make a difference to others. When the dark clouds gather over him, he slots back to what he calls 'The Hibbert Mindset'. 'Crack on' is one of his favourite go-to sayings.

Martin's dad was a police officer in Bolton and his mum was a pharmacy dispenser. Growing up he spent a lot of time with his grandad who had a big influence on his outlook. He always used to tell Martin that life was littered with lumps in the road but the secret was just to keep on running.

'My mum would always say that she was waiting for her ship to come in – something that would change everything – and that used to really annoy my grandad. He would always challenge her on it and, when I was six years old, he told me something that I still think about now. He took me to one side and said, "Martin, never wait for your ship to come in. Row out there and meet it" I have always had that thought in my mind. When everything is going wrong, when the world is falling down around you, I look for the opportunity. I think it's a Bolton thing, a northern thing. I refuse to let things drag me down.'

Martin has always been a grafter. He had a paper round from the age of eleven and got up at 6 a.m. every morning until he was eighteen. He would clean dishes in the evenings to make extra money.

That day he went to see Eve for the first time, his birthday, he knew that coming out the other side would require the most 'graft' he had put into anything his entire life.

'She comes into my head quite a lot,' says Martin. 'The picture of her lying in her bed that day. She was covered in pipes, pipes that were keeping her alive. I say "keeping her alive", but she didn't look "alive" at all. She was still and lifeless. There was nothing there. I asked if I could hug her, which you can imagine was quite difficult with a bloke paralysed from the waist down and a girl in a vegetative state. It took four staff to help to get us in position but, even though it was awkward, it was beautiful. I can't explain to you why or how, but I knew in my heart that she would survive. That hug was so special.'

Weeks became months, but slowly Eve was making progress. The big turning point came the second time they tried to take her off the ventilator . . . she could breathe on her own for the first time! Martin constantly has to remind himself of what the consultant told him, that his daughter may never be able to walk, talk or eat on her own again.

'She just keeps getting better and better,' says her dad with a giant smile across his face. 'I've got a video that I look at sometimes of Eve putting triangles through holes. I never thought she would have the mental capacity to do that. She was mute for two years because of all the trauma and then, I was in Australia, getting some treatment and I remember we were on FaceTime and she just started talking to me and eating on her own. It was incredible. She said, "Hello Daddy". Her speech was broken and you could tell the PTSD was hitting her hard but it was her . . . it was Eve. The medics threw out the book when it came to her a long time ago. She keeps on proving them wrong. She keeps on breaking boundaries. She's amazing.'

Stuart Wildman, the consultant nurse, had witnessed Martin's meeting with Eve on his birthday. Like everyone who works on a major trauma ward, Stuart has seen his fair share of grief and heartache. There are some things that stick with you, some people you never forget. Martin is one of those patients.

'I see a lot of sad things in my job, but that day, Martin's birthday, when he saw Eve for the first time, I went home and cried that day. It was all just so real. I have a daughter who is two years younger than Eve. I just kept thinking about her and what I would be like in that situation. I've been to the MEN with my daughter. My friends have been there. This is my city. For any of us Manchester dads, we all know that that could have been us. We could have been there like Martin, struggling to hug his daughter. I remember his determination to give her a kiss. There was no way he wasn't going to do it. It was almost physically impossible, but you could tell from his face that he wouldn't be taking no for an answer. That was the first time I saw the determination. That was the first insight into what drives him on. If there is even a 1 per cent chance of something happening, Martin is one of those people who will do absolutely everything in his power to make it work, to bring it to life.'

After seeing Eve, Stuart took Martin to St Ann's Square in the centre of the city so that Martin could light a candle for the victims of the Manchester bomb. From that day forward, Stuart saw a new motivation in his patient.

'He had down days but he never turned down a therapy or a care session. You get some people in Martin's situation who just can't see a way out. They get lost in the grief or the pain and they just start to waste away. You can see the depression ruling them and it just keeps getting darker and darker. Some people don't want to get out of bed. They don't want therapy, they don't want help, they can't see a way out. Martin was the complete opposite. He couldn't wait to get out of hospital. He quickly became one of the reasons I love my job. I have always thought it is a real honour to give someone personal care, for them to allow you into their personal space. That is a rare privilege and, once you're in there, you form a special relationship. Sometimes dressing his wounds would take up to two hours. You get to talk, you share stories, you see what makes someone tick. I was helping him, but caring for Martin gave me so much reward and reaffirmed why this is the job I was born to do.'

When Martin finally left Stuart's care, Stuart didn't think the friendship would continue, they rarely do. But, every time Martin returned to the hospital to visit the Spinal Injuries Unit, he would go back to Stuart's ward and make sure everyone was ok.

'He would always ask us all how we were,' remembers Stuart fondly. 'Despite what he'd been through, he never made it about him. He was always more interested in us, in other people.'

The second time that Martin came into the *BBC Breakfast* studio, he brought Stuart with him. They spoke about their friendship, the shaving incident and Martin said something that I still think about all the time. I ask Stuart if he remembers what it was because I remember looking at Stuart's face as Martin said it and I felt it had a similar impact on him that it had on me.

'The thing about feeling disabled?' Stuart said.

That was precisely it. Towards the end of the interview, Martin was talking about his new life in a wheelchair and why he felt so passionately about campaigning for others to have access to the spinal care that he had.

'It's not my injuries that make me feel disabled, it's people's attitudes that make me feel disabled.'

'I think about that a lot,' says Stuart. 'He's right, isn't he? It's so easy to get stuck in that mindset where you concentrate on what people can't do rather than what they can. Do you know what, Dan?' says Stuart as he shuffles in his chair. Stuart is always smiling, but now there is also excitement in his voice. 'I talk about Martin a lot to other patients. I can't tell stories like Martin can, but I can tell other people about Martin. He is the example I use to so many.'

Martin has also had a profound effect on Paul, the paramedic who took him to Salford Royal that night and saved his life. Paul picks up the story. 'I'd checked in on him that night and the following morning to make sure he was still alive but, after that, it was difficult to find out what had happened to him. Then, one day, my wife (Louise) saw him being interviewed on Channel 5!'

Louise jumps in. 'That's right. I messaged Paul straightaway. I took a picture off the telly and said, "Is this him? You know, the guy from the arena?" and then Paul came back with . . .'

'That's him!' says Paul. 'I did a bit of Facebook stalking and then I thought I would send him a message and see if he wanted to get in touch. We've been friends ever since.'

'Do you remember that ball we went to?' says Louise.

'Yes, that was the first time we actually met him,' remembers Paul. 'Martin was doing this black tie charity do at the Midland Hotel in Manchester. Ron Atkinson was there! We met Martin and we just got on straightaway. He sat us on the top table and then, when he made his speech, he introduced me to the crowd and said, "This is Paul, the paramedic who saved my life."'

The other thing that Paul and Martin share is a love of Manchester. One thing that has always struck me about this city is the way people come together in grief. Where terrorists try and sow discord and pain, Manchester gives birth to strength and togetherness. The Manchester bomb made those bonds stronger than ever.

'We've both got bee tattoos,' says Paul proudly. 'Me and Martin, we both have them.' The bee became an even more powerful symbol for Manchester in the aftermath of the bomb. The worker bee has long been a symbol of the city's hard-working past. In the 1800s Manchester was full of textile mills and they were often described as 'hives of activity' and the workers inside them compared to bees. The bee symbol was a part of Manchester's coat of arms which was given to the city in 1842. After the bomb, it was associated with unity and defiance; it represented Manchester's indomitable spirit. People added it to their social media profiles as an act of solidarity and many, like Martin and Paul, got tattoos. If you ever visit the city and go to the Koffee Pot building in the Northern Quarter, you find an image of twenty-two bees on the side of it. Each bee is swarming around a honey pot and each one represents a victim of the attack.

'I've got bees painted on my garden fence too. Just to remind me.' Paul, like many Mancunians, was moved when he heard the words of the local poet Tony Walsh and his 'This Is The Place' poem which he read at the memorial service in St Ann's Square.

'I've got those final words on the inside of my left forearm,' says Paul. *Always remember, never forget, forever Manchester.*

Paul has another reason to use Martin for inspiration. In July of 2021 he had an accident on his road bike. He hit some debris on a road near Wigan and ended up with fractured vertebrae, broken ribs, a brain injury and underwent spinal surgery in the Salford Royal. Guess who has been his great encourager during recovery? Martin Hibbert.

'Watching Martin has helped me come out the other side of all this,' says Paul. 'We all know people who work hard to support a charity but Martin just takes things to another level. He's superhuman. I am determined to show my family, to show everyone, that I can be just as positive as him going forward. Martin is a permanent reminder to me to make sure that I don't accept average. I want to push the boundaries just like him.'

As I write this, Paul is back in the office just seven months after being in a drug-induced coma. He says that Martin's example pushes him every day but, because of his injuries, he wasn't able to take part in Martin's greatest challenge: climbing Kilimanjaro in a wheelchair.

'I was talking to him about the trip the week before my accident,' says Paul. 'He was like a little kid. Once he gets something in his head there is no stopping him. As soon as I came round after the accident he contacted me and told me not to worry and that, even if I couldn't be there, I'd be part of the team. I know some people laugh at him and think he's mad. I've seen the way some people look at him when he talks about climbing Kilimanjaro, but if there is one thing I've learned in the last few years . . . never doubt Martin Hibbert.'

'Where did the idea of Kilimanjaro come about?' I ask Martin. 'That sounds like one of yours.'

'It was,' says Martin, 'but it wasn't all my fault. I was asked to speak at an event in London for the Spinal Injuries Association. I was addressing a load of multi-millionaires. We were pitching to them to see if they would take us on as their charity of the year. Anyway, we had a dinner and it raised just short of a million quid. One of the guys from the charity jokingly said, "That's amazing, what are you doing next year to raise a million quid?" My brain started ticking straightaway and I thought, if this is going to work, you've got to do something that is an actual risk to your life. Otherwise what's the point? My first suggestion was to climb Everest but then I discovered that I'd have to be carried about 90 per cent of the way, which didn't really seem fair. I looked into things and Kilimanjaro was actually possible. I would only need help 10 per cent of the way and it was tough enough to be worth it. Only 6 per cent of able-bodied people make it to the top, only two other people have done it in a wheelchair. I look at it this way, Dan, every day I have to climb a mountain so I might as well actually climb one.'

Martin has assembled an impressive team around him for the climb. Paul is unable to go because of his injuries, but Stuart will be there alongside him on the trip. The phone call from Martin came through one Saturday morning.

'I was lying in bed and I saw this WhatsApp message arrive,' recalls Stuart. He is laughing as he remembers the story, but he tells me that's because it still all feels a bit bonkers. The messages between the two of them went like this:

Martin: 'Hi, Stuart. Hope you're ok. I've got a challenge I want you to be part of.'

Stuart: 'What is it?'

Martin: 'You might need some time to think about it? I want you to climb Kilimanjaro with me.'

Stuart said 'yes' immediately.

'I turned around to my wife and said, "What on earth have I just volunteered myself for?" There was a mixture of excitement but also apprehension, but I know all about Martin's drive and determination and I know that, at the heart of it, he just wants other people to have the same access to the best care that he had. Having a spinal injury turns your entire life upside down. It's not just the practical things like bladders and bowels, it's everything. The Spinal Injuries Association are amazing but they need money to make a difference and help people to live a fulfilled life.'

Martin Hibbert is a pretty amazing man. You don't have to spend much time in his company to realise that his passion and enthusiasm can convince anyone to do virtually anything. I haven't often seen him without a smile on his face but, as you would expect, there are dark days. There are flashbacks to that night at the Manchester Arena and the time spent in hospital. There is the lingering spectre of PTSD. He has visions of seeing Eve for the first time after the incident and it can hit him at any time and anywhere. Sometimes it keeps him up all night. He has to keep busy. He always wants something to look forward to so that he doesn't have to look back.

I don't know about you, but Martin is one of those people who makes me think about how I would act if I was in the situation he has found himself in. I wonder if I would be able to think as quickly as he did on the night itself. I wonder how I would react to being told I would never be able to walk again. I wonder what it would have been like for me to see one of my daughters under the same circumstances that Martin saw Eve, and I wonder whether I would devote myself to helping others when life remains an uphill struggle every single day.

Martin isn't religious but does enjoy talking to friends about what he describes as 'life, the universe and everything'. He doesn't have an answer to why that night happened to him and his family but, within a few minutes of meeting him, you realise he is a deep thinker. So what does he see as his reason for being here?

'There has to be a reason I survived,' he says, more earnest than at any other point in the interview. 'The bolt went through my neck. It was travelling at about 100 mph but somehow I swallowed it. No one can understand either why, or how, that happened and believe me, I've asked everyone. My story has given me a voice that I never dreamed of having and that is what I use as my motivation, my reason for still being around.'

When Martin tells his story at events, the whole room falls silent. His tale is solemn, painful, but also inspirational. He talks about the fact that he has never wanted revenge for what happened to him that night.

'Forgive me if I don't use his name, Dan,' says Martin carefully, 'but I don't hate him, you know, the bomber. I use him. On the bad days, I use his face to get me out of bed. Sometimes I want nothing more than to stay under the covers. I know that's what he would have wanted and, if I stay in bed, hiding, even for one day, then he wins. I'll happily admit that sometimes I cry in the shower, but I always come out and think . . . right, crack on. I was at the re-opening of the arena in September 2017,' says Martin proudly. 'I wanted them to see that they couldn't stop me. I virtually broke out of the spinal unit to be there but it was important to me. Yes, I got in trouble for it when I got back, but every little win for me is a little defeat for the people who wanted to detonate a bomb at a concert. When I climb Kilimanjaro, they fail. When I get my message around the world, they fail. They nearly took my life away; they did take my legs away but they've actually made me stronger than ever.'

Martin often thinks about the people who didn't make it that night, particularly Saffie Roussos, the youngest victim, who was just eight years old. He has survivors' guilt over why he made it and she didn't. He wants to know why a forty-year-old man who had 'lived a great life' made it home and she didn't. But that has also driven him on to make a difference for others.

'I had no idea about disability before it happened to me. You very rarely see disabled people out and there are many reasons for that. It's because of parking, it's because of a lack of lifts, it's because there are no ramps where they need to go or there just simply isn't enough space. When I'm out and I see another disabled person, I always wave at them because it's so rare. I went to Bond Street in London and I couldn't get in the shops. You go in and ask where the men's stuff is and they tell you it's on the first floor. "Where is the lift?" you ask. "We don't have a lift." It doesn't have to be like this. I go to Australia for treatment sometimes and, when I'm there, I hardly feel disabled at all. Facilities are incredible and so far ahead of what we are doing here. We have the equality act in this country,' says Martin passionately, 'imagine if someone from the BAME or LGBT community was told they couldn't use a shop, or a service, because they didn't have the facilities? This is what I'm trying to change for disabled people and I will use the rest of the time I have on this planet to sing and shout about it. We have to change the mindset. When we look at disabled people we only ever see either a Paralympian or a benefit scrounger. I am neither of those and nor are the vast majority of disabled people. They want to work, but they can't get there. When they do get there, it can be a struggle to get in and, if they do get into the office, they can't get their wheelchair under the desk. I'm sorry, but that's just not good enough.'

Martin's real gift is that he is a campaigner. He doesn't make you feel guilty for not doing or supporting something but he convinces you that things need to change by the sheer weight of reason and enthusiasm. It's hard to disagree with that, particularly when you consider the path he has taken to get to where he is. Martin doesn't wear slogan T-shirts but, if he did, it would read 'Don't Write Me Off Because I'm In A Wheelchair'. I don't think there is any danger of that happening.

Martin wants Eve to be able to live her life to the full too.

They now talk about what happened that night in Manchester. It has helped Eve to deal with the trauma and eased her PTSD. Martin has reminded her that, throughout that night, while she was unconscious on the floor, he was never more than a few feet away from her. That reassurance is as much a help to Martin as it is to Eve. Neither of them like the idea of being alone.

They haven't been back to a concert at the arena yet, but that is the plan. At the moment, loud noises and bangs are too triggering but, eventually, Martin is confident they'll get there. He knows it will be a hard day, but also a hugely important one.

Eve is always making progress. At the moment she is in a wheelchair. At the time of writing this, she is twenty years old and currently doing work for a nine to ten-year-old. 'I know life will be tough for her,' says Martin. 'She probably won't be able to hold down a relationship, but she's here, and that's the important thing. All the time there might be chances of seizures and strokes. There will be constant trips to hospital but, listen, I often laugh when I think about where she was five years ago and where she is now. I have my daughter back and, for a long time, I never thought that would be possible. Ever since that night, she has been defying the doctors' predictions. Look at her now, back at sixth form, kicking ass. She will inspire the world when she's ready to do it.'

I love talking to Martin. He makes you look at things in differing ways. He allows, and occasionally has to persuade you, to see things from a new perspective and his motive always seems to be to improve the lives of those around him. I have no doubt in my mind that he will go on to achieve great things in life and, if Eve is anything like him, she will too. He may well spend the rest of his life in a wheelchair, but standing on his shoulders gives me one of the clearest views possible of what it is to cling on to the positive in the bleakest of situations. That's what I told him at the end of our long conversation. I thanked him for his time and thanked him for coming out from under the covers every day and inspiring me and many others. He answered in typical fashion.

'We could all sit in a corner and cry. It's much easier to mope around and feel sorry for yourself and blame others, but I want to use that as my drive, my motivation, to live life to the full.'

And that's exactly what Martin was trying to do when he set himself the enormous task of climbing Kilimanjaro in June of 2022. If you followed any of his journey on TV, or in the press, you'll know that he managed to make it, but when we caught up a few days after he made the summit, he was in typically down-to-earth mode.

'I don't think it has sunk in yet, I have just come back from having my catheter taken out, so it's been back to normal with a bump. I've had messages from all over the world,' says the proud Mancunian. 'America, Pakistan, India, Australia . . . so many messages from so many different people who all seem to know that we managed to do what most people thought would be impossible.'

Martin made it to the top on 9 June but the last few hours of the climb produced so many doubts. 'Walking through sand is hard enough, but imagine trying to shift a wheelchair through it. I have never done anything like that before. We were spending ten minutes going up and then slipping back to where we started. I told the porters who were helping us that I just didn't have anything left in the tank. One of them just kept saying, "Twenty minutes, twenty minutes," but it was the longest twenty minutes I have ever experienced.'

Martin and his team had already seen the mountain bare its teeth. His best friend, Steve Lloyd, had to pull out on day two with altitude sickness, and the team lost their medic, Chris Paton, on day four in similar fashion. 'Chris was the man looking after my skin sores but also checking on my bowel and bladder movements. They were my wingmen so once they had gone I felt totally alone. I had to sleep with the light on. I felt so incredibly vulnerable, which is strange for me. I hardly slept at all and then we set off at 5 a.m. the next morning. I remember what you told me though, Dan, and I did it.'

When Martin first informed me about his attempt to climb Kilimanjaro he asked me if I had any advice from the time I went up there for Comic Relief. I told him to make sure he had plenty of snacks and, even though it was easy to get distracted by the seemingly endless final morning, I said don't forget to turn your back on Kilimanjaro and enjoy one of the greatest sunrises you will ever see crack across the horizon.

'I remember that picture you showed me,' says Martin, 'and, when the sun rose, I got really emotional. It was the sort of thing you only ever see from a plane. I thought about our talks quite a bit that morning, Dan. I took a photo with the team (which you can see in the picture section) and I had a little cry. There is something amazing about being that free, that silent, that in touch with your surroundings. It was magical.'

Martin also got to keep his promise to his mum. He sprinkled some of her ashes at the top and played their favourite song on his phone. 'I know I was raising money for the Spinal Injuries Association and raising awareness but, from a personal perspective, it was all about my mum. I wanted to have a picture at the top with my Manchester United flag but I knew my mum was with me all the way. It was a really emotional moment when I played "For All We Know" by The Carpenters on my phone. I cry every time I think about it. She knew all about the climb and knew how much I wanted to do it before she died back in October 2021. I had a good sob and sent my two brothers the video from the top and that was pretty special.'

Martin is rightly proud of becoming only the second paraplegic to climb Kilimanjaro and has been staggered by the reaction to his successful summit. 'A guy came up to me on the way down and said, "Martin, you don't know me, but my name is Paul. I was up there a few days ago but I stayed on at base camp for another two days because I wanted to see you." I was really touched by that but also by the porters. Lots of them kept telling me that they had never seen a wheelchair on the mountain. They nicknamed me "Lion" because of the tattoo on my arm. At the end, one of the guys took me to one side and said, "You have inspired me. I have never seen anyone like you before. I am not going to live my life like this anymore, I am going to live like you, live like Martin." I will never forget those experiences.'

On the day that we speak, Martin tells me the total raised has gone up £100,000 in the last forty-eight hours. The million-pound dream is within reach and there is no sign of him taking his foot off the fundraising gas.

'I want to do base camp at Everest,' says Martin, giggling at how crazy it sounds. 'It has never been done in a wheelchair and, since I've come back, I've been contacted by two Royal Marines and two Gurkhas who have told me it's possible and they'd like to help. I know I still need to do a lot of checking but I'll keep going until ministers listen and we get those changes to social care and everyone gets access to the care that is available. Seven people a day get a spinal cord injury and only one in three get help and support. That means four of those seven go home without any rehab, any help or any education. How is that possible? How can they be expected to get on with their lives? During the pandemic I was constantly hearing stories of people in a wheelchair being left in a bed, in their own mess, for two days, or left waiting at the bottom of a flight of stairs for the same amount of time. While that is still happening, I'll keep going.'

I ask Martin if he has taken the time to reflect that it's only just over five years ago that he was lying on the concrete floor in the Manchester Arena on the night his life changed forever. 'I have thought about that, Dan,' says the forty-five-year-old. 'I have thought about the fact that I was told I would never walk again. I thought about that at the top quite a bit. I was lying in a bed in hospital back in 2017 and the only thing I could move was my head and here I am at the top of Kilimanjaro. What a message that is to disabled people everywhere. I've had wheel-chair users contact me this week and tell me they've watched what I did and have left the house for the first time in ten years. I am so humbled that I have inspired anyone by what I have done. It's not just a message to disabled people but it's a message to the people who tried to blow me up. They wanted me dead, and if they couldn't have that, they wanted me terrified and silent in a corner somewhere. We'll, I'm very much alive and, I might spend most of my life sitting down, but I won't be in a corner and I won't be quiet. There is too much to do.'

A ROSE IN BLOOM

'My mum always made me feel like I could do anything,' says Rose. 'She would always tell me that there was no job that was beyond me.'

'Maybe not a telephonist,' interrupts Donna. 'But anything else, Rose. Anything.'

Rose Ayling-Ellis was the undisputed star of *Strictly Come Dancing* in 2021. She will probably go down as the greatest contestant in the history of the show. She is also the only celebrity ever to take to the dance floor who hasn't been able to hear any of the music. If you didn't know, Rose is deaf. What she did over those thirteen weeks was truly incredible. Giovanni Pernice was with her every step of the way on the floor, and her mum was just as supportive off it – as she has been for the whole of Rose's life.

'I've always had people telling me there are things I can't do. I always think that's the wrong way round,' says Rose with that permanent smile on her face. 'Mum was always fighting my corner, weren't you?'

'I was, but that's because I was always getting told what was the best thing I could do for you,' says Donna. 'Most parents get that, but it happens even more when you have a deaf child. "Teach her this", "Make sure she doesn't do that", "Don't teach her sign language", "She's never going to be able to speak". I know you're the deaf one, but I learned very early not to listen! Every deaf person is different and, when I watched Rose, the way she was with people, from a very early age, I just knew there would be no boundaries for her. I knew, I was convinced she could do anything, and I just kept telling her that.'

I first met Rose on week one of *Strictly* when we were all saying 'hello' to each other. My dad is deaf. He has no hearing in one ear and has a cochlea implant for the other. He hates rooms with lots of people in them. The background 'fuzz' drowns everything out and he normally just switches off the box on the side of his head and keeps himself to himself. Rose was nervous – as we all were – but she was also positive and confident. She stood out.

'She's always been like that,' says Donna as I recount to her my first meeting with her daughter. 'When she was young, you know, at school, everywhere she went, she used to blow people away. Everyone would be taken aback by her. She has always had that effect on people. She would get the "poor little deaf girl" reaction, but she was the complete opposite. People would always expect her to be the quiet kid who would hide in the corner, but Rose has always been full of life.'

'You used to send me to everything, didn't you, Mum?' chirps Rose.

'Exactly,' replied Donna. 'She didn't care. I would send her to every club going. I never wanted her to think that a door would be closed to her because she was deaf. She was at Brownies, swimming clubs, after-school stuff. If it was on, Rose was there.'

Rose and Donna have this endearing way of talking when they are together. They have a gorgeous habit of teeing each other up.

'You used to like surprising people, didn't you, Rose?' says Donna, encouraging Rose to share.

'They would always be surprised if I could write a sentence, weren't they, Mum? I felt like saying, "I'm deaf, I'm not stupid."'

Donna jumps back in. 'If she ever had a bad day or had a knock-back, I would always remind her that she could do more than people expect, that she could be more. The great thing about Rose is that she was always so enthusiastic. Do you remember the doctors, Rose?' asks Donna. Rose nods.

'When we used to go to the doctors, or somewhere like that, they would always talk to me and not her.'

'I used to hate that,' says Rose with a smile.

'Do you remember, Rose? I would deliberately turn my head away. They would be talking to her but looking at me. "I'm so sorry" was another one. "Why are you sorry?" Don't be sorry. She's happy and she's fine. I know almost all of it comes through ignorance. It's just because people don't know.'

Rose lifts her hand to jump in. 'And that's what we are trying to change, Mum!'

'That's what you're changing,' says a proud Donna. 'There wasn't a Rose Ayling-Ellis to look up to when she was growing up.' She turns to me and points at Rose. 'Now there is, and that's my daughter.'

That is exactly what Rose did during her time on *Strictly* and is continuing to do. The week after I spoke to her for this book, British Sign Language became an official language – a huge step forward for the deaf community and directly linked to the awareness associated with Rose's time on the biggest show on telly. Everywhere she goes she makes practical suggestions, things that make you feel daft for not thinking of yourself. In the first week of our *Strictly* experience, Rose put a message on the group WhatsApp.

'Hi guys. I would love to be able to follow all the training on your Instagram stories but it's really hard without captions.' She then sent through a how-to video link which explained how simple it was. We all apologised for not thinking of it but thanked her for the heads-up and most of us will keep doing it forever. She wasn't judgey, she wasn't angry, she wasn't frustrated, she just calmly explained why it was important and it all just made perfect sense. She opens up the doors to her world and lets you in. She does that a lot. She's very good at it.

'When I was a child, I thought I was the only deaf person in the town,' explains Rose. 'I went to a deaf club once a week. There were a lot of older people there and occasionally we would go on camping weekends together. My mum is right, I never really had a role model.' She giggles. 'Do you remember, Mum? My nan used to give me books about Helen Keller, that American author who went deaf and blind when she was about 19, but I couldn't relate to her. She would tell me about Dame Evelyn Glennie, who is a deaf percussionist, or the film called *Children of a Lesser God*. I do remember, from a very early age, I wanted to be an artist. I found that I could communicate through drawing, and I loved it. It wasn't until I was older that I realised acting could be art.'

Donna jumps in. 'She was so creative, Dan. She was really gifted.'

'Stop it, Mum. You'll be getting my old pictures out next. She's kept them all, Dan. It's so embarrassing: fabric, textiles, arts and crafts. She's got everything.'

Donna is laughing into her cup of tea. 'There is nothing wrong with being a proud mum, Rose. Tell Dan about that weekend you went on, the acting one.'

Rose picks up the story. 'I didn't really have any interest in acting at all at the start. I saw it as something for the popular kids. How old was I, Mum, when I went to the weekend?'

'Fourteen or fifteen?' offers Donna tentatively.

'That sounds about right. I went for a weekend. I was convinced that all the kids would be younger than me and I was worried because I had never done it at school. It was like a deaf children's acting weekend, wasn't it?'

Donna nods. Rose continues. By this point they are just telling the story together, one sentence at a time.

'It was run by a charity.'

'You made a short film, didn't you?'

'Yes, I thought maybe filming could be something to do but I didn't enjoy it.'

'And the director, he asked you if you wanted to act.'

'That's right, and I remember that I wasn't intimidated for the first time.'

'Later on, Dan, I got there to pick her up and she was this star and she'd had a lovely time. I honestly thought she would hate it.'

'And,' says Rose, 'that director asked me to be in his short film and that was really the start of it all.'

Rose explained that throughout her early childhood she knew she was different to most other children, so she was determined to make sure she had no other reason to stand out. She didn't mind going under the radar.

Donna is listening carefully and asks a question. 'Do you think that's why you didn't want to be on stage at the start, Rose? Maybe it was because you wanted to hide that from people?'

Rose thinks about her answer. 'I was always confident, but I didn't want to be front and centre. I was blurred into the background. It wasn't until year 10 or 11 that I grew in confidence, and I became more of myself.'

Rose's first job was at a dog school. She was a gardener for two summers and then she got a gig at Sainsburys. 'I was stacking shelves,' she says proudly. 'I specialised in the fridge section.'

'She was so amazed when she got that job,' says Donna. 'I think she convinced herself that, because she was deaf, she had no chance.'

That supermarket job also gave Rose a first taste of discrimination. 'I loved that job and sometimes, during an emergency, when there were loads of people in and it was really busy, you had to jump on the tills to help. They would train people up to do it, but I was the only person who was never trained to work on the till! That's the problem with discrimination. It's hard to prove. You're never told that you don't get the opportunity because you are deaf, but you also never get the chance to prove that being deaf isn't a problem.'

Rose was destined for much bigger things than a life on the tills. The short film after the acting weekend led to wider recognition which eventually brought the offer of a job on *Casualty*. There was no agency which represented deaf actors, so Rose was getting her opportunities through Facebook.

'What about *Summer of Rockets*, Rose?' says Donna. *Summer of Rockets* was a cold-war drama series directed by Stephen Poliakov for BBC Two. 'I remember the night before the audition for that,' continues Rose's mum. 'I remember she went to bed early, and I thought she was so professional. I tried to manage expectation and told her it didn't matter if she didn't get it, but I was excited. Most of her jobs just came from impressing people when they met her for the first time.'

'I enjoyed that one,' says Rose, managing to get a word in. Donna is on a roll.

'*EastEnders* was massive, Dan. We used to watch it together, didn't we, Rose, when she was a little girl. I know *EastEnders* is mad and completely over the top, but you can use it sometimes in a way to explain situations. That's why we used to watch it. When she got that job, I couldn't believe it. It was all so surreal. We sat and watched that episode, do you remember, Rose?' Donna pauses and the pair of them laugh and then she pretends to take a picture with her phone.

'I paused it and I took a picture of you there, with you in the background on the telly.'

As Donna is talking, you can see it all coming back to her. All the battles she had along the way. All the times she was told 'no'. All the times she had to fight for Rose to be included. All the times she was the only one who believed in her daughter.

'I always knew she could fly this high,' says Donna, staring at Rose as only a mum can. 'I have always seen her work so hard to get to the same level as other people. I knew she was unstoppable. That's why, when *Strictly* came calling, I had no doubt she'd be brilliant. I know some people just couldn't understand how a deaf girl could dance on the telly like that, but I was like, that's my Rose. She can do anything.'

Donna works in a local hospital in the outpatient's department in cardiology. She was at work when Rose gave her the call about *Strictly*.

'I answered the phone and she just said, "Mum, guess what, *Strictly Come Dancing* want me." I couldn't tell anyone. I was so excited.'

Rose was invited in for a trial with Executive Producer, Sarah James. She would be dancing with Giovanni Pernice. 'I was terrified,' remembers Rose. 'He made it so easy, and we got on really well, but it was so difficult. I had never danced before. If I was a bad dancer, people would think that it was because I was deaf. I didn't want to let down the deaf community. We did some jive, and I was quite bad at it, and we did some ballroom and I left. I thought that might have been it.'

Her future professional partner had other ideas. 'Quite a few of the celebrities are asked to dance before they go on *Strictly* and I was told the next one would be a deaf girl called Rose,' recalls Giovanni. 'We got on straightaway. I tried to make her feel comfortable and I was really careful in the way I explained things to her. I could tell she was nervous, but she was great. As soon as she left the room, I went up to Sarah James and said, "She has to do the show! I am not asking for much, but please, I want Rose. I would love to dance with her."'

Sarah James remembers the conversation well. 'He was desperate to have her as a partner after that session. I couldn't tell Rose at that point because we were seeing other people, but I knew we already wanted her on the show. We had met her on Zoom, and we were blown away by how much she had thought through everything. In our first meeting she talked about interpreters, about music and subtitles. She explained to us all that she hadn't really watched the show before because it wasn't accessible to the deaf community. I remember being ashamed as she told me that the live subtitles were totally unreliable and that all she was able to do was watch catch-up clips of the dancing. She was already improving the show and making it more accessible before she'd even started! The dance session was more for her than for us. We just wanted to see how it would work and Giovanni was amazing with her straightaway. She could lip read him really easily and she'd already told us that Italians were easy to lip read because they were so expressive. He didn't patronise her at all and they were already taking the mickey out of each other. We knew it could be a special partnership.'

'There was a connection straightaway,' says Giovanni. '*Strictly* lasts a long time and I wanted to be with someone

I could get on with. She didn't feel worried and she was very comfortable with me. I was hopeful that we'd be paired together but there were some nervy weeks ahead.'

Three days later, Rose had a call from her agent to confirm her place on the show. She had just done a night shift filming *EastEnders* and was told she could only tell her mum and her then boyfriend, Sam. It had to remain a secret.

'I'd not even been in *EastEnders* for a year, had I, Mum?' says Rose, laughing.

'I know,' replies Donna, 'but no one turns you down after they've met you, do they? I knew she'd get it,' says Donna confidently. 'As soon as Rose told me she was going to meet the team at *Strictly*, I knew she'd be dancing.'

'Stop it, Mum,' complains Rose, rolling her eyes.

'No, I won't,' replies Donna giggling. 'I'm your mum and I'm meant to be your biggest supporter. At least I was able to keep a secret!' Donna widens her eyes and flicks an accusatory glance at Rose.

It was all coming out now. The pair of them were chuckling away. Donna told no one, not even Rose's brother. Her daughter's lips were a little looser.

'I told Danny Dyer the next day on the set of *EastEnders*!' confesses Rose with her head in her hands. 'I kept having a big mouth. I am so bad at keeping a secret. They always ask someone from *EastEnders* to do *Strictly*, and everyone kept asking who it was. I told Danny and he was great. He cried and was so proud of me. I told him it was a secret and that he couldn't tell anyone.'

'Didn't someone find out though, Rose?' says Donna, laughing.

'That's right,' says Rose. 'The next week someone from *EastEnders* asked me if I had talked to anyone on the show about doing *Strictly*. I just panicked.' At this point Rose is laughing her head off. 'Guess what, Dan? I was so embarrassed that I just told them I hadn't said anything to anyone. I was becoming really stressed holding on to the secret. That's why I was so happy when it finally came out.'

The *Strictly* announcements are incredibly carefully choreographed. They are meticulously planned by the team with everyone having a certain slot on a certain show. I was announced alongside Katie McGlynn on BBC *Breakfast* and there are various other segments on shows like *The One Show*, Zoe Ball's Radio 2 *Breakfast Show* and so on.

'I remember being on BBC News,' says Rose. 'It was really positive. I hadn't even started dancing and everyone was talking about it already. I started on *EastEnders* during Covid so I think I managed to be under the radar a little, but this was big news and there was no going back.'

The memories are all coming flooding back for Donna. 'I was so excited. I didn't really sleep well at all the night before. Loads of my friends were messaging me. I was also a little worried about Rose, to be honest. Would she be able to cope with being in the public eye? I worried about the press, you know, how they would portray her. I never worried that people wouldn't like her, but I was worried that she would be put out there in the wrong way, but it was ok, wasn't it, Rose?'

'Yes, it was great, Mum,' replies Rose. 'I worried about being the first deaf one. Do I need to behave in a certain way? The day before I went for my first interview I spoke to Danny Dyer. "Do I need to put on a personality, Danny? Maybe I should pretend to be someone." Danny just said, "The best advice I can give you is, be yourself and just own who you are." He told me that I would feel like it wasn't real, and he reminded me that people will always see if you're faking it. He reminded me that was the only thing I could control. It was just what I needed to hear.'

Donna is giving her daughter the proud-mum look again. 'She was just being herself, Dan. That was her. Quirky, geeky, funny. As her mum, you watch that and think, "There she is. YES!"' She turns to Rose. 'Don't you think, if you hadn't stayed yourself, you wouldn't have been able to do it? No one can keep an act up that long.'

'Yes,' says Rose, 'but it's also hard, because being yourself is much more vulnerable. I think that's why some people put on an act, because if people don't like it, you can always say, "It's not really me." I also think Gio helped a lot with that. He just let me be me from day one.'

'Day one' for Rose and Gio was actually their 'meeting VT' at a pie and mash shop in the square that provided the inspiration for *EastEnders*.

'It's a bit strange really,' says Gio laughing, 'because I don't eat that sort of stuff and Rose is a vegetarian.'

'It took a lot for him to eat that,' admits Rose. 'I'm not even sure if he'd ever watched *EastEnders* before.'

I ask Gio if that's true. 'I'm a busy man, Dan,' he laughs. 'I was hoping I was going to get Rose, so I'd done my research, like I always do. I was so happy when it was her that I even forgot how bad the pie and mash tasted. I don't watch *EastEnders*, but I know we always have someone from the cast on the show. I knew that Rose was special from when we danced together at her first session, and I was looking forward to a brilliant season on *Strictly*. Like all good partnerships, it wasn't always smooth, but I will never forget it.'

Things were always going to be different with Rose. *Strictly's* first deaf contestant was going to open the eyes of her profession, her professional dancer, the production team and the watching public to the deaf community.

'We can't train in here. It's just too echoey.' That was day one. Gio had taken Rose to one of his favourite studios, but she couldn't hear a thing with all the sound bouncing off the walls.

Gio realised he had to completely change the way he had done *Strictly* in the past. 'When you dance with someone who hears, you don't think about sound. You don't think about the size of the room. Rose was lovely about it, but she just said, "I can't hear you. I can't be in here. I can't learn in here." We looked around for a new studio for a few hours and eventually we settled on the rehearsal room at Elstree which was much better for Rose. That was my first big lesson. The second one was a reminder that, when someone has never danced before, jive is a tough one to start with.'

'I think Gio was really worried that first week,' remembers

Rose. 'The room was bad, we'd had to move and I was really struggling with jive. I get asked a lot about what I can hear during the dance and it's hard for me to explain because I don't know what you hear. I have nothing to compare it to. I don't hear the music. Sometimes, I can feel it. There is like a hum in the background, but that's it. What Gio did really well was never letting go of me. I followed him really well and that's how we survived those first few weeks. That and a lot of ice-packs!'

Rose isn't joking about the ice-packs. I remember seeing her in the studio on the Friday before her opening dance and her ankles were the size of melons. 'I haven't told many people this, Dan,' says Gio, 'but I didn't know if Rose was going to make it through those first few weeks. I pushed her too hard for someone who had never danced before and for someone who didn't do that much exercise. It got to the point that I was going to ask the bosses if we could have a week off because Rose could hardly walk. I thought I might lose her. I told her it would be ok, and I changed the choreography for our jive to make it less intense and less jumpy and I did the same for the salsa in week two. I think that helped.'

'There was no way I was going to stop,' says Rose. 'I had to prove to myself that I could do it. No one was going to stop me getting on that dance floor. My ankles were massive, but I couldn't let people down. I couldn't bear the thought of someone saying, "It was probably too much for her" or "The poor deaf girl couldn't do it". I didn't want it to be an excuse.'

'I was really worried,' says Donna. 'I knew mentally she was so strong, but her body was stopping her. You were on those painkillers, weren't you, Rose?'

'I took painkillers but it still hurt. I would wake up my boyfriend in the middle of the night and ask him to carry me to the toilet so that I didn't have to walk. The team at *Strictly* were so supportive too. Ugo (Monye) got me this ice machine and the production team took care of everything. Gio just carried me around everywhere. The only thing I had to do was dance, so by the time we got to our first ballroom dance in week three, things were much better. I really like ballroom.'

I don't mind telling you that I voted for Rose from week one. I told Donna that too. I told her how amazing her daughter was and explained that, as the son of a deaf dad, it was blowing my mind how she was doing it. I found dancing hard enough and I can hear everything. Everywhere I went people were saying the same thing. 'Dan, we love you and Nadiya on *Strictly* but . . . how amazing is Rose?' She had captured the attention and the hearts of the nation and the fella who got to dance with her every week was equally enraptured.

'She is different to everyone else,' says Giovanni with a huge smile. 'I love *Strictly* but every year it can be the same for me as a professional. It depends on your partner a little, but you teach each dance the same way. Not with Rose. She made me change the way I choreograph. She made me think in a different, deeper way. She helped me to grow as a dancer, as a teacher and as a performer. Rose reinvigorated my love of *Strictly*. Dan, you saw how it works with Nadiya. It's a waltz . . . we teach you how to waltz. I have always taught waltz the same way, but with Rose, everything is different. Everything is better. She made me fall in love with the show and fall in love with teaching again. I will always be thankful to her for that.'

I'm about to ask Giovanni a question about when he thought Rose could go all the way and, before I was even halfway through, he says, 'Week three. Movie week was a big one. Ask Rose about movie week.'

When you talk to Rose about dancing, she doesn't talk about it like anyone else. Maybe it's the natural performer in her. Maybe it's the fact that she doesn't need the music but, while the rest of us could easily get bogged down in the fog of technique, concerns about hand position and whether it was a heal-lead, Rose was all about finding the character. The breakthrough was when Rose found Rose. When Rose from *EastEnders* found Rose from *Titanic*. I did exactly what Giovanni told me to do; I asked Rose about movie week.

'I didn't really listen to the music at all, Dan, to be honest. In my head, there wasn't any. It all became about muscle memory. During the week I would learn the technique and just religiously follow Gio. On a Saturday night all I could hear was a little bit of noise, the rest was all about the character.'

I ask her to explain how it works. 'Dancing for deaf people is just totally different. It's still beautiful but it has nothing to do with the music. All I'm trying to do is tell a story. I love telling stories. With *Titanic*, I watched the film, I learned as much as I could about that character, their personality, I read the subtitles and then, that's who I would become on the Saturday night. It was the same when we did the dance from *Frozen*, and

I was Anna. I don't know any of the songs from *Frozen*, but I can understand who she is and what makes her tick. She's a bit clumsy, lots of fun and a bit daft. She's a lot like me.' Rose laughs before declaring, 'I would love to play a Disney princess.'

I ask her what she does if there is no character and it's just a song? 'I would study the lyrics and find a character in the lyrics. You should see my Spotify playlist,' says Rose proudly. 'I went through all the lyrics carefully every week and then, when the time came, I gave it 100 per cent every single time. On Saturday night, you saw it, I was a different person. During the show, with the costume, the hair and the make-up, I wasn't Rose anymore, and I loved it.'

It's incredible, isn't it? It's easy to see why most of the professionals watching Rose dance every week were open-mouthed at what she was able to do. Giovanni had to keep his mouth closed on the dance floor.

'I still don't know how she did it,' he says. 'When you dance with her you can't understand that she doesn't hear the music. You get reminded every now and again. I have been a dancer for 23 years and Rose made me realise that music is not as important as I thought it was. She made me look at dancing in a different way ... and I thought I knew everything. Her connection to the dance was stronger than anyone I have ever met and, because she doesn't hear the music like I hear it, that meant our connection was so important. She had to connect to me. She needed me to touch her to help her, to guide her and that meant we were so finely tuned to each other which, in dance, means everything. Sometimes your partner gets distracted by the audience, the band, the music, the noise, the occasion, but never with Rose. It was just me and her.'

It was just the two of them on the dance floor, but it was the rest of the country falling in love with them every week. Rose was changing opinions, starting conversations and also breaking records. In week six, their tango produced the earliest ever perfect score in *Strictly* history. Four 10s from four jubilant judges.

'I felt the pressure that week,' says Giovanni. '*Strictly* always makes this big thing of me being the "King of Halloween" because I'm always top of the leader board each season. Rose and I were doing a tango. It was a good tango, but it was not a 40-point tango all week. Something happened when the music started in the studio. I felt like I was dancing with a professional. We had made a mistake in the dress rehearsal, and I think Rose used to like doing that because she only wanted one routine to be perfect. I can't describe how good she was that night. She was incredible. She came to life. I could see the public were falling in love with her. That tango, for me, will go down as one of my best ever dances on *Strictly*.'

Rose had become the overwhelming favourite to win the show in a year when the standard of dancing was the highest it has ever been (with the occasional exception). It was all getting a little tense for Donna.

'I went to five shows in total. I would spend the whole week talking to her. She would be the same every week. Monday and Tuesday were the "I can't do it" days and then, by about Thursday, she would start to say she had it and then I would spend the whole of Saturday a nervous wreck.'

'Did it get easier to watch me as I went further, Mum?' asks Rose.

'I think it was easier after week three – when you did *Titanic*. I think that was your breakthrough week. My favourite week was your Couple's Choice one. I think that was everyone's favourite. People still talk to me about that one all the time.'

Rose and Giovanni's dance to 'Symphony' by Clean Bandit was the standout moment of the 19th series of *Strictly Come Dancing*. I don't think it's going too far to say it was the standout moment of TV in 2021. The dance has picked up award after award, including a BAFTA for TV's 'Must-See Moment'. It was such a privilege to be sitting there on the night and witness the magic from just a few metres away.

At the point when Rose put her hands over Giovanni's ears and the music stopped, everyone in the studio, and I imagine everyone at home, held their breath. I was sitting next to Nadiya at one of the tables and I remember she reached out and grabbed my hand. When the music kicked back in, she just burst into tears and after the show she went up to Rose, still in tears, and thanked her for letting us all into her world. It was an epic bit of TV; an epic bit of TV that took an awful lot of planning and an epic bit of TV that almost went horribly wrong.

'We spoke to Giovanni about the idea really early on in the series,' says Sarah James, Executive Producer. 'The whole idea was that we wanted to try and give people an idea of what Rose's world was like, but at the start we didn't really know how to do it. We had so many meetings about whether we cut the music completely, whether there was complete silence, or should we have some background noise? Giovanni was totally invested in it and wanted it to be perfect. We all did.'

'I remember that Giovanni told me what he was planning,' says Rose. 'He said, in week eight we are going to dance in a silent moment. The music would stop and then come back on. I told him that I loved the idea but that I didn't want it to be sad. I don't want people to watch it and think, "Oh, look at the poor deaf girl". I've had enough of that in my life. I love being deaf. I wanted to show people that, if they came into my world, we'd be having a party.'

Lead choreographer Jason Gilkison, who works with all the couples and is a genuine genius, came up with the music and Giovanni was determined that Rose had to be happy with the dance.

Sarah James knew it was going to be a big moment. 'Some things happen for a reason, don't they? Jason had been wanting to use that song for a while. We had actually offered it to a different celeb the year before, but it didn't work. We wanted it to be emotional but also uplifting. Whenever you do a Couple's Choice on *Strictly*, the professional dancers are always assisted by our choreographers. Rose was really clear on what she wanted.'

'When I first saw the choreography, I didn't think it was right for me,' remembers Rose. 'The choreographers who worked with Jason, Ash-Leigh (Hunter) and Arduino (Bertoncello), had got to know me really well so we worked on it together with Giovanni. They both knew that I was so positive about being deaf and they poured all of that into the dance. Gio kept saying, "Is there any bit in it you don't like?" and we kept changing things right up until the Thursday morning. The thing I love most about it was, if you watch it closely, up until the silent moment we were dancing little bits from our routines in the previous weeks then I put my hands on his ears and open the door into how I dance.'

'I had so many meetings with production about that moment,' recalls Giovanni. 'At the start we were going to have the silence at the beginning, then we thought about doing it at the end but, eventually, we got it just right. Sarah James was amazing. At one point I think we were going to do the whole dance in silence, but I'm so glad we did it the way we did. It was perfect.'

One of the big concerns about the moment of silence was how Rose and Giovanni would get back into the dance. Rose couldn't hear anything but, for the first time, neither could Giovanni. They settled on a loose spin to get themselves back in time. Giovanni could control that but there were still worries over following the beat in the music when there was no beat. *Strictly* provided Giovanni with a belt that would pulse with the music. He could wear it underneath his clothes and that would keep him in time.

'We tried the belt in rehearsals a few times,' says Giovanni. 'It worked but it didn't feel right. Those ten seconds of silence were going to be the most powerful thing I had done in my life. It was all about the message and it had to be authentic. It had to be real. I called Sarah James and told her I couldn't wear the belt. I told her it was about Rose. The whole point of the dance was that I was experiencing what Rose feels, we all were. The belt defeated it. I would have been cheating. I needed to feel what she feels. When I told Rose I was getting rid of the belt she was so thankful. She knew that I understood her. She said, "Welcome to my world." It was beautiful.'

Strictly Saturdays are busy. Everyone arrives at some point in the morning, depending on how much time you need in hair and make-up. To give you an idea, when Nadiya was dressed up like Sleeping Beauty in week three, just her hair (crafted by the brilliant Anna Winterburn) took about five hours. All the couples have the chance to go through their dance twice with the band playing the music live. It always sounds very different to the track you rehearse with during the week so it's invaluable. That gives you the chance to iron out any issues and make a few tweaks. The rest of the day is filled with interviews, lunch, filming for social media, meetings about music, physio and then, at about 2.30, there is a full dress rehearsal.

Rose and Giovanni's dress rehearsal did not go well. I have to say that the band and singers on *Strictly* are the most phenomenally talented bunch of musicians I have ever seen but, during the 'moment of silence', there was quite a lot of noise. Giovanni had a word.

'I told Dave Arch that this was the most important thing I had ever done. I wanted it to be perfect. Dave is so good, and he promised me they would get it right when it mattered, but the pressure was on. I could tell everyone was nervous. We only had one opportunity to do it. They were amazing. Rose was amazing. The whole thing was amazing.'

'I was confident it would work,' says Sarah James, 'and it was wonderful. I was glad that we had achieved what we wanted. I was glad that Rose was happy. I had no idea just how huge it was going to become.'

'When we finished the dance,' says Gio, 'I could feel it. It was different to every other dance. I looked at Rose and she could feel it too. You don't get many moments like that in your life.'

When I speak to Rose about it, her partner at the time, Sam, is working on the table behind her.

'Sam was there that night, Dan. With his mum,' says Rose.

'What did he think of it, Rose? Can you ask him?' I said.

'Hold on. He's deaf. I'll have to tap him on the shoulder.' She reaches over the back of the chair and gets Sam's attention. 'Dan wants to know what you thought of the Couple's Choice.'

Sam turns round. 'It was wonderful,' he says with a smile. 'When I watched it, I knew it was a huge moment for the deaf community, but also for society. It was beautiful and I was just really proud of what Rose had done and I was so happy to be there.'

He turns to Rose. 'It was only you and me in the whole studio who were deaf that day, wasn't it?'

Rose nods. Her former partner continues. 'When you're deaf, we are really careful about how we share what our world is like. It's hard to explain to a hearing audience who have such a small knowledge and can never understand. We have our own culture, and we talk a lot about how positive it is to be deaf. What Rose did that night was invite the whole of the UK to experience what she sees, and what she hears every day. That is a game changer for the deaf community.'

Rose extends her hand and holds Sam's. Donna joins back into the conversation.

'She showed everyone that she was happy, Dan. The whole story was one of happiness. She showed the audience that too.'

'She showed that there was nothing wrong with me,' says Sam. 'I can't tell you how powerful that is for me and every deaf person out there. It's society that makes me feel different.'

This is why *Strictly* was so important for Rose. She wasn't just dancing. She was on a mission.

'*Strictly* gave me that access,' she says. 'We don't give disabled people a chance. Ask anyone. They will tell you the same thing. Every day is a battle sometimes because, as a society, we put all these obstacles and barriers in the way. The world is designed for hearing people. We are so proud of being deaf and we are very good at adapting to things.'

'People started to learn about our culture,' says Sam. 'Rose made the deaf community step forward years. She didn't do it by shouting or screaming or slashing tyres. All she did was open the door.'

'Lots of people just didn't know,' says Donna. 'What Rose did was educate a whole nation in the comfort of their living rooms, as part of Saturday-night telly. I told you she was amazing.'

'I didn't want to shout at anyone,' says Rose. 'I always try and teach with humour. It's so easy to be angry about it, because it hurts so much when you are discriminated against. Some days

I want to scream but all you get is, "Oh, she's a bit angry" or "She's too aggressive". I wanted to be positive.'

'That's who you are, Rose,' says a proud mum. 'You are such a positive person.'

On the day I spoke to Giovanni, British Sign Language had just been recognised as an official language: a campaign supported and inspired by Rose. The Italian still can't quite get his head around the impact that his partner has had on wider society.

'I knew we were going to do something so special for the deaf community and I knew it was going to be a big statement for Rose, but since then things have gone crazy. She has changed the world. Rose has opened everyone's eyes. After years of waiting, who would have thought that just ten seconds of silence on BBC One would make such a big difference?'

If you talk to Rose about the impact she has made, both during and since *Strictly*, she is quick to point out the support she received from the whole team on the show and particularly Sarah James and Stef Aleksander, the talent executive.

'They listened to everything I said from the start,' says the *Strictly* champion. 'I talked to them a lot about the interpreter. I didn't want all the attention and the camera to be on them all the time like it normally is. They are not here to help me, they are here to help hearing people to communicate with me. I had a responsibility to every other deaf person in the country. I wanted it to be about the deaf person and not about the interpreter. I didn't watch *Strictly* before I was on it, because the live subtitles are so slow, and you don't feel part of the show. Even twenty-four hours later, it's still live subtitles. Even a year later, it was still the live subtitles. Sarah James changed all that. We now have subtitles which will be on time within twenty-four hours and an interpreter on iPlayer and they have also added audio description for blind people.'

Donna has been listening carefully to her daughter. 'She won't say it herself, Dan, but she's changed TV forever. That's what everyone keeps saying. Everyone on the show had deaf awareness training too, didn't they, Rose?'

Rose nods and smiles. 'It was amazing. They couldn't have done more for me.'

'You know,' says Donna, 'I started following you all on Insta-gram and I watched you all putting these captions on for Rose. I was so proud. My little daughter changing the world. There is not a word that is big enough to say what it means to me as her mum. I've always been proud, since she got that first job in Sainsburys.'

Rose laughs. 'It's a bit bigger than Sainsburys, Mum.'

'I know. I know,' says Donna. 'It's also just a bit surreal. I always knew you'd do something like this.'

'She has always said that, Dan,' says Rose, giggling again but looking lovingly at Donna.

'I did. Maybe every mum thinks that. I didn't know she was going to be famous; I just knew she was special. She always had an impact on everyone, wherever she goes, and she has always worked so hard and . . .'

'Tell Dan about the World Cup,' interrupts Rose. 'You know, the score.'

'No, he'll think I'm daft,' says Donna, throwing her head back.

'Tell him, Mum, he'll love it.'

'Ok,' Donna admits defeat. 'I've always been a bit of a dreamer. I don't watch football at all, but once, England had a big game in the World Cup and, the day before, I dreamt the exact scoreline and then it came true.'

'She should have gone to the betting shop,' howls Rose.

Being in the studio for Rose and Giovanni's Couple's Choice was amazing. That weekend I gave Rose all three of my online votes. She normally got two and then I'd give the other one to either my favourite dance of the week or whoever had been in the dance-off the week before and survived. Channels will keep showing that dance for years to come. I watched it four times the next day with my kids, I'm sure lots of people did. What they did the following week in their paso doble was even more impressive. For much of the competition Rose would be in close contact with Giovanni to help her keep time with the music. For the paso, Rose started on her own on the stage and Giovanni was completely out of shot behind the camera. There is no footage of what he did anywhere, but it was incredible to witness.

'She was getting better every week,' recalls Giovanni, 'but I wanted her to be able to dance on her own. Sometimes when I was dancing with her, she was so good, I forgot she was deaf, and I wanted people to see that.'

'I remember that week,' says Rose. 'I was having a bit of a panic because I didn't want to look stupid. Gio was dancing behind the camera and I just had to follow him. It was really complicated, but it worked.'

'We tried it in rehearsals,' explains Gio, 'but she was always a little behind. I had to count her in and then dance one beat ahead of the music. If she copied me straightaway, we found out she was on time. I'll be honest with you, Dan, it felt completely wrong for me as a professional. Every time I did it I was like "WHAT ARE YOU DOING?" but she was amazing and it was perfect.'

That perfection, or as close to it as possible, continued right the way to an emotional final. AJ was out injured, so she and Kai had to watch from the sidelines. John and Johannes were equally sensational, but it was impossible to stop Rose and Giovanni from lifting the glitterball trophy.

'I was exhausted that week,' remembers Rose. 'My body started to shut down. That Monday after the semi-final was one of the worst days. Gio wasn't happy. "What is wrong with you? Why are you giving up?" he said. "This is one last week. You've got to go for it." He was quite military about it all, but it did help me get my head together. I just told myself that this was my last ever week on *Strictly* and I was going to enjoy it, every second of it. The one thing that caught me out was the emotion of the final. It just hit me on the day that it was going to be the last day that we would dance together, and I was overcome by the sadness of that. I cried all day.'

'I have never cried before over *Strictly*,' says Giovanni, 'but that final day with Rose was ridiculous. Every time I heard her name, it would set me off.' He starts running through some of the things Rose had to do to prepare for the final and then making the sound of someone sobbing.

'Rose needs to go to make-up.' [tears]

'Rose needs to get her hair done.' [tears]

'We need Rose for an interview.' [tears]

'Rose is in the toilet.' [tears]

'I know,' says Giovanni, gesticulating wildly as only an Italian can. 'I even cried when she went to the toilet! I didn't want it to finish. I was a complete mess. I am addicted to her. She wasn't just a great dancer. She was wonderful to be around and just so funny. When we went up to see Claudia, I had no idea what she was going to say. I have got to tell you; she completely ruined my reputation. She killed off the "Italian Stallion",' he says laughing.

'People keep telling me I have changed, but I think the truth is that Rose brought out a different side of me. On *Strictly*, you get used to people saying you are sexy or attractive, but with Rose it was completely different. After our amazing Couple's Choice, the whole nation is in tears, and Rose tells Claudia that I have horrible feet, like Gollum! She said she didn't like being so close to me in the Argentine tango because I had "smelly breath". She would always talk about me being too sweaty and I used to tell her that people would pay a lot of money for that. She didn't care. That's Rose. I have never had a partner like her before and I loved it. I wasn't nervous when we were in the final like I have been in the past, because I knew that what Rose had done was bigger than all of that. In one sense, we had already won.' He stops and has a little giggle to himself. 'But, it was still nice to lift the trophy.'

'I reacted when Gio reacted,' says Rose. 'I didn't hear my name, but I knew from his scream that it was us and I just went completely blank. I was out of my body. I couldn't feel anything. It was like my eyeballs were coming out of my head. Everything closed in. I felt like . . . that's it. We've done it.'

Donna was even more of a mess at the side of the dance floor. 'I remember thinking, "It's going to be Rose", "It might not be Rose", "She's going to win" . . . "It's going to be John and Johannes". It went on for ages. I was trying to take everything in and enjoy the moment, but I also just wanted Tess (Daly) to get on with it. And then, before I knew it, it was all over. I remember crying because I was sad that I wasn't going to watch her dance again.'

'I felt the same,' says Rose. 'If you'd have said to me that night that it was possible for me to dance for another ten weeks, I'd have done it in a heartbeat. We spoke to Claudia and then Gio and I just burst into tears. We knew that was the end.'

It was an emotional night for Giovanni. 'Donna came up to me and thanked me for what I had done for Rose,' he says, 'and that set me off again. She told me that I had made her feel more confident and that I had changed her life forever. I am just a dance teacher but that was so special. I went off to thank everybody and Rose and Donna had some time on their own.'

I took a photo of Rose and Donna having that 'time on their own' and the following morning, I posted it on social media. You can find it in the photo section. The caption said this:

Of all the photos from last night ... this might be my favourite. Rose's mum knows how hard she has worked, how many barriers she has had to run through, how many times she has been told 'no' and how much all this means. That's why I voted for her from day one.

Donna remembers the moment well. 'The lights went off and the sparkle just sort of disappeared. I was watching as everyone was looking at my daughter and I needed some "mum-time" with her. I think I just said, "Well done." I think that was enough. I couldn't really speak.'

'I was still in shock until Mum came and gave me a hug,' remembers Rose. 'She sort of snapped me out of it. Do you remember, Mum? I was surprised that it affected you so much.'

'I know,' says Donna. 'I wasn't sad. I was so happy for you. I didn't need to say anything because you knew it already. You had worked so hard for so long, doing everything in the public eye with everyone talking about you. I had bottled all of that up and it just all came out ... It was just little Rose up there.'

They look at each other for some time. Remembering the moment before Rose breaks the silence. 'The only person who knew me before all this was my mum. She is the one who understood why it was important. I didn't want to get a pity vote, and I think we won because I became a good dancer and that was all because of Gio. He always wanted more from me. He wanted quality in my movement. He kept teaching me to finish and to shape things and to use my body. He was never happy to just do well. "You can always give me more," he used to say ... and he was right. He believed in me more than I believed in myself. He was exactly the person I needed him to be.'

I loved my time on *Strictly*. I don't think I will ever have as much fun as I did in those three months of dancing and learning alongside Nadiya, but a huge part of the enjoyment came from being a small part of a very special series. Each Saturday, I was mesmerised by Rose and, sitting on the *BBC Breakfast* sofa every week, I got to see that the rest of the country felt exactly the same. Every couple would get letters sent to them each week which would arrive at Elstree on a Saturday morning. Most of us could carry them in one hand; Rose and Giovanni needed a bag for life! I was desperate to include them in this book because they are the epitome of what it is to lift others up. Donna never allowed Rose to think she was anything other than special. At times it was a fight, but she dug in, time and time again, and made sure that her daughter had the same opportunities as everyone else. Giovanni lifted Rose up – literally – to allow her to shine on that dance floor. He worked hard to make sure her deafness was never an obstacle. He turned it into a superpower! And then there is Rose. The 'deaf girl' who fine-tuned all our senses, and gave us a much-needed kick up the backside at the same time.

She inspired and highlighted the deaf community.

She made the biggest show on the box far more inclusive and turned Saturday-night television into a force for societal change.

While changing others, I asked Rose, Donna and Giovanni how the experience has changed them. 'I woke up on a Monday morning after *Strictly*,' says Giovanni, 'and I think I was talking to you on the TV and it hit me . . . I am not going to see Rose today. It was horrible. I don't mind telling you, I am addicted to Rose! You cannot stay away from her. She is contagious. I have to talk to her every day'

'But seriously,' he says, composing himself, 'I have done the show for seven years and I have never thought about deaf people. I learned from her that all things are possible, and I think I have a responsibility now to make other people aware. At my solo tour now, we have a section where we do the sign for clapping instead of clapping, like we did on *Strictly*. I do a little bit of sign language myself in the show. We can all do that – just a little bit. I have deaf people coming to the show for the first time. I have an interpreter for the first time. We had the same thing on the live *Strictly* tour. It's better than a standing ovation and it's all because of Rose. She should be a dame. She has changed the world. She has made me think about so much. What do I do as a dancer? What can I achieve? I can do a good dance. I can win a competition but, what she did, what we did together, is so much bigger than any of that. If she was here now, I would say . . . I would say thank you "Rose," he says, as if speaking to her, "you made me a better person, you made me more kind, you made me more aware, you made me less selfish and you taught me to enjoy what I have and to remember to not be in a rush. You showed me the importance of joy and happiness." We all forget that sometimes. Rose can do anything she wants in life. A deaf person can win *Strictly*.' He says it again and shouts it at me. 'A DEAF PERSON CAN

WIN *STRICTLY*! I know you don't swear, Dan, but write this down . . . If Rose can do that, if you have the right mindset, you can do whatever the $%££ you want. I'm dreaming big for Rose. I look forward to her inviting me to do the opening dance at the Oscars one day when she picks up the top prize. There is no stopping her.'

Rose and Donna are sitting having a chat, like they do most days. This time, they are reflecting on that *Strictly* win and what it means to the pair of them going forward.

'I learned that I can be confident in myself,' says Rose after much thought. 'I can be myself. I learned most of all about how, even at your lowest, you can still keep going even if your body is crashing. I didn't think I had that in me. I was always comfortable when I did exercise. I did swimming or yoga. I never understood why people pushed their body to the limit, but that is where you learn so much about yourself. You go into survival mode, and you realise what and who you really are. I was confident in private before *Strictly*, but I am now that way in public. I used to have to be so careful but, during the show, I would just go up to Claudia and whatever came out was fine. I don't need to plan what I say anymore. I can just be me.'

'What about what you showed people about the deaf community, Rose?' asks her mum.

'I think people saw that sign language is beautiful,' says a reflective *Strictly* champion. 'They learned how different deaf people could be. When I talk to deaf people now, they say, "You started the conversation". People aren't frightened anymore. Anyone can do anything.'

'For me,' says Donna, 'people have learned that it's ok to ask questions. They will ask me all sorts of stuff and, for the first time, they are interested in the answers. That's a big change. Rose won't like this, but she taught me to be brave. Rose was so courageous to go on a show that was about dancing and music. I know she did it to make people more aware and that makes me feel even more emotional. She showed me that I could be brave. I'm more confident now. I'm quite a shy person. Everyone wanted to talk to me, and I have become more confident and don't worry so much. That's all because of Rose.'

'It does get a bit scary sometimes,' admits Rose. 'I went on the tour and there were posters of me, books with me on them, T-shirts and everything. Before *Strictly*, I could do anything, and people didn't care. I was wondering if this is what my life is going to be like forever, but thankfully it has relaxed a bit now.'

'You can go back to Sainsburys now, can't you, Rose?' laughs Donna.

Rose rolls her eyes and brings things back to the big issues. 'I'm glad we've managed to use the awareness to make a difference and get British Sign Language to be recognised as a language. The government can't just sweep it under the carpet. They can't do that anymore. It has to go further. I want to make a documentary about that, and I still want to do what I love. I feel responsible, I'll keep fighting, but I also want to enjoy life. I know we used to say, "Keep dancing", Dan, but it's "Keep acting" for me now.'

'I would love to see her play an evil character in a movie!' says Donna. 'I want her to be in a film which really pushes her ... a baddy! Something to really test her. I know she can do it. She can do anything.'

'Mum!' says Rose.

'What?' says a proud Donna. 'I watched you at the BSL [British Sign Language] rally in Trafalgar Square. Tell Dan about it.'

'It was amazing, Dan,' says Rose, full of enthusiasm. 'It's the first time I have seen such big a group of deaf people and they were so kind. They said I had changed their lives and one said that she had been discriminated against at work for so long and had taken them to court. She said she saw me on *Strictly* and thought, "I will never give up." Soon after that she won her case because, she said, attitudes were changing. Isn't that amazing? It's a bit overwhelming sometimes. I only danced on a show!'

'It was brilliant to watch her that day,' says Donna. 'It was a big moment for me, as her mum. She got on the stage, and she signed a speech. She presented it really well. It blew me away. She signed a poem. It was like watching someone from the UN. I cried!'

'Oh, Mum,' says Rose, in a mixture of embarrassment but obvious love.

'I have to remind myself,' says Donna, 'my daughter won *Strictly Come Dancing*!'

They both laugh.

'You're never going to stop going on about it, are you, Mum?'

'No, and why should I? A deaf girl, my daughter, won *Strictly*, and millions of people watched you do it. You showed me, you showed everyone, that nothing is impossible.'

THREE DADS, THREE DAUGHTERS

I want to tell you about Sophie, Beth and Emily – three young women with so much to give.

Sophie was bold and brash. She was very loud, always entering a room with a raucous 'hiya'. She was just a fun person to be with. She had always been incredibly sociable. For much of her life, Sophie lived in Kendal in the Lake District and used to love walking the fells with her dad.

Everyone always said how considerate she was. She always thought about other people and was really well liked. She was deputy head girl at senior school but she also discovered alcohol and boys before going to Newcastle University to study history. She hated it and by Christmas had dropped out. She made a pact with her parents that she wouldn't just lounge about and she learned to drive, had her tonsils taken out and ended up going to Kenya for four months where she worked in an orphanage. Sophie came back from that trip and announced she was going to be a nurse. Her caring and empathetic nature made her a brilliant nurse. Sophie met a lad called Sam. They fell in love, moved to Edinburgh – where she worked at the Western General Hospital – and got married.

Beth was a wonderful person. She was tactile, loving and happy. She was born later in the year so was always the youngest in her class, but was incredibly popular at school – always the centre of attention. She loved going out and was a huge fan of Harry Potter and Johnny Depp.

During her time at secondary school, Beth developed a talent for singing. She was a natural dancer and was always right at the front of any performance. Her mum was a professional dancer and Beth had clearly inherited that talent. All her friends saw her as loving and loyal.

She went to a performing arts college after school and was brilliant. She started gigging around Manchester. It was her dream to be on the stage.

Emily was a brilliant artist. She was also the life and soul of every party, but the public perception was very different to what was happening in private. She was struggling through life. At 16, she was diagnosed with autism. That private diagnosis was a huge breakthrough. It helped Emily know why she was different and her family all noticed a big change. She wanted to keep the autism quiet though, and only her family and a few close friends knew about what she was going through.

Disguising the autism took a lot of effort – effort that would leave her completely wiped out. After her GCSEs, Emily went on to art college, did a personal training course and she learned to drive. That was so important to her because it gave her the freedom she was lacking. She worked in the village pub which had been bought by the local community. It was never her plan for that to be her forever job, but it was really good for her. The job, combined with the freedom of being able to drive and the ability to regularly go to the gym, kept Emily going.

Sophie, Beth and Emily: a nurse, a performer and an artist.

Three young women adored by their families.

Three young women with so much going for them.

Three young women who all took their own lives.

Three young women who all left behind three broken dads.

Three dads who it has been my privilege to meet and interview on several occasions.

Three dads on a mission to make a difference.

Andy is Sophie's father. Sophie was a daughter from his first marriage to George. Andy is now married to Fiona but everyone had a great relationship with Sophie. Andy and Fiona have a son, Gregor, who is nine years younger than Sophie.

'When I look back now,' says Andy, 'I can see that she struggled to get her head around who she was. There was a period, when she was at university, where I think she had that feeling of not knowing what she was going to do with her life. There was a weight of uncertainty. She was very much like me.' He pauses and looks upwards. 'She was always internalising. You convince yourself that you don't need help and you are sure that the best thing to do is just deal with it yourself.'

Sophie was in her late twenties and living in Edinburgh with her husband, Sam. 'I was in contact with her all the time,' says Andy with a huge smile on his face. 'We saw her regularly and, every time we did, she seemed fine. Her and Sam were living what looked like a great life. We talked about stuff. If I was worried about her, she would listen to me and would always answer questions.

'In September 2018, they came and stayed with us in Kendal on a Saturday night. During the day, Fi and I had taken Gregor to university in Liverpool. We expected Sophie and Sam to be there when we got back but, as we were driving back down the road, we got a tearful call from Soph to say she'd left Sam and she was struggling. She said she didn't love him anymore. Both Fi and I were stumped. Where had this come from? We went to Edinburgh the next day and brought her back home with us. I had never seen her that low . . . it felt like she was self-destructing.'

Andy knew that relationships changed and that people split up all the time. Sophie was sad, but there was nothing that suggested what she was going through was life-threatening.

Andy continues, 'For the next couple months she tried to sort herself out. She got herself a new flat a little nearer to the hospital. She had a new job to look forward to which started just after Christmas, and it looked like she was pulling her life back together. Sophie was down every now and again, but there was nothing that I looked at that made me worry. Things were looking up.'

Sophie turned twenty-nine on 12 December 2018. She took her own life seven days later, just before Christmas. Andy will never forget that day.

'I remember we were in Boots in Carlisle on the afternoon of the 19th. It sounds crazy now, but we had booked in to get our yellow fever injections because we were planning on going to visit Fi's brother who lived in Gambia. Like a typical dad, I had somehow managed to bum-dial Sophie while this was happening. She was in the car at the time.' Andy pauses and smiles as he remembers Sophie's response to a typically embarrassing dad. 'She was telling me how stupid I was and we were laughing together. I apologised for being daft and we said goodbye and I put the phone back in my pocket.' Andy later found out that at that precise moment, Sophie was on her way to take her own life.

I cannot imagine what it must be like to lose a daughter or a son like that. I know you're probably reading this at the moment and thinking . . . where is the light in all of this? Where is the way out? Where is the hope? Believe me, it's coming and, strangely, Andy is one of those who provides the hope with a little bit of help from two other dads called Tim and Mike.

Tim is Emily's dad. I'm sure everyone reading this will have very strong memories of what it was like when we went into coronavirus lockdown in March 2020. Tim has a particularly vivid memory because that was the week that things started to unravel for nineteen-year-old Emily.

'It was the week when everything was changing. Gyms were closed, the pub was closing and then on 16 March some people in the family started to cough. The next day Emily started to cough. There were three things she really needed in her life to keep things ticking over: the gym for the physical release, working in the pub for money and being able to drive around in the car for freedom. All of those were taken away in the space of a few days. Things changed very quickly with Emily. We were locked down in the house and had a lovely Monday and Tuesday watching Disney films but she woke the next day incredibly agitated. She was desperate to take the car to the coast and take our dog for a walk but we said "no" because she had symptoms and we were one of those families who were carefully following the rules.'

By the end of that day Emily had tried to take her own life. The family have understandably asked that I don't go into details of what Emily did, but she was in a bad way. Her own dad tried to resuscitate her after finding her at the family home. After twenty minutes of CPR, he'd managed to find a heartbeat but then came the hospital experience that so many people found during the middle of the pandemic.

'Because of her symptoms, Emily went into a Covid ward and we couldn't see her for two days,' says Tim. 'She tested negative and we finally got to see her on that Friday in a normal intensive care ward. Things weren't looking good. She'd signed up to be an organ donor when she was younger and by Friday evening, we were having that discussion with the team at the hospital. The Saturday was a long day as the transplant team tried to line up recipients. You can imagine that the pandemic was causing all sorts of issues for the people involved. On Sunday, just after midday, Emily's life support was turned off. The fact that her organs were donated was the only light in a sea of darkness. Thinking about that is what gets me through some days. It was the following day that the Prime Minister appeared on television to announce the nationwide lockdown.'

Tim is married to Sue. Annabel, Tom and Evie are Emily's surviving siblings. Tom, who was fourteen at the time, was the one who called 999 that day. Both Tom and Evie, who was only nine, saw their dad performing CPR on their sister. Those are scars which don't heal easily and the whole family had the gruesome experience of a lockdown funeral and the brutal brevity of saying goodbye to someone you love.

'We couldn't see her at the undertakers,' explains a tearful Tim. 'We were all so terrified of getting Covid and not being able to go to her funeral that we just kept ourselves to ourselves. People dropped off food at the house but we didn't spend time with anyone in the build-up to her funeral. There was only a twenty-five-minute service at the crematorium. That was it. Just six of us went to the funeral – the five of us and our eldest daughter's boyfriend. It was all over in a flash, and we were back home by 10.30 in the morning with the rest of our lives – without Emily – ahead of us. I've never seen someone in as many pieces as my wife was that day. She was totally broken. I remember that after the funeral, Sue said, "She's gone and no one will remember her in a year's time." That is one of the hardest things to get your head around, but it was also one of the things that convinced me that I had to find a way out of the pain and the misery. I had to try and find something to cling on to.'

One of those things which Tim found was companionship.

Strength came from talking to people who had been through the same heartache as him. Eventually it would be Andy, but it started with Beth's dad, Mike.

Mike lives in Manchester with his wife Helen. He has a daughter, Charley, from his first marriage, and Emily, who was Beth's sister, with Helen.

Beth was seventeen when she took her own life. It was just five days after Tim's Emily had died in Norfolk. Mike, like everyone who has lost a family member or friend to suicide, has spent hours, sometimes days, mulling over things she did and said before she died.

'Looking back,' says Mike, 'I can see she was losing hope. She was great at the singing, but I think her music was becoming slower, maudlin. I can see now that she had lost the bounce and the power. In the months before she left us, she had become quite moody and dark with the music. I remember all the conversations.'

He pauses. It looks like he is going back over things in his head. Suddenly, he jumps back into the conversation. 'It was at that time that only one person was allowed to go shopping. I remember that week I'd worked hard in the garden so we could spend time in there during lockdown. Beth had been going for a few runs with her sister, but she wasn't really herself. The day before it happened, she hadn't got out of bed, so I went into her room at midday and told her to get up. She told me she was having a bad day. I told her to stop being ridiculous, to get things together and to come downstairs. She did come down and played with the dog. The next day I remember her coming down from her room. I had loads of phone calls that day and in the evening I had to go to work.' Mike is a firefighter at Manchester airport.

'I was doing a bit of a workout just outside the house and I looked inside to see that Beth was chatting to her mum. She went down into our cellar which is where she used to go to practise her signing. I heard her voice in there. I used to love listening to her. She had such a beautiful voice. I'd finished my workout and I was getting ready for work. I went down to the cellar to get my coat, but I remember that I decided not to go in because I didn't want to interrupt her recording. I went to work and came home early in the morning and me and Helen went out for a dog walk. We talked about getting the girls out a bit more, so they didn't feel so cooped up. We got back to the house and had breakfast. The girls weren't down yet but there was nothing unusual about that.'

Mike, as he usually did after a nightshift, went for a snooze on the sofa. 'I was woken up at about 12. I heard screaming. Helen had gone into Beth's bedroom and found her body. I ran upstairs . . . my legs were like lead . . . I knew she was dead as I sprinted to her room. Emily was up and I raced into Beth's room and slammed the door on the rest of the family. I wouldn't let them in. I didn't want them to see her. I am a first responder. I'd used defibs many times and I knew she wasn't coming back. It wasn't long before the paramedics arrived, and they confirmed what we already knew. She was gone.'

'That is the worst day of your life. A nightmare that never finishes. Tears wouldn't come at first. It just didn't happen. It was just absolute horror and shock. The police turned up, a friend across the road turned up. That day will never leave me. I go through it every day . . . every day.'

The words are just pouring out of Mike at this point. 'The guilt comes from missing behaviour that is unusual. Beth had maybe started to become a little eccentric and annoying at mealtimes and that wasn't her. She was pushing the boundaries of going out, but she was seventeen and she was at music college. "Dad, you don't understand," she would say. "I'm having a bad day." I just wish I'd opened my eyes a bit more,' says Mike. 'Why couldn't I see that she was going from a high to a low so often? I remember talking to her about getting some new equipment for her singing and she just wasn't interested. Now I look at that like a red flag. I wish I'd had the knowledge then that I have now.'

In my last book I wrote about the death of Gary Speed. That was over ten years ago, and I still think all the time about the final day I spent with him before he took his own life. There are many questions I ask myself about things I could or should have seen, things I could have asked about and whether he'd still be here if I'd done something differently that day. I have gone over the day in minute detail. Gary was a good friend of mine, but I imagine when the person you lose is a daughter the pain is magnified, and the questions never stop. That is certainly how Mike feels.

'The opportunity arose to talk to Beth the day before and I

missed it,' he says. 'My wife Helen feels the same and she, just like me, is wracked with grief and remorse. Helen couldn't be a better mother. She doted on Beth and couldn't have done more for her, but here we both are without a daughter, wondering if we could have done more to help her.'

Mike himself needed help. He was spiralling into a dark place. That help would come from an unusual source. In Norfolk, Annabel, Tim's eldest, sent a message to Mike's daughter, Emily. She'd seen what the family were going through and decided to reach out. Emily showed the message to Mike, who ended up talking to Annabel on the phone.

'She suggested that I talk to her dad, to Tim,' remembers Mike. 'I was desperate. I had tried a support group, but I just didn't get it. I didn't know what to say or how to say it, but for some reason, I thought I could talk to Tim. It was the best thing I ever did.'

I have had the privilege of meeting hundreds of people over many years of interviews who have been through incredibly low moments in their lives. It may be illness, trauma, loss, fear, so many things which have the ability to bruise or crush us. I have always been fascinated by the way people pull themselves out of the mire. So many of those stories involve talking to someone who has fallen into the same hole as you; someone who carries the same scars, who has had the same thoughts and carries the same burdens. Tim, Mike and Andy are a classic example of gathering strength and finding a reason in a shared experience, however grim that experience continues to be.

So how was it for Tim to find out that his twenty-one-year-old daughter, Annabel, was talking to a dad in Manchester? I ask the pair of them that question together and they both laugh. Mike turns to Tim with a look on his face that suggests he is quite interested in the answer.

'It was so odd at first. Forgive me, Mike,' Tim says with a big grin on his face, 'but it is a little weird to discover that your daughter is speaking to a strange bloke hundreds of miles away. This was just three weeks after the deaths of our daughters. It was a strange way to start a friendship, but we quickly found common ground. Mike is a firefighter and I used to fly Tornados. Both our daughters were very artistic and brilliant singers. We were both in a very similar place and we both had other children. I remember being really frank about where we were. We just held each other's hands all the way through the inquests. We were just speaking to each other and going through what we could learn from each other. Everything we had planned and built for our families had gone. It's a strange foundation for a relationship but it worked.'

Mike jumps in. 'You've got to remember, Dan, I had no one. I was desperate. I'd tried grief counselling, but it just wasn't working. I was in a place where I didn't even know how to talk to anyone about it. What do you say when you've lost a daughter like that? How do you even begin to see your way out of that? My way out of that started with Tim.'

Tim has an incredible memory for dates and names. Out of the three dads, he is the one who writes everything down: when things happened, who was there, who said what. Several times during our conversations he asks me to wait a moment while he flicks through his notes to check the name of someone or the exact time that something took place. Unsurprisingly, he has a clear memory of that first conversation with Mike.

'I remember we had so much in common. We both had a link through aviation. I was in the RAF and Mike worked at Manchester airport. We both had families; families who were struggling. Most painfully, we'd both given CPR to our daughters. We spoke graphically about those final moments; things you wouldn't think you could say to anyone, but with that openness and honesty you find a validation for how you are feeling and how someone else feels. I needed Mike and he needed me. I just instantly knew that this was a man who knew what I was going through. I didn't have to explain to him the depths of my feelings because he was there too.' Mike nods in agreement and adds that Tim was always there in the dark times for him.

'The best thing about it,' explains Tim, 'is that I could call him at any time. Professional help really works for some people but it's always at an allotted time. We could call each other whenever we needed it.'

'The most important thing for me,' adds Mike, 'is that I felt no shame talking to Tim. There were no areas that I felt I needed to conceal from him. Sometimes the tears just flowed. Sometimes you couldn't find the words and you just listened. We just discussed everything brutally and openly and with no shame, which was so important for me.'

Grief is such a complex issue. It affects people in all sorts of ways. One thing that all three of the dads said to me when they spoke to me in the studio, on the phone or in person was that they felt I understood what they were going through. All three of them referenced the death of Gary Speed and how they had seen how that had affected me deeply. I am well aware there is a big difference between losing a friend and losing a daughter, but there is common ground. There are the complicated feelings of guilt mixed with sadness and anger. There is an overwhelming sense of loss combined with a helplessness and a nagging – sometimes crippling – feeling that you should and could have done more to help. That 'why didn't I see it?' scream that wakes you up in the middle of the night or lingers for hours in the back of your mind.

All three of the dads have been through all those emotions time and time again. What Tim and Mike felt they both needed was to know that there was a way through it all. Tim has always been incredibly practical about navigating the grief of suicide, it's the way his brain works. He saw things quite clearly quite quickly. If he and Mike were going to come through this, to find a way of living without their daughters, they needed the support of someone who had walked the path they were tentatively stepping out on. They needed Andy.

At this point, I need to mention Papyrus. Papyrus is a charity which is dedicated to the prevention of suicide, particularly in young people. Their vision is all about encouraging society to talk openly about suicide and equipping young people with the tools to deal with thoughts that could lead to them thinking about taking their own lives.

The three dads have all benefited from the work of the charity and are all passionate advocates. We'll talk about that more a little later. Papyrus was also responsible for bringing Andy into the equation.

'Our son, Gregor, was at university in Liverpool,' explains Andy, 'and the head offices of Papyrus are in Warrington. We dropped in and Gregor registered on one of their courses. He was always keen to learn and to help others. You'll never guess who he sat next to on one of his courses?'

'Gregor told me all about his rough Cumbrian dad,' giggles Mike. 'I'd already heard a little bit about him because I knew he liked walking and I'd had this silly idea about doing some sort of charity walk. I'd watched some of Andy's films online and that had got me thinking. Now, here I was sat next to his son. I thought to myself, "I'm no good at map reading, I could do with finding someone who is." Gregor said that his dad might be interested. That's where it all began.'

Andy and Mike met for a walk. It was an incredible, emotionally charged occasion. They were open and they were honest. Andy laughs as he remembers Mike producing a 2010 AA Road Map with some lines on it. Penrith was marked on there, so was Mike's house in Sale in Manchester. There was a dot at Derby and another one at King's Lynn, Tim's hometown. Mike told Andy all about Tim, and the idea of a walk between their three homes to raise awareness of suicide prevention was born.

Each of the dads was leaning on the others. The walk provided a focal point for all of them; something to concentrate on. They all speak powerfully about those dark days when death comes calling on the family home.

'I was desperate,' recalls Mike. 'I was surrounded by so many people, but I was totally alone even when I was stood next to my wife. The world completely changed. I had to go out very early in the morning to walk the dog. It was like I was walking in a parallel universe. It's quite hard to describe it to you . . . I could recognise things but nothing felt right.'

Mike composes himself for a moment and addresses the heart of the issue. 'The thing is, I couldn't have loved anything more than Beth and to lose her like that, it's overwhelming. If I'm honest, at times, I struggle with still wanting to be here myself. I even got to the point of planning it, but every day something would happen to put me off: the phone would ring, I'd have to do something for one of my daughters, or they'd say, "Dad, I'll call you tomorrow." My sister was great. I would call Lindsey in the middle of the night, just like I would call Tim. The pair of them were massive for me and there were other people like the chaplain from Manchester airport, Chaplain George. I'm not really a man of faith but he listened to me. He didn't say much but he just listened. One of the things you think about is, what happens when you die? Is that the end? It was wonderful to talk those things through with George. I started to read a lot of stuff about the afterlife.'

Mike pauses again before returning to thoughts of his own future: 'I'm not proud of it, Dan, you know, planning it. I've dealt with a lot of death through my job. I always work absolutely to my limit to save people. I was good at it. This was totally

84

different. She had taken her own life. What went wrong? What had I done? Sometimes the knock-on effect of suicide is suicide. Every day I have to look at my wife, my daughters and the rest of the family and see the pain that they still go through.'

Sometimes anger grips Mike hard. 'It's still very much there, if I'm honest. I see what it has done to the people she loved. I think a lot about the whole issue of forgiveness. Is it a case of us forgiving Beth for what she did, or is it about us forgiving ourselves for not seeing her pain? It feels like life is a fight. A fight with your mind and for positive mental health. There are so many questions I will never be able to answer. Was it a teenage thing? Was she cross with us? The police took her laptop and her phone and there was nothing on there to indicate she was thinking about it. The thing is she's gone . . . I can't talk to her but there are two things that drive me on: trying to better understand why Beth might have taken her own life and trying to stop others from doing the same. That is a huge part of the healing process for me. I was a dad. I was Beth's dad, and I didn't see this coming. I just want other dads, other parents out there, to be able to see things more clearly than I did and to talk to their children before it's too late.'

Tim asks himself the same questions that rattle around Mike's head. 'I often wonder why she felt she couldn't tell us how she was feeling,' says Tim. You can tell by his delivery that it's a question which weighs heavily on his mind. 'Why didn't we let her go out driving that day? If only we had let her. We all think that if we'd let her go to the coast that day then she'd have been fine. She'd still be here. We have a nephew who lives in Northern Italy, and he was telling us how bad it was there, and we all felt that we were just a couple of weeks behind. I think that concern about the future just got on top of Emily. She couldn't see a way out.'

Tim pauses and gathers his thoughts for a moment. 'What could I have said to her? I think about that a lot. We were doing the right thing by society by not letting her go out, but not the right thing by our family.'

When I first spoke to Tim for this book it was right in the middle of the revelations about parties at Downing Street during lockdown. I asked him if he found that hard to process given that he and his family tried so hard to stick to the rules during that period and they still feel that Emily might be here now, if the government had been willing to relax them slightly. He takes his time to respond. A smile comes across his face, and he looks at me. I can see there is great wisdom behind his eyes. 'I think I need to be very careful about what I say here, Dan.' Safe to say that Tim and his wife share the view of many people who lost loved ones during the pandemic. 'We felt we were doing our bit to save lives, to help others. We listened to the politicians. We followed what they said. We did what they asked and because we did that, we lost Emily that day. The idea that the rule-makers weren't following their own regulations leaves us with a bitter taste in the mouth.'

Emily's ashes were scattered down in Cornwall. The family are trying hard to move on. Emily's brother and sister started to go back to school in the September after they lost her, but every little step has been hard. Tim couldn't handle the memories of their old house. He couldn't bear to be there. 'We'd spent our whole lives dreaming of this house. I built it. It was overlooking fields and it was beautiful, but it was also the place our daughter died and it will always be stained by those memories. All our life plans were completely blown out of the water.'

There were two incidents which had a huge impact on Tim. They were two crucial steps on his way out of the grief. The first is something we've already mentioned. It was his wife, Sue, saying after Emily's funeral that no one would remember her. That forced Tim to think about doing something to make sure that never happened. The second was a bizarre situation which came about after his mother-in-law fell down the stairs of her home in Coventry.

'About four weeks after Emily died, Sue's mum hurt herself. She broke her ankle falling down those stairs, so we all decided that the best thing for her to do was to come and stay with us. We didn't have a spare room so that meant our only option was to clear Emily's room for her to stay in. Up to that point we hadn't touched a thing in there. The police had gone through all her stuff, but it was exactly how she had left it. We started clearing it out and I took a cloth bag out of her wardrobe. As I picked it up a piece of folded paper fell out of it. It was a suicide note.' Tim stops for a moment, recalling the emotion of that day.

'The police must have missed it because it was so thin and easy to gloss over. I opened it up and collapsed as I read it. I'm so glad she wrote it, but I can't tell you how hard it was to read. She said she felt she was a burden and that she couldn't cope.

She wrote that she could see no other option and she asked us not to worry about anything.'

I am struggling to hold in the tears as I think about Tim finding the precious note from his daughter. He is taking regular pauses as he recalls perhaps the most important thing he has ever read.

'Two sentences really got me. There were two things in there which changed my life. Emily had written "don't be ashamed of what I've done" and also, and even more importantly, she said "if others can learn from what I'd done, please let them". I knew I had to do something. I knew that Mike had rowed the Atlantic before, so he was intrepid. I knew he was planning some sort of walk but what we needed to make it all happen was someone like Andy. Not only was he an expert adventurer but he became the man who showed me what the next chapter of my life could look like. I kept thinking, how do I get out of bed in the morning? How do I get beyond today? Andy was the man with the answers.'

'Do you remember that day when I called Sophie in Boots from my pocket?' says Andy. 'Well, that night we came home, Gregor was back from university and he was working in a pub up the road. He'd done it since he was fifteen. I remember there was a ping on the family group chat: a message from Soph. "I love you all so much," it said. The words just didn't seem right. They didn't ring true. That wasn't Sophie. The house phone went, it was her mum, George, in a right state. She had been called by

Sophie's husband, Sam, who had just had a long text from Soph saying "sorry" and telling him that she was going to kill herself. She told him where to find the car and said please don't bury me. He'd called the police.'

When Andy told me this I was rooted to the spot. I was meant to be taking notes on the interview, but it's one of those times when your mind races and you think about what you would do in the same situation. How would any parent react if they are told that their daughter, who is about 130 miles and three hours away in a car, has probably taken her own life? The shock and despair kick in straightaway. It's not a scenario that ever crosses your mind. Andy did the only thing that he felt he could do. He got in a car and drove to Edinburgh. That was the worst journey of his life. Sophie's mum, George, and her uncle, Bill, also made their way to Scotland. They were all as lost as each other.

'It's amazing how so many things bring it all back to you,' explains Andy. 'I was watching TV recently and that show *Anne* was on; the one where Anne Williams (played by Maxine Peake) loses her son at the Hillsborough Disaster. Her son has gone missing, and she and her husband face that awful drive from Liverpool across to Sheffield. That's what we felt on the drive up to Edinburgh that day. What were we heading into? What would we find?'

They got to Sam's flat. Sophie's friends and the police were there. All the family could do was to sit and wait. The police found the car but there was no sign of Sophie. No one was able to sleep. Andy was still awake in the early hours of the morning.

What were they meant to do? They went and checked into the Premier Inn down the road feeling desperately lost and alone.

'We phoned as many people as we could,' remembers Andy. 'I was just trying to get the message out there. I put an appeal out on social media just trying to get people to help us find our beautiful daughter. I'd had some dealings with Alison Freeman who worked for the BBC in Newcastle. She was presenting the regional news programme that night and she mentioned the appeal. We were helpless. We sat there for a couple of days and eventually decided there was simply nothing we could do. We came back home and just sat and waited. We got a phone call on that Saturday morning to say that they'd found Soph's body. That was it. Confirmation of what we had known. She had gone. Our daughter had gone.'

Suicide leaves a mess. There is so much wreckage to try and sift through both physically and emotionally. Sophie had signed up to run a half-marathon which finished in Bamburgh. Andy knew he needed something to fill the void, so he tried to sign up to do it himself. There were no places left so he had to call the organisers and explain that his daughter had died, and that he would love to take her place in the race. That was the start of *#RunForSophie*. Andy started a video diary of his training. The physical effort gave him something to occupy his mind. It was essential to his well-being in those first few months after Sophie's death.

'I didn't really realise what I was doing,' says Andy, who used to run mountain marathons in what he describes as his 'more active' days. 'It gave me this laser focus going forwards.

My only concern was what was going to happen to me after the run. Thankfully, what actually happened was, over the space of a few months, I became heavily involved in Papyrus. It was a real help to me. In a relatively short space of time, I became some sort of suicide prevention guru. It wasn't long after that that I met these two fellas called Tim and Mike.'

Andy saw quite a bit of himself in the other dads when they all met up together. Mike was the one who carried the heaviest weight of guilt. He often finds himself in a trough of despair. He finds himself getting stuck in the anger and the guilt. It's lovely that they are able to help each other through the darkness. Mike reminded Andy of himself in those early days. 'He was in the desperate place,' recalls Andy. 'You try and live your life, but you just can't help yourself falling into it. Mike was going there regularly. I just saw the pain and the anguish. Tim and I have a very similar attitude to it all and we've been able to bring Mike with us. I think we can see where we want to start and where we want to get to.'

What really strikes you when you speak to Mike, Tim and Andy is their determination to try and find a way out of the wreckage. They all came to the realisation that the best way to help themselves and their families was to help others. 'I would sometimes sit there and say, "we can't let this knacker our lives forever,"' remembers Andy. 'None of the girls would have wanted the situation to strangle us and that's why the walk became such an important focal point.'

The idea of walking between their houses seemed like a simple one. No one ever expected it to turn into the epic journey it became. In September of 2021 they set a tentative target of raising £3,000 each. The premise was a pretty simple one: three dads, three homes, 300 miles raising £3,000. 'Do you remember how guilty we all felt when we made it £10,000 each guys?' asks Tim. Mike and Andy drop their heads in mock shame with big smiles on their faces. 'We felt bad because we didn't want to ask so much of our friends and families,' says Tim, 'but, for whatever reason, it just felt like it was the right thing to do.'

The plan was to walk for fifteen days, starting on 9 October at Andy's house in Morland, and finishing on 23 October in Shouldham with Tim and his family. The whole route with timings was posted on the 3 Dads Walking website so that people could come and support them or join them on the way.

It was at this point that I met the 3 Dads for the first time. I got to meet so many guests on the *BBC Breakfast* sofa but there are always some individuals who really stick with you. Mike came on the sofa with Ged Flynn, the CEO of Papyrus, and was captivating. I could see the sadness in his eyes but also the hope that the walk had given him. He talked with such love about Beth, and the heartache was just as real as his obvious desire to try and see if they could do something to help anyone who found themselves in the same position as his daughter.

The *BBC Breakfast* audience is loyal and generous, and when they get behind a story it is something quite special. Mike came on the sofa on 28 September with the total hovering around £10,000. By the end of the day, it was five times that.

In the weeks before the walk started, we spoke to all three of them on the sofa and their story was gathering pace and some high-profile supporters, as Tim can explain.

'I was at Wigan station catching the train to see Andy when I heard that Daniel Craig was going to donate £10,000,' he recalls. 'The actual James Bond! I read the WhatsApp message from the charity, and I just sat on the floor and started crying straightaway. I must have looked like a complete idiot.'

'What about the letter from Prince William?' chirps Mike. 'It was so touching. It doesn't matter where you are in society, it affects all sorts of people'. I told the dads that I made a documentary about mental health with Prince William a few years before. It was all about addressing the stigma that surrounds men and how they feel. We sat in a dressing room at Cambridge United and William (he said we could call him that) was alongside the England coach Gareth Southgate, French World Cup winner Thierry Henry, England international Danny Rose, pundit and presenter Jermaine Jenas and former footballer Peter Crouch. They all spoke about some of the struggles they had faced in their careers. It was incredible to watch how, as each one of them opened up, it encouraged the others to follow. William was so engaged that day. I think he wanted to lead from the front and show that if he was willing to speak honestly it might encourage and help others. The 3 Dads were following in the same footsteps.

James Bond was followed by another £10,000 donation from Nicole Kidman, who had seen the interview on *BBC Breakfast*. 'I was over in the UK filming *Aquaman 2*,' says the Hollywood superstar. 'I was getting ready to leave for filming that day when I caught the item on *BBC Breakfast* about the 3 Dads. I had a huge mix of emotions. It was utterly devastating to think about what they had been through and what they were doing in memory of their daughters. Despite that, they were so strong, and determined to make a difference for every child. You couldn't help but be truly inspired by them and the journey they were on.'

I asked her about that leap from being moved by a story to wanting to help. 'Who wouldn't?' says Nicole. 'Their story inspired not just me, but people around the world. What they did, what they started, and why they did it, mattered then, and continues to resonate. I honestly think it would be impossible not to be deeply moved by theirs and their daughters' stories. As a parent, we all do everything we can to protect our children, and so the loss of a child hits hard, and I can feel nothing but huge empathy for them.'

Nicole doesn't want to go into any details about personal loss but, like many people who watched and supported Tim, Mike and Andy, she was touched by the beautiful bond between father and daughter, between fathers and daughters. 'As a daughter to the sweetest father,' she says, 'I really connected with them. The care and the love they showed really reminded me of my own dad.'

Nicole's testimony says a lot about her but also a lot about the power of the story and the impact the 3 Dads were able to have on so many people. She's right, it was impossible to watch them and not be moved, to not be touched by their love and their loss and their desire to try and protect others from the pain that had ripped their lives apart. Nicole, like thousands of others, has continued to follow their stories since watching them for the first time that morning.

'I keep an eye on them on social media and it's incredible to see their continued work, and the difference they are also making to Papyrus, who they were fundraising for. If I could pass on a message to them it would be this: I would send them love, I would send them strength and I would want them to know about the huge admiration I have for them, both now and always.'

The donations just kept coming. There was £10,001 from former Manchester United footballer Lou Macari, who said he didn't want to be outdone by Daniel Craig. Despite the stardust, it was Macari's donation that really put a smile on Andy's face.

'Nicole Kidman and Daniel Craig were amazing; especially with the timing of the new Bond film, it couldn't have been any better, but meeting Lou Macari was a real highlight for me,' beamed Andy. 'I am a Manchester City fan, but when we were in Manchester, going to Old Trafford, meeting Lou was amazing. What a lovely bloke he was. He lost his son to suicide all the way back in 1999 so he knew about the importance of what we were doing. The extra pound was just a bit of fun. Like everyone else, he just wanted to help.'

The dads were live on *BBC Breakfast* again on the morning they set off. By lunchtime on that first day, Tim decided to turn off the JustGiving notifications on his phone because there were 2,708 of them! The money was great, but more important to all of them was what they wanted to happen along the way. They wanted to engage, they wanted to start conversations, they wanted people to come and find them and see a safe space where they could talk about loss and grief and share that burden with people who had been through it themselves. They were all blown away by what happened during those fifteen days. I asked each one of them to pick one or two people who had the biggest impact on them.

Tim has lost friends during his time in the military, and he'd had to train to deal with that loss. After losing Emily, he was self-aware enough to understand that he didn't have the toolbox to deal with the grief that was tearing into his family. He knew he needed help. He was brought up in a Baptist church but had grown cynical about what happens to religion when humans get involved. After Emily died, the local padre from RAF Marham used to come around and talk to Tim at a social distance in his back garden. They talked about everything and that helped Tim to see the importance of discussing what he was going through.

'There were so many people on that walk who, just like me, needed someone to listen,' remembers Tim. 'We met Angela and her daughter Tash who set up a charity called Bags for Strife. Angela had lost her husband and daughter to suicide, and they were both struck by the lack of practical support that is available for people when they are at their most vulnerable. They wanted to change that by allowing people who were suffering to get simple things like a water bottle, tissues – the stuff you don't think about. There were moments of laughter followed quite quickly by a huge emotional switch. I remember one day we were all eating ice-creams and started talking to a dad who had lost his wife just a couple of weeks before. He was there with his two children who just looked completely lost; like their world had imploded. We spent some time with them and then, as we left them and wandered out of the town, we all just wept as we walked.'

There were also tears when the 3 Dads were sent a poem by a lady called Helen Taylor. Mike started to read it and 'we were all blubbing,' says Tim. 'I'll send it to you, Dan, maybe you could put it in the book.'

Each day on the walk was just as emotional as it was inspirational. Each day they would set off and find various people waiting for them along the route. 'Nothing was ever forced,' says Tim. 'Most people would just say "Can I join you for a bit?" and then, after a while, we'd ask why they had come, and they'd just share their story. You learn to see grief. You can tell from people's faces what they have been through. A couple had lost their son just three weeks before they came to see us. All they wanted to do was tell us about him. They weren't ready for anything else. What really struck me was the number of people who had never spoken to anyone. A guy near Buxton had never told anyone about what happened to his son seven years ago. A lady came and told us about her dad who had taken his own life seventy years before. She finally felt able to tell someone how she felt about it. It really helped as people unburdened themselves on us.'

When I ask Mike if anyone stands out to him from the walk, he launches into a story without a breath. 'Right at the beginning, day one, there was a couple who came to see us maybe a mile from the start. They had come from Lancaster.

I could see the mum was desperate to talk. She had that pain in her eyes and she told me about their daughter. Suicide had taken her in August, and they only just had the funeral a few weeks before. She showed me the order of service from that funeral. I told her I would carry it with me for the whole walk. I kept it in a plastic bag. It meant a lot to her, and it certainly did to me. A few days later, I met a man in a Mazda sports car. He was there with his wife, and I stopped, and spoke to them. I remember he simply said, "I've joined the same club." He told me about their daughter-in-law who had died a few weeks before. A little later we came into the town of Kirkby Lonsdale. We met the dad who Tim told you about, with the two kids. We talked to him about his wife who had taken her own life. It was just so sad. Once the walk had finished, I had taken the details of the mum I spoke to on day one about the funeral, so I gave her a call to make sure she was alright. We talked about some of the other people I had met on the walk and, incredibly, it turned out that the couple in the Mazda car were talking about her daughter! They were the mother- and father-in-law of the girl whose mother I spoke to on day one and . . .' Mike continued, still amazed by what happened, '. . . the dad who we met in Kirkby Lonsdale, that was her daughter's husband, and those two children were her grandchildren! I had no idea who they were at the time, and they had no idea that I was carrying the order of service of the funeral of the gorgeous daughter-in-law, wife and mum they had so sadly lost. I will never forget that.'

Wherever they went there were people who needed them.

There was a lady waiting for them on the sea wall in Lincolnshire. She was standing on her own, getting battered by the wind. 'I've been waiting for you,' she simply said as they approached, before telling them all about her son.

'Some would spend a day with us and some just a few minutes,' said Mike. 'Suicide is a powerful word. It's a horrible word. It's hard to say, particularly if you've been affected by it. Other people really find it hard to talk about. All three of us have seen that in our own lives. You lose friends, people you've known for a long time find it impossible to mention and almost run away from you. If you can't find the right words to say, then some people find it easier not to say anything at all. I think because we'd been so open, it gave them the strength to talk about it.'

That has certainly been my experience, to a much lesser extent, since writing about Gary Speed's death. So many people have felt able to reach out since my first book *Remarkable People* came out. I still think about Gary a lot and, for the tenth anniversary of his death in November 2021, I was asked to film a piece for BBC Sport to remember him. You can read a little bit more about that in the chapter about Nadiya and our time on *Strictly Come Dancing*.

Initially, I'd said 'no' but the family said that they would like me to do it, so I did. It went out on the Saturday afternoon, and it also went on social media where it quickly picked up millions of views. I think his death still touches an awful lot of people. I still regularly get stopped in the street by people who want to talk about Gary and, after the tribute was shown on telly that weekend, I received hundreds of emails, letters and messages from people who had also been touched by suicide.

There were people who, like me, felt that if they'd said something on the final day before they lost someone it could have made a difference. There were people who opened up about their own suicidal thoughts, depression, abuse, bullying or wanted to talk about the person or people who had helped them at their lowest point. There were some who wanted to talk about how much they loved Gary, how they were still scarred by his death and how the film had helped someone in their life. One loving mum sent me an email describing the joy at how her daughter had watched it and finally found the courage to tell her friends about the attempt she'd made on her own life five years before. She had shared links to the film on Facebook and spoken to her friends in the hope that it might help others to see a way out.

There was one email which I keep coming back to. On the day I received it, I sent it on to the then editor of *Football Focus*, Helen Brown, who was the one who persuaded me to do the piece about Gary. I didn't want it to be about me. I wanted it to be about the need to talk, and the importance of looking out for your friends. This was the email.

> *Dear Dan,*
> *I've had a really, really, rotten year. I know lots of people have and unlike them, a lot of my woes are self-inflicted but on top of all the travails involved with Covid (which I also had a rotten time catching) I have lost my job, run up huge debt, had major health issues and now my wife*

has rightly left me so I am barely seeing my kids. I really was at rock bottom, then, as a huge football fan I watched your Gary Speed tribute.

It saved my life.

Particularly after watching the part about his sons, I have begun talking about my issues and whilst I have a long way to go I am miles away from the darkest of places I was in not so long ago and I will hopefully now be able to play even a tiny part in watching my daughters grow up.

So, thank you.

Thank you, a million times. You have no idea what an absolutely wonderful human being you are.

Keep doing what you are doing. You are an inspiration.

Thanks again.

I remember reading that for the first time in my *Strictly Come Dancing* dressing room and having a gentle sob for about ten minutes. I am so glad it made a difference. Gary's family were keen for me to do the piece because they wanted people to be reminded of the importance of communicating with each other before it's too late. I think that really resonates with the message at the heart of what the 3 Dads are all about.

Their big push now is all about teaching suicide prevention in schools. In February 2022, Mike, Andy and Tim all met with the Health Minister, Gillian Keegan, to start the conversation about adding suicide prevention to the Personal, Social, Health and Economic (PSHE) curriculum in schools. For Tim, it seems like a no-brainer. 'It's so simple. Our children learn about drugs and knife crime. They learn about county lines gangs and pregnancy. Statistically, the biggest risk to their safety is actually suicide. Why don't we teach our children about that? If you're at school and your mate is really struggling, what are you going to do? If that kid takes their own life, you've got to live with that for the rest of your life. Knives, road safety and drugs are all huge issues, and we rightly make all this effort with those subjects, but the numbers affected by suicide are just so much higher.'

It's a subject I often think about with my own children. How do we best arm our kids to deal with the toxic landscape they sometimes have to live in? We need to teach our children to be resilient, to realise that it's ok to feel stressed and anxious, that it's normal to feel worried about an exam, a boyfriend or girlfriend or what someone has said about you on social media. There is no break for this generation of children. Issues like bullying don't stop at the school gates. It can be a non-stop, twenty-four hours a day drip, drip build-up of pressure. There can be no release and no let-up. Tim is convinced through his own experience, and through spending time working with Papyrus, that there is such a better way of doing things. 'If we train them young,' he says, 'if we give them the tools, they can use them. If we just simply talk about these things, then maybe we can save some lives.'

At the time of writing, the 3 Dads are not far off raising £1 million and they haven't stopped there. They will keep walking, but they are also keen to put the money they have already raised to good use. 'Awareness is the key,' says Mike, sitting up in his chair. 'Suicide is the biggest killer of under-thirty-fives in the

UK. Parents have lost children and only then found out that the most dangerous thing in the kids' lives were the kids themselves! We want to use the money to encourage suicide prevention and get the kids to talk to their families. Everyone we spoke to and met along the way on our walk said they were very grateful that we have encouraged people to have conversations. I know that is already making a difference, but there is so much more we can do.'

When I ask Andy if someone he has met really stands out, he tells me about Sandy. Whenever you talk to anyone who has been touched by suicide, you instantly realise that it affects so many people. The ripples spread far and wide. Sandy was one of those caught in the ripples.

When the police found Sophie's body, they didn't tell her dad much other than that a man had called them with the information and that he'd stayed with her body until they had arrived. Understandably, that meant an awful lot to Andy at the time. Sandy was the man who found Sophie's body.

'We live right by the side of the water,' says Sandy in his beautifully soft Scottish accent. From the moment he picked up the phone, I knew he was kind. I could tell in the lilt of his voice and the way he asked if I was ok. 'I'm so glad you're writing about Andy,' he says. 'He's an amazing man and it's been a pleasure to get to know him.'

Sandy and his partner, Anna, live in South Queensferry on the banks of the Firth of Forth. Sandy is an architect who works in Edinburgh, and he has a painful memory of looking out of his living-room window that December morning.

'It was 8.30 a.m. I looked out to the beach and my first thought was disbelief. I instantly knew what it was I looking at and I knew I didn't want Anna to see it. She had been at a Christmas party the night before and is far more sensitive than me. I ran to close the curtains as quickly as I could. I went outside and I called the police and waited for them to arrive. If I'm totally honest with you, when I first saw the body, I went into shock. It seems a bit of a blur. My heart just completely went out to her. I remember feeling angry that no one had been looking after her. I waited next to her and presumed she'd had a hard life and I was upset that it had come to this for her. I passed on my details to the police and said I would happily talk to the family. For whatever reason, the police never passed on my details, but I couldn't stop thinking about her.'

Sandy did his own research and found Andy on social media. He saw when and where Sophie's funeral was going to be held and decided that he had to go to try and learn a bit more about the woman he had found. He drove for hours.

'I knew her name,' he says. 'I knew where she was from, but I was compelled to go to the funeral. I thought I would be one of just a handful of people there and I wanted to pay my respects. I just sat in the car outside and watched people go in. I was so relieved to see so many people there. I knew she was loved. Don't ask me to explain why, but that just meant an awful lot to me. In that moment all the anger, the questioning and the concern subsided.'

Sandy went to the wake afterwards. He stood in the corner: shaking, waiting, thinking what he should do. 'Do I talk to someone?' he thought. 'I didn't want to make their life more difficult. I was standing at the bar deliberating. One of the gentlemen who had been talking to the family came to the bar to get a drink and I managed to pluck up the courage to tell him who I was. His name was Nigel and I told him why I was there, explained that I didn't want to get in the way and asked him if he knew the family well enough to know if I should tell them that I was the one who had found their daughter's body.'

Nigel immediately introduced Sandy to Fi, Andy's wife, and, fighting back the tears, Sandy explained why he had driven three hours to attend Sophie's funeral.

'Fi is never normally rude,' says Andy, 'but she was that day. I was standing at the wake talking to some of Soph's university friends when she came over and said, "Come and meet this bloke." I could tell that she wouldn't take no for an answer, so I walked over, and she introduced me by saying, "This is Sandy. The man who found Sophie's body."'

I ask Sandy about that moment of meeting Andy for the first time and there is a long, pregnant pause. 'I'm sorry,' says Sandy, quietly. 'Just . . . give me a moment . . . this is the bit that I always struggle with. I have hardly told anyone about Sophie other than close family members, and meeting Andy for the first time and telling him about his daughter, is still the hardest part.' I tell Sandy to take his time and only tell me what he feels is right. He thanks me, takes a deep breath and continues.

'He was so lovely and gave me a hug and thanked me.' Sandy has to stop again and compose himself. 'I know this probably sounds a bit silly. Here I am talking to the father of a girl I had never met and I'm grieving her loss. I was grieving someone I knew nothing about. It is a very strange experience. I am a bit jealous that I never got to meet her, but I also feel the shock that she is no longer here.'

On the first anniversary of Sophie's death, Andy, Fi and her mum, George, all went to Sandy's house and stood on the water's edge where Sophie's body was found. 'I knew he felt better knowing that I had stayed with her body at the end, even for a short time,' recalls Sandy. The connection these two men have is as strange as it is captivating. The most unusual and awful circumstances have produced an incredibly strong bond.

In the months after Sophie's death, Sandy wasn't in a good place. He still sometimes walks the paths around his house and wonders if he could have done something to save Sophie. 'Did I walk past her on the day she took her own life? Could I have stopped her? Could I have helped her? It's so strange to have that guilt when I never met her. I just wish there is something that someone could have done, because I see that mess her death has left behind.'

Sandy spoke to an old friend who had served in Afghanistan about his feelings, and he told him about post-traumatic stress disorder (PTSD) and how it can affect people. He told Sandy he needed to try and turn whatever he could into a positive rather than let it eat away at him. When Andy ran the Northumberland half-marathon in Sophie's place, Sandy cycled for two days from Edinburgh to Bamburgh to meet him on the finish line. Sandy is a remarkable man.

When the police went to Sophie's flat on the day she died,

they found her final purchase on her kitchen table. It was a Christmas present for her dad: two tickets to the Scotch Whisky Experience on the Royal Mile in Edinburgh. She and her brother, Gregor, had bought it together.

'You can understand that, for a while, we never felt like using it,' explains an emotional Andy. 'But things change with time and this year we went and did it together. We went to see *Hairspray* too. Sophie would have loved that.' Andy and Fi also took the opportunity to meet up with Sandy and Anna. 'The whisky was very popular that night,' remembers Andy.

'I do feel like a bit of a fraud,' explains Sandy when I ask him about his continued friendship with Andy. 'I suppose you never realise the implications and the depth of the effect that these things have on you. I think I thought I was anesthetised to it, but that couldn't be further from the truth. It has had a much bigger impact on me than I ever thought possible. I wish I'd had the opportunity to meet Andy under different circumstances, but maybe this is the way it was meant to be. He's amazing and I find his strength and determination a huge source of inspiration.'

Sandy isn't the only one. Every time I speak to the 3 Dads, I am impressed by the way they carry themselves. They have all been to some dark places but are constantly searching for the light. It must be impossible to imagine what it is like to have the life you build for your family explode like that overnight. Everything that feels normal changes in an instant. There is that first awful scream of realisation that life is never going to be the same again.

Tears aren't enough. Every emotion is turned up to eleven.

You are completely overwhelmed. The shock blinds you and is only broken by the feeling of sheer horror at what has happened and the constant questions. How did they get to a place where they felt that this was their best option? What didn't I do? How could I have helped? If the noise ever dies down there is the unbearable, heart-breaking desire to turn back the clock, but you know it's impossible.

'If I could speak to Emily now,' says Tim, 'the first thing I'd do is just cuddle her. I'd tell her she was an idiot and tell her how much we love her. She genuinely thought she was helping us and unburdening us. Her little sister, Evie, will struggle with this for the next seventy years of her life. The thing that crushes me is that all three girls were so talented – a nurse, an artist and a musician – and they couldn't see it. You worry about the scores of kids who are in the same situation. We aren't a mega rich family, and we aren't destitute. We were a normal middle-class family. You think you are doing everything right and it makes it feel worthless at times. Spending time with Andy and Mike has given me something that it's hard to see at first; it's hard to see the hope.'

'That's the key word for me, Dan,' Mike jumps in. 'We are not qualified in counselling or anything like that. I have some mental health training now because of Papyrus. Did it help me? I hope it has helped both me and others. We will never be the same, but trying to do something positive was massively important for us. We are hoping that positivity has transferred to others.

'If I saw Beth now, I think the first thing I would do would be to boot her up the arse. I always used to say to her before she went out: "Don't be a d*&*head, be wise." I'd just tell her I love her. I see the anger and the pain she left behind every day, but she is still loved.'

The 3 Dads have a fascinating relationship. A deep and meaningful friendship has emerged from a situation that each one of them would have given everything to avoid. From just a few minutes in their presence, you realise that their bond is such a strong one, cemented by the love of father for a daughter and soaked in tears. They have the utmost respect for each other, and they truly do want to make a difference. They cannot understand why they've lost their girls, but the driving force behind all they do is the desire that other families would be able to avoid the paths they have had to walk down. Friendship has helped them rebuild their lives.

'I dread to think where I would be without these two,' says Mike. No one speaks for a moment. 'They are diamond geezers. I am not the person I was. I'm smiling now but I'm still a mess. I struggle to work. I have PTSD. Everything has changed and I find life so hard to deal with at times, but Tim and Andy are always there, and believe me, this journey is far from over.'

I get the feeling the 3 Dads are going nowhere. They have so much more to do.

As promised, I wanted to finish this chapter with the poem that Mike, Tim and Andy were sent by Helen Taylor during their walk. When I approached Helen to ask her if I could print her poem in this book, she said she would be delighted. 'I was prompted to write it after seeing them on *BBC Breakfast*. Their story gripped my heart and I was so pleased to meet them. The poem simply fell out of the end of my pencil.'

Helen not only wrote 'Our Girls' for the 3 Dads, but she and her husband also drove all the way from Coventry to Buxton to see them during their walk. Making an effort to help someone else goes a long way.

Our Girls

We can still hear all the giggles,
See the smiles and feel the love
For our gorgeous girls who left us
Yet have given us a shove
To step out into all weathers
As the road ahead uncurls.
We're out walking,
We're out talking,
We're out walking with our girls.

We three know the depths of sorrow.
We've lost count of all the tears
But we've found our hearts and legs again
And hope to crush the fears
Of the lonely, frightened, helpless
As their turmoil twists and swirls.
We're out walking,
We're out talking,
We're out walking with our girls.

So, we're striding down the country.
If you see us, give a wave.
Even better, find your wallet
Or look up our 'giving' page.
If we help a few and save them
As these scenes of life unfurl.
Now you're talking!
We're out walking.
We're out walking for our girls.

For Beth, Emily and Sophie.

FOUR NOTES

'And for that week, he was the biggest star on social media!'

'Who was?'

'You were, Dad!'

'Was I? What did I do?'

'You played your piece based on those four notes.'

'Well, that sounds nice.'

Paul Harvey is a brilliant musician. He has an incredible musical ear, perfect pitch and a remarkable ability to create on the spot. Paul also has dementia. His story is sad in places, but it is packed with joy, laughter and talent . . . so much talent. For much of his life he was a teacher, inspiring his students for decades, and now, in his eighties, his music is reaching millions more.

I first met Paul on social media thanks to his son Nick. Nick is also an accomplished musician and has always been amazed by his dad's party trick of being able to compose a piece from any four random notes picked for him.

In the depths of his dementia, in October 2020, Nick recorded his dad doing just that and posted it on Twitter. It was picked up by Radio 4's *Broadcasting House* programme and the host, Paddy O'Connell, helped to arrange for the song to be recorded by the BBC Philharmonic orchestra, conducted by the man who wrote it. It was the culmination of a life-long dream for Paul Harvey.

This is Paul's story.

We spoke to Paul and Nick on many occasions on *BBC Breakfast*. I used to love it because Paul was so full of life, and I enjoyed watching their beautiful relationship. You could see how much Nick loved his dad and how proud he was of him. You could see the dementia was taking its toll on Paul, but it was also clear that their coping mechanism was a gorgeous mix of care and humour. All this was happening when the world was in the grip of coronavirus and, alongside the actual vaccine, it gave us all a much-needed injection of inspiration and reminded everyone of the power of music.

One of the great things about chatting to the Harveys is that you never quite know where the conversation will go. Both Paul and Nick are gloriously unpredictable. The only thing you can be certain of is that they will never be far away from a piano.

'Hello, Dan,' says Nick, as the Zoom kicks in. 'It's Dan, Dad,' says Nick, pointing at the screen.

'Hello, Dan. How are you doing?' says Paul with that giant grin that has become so familiar. He is sitting with his regular red jumper on, next to his son, with his famous piano just slightly out of reach on his left.

When I used to speak to them on *BBC Breakfast* we'd only have about five or six minutes, so I remind them that we have loads of time and there is a lot to get through. With that in mind, I ask them to take me back to the beginning.

'It's a good job we are talking about the old stuff,' says Paul. 'I can remember the old stuff. It's the new things I struggle with sometimes.'

Paul was born into music. His parents called him Paul Ragle Harvey. His middle name is 'Elgar' spelt backwards, as the famous composer was a big favourite in the Harvey household.

'Imagine if they'd liked Shostakovich,' says Nick, laughing. He regularly punctuates the conversation with jokes and his dad loves them.

'Ha!' snorts Paul. 'That's a good one!'

'That's one of the benefits of dementia,' says Nick. 'I can tell Dad the same joke a hundred times, and he'll laugh a hundred times because he can't remember me telling it before.'

Paul's dad – John Augustus Harvey – was a working-class man who taught himself the piano in his twenties. He started up a music school in Stoke-on-Trent and Paul was always surrounded by a love of music. He took his first exams at the age of four and his progression was incredibly quick. He received the highest marks in the UK in his grade 8 exam and went on to study at the prestigious Guildhall School of Music.

'I was quite a good footballer, you know,' remembers Paul. 'I had a try-out with Port Vale as a keeper, but I was desperate to go to music college and that is what happened. I think that's what my dad wanted too.'

'Your dad was great,' says Nick. 'Our youngest son has "Augustus" as a middle name because of your dad.'

'I'd forgotten that,' says Paul. A smile breaks out across his face. 'Isn't that lovely? I'll have to write that in my book.'

More about Paul's 'book' later . . .

The talented Mr Harvey got a highly sought-after scholarship with the Russian pianist, Iso Elinson, and went on to become a concert pianist and composer. His 'Rumba Toccata' is still used in grade 6 piano exams. He used to play on the BBC Home Service in the early 1960s.

'It was just before we won the World Cup,' says Paul enthusiastically. His memory of that part of his life is still razor sharp. 'I used to play on a programme called the *Variety Playhouse*, Dan. It was the most popular show on the wireless, presented by a chap called Vic Oliver. He was a comedian but also a very good musician. Do you remember that Mozart piece, Nick?' he says, turning to his son.

'Dad found an old CD in a box, and it was some of his old performances. It was amazing, Dad, wasn't it?' says Nick, encouraging his dad to recall the story.

'I don't think I could play them now. There were fingers all over the place,' he says, laughing.

'Why did you leave all that behind?' I ask.

'I was born to teach,' says Paul. 'I just loved it. I had inspiring teachers and I wanted to do that for others. I wanted children to love and appreciate music and sounds. I wanted to bring it to life for them. It gave me so much pleasure for so many years.'

Paul puts his hand on his chin as he launches into a story. 'I used to love getting a new class from the primary school. It was always full of kids who thought that music class was going to be dull and boring. I loved that challenge. "Listen to this," I would say and I'd bring out the *Match of the Day* theme tune and I could see their ears prick up. I had got them. Nick understood that too. He's a wonderful composer too, aren't you?'

'That's what happens when you have a mum and a dad who are music mad,' says Nick. 'I was taught to play the violin, but I taught myself the piano. When Mum and Dad used to argue, I would disappear into the piano. You remember that, don't you, Dad?' he says, poking his dad, who giggles.

'Some of my favourite memories are when Dad used to say, "Nick, do you fancy having a play?" And we would just go off and improvise on the piano. Those moments will stay with me forever. Do you remember that, Dad?'

'I do now you've told me. I'm sorry.'

'Don't be sorry,' says his son.

There is a lot of that between them: Nick gently probing his dad's memory and Paul being totally honest about what he does and doesn't remember. There are a lot of gaps, there are a lot of sketchy patches, but the real magic still happens when he sits in front of a piano.

'It's just something I can do,' says Paul. 'I used to do some teaching at a jazz summer school and one day I thought, "Let's try something." Somebody picked four random notes and I started improvising.'

Nick was also there. 'I was ten at the time and it was incredible. I just remember thinking, "That's my dad . . . he's amazing". I can't tell you how beautiful it was. It's hard to put it into words how difficult it is to do what he does. If you gave me four notes, I could do something with them, but Dad's talent is outrageous.

'Maybe this is the best way of describing it,' says Nick,

gathering his thoughts. 'Lots of people play music, but Dad lets the music inhabit him. He's made of music and now he has shown the world what he's made of.'

If you ask Paul how he's feeling now, he normally makes a joke about his ears going or the hearing aids he has to wear or the fact that he's falling apart. His family first noticed something was wrong a few years ago.

'I've known for years that my memory was going a little,' says Paul.

'I think you try and ignore it for a while, don't you?' says Nick. His dad nods quietly. 'I remember that day we knew we had to do something. It was maybe four years ago when we invited Dad round for Sunday lunch, and he arrived at 6 o'clock in the morning. He started to struggle.'

Nick turns to his dad.

'Do you remember you had a fall at home, Dad?' he asks, putting his hand on Paul's arm.

'Did I?' says Paul.

'You did,' replies Nick, before turning to me to explain. 'His cognitive state reduced considerably during those weeks in hospital.'

Paul jumps in with a question. 'What does cognitive mean?'

Nick answers with his usual patience. 'It's to do with your brain, Dad.'

Paul nods, almost looking like he's been told that before.

'He was there for nearly three months, and, in all honesty,

we thought he was drifting away. The medication has been amazing but his short-term memory particularly is shot to pieces.'

I ask Paul how his dementia affects him day to day. Does he think about it a lot?

'I suppose I have to,' he says. 'Things have to be in the right place for me. I get rattled sometimes when I wouldn't have done before. Routine has become so important to me, which is frustrating, but I know that it helps.'

Once Nick had his dad back at home, he knew there was only one thing that would really get his dad's brain firing again. It was the thing he loved more than anything else. It was his music.

'There was just one day when I was at home with Dad, and he was really struggling. As I often do, I persuaded him to get on the piano and play something. He was sat there with a classical piece of music in front of him and it wasn't happening. He couldn't find the notes, he couldn't get his feet on the pedals, and you could tell he was frustrated. I remembered his old party trick and asked him if he could do it. I love watching him play so I just recorded it for posterity. It was so amazing that I decided to put it on Twitter and, well, that was the start of all this but, more importantly, it brought him back to life. I got my dad back.'

And with that, they both turn and looked at each other as only a proud father can look at his son and an adoring son can stare at his father. It's a beautiful moment to witness and that is one of the reasons why Paul's story has spread so far, and his music has been heard by so many. There is an unstructured warmth when you watch them interact with each other. You can tell that Nick loves spending time with his dad, cares for him deeply and nothing gives him more pleasure than seeing those little flashes of the father he grew up with who loved to teach him about music. The other thing I love about their relationship is the brutal British humour. Nick breaks the adoring look with a zinger.

'Before all this you were just sat watching TV all day, weren't you?'

'I just didn't want to see anyone,' says Paul.

Nick jumps in. 'The good thing about this was that it gave you the lift you needed; like a firework up your arse.'

Paul leans forward in his chair, roaring with laughter.

'Oh, that's good . . . I'll remember that one,' he says.

'No, you won't!' retorts Nick.

And that's the beauty of it. Dementia is brutal, painful, heart-breaking, but everyone deals with it differently. Paul and Nick do cry about it, but they also love to laugh.

'I took Dad out for dinner last Friday,' says Nick. 'We had fish and chips. There was half a lemon on his plate and Dad just ate it. You should have seen his face.'

Paul starts giggling. 'I'd forgotten what you're meant to do with it. Do you squeeze it on or something?'

Paul's dementia is getting worse but it's such a treat to talk to him. You get wonderful sparks of humour. You get powerful recollections from half a lifetime ago and then, every now and again, you catch a glimpse of a musical genius.

'Shall I play you something, Dan?' he says out of nowhere.

'Off the top of your head, Paul?' I ask.

'Yes! Let me get around to the piano.' He hauls himself up onto his Zimmer frame and shuffles over to the piano and collapses onto the stool.

'Now,' he says, pointing at his instrument, 'I must confess that this hasn't been tuned for a while, but we'll see what we can do.' He stretches his fingers.

'This is for you. It's a one-off because, once I've played it, I won't remember it,' he laughs.

'Are you ready? This is Dan's tune.'

For the next ninety seconds, Paul plays the most gorgeous piece of improvised music.

It's all off the top of his head and all mesmerising. I'm struggling to stop the tears from pouring down my face. As he finishes, I applaud and Nick rushes in to hug his dad, but someone is still clapping in the background. 'That was beautiful, Paul,' says a voice from the depths of the living room.

'Have you got an audience?' I ask.

'That's Louisa,' says Nick, helping his dad back to his feet. 'She is dad's home help, and she's popped in to bring him his lunch.'

'Hi, Louisa!' I shout from the other end of the Zoom call. 'Wasn't that great?' I ask her.

'I love listening to him play,' she says.

'Did you get that?' asks Paul. I explained to him that because my AirPods were plugged in, even though I was screen recording, I didn't pick up the sound. 'Let me do you another one,' he says with a skip in his step. He sits back down and produces another ninety-second improvised masterpiece. It is completely different to the first one, just as beautiful and emotional, but more haunting. It is just pouring out of him as his fingers caress the keys. Nick and Louisa are standing either side of the piano, just out of shot; I'm filming the screen back in Sheffield and we are all in total silence watching a master at work. There is a big round of applause as he finishes, Nick gives his dad another hug and Louisa puts down his lunch as Paul shuffles back to his armchair.

In the days after Paul's original video went on social media, there were various appearances on TV shows and pages of coverage across the papers. 'Four Notes: Paul's Tune' raced up the charts and things were put in place for Paul to conduct the BBC Philharmonic playing the piece he had written. Did they have a chance to stop and think about what was happening?

'No, is the simple answer,' says Nick. 'It was lovely to see the impact it had on people, and I love the fact that it came from a dark place. Dad was feeling really low, and me giving him those four notes somehow gave him a path out of that. We were all in lockdown at the time (October 2020) and we all needed an escape. The piece is beautiful, and what makes it beautiful for me is that Dad wasn't just playing the music, he was communicating with it. He wasn't really talking too much at the time, but he told all of us how he was feeling with "Four Notes". There was sorrow in there but also great uplifts of joy. If you listen to the end of it, it's almost a question mark, it's almost like it doesn't end at all. It's so clever and that is what he was going through. He told us with his piano.'

Nick is also convinced that the planets aligned to make it

STANDING ON THE SHOULDERS

special. 'It was meant to be, Dan. Twitter has a video limit of two minutes and twenty seconds. Obviously, Dad has no idea about that, but he played for just short of that, so I was able to upload the whole thing.'

I remind them both that it wasn't just the music that people fell in love with; it was their relationship, that father-and-son magic.

'That really surprised us,' says Nick before laughing, 'I have this habit of saying the most inappropriate things, but I will never tire of telling him how great he is.' Paul turns his head towards his son, and they share each other's gaze. It's another beautiful moment before Nick again breaks the silence . . .

'He is very annoying, too.'

'Who is?' says Paul in mock disgust.

'You are, Dad,' laughs Nick.

'Am I?' responds Paul before a glorious change of direction. 'I do like your car though.'

'I'm sorry you keep banging your head on it when you get in it. Every time, Dan,' says Nick.

'Do I?' says Paul. 'It's a good job I don't remember that or I'd never go anywhere with you.'

The pair of them are once again lost in laughter.

If you ask Paul how he sees himself, he answers as quick as a flash: 'I'm a composer, a pianist, a conductor and a teacher. I spent much of my life teaching and that was a real pleasure. I just wanted to show people the joy of music.'

And that is precisely what Paul Harvey has done his whole life. That is why I was so happy when he and Nick agreed to feature in this book, because Paul is exactly the sort of person I love to write about. He inspires those around him. He lifts spirits with that beautiful mixture of talent and enthusiasm, and I'm going to demonstrate that to you now by introducing you to six people. Three of them are former students of Mr Harvey, one of them is a former colleague, one is from a dementia charity and the other is a millionaire who was watching Paul's first appearance on *BBC Breakfast*.

'The most important thing a teacher can do is try and connect with a pupil and offer them options in life. That's what Mr Harvey did for me and many others.' Nick Van Eede was one of many taught by Paul at Imberhorne School in East Grinstead in the 1970s. He went on to become a musician, producer and lead singer in Cutting Crew whose single '(I Just) Died In Your Arms' was number one in nineteen different countries.

'I went to Imberhorne when it was changing from a stuffy grammar school to a comprehensive. There was a big influx of fresh young talent and Paul Harvey was part of that. We used to call him one of the 'Three Ps'.

The Three Ps were Paul Harvey, drama teacher Pete Talman (who we will meet later) and music teacher Pete Caruana. Between them they would put on big school productions. Pete Talman would write the lyrics to Paul's masterful score.

'Mr Harvey was always so generous with his advice,' remembers Nick Van Eede. 'He would come in with his keyboards and microphones and it was the first time I'd seen anything like that. I'd write some songs and he'd suggest different notes. "Try a B-sharp instead of a G, Nicky," he'd say. He always called me "Nicky". I know that most music lessons were all about "London's Burning" on the recorder or getting out the tambourines, but his lessons were never like that. He wanted you to love and appreciate music like he loved and appreciated it. He taught me to never lose that. Sometimes, it's easy to forget what makes you tick. We used to go on tour with Cutting Crew for six months. It was amazing but then you'd spend six months talking to lawyers and managers and you'd forget about the magic of making music. Then you pick up your guitar again and you're back in the right place. I don't think Mr Harvey ever lost that. I have a rehearsal in thirty minutes. My voice will be croaky, but I know I will love it.'

Nick was inspired by those epic school productions, but so too was Alix Lewer who now runs a music charity. 'Mr Harvey drove a Ford Capri, he was cool. He loved it and we loved that he loved it. The job that I'm doing now, using music to include and help people with learning difficulties, all goes back to him.'

Alix runs a charity called Include.org. She loves her job but found life at school hard. 'I was mercilessly bullied. I was academic, my mum would never buy the trendy clothes and I'd arrived from a small school, so no one knew who I was. I was a moving target every day, but music was my release and Mr Harvey was the man who opened the door. He just had the ability to bring the best out in people, no matter how hard he had to dig. If you were willing to work, he was on your side, whether you could play an instrument or not. I remember once, he asked me to play the clarinet in assembly. I was terrified and thought that everyone would go for me, but I loved it. He was the cool teacher and was so proud of me, and that gave me the confidence to be myself. Life was fun when he was around. He built teams of good people and you just wanted to be around him. He built these wonderful environments that we wanted to be a part of; places where you could be yourself. That's exactly what I try and do now in my job. I'm just trying to be like Mr Harvey.'

I ask Alix if she, and the other students, knew how talented he was, or was it all about the Ford Capri. 'This is weird,' says Alix, 'but I actually played the piano at his leaving do! I wasn't even a pianist but the guy who was meant to be playing couldn't be there, so I had to do it. I was pretty average, but Mr Harvey came over and was so complimentary about my playing and, later on, he sat at the piano and the whole room was like "Wow!" We knew he was a great teacher but that was the first time we saw he was really special.'

Dominic Glynn, a prolific composer of music for TV and film, is a third former student of Paul Harvey's. 'I always looked forward to his lessons. The school was very progressive, and Mr Harvey was at the forefront of that. He would sit there, play something on the piano and just talk to us about the music and why it was important. Over the years, he inspired me. When I was in the sixth form, we started a band and Mr Harvey was in charge of the music block. He would always encourage us to use the facilities and even trusted us with the keys. He just wanted us to experiment and find our feet. We'd play him something and he was always encouraging. You could tell he was desperate for us to do well.'

Paul kept a close eye on his students even after they had left school. I remember when we reintroduced him to some of them on *BBC Breakfast* and you could see the joy on his face. One of Dominic's most well-known arrangements was the iconic *Doctor Who* theme tune and he was so touched that Mr Harvey had followed his career.

'It was wonderful when Nick said that his dad remembered me. Nick said he used to bring me up during his lessons with other students, which is remarkable and really humbling. When I spoke to Paul, that was the first time we'd seen each other in forty-five years. He was the man who set me on my way and it was great to get the chance to thank him for all of that.'

While Nick, Alix and Dominic all studied under Paul Harvey, Pete Talman shared a staff room with him at Imberhorne. 'Paul was a born teacher,' says Pete. 'I was head of drama, and he embodied the music department and was a larger-than-life character. I didn't go in his classroom much but, when we worked on the school shows together, the enthusiasm just poured out of him. My fondest recollection is of composing with him. Paul wrote the music, and I would take care of the lyrics. I would go round to his house on a Sunday morning with a lyric in my mind and he would just sit at the piano and the magic would happen. It was like his hands were remote controlled, searching the keyboard for a melody that suited the words. It was fascinating to watch it evolve in his mind, in front of your eyes. The piano was his best friend, and he just couldn't stop himself.'

Pete and Paul lost touch for a few years, but Paul's first wife contacted Pete to let him know that Paul was ill and the pair of them got back together. 'His dementia is sad but also fascinating. When I saw him at Christmas,' says Pete, 'his recall of students he taught was remarkable. I was running through some of the children and would ask him, "Do you remember Alison? You wrote her a song," and he would say, "Yes! Alison, restricted vocal range and sometimes I had to play a little louder to cover for that." That was nearly fifty years ago and it was there at the front of his mind. His mind is still brilliant but the more immediate seems to just drift away.'

I ask Pete what it was like to watch his old friend play 'Four Notes' in his eighties and go on to conduct the orchestra. 'I was just so moved by it all,' says Pete. 'When I watched him, I just felt that he looked at home – that he belonged there. In another life, that's where he should be, that should have been Paul. He could have gone on to fulfil that dream and ambition of being a musician, but he found that fulfilment in teaching. He's not a frustrated musician because teaching was always at the very centre of his being. I know his mind is failing him, but I like to think the dementia can't get to his music because he plays with his soul. Music and Paul are indivisible.'

It wasn't just Pete Talman who was mesmerised by Paul's performance. His old students couldn't take their eyes off him. 'It is impossible to watch it without a tear in your eye,' says Dominic Glynn. 'His talent is just so visible. I'm not surprised it caused such a stir and went around the world when you think about what he is going through and how much skill it takes to do what he did. It's not just that,' adds Dominic, 'it's the fact that it's technically beautiful. The way it ends, the very last note, is perfect. You wouldn't put it there. It's not a cliché and a lesser composer wouldn't see it or hear it the way he does. With every note he's telling us a story, he's telling us how he is feeling and that is wonderful.'

Alix Lewer was equally inspired but also sad to watch her old teacher struggling. 'I'm a speech and language therapist. My musical journey began with Mr Harvey. He gave me the confidence to do what I do now. I set up the charity and we help people with dementia and there he was playing music with dementia. It was a little overwhelming. For me, he was always a brilliant teacher, but I also looked up to him and you always put him on a pedestal, so it was hard to see him so upset, with his emotions so open and near the surface, but that's what happens with dementia. The thing that encourages me is that, even though he has dementia, he's showing us all his skills. What an example to others! By playing the piano every day, he is keeping that part of him alive. It's coming from his soul, it's so much deeper than cognitive function.'

When you talk to Alix, it is obvious very early on that she is one of those wonderful people who searches for the positive. She talks with great passion about the work she does and, because of that, she focuses on the inspiration in the life of people like Paul, rather than the sadness.

'My first experience of dementia was working in a nursing home at sixteen. You got the patients up, they had lunch and then you put them to bed. There was no investment in finding the things that made them who they are. That is the problem with social care. Paul is in a position where Nick can help and encourage him to share his gifts with the world. Nick is integral to all of this, and Paul is proof that people with dementia aren't gone, they can still contribute. I know that there are so many more Paul Harvey's out there. Not all of them can play the piano like him, but they can all teach us something. That's why I loved watching him conduct the orchestra,' says Alix, once again getting emotional. 'I just sat there in tears watching him because that is where he was meant to be: not in a nursing home watching TV, but living his dream and lost in the music. He was so proud, and how often do people with dementia get to feel pride rather than shame? He was eighty, he has dementia, but he's not finished. He has so much more to teach us.'

Nick Van Eede was just as emotional when he watched his old teacher in action. 'When I was a lot younger, I played some songs at what used to be called the Horsham Mental Institution. It tells you how much things have changed that we don't call it that anymore, but I was playing some Tom Jones to the residents and one of the women there came up and sang the song with me. Afterwards, the doctor told me she hadn't spoken in three years. That's what music can do to you, that's how deep it sits in our bodies and that's why watching Paul was so wonderful. What really struck me was . . .' he pauses to find the right words . . . 'it was brilliant. I love classical music and what he captured in that piece was how he was feeling at the time, at that precise moment. It was beautifully sad but also uplifting. He couldn't tell me how he felt, but he played to me how he felt and that is the very essence of a musician. There is nothing sadder than watching your loved ones drift away. I am very thankful that my mum is eighty-seven and currently sharp as a button, but watching Paul was inspirational.'

I am about to thank Nick for his time when he jumps back in. 'There is another thing, Dan,' he says, with a degree of urgency. 'What he did will last forever. That will probably never happen again. You get moments like that, and they don't come around very often so you must treasure them. I had one a few months ago. I was at the London Palladium with Cutting Crew performing with a thirty-two-piece orchestra. I sang the first line of "(I Just) Died In Your Arms" and it was a forever moment. I knew I would never get the chance to do that again. That is what Paul created with his son. That is his hand-me-down to the rest of us. I know what it's like to sit down and write a song – a good one and a bad one. I know what great musicians look like and he is one of them. I hope he realises how special he is, because it all works through him. It's a lovely story, it's a lovely piece of music, but it's Paul who has the charm and the talent, it's Paul who can see the humour in the darkness, it's Paul who provides the magic.'

His former students and colleagues weren't the only ones who saw that 'magic'. There were millions watching Paul and his piano and one of them was sitting at home with his wife in Scotland, businessman Sir Tom Hunter. Sir Tom's tale is a book in itself – a young man borrows £5,000 from his dad which he uses to start selling trainers from the back of a van. He turns that into the retail chain Sports Division which is sold to JJB

Sports in 1998 for around £290 million. More importantly for this story though, Tom had lost both his parents to dementia.

'My wife and I were watching *BBC Breakfast*, like we always do, and on came Paul and his son. We just sat there in silence. I had never really talked about my mum and dad's dementia, but it all just came flooding back to me. It was the father-and-son element, the bond over music and the way that the music was able to reach into this man's mind. We were both sobbing.'

Tom's dad was called Campbell. He owned a small grocery in New Cumnock when 90 per cent of employment was down the coal pit. Tom worked in the shop with his dad from the age of six. When the Miner's Strike happened in 1984, the business disappeared. 'He had to sell the shop and he thought he was a failure,' explains Tom. 'He put a little bit of money in with another man selling slippers in markets. I noticed that trainers were a big part of what they were doing, and I thought I would start trying to sell them. I wrote to a shop and asked if I could start selling some trainers in their store. Remarkably they said "yes" and asked if I could start with their shops in Leeds, Sunderland and Aberdeen. I told them I would see as our shopfitting team were really busy. I didn't have a shopfitting team; I didn't even have any trainers! I told my dad what was happening, and that's when he loaned me the £5,000.'

That money enabled Tom to enter the trainer business at just the right time and he went on to have enormous commercial success. When he became Sir Tom Hunter, he was allowed to take three people to Buckingham Palace and he took his wife, Marion, his son and his very proud dad.

Tom's mum was the first to be diagnosed with dementia in the family and his dad became her full-time carer. 'That was one of the things I loved about Nick and Paul. I saw that love and that care. My mum was much worse than my dad. It was death from a thousand cuts. She was drifting away and then he started to deteriorate. It wasn't as sad with my dad. We had said all that we had wanted to say to each other. My mum was much harder to watch. She just vanished in front of my eyes. I would visit her at the nursing home and then just wept as I left. She disappeared. She couldn't talk, walk or speak and when you held her hand it was like she just wasn't there. She had always loved her music. She was Welsh and had a great voice. We would listen to Andy Williams, Matt Munro and the Mike Sammes Singers'.

I ask Tom if that was another reason why Paul Harvey made such an impact on him. 'I don't cry, Dan,' he says, 'but Marion and I were just quiet for a few minutes. I loved the way that Nick looked at his dad: a father's love for his son and a son's love for his father. That did it for me. The music was beautiful, but I don't even think you need to have had an appreciation or a love of music to be affected by it all. I was crying because of the way my mum slipped away too. I wish we had known some of what Nick and Paul had for my mum. I turned to Marion and said, "I think they are on to something. I am going to do something." My wife just said, "On you go."'

That morning I was sitting on the sofa alongside Louise Minchin. She had met Tom at a charity event, and they had swapped numbers. At the end of the show Louise said, 'I've had a message from Tom Hunter. He says he wants to support the charity.' You only have to do a quick Google search on Tom to see how wonderfully generous he is with his money. There are so many good causes he supports, and after a few phone calls and emails, it was all organised. Tom was donating £1 million to dementia charities after being inspired by Paul Harvey.

A few days later we got Paul and Nick back on *Breakfast* and made the announcement live on the television to Grace Meadows from one of the charities, Music For Dementia. Everyone was crying.

'I still sometimes watch it back in absolute shock and euphoria,' says Grace, laughing. 'The lift that it gave during a lockdown and a pandemic was just so memorable. It validated all the times I have stood at a conference and talked about the power of music. It reminded me that someone was listening, it was worth investing in and it was life-changing and life-affirming. You know that Tom still sends me messages, Dan?' says Grace, full of enthusiasm. 'Just little things like, "Keep up the good work." For this to be on his radar is incredible. He is so busy, but he has shown us all that recognition makes such a massive difference.'

Every penny of that donation has already been spent across thirty-one organisations in all, covering a huge number of schemes and courses: dementia discos, orchestral work, therapy, singing groups, music in care homes.

'That money has genuinely changed lives and saved a lot of those organisations from money lost in the pandemic,' says Grace. 'But it's not just the money. People come up to me and say, "You did that piece with that old guy." Paul has allowed me to go and have conversations with people because they have been emotionally moved by his music and what it does. He has opened the door for so many people living with dementia.'

Grace is a bassoonist. She plays in the World Doctor's Orchestra, and she has also been a music therapist for the past decade. In 2018, she became campaign director for Music For Dementia. I have to say that Grace is one of those wonderful people who inspires you the second she starts talking. She has so much passion for what she does, it spills into all those around her.

'I have always known about the power of music,' beams Grace. 'I will never ever forget when I was doing a session at the Chelsea and Westminster Hospital in London. Two people were getting married and one of them had terminal cancer. They had a full-on wedding but there was no music so I stopped and offered to play my keyboard for them. It was really poignant for me. I will never forget that. I just think that music enhances relationships in the same way that it has for Paul and Nick.'

I tell Grace that what really strikes many people about Paul is just how talented he is. 'That's it!' she says, beaming even more than before. 'My uncle has dementia and is a musician. He can sit and play but it's not coherent. It just sounds like random notes. Paul is quite special in terms of what he can do. He is a standout. I often think about what happens to all those amazing musicians who will get dementia in the next twenty years? How painful will it be for those who can't do what they once did? If I get dementia one day, will I know how to play?

Will I forget that I ever played? What Paul demonstrates is that there is something extraordinary about the way that music touches the brain. It's not just cognitive, it's emotional. There are some studies that suggest it's all tied in with sounds we hear as a child but, whatever the answer, music is part of Paul's fabric.'

I don't know about you but I am fascinated by music therapy and how we interact with it. Music is so intrinsically linked to so many of our memories and standout moments in our lives. As soon as I hear the first note of 'Killing Me Softly' by The Fugees, I am instantly transported back to our university corridor in 1996 where my next-door neighbour, Jason Power, started each day by playing it at full volume. All the songs we danced to on *Strictly* instantly take me back to the dance floor, and just a few strums of Chas & Dave and it's 1987 and the FA Cup final again when Coventry City beat Tottenham.

I ask Grace how she uses it in her therapy. 'You might start with a piece of music that they know,' she says. 'They may know the lyrics. You may start with the la la la's. You use anything to bring them into the session. You wait for that moment when they are there in the room and then you can build on that connection with them. You can then watch carefully as that music plays out.

'Are they grasping for something?

'Are they looking to you for guidance?

'Are they following the tune?

'Do they need help?

'Are they waiting for the next verse or the chorus?

'Are they agitated?

'You are constantly micro-analysing to see if there is any reaction to what you play. You are constantly creating a stage for them to be on beyond their diagnosis. Whatever they give you, you can work with it. With some brain injury patients, you might be working with something as small as a finger movement or an eye flicker. You are always looking for a call and response and then, suddenly, you have a conversation going with someone who can only tap a finger. With someone with dementia, they might not be able to speak, but you might mirror a sound or a motion. You do all that you can to find a means of communicating with them. There is also some powerful work you can do with families. You are creating musical memories for that family, which happens a lot in palliative care. Lots of people work with the music therapist and maybe rewrite a song to create a musical legacy.'

'What difference did Paul and Nick make to all that?' I ask.

'Dan,' says Grace, 'I cannot even begin to tell you. They took awareness to a stratospheric level with "Four Notes". Their relationship was inspirational for so many people because Nick can see his father and his dementia. He still feels and sees his dad through the music that he plays. I will never forget him playing with and then conducting the Philharmonic. It was the most thrilling thing I have ever seen; just the sheer joy of watching a man fulfil his lifelong dream. I was sobbing already before I looked across and saw Nick arm in arm with his brothers, watching their dad. The pride was pouring out of them. It was such a powerful celebration of family.'

I don't mind telling you I was in tears listening to Grace. She gets me every time. I think it is the fact that she understands and explains the subtleties of dementia so beautifully. It is scary and sad and painful and heart-breaking, but there can still be joy and fun and a celebration of talent that shouldn't be allowed to go to waste.

'Paul has allowed people to see the power of music,' says Grace. 'There are so many families who are now doing music therapy with their loved ones because of him. He has inspired people to set up their own programmes, inspired a £1 million donation and he has changed lives. Aside from the help he has given others, there is so much to admire about his music: the harmonic progression, the lyrical phrasing and the way he feeds rhythm into that. There is so much depth and richness and colour. The way he gently lifts his finger off the keys. You can see the musicality is still there; he still feels it through his body. I love that he decided to teach all that to the next generation and now he shares it with everyone. He has radically changed how many of us see people living with dementia. He is one of a kind. He has shown how music can keep connections that can keep you alive. His son thought he had lost him. Dementia can be such a painful, drawn-out process as you watch that daily decline. Anything that can give you back a sense of connection or togetherness is so powerful and gives everyone the strength to keep going. I hope Paul keeps playing for many years to come.'

'Can you still remember what the four notes were that started all this, Paul?' I ask.

'F, A, D, B.' He sings them back to me. Nick is open-mouthed next him.

'How do you remember them?' asks his amazed son.

'I don't really know,' says Paul. 'Maybe I wrote them in my book.'

I did tell you I would come back to the book. Paul keeps it by the side of his piano.

'I write things down in here,' he says. 'As soon as I get to the point where I think I might forget something, down it goes.'

He starts to giggle. 'I've even written "diarrhoea" in it,' the giggle develops into a belly laugh, 'but I can't remember why.'

Again, this is what I love about these two. As the conversation shifts, you go through all the emotions with them. One minute you're crying and the next you are spitting out your tea. It quickly shifts from diarrhoea to something far more serious.

'Haven't you got Alzheimer's written on the first page, Dad?' says Nick.

'Yes,' says Paul, sighing. 'That's because I can't sometimes remember what I've got. It's not the nicest thing to be reminded of, but I suppose it's important to know.'

The conversation jumps again. 'I love snooker, Dan,' says Paul. 'I was watching the snooker with Ronnie, and I couldn't remember his surname. I could remember The Two Ronnies, but I couldn't get Ronnie . . . Ronnie . . . and then it came and I wrote it in the book because I don't want to forget that.' He checks the book. 'Ronnie O'Sullivan. Usain Bolt too! I forgot his name and you can't have that, so I wrote it down straightaway. I knew I was going to forget. The book is very helpful.'

'Do you remember when you asked me who wrote Bernstein's *West Side Story*?' says Nick, giggling again.

'No,' says Paul, but he seems to know it's funny.

'I just said "Bernstein"' says Nick, 'and you said, "That's it!"'

They are laughing again.

'It doesn't annoy me that I forget,' says Paul. 'Even Beethoven, who was deaf, sawed the legs off his grand piano so he could feel the vibrations through his feet!'

'Did he?' says Nick. 'Do you want me to do that for you?'

'Don't be daft,' says Paul.

'Do you remember playing "Four Notes" and all the things you did on the television?' I ask.

'I can't really remember it at all,' says Paul.

'We watch it a lot, don't we?' offers Nick, who explains that he has all the performances and appearances saved on his YouTube channel so his dad can watch them every time he turns on the TV.

'Do you worry that you will forget how to play, Paul?' This time there is a long pause after my question.

'I don't think so,' says Paul eventually. 'We've all got to go sometime.'

'We both live in the moment, don't we, Dad,' adds his son. 'I've seen him at his worst and at his best. At his lowest, in hospital after that fall, he was spending every hour crying and confused. Look at him now! Fundamentally, he is back. This is my dad. I don't think of the future. Right now, things are ok.'

'I can't remember anything really,' says Paul.

'I think it frustrates you sometimes, doesn't it?' adds Nick.

'When you forget the names of people. He forgot my wife's name and he adores her, or the names of his grandchildren. That upsets you, doesn't it?'

'It does,' replies Paul, 'because I love them, but I am happy. Dementia robs you of so much, but I still know who I am, and I still know that music means everything to me and I'm just glad I got to share it with so many people before it was too late.'

Nick knows that the best way to keep his dad going is to keep him at the piano. They are always looking for the next piece to play, for the next challenge. 'I want to keep going until at least Christmas,' says Paul. 'I've written some carols.' He's worked with Aled Jones and would love to write something for Katherine Jenkins.

I ask the pair of them what they think about all the money they raised through the single and the donation from Tom Hunter. 'It's amazing, isn't it?' says Nick. 'All the money, Dad, you know, from "Four Notes" . . . with Grace from the charity.'

Paul's eyes light up. 'She's in the book,' he says. 'Grace is one of my special people.'

I tell Paul that Grace thinks he's amazing and that he's made such a difference to so many people. Nick reminds him about the message he got from his hero, the composer Stephen Sondheim on the day he composed the piece with the BBC Philharmonic. 'That was special,' says Paul. 'I cried a lot that day.'

The conversation moves on to how he'd like to be remembered. 'It's pretty simple really,' says Paul. 'If I brought any sort of pleasure through music, I'll be very happy.'

'What about your Dyson vacuum trick?' says Nick. 'Dan,

he can tell you the last two notes of our vacuum cleaner as it shuts down. He's got the perfect pitch. He hears a note, and he can tell you what it is. Watch this.' Nick sprints to the piano. 'Dad, don't look . . . what is this note?' Nick taps the piano key a couple of times as Paul turns away with his eyes looking into the middle distance, listening intently.

'Well . . .' he says with a fair degree of confidence. 'It's very out of tune but it's either an A or an A-flat.'

'He's right!' exclaims Nick. 'It's an A!'

As Nick sits down, I remind him that so many people love the way he cares for his dad but also celebrates his skill and wants the rest of the world to know about it.

'I've always known that Dad's music was world class. I'm so proud that, as an eighty-year-old, you got there,' he says, turning to his dad and addressing him directly.

'You never wanted to be famous, you just loved teaching, but I knew that the quality of your music deserved a bigger audience. The songs you wrote for school productions were as good as anything on the West End and you chose to be a teacher and . . . they were so lucky to have you. And then, after all that, we got you out there and you broadcast your talent to everyone. That meant the world to me, Dad. It was wonderful. You deserve all the love.'

They embrace.

I think about Paul Harvey a lot, I think a lot of people do. I am so glad he is in this book. He is a musical giant who has allowed us all to spend a little time on his shoulders.

I love listening to the students he inspired almost as much as

I love listening to his music. I love the way his son talks about him. I love the way they poke fun at each other and laugh alongside the sadness. I love that he has done so much to change our perceptions of the cruel beast that is dementia. I love that when he was meant to be at his weakest, he showed his strength. I love that he has shown us all that although it might rob him of his memories, it cannot steal his worth.

After their long embrace, I thank them both for their time and talent.

'You are a remarkable man,' I offer.

'Thank you,' says Paul, bowing his head.

'He was talking to me,' retorts Nick and, once again, as it often does when the Harveys are around, the sound of laughter fills the air.

THE MAN WITH THE NARWHAL TUSK

When Darryn was four years old, he was bullied at school. An older boy, called Troy, pushed Darryn to one side and looked the aggressors in the eyes: 'If you want to get to him, you have to come through me.' The bullying stopped.

When Darryn was a lot older than four, he was on a train on his way to Northampton. There were two football fans harassing a young girl. They were sitting behind her making inappropriate sexual comments. She whispered, 'They just won't leave me alone.' Troy wasn't around this time, so Darryn stood up and said, 'If you want to get to her, you have to come through me.' The men were abusive but, when the rest of the carriage showed they were also ready to take action, they quickly sunk back into their seats and nothing more was said.

Darryn was in New York when he witnessed a man on a train swearing violently at the woman who the man was with. Darryn told him that it wasn't right to speak to a woman like that, especially in front of young children. The man turned his aggression towards Darryn who stood his ground. The man backed down and got off the train at the next station. An elderly lady came up to Darryn and thanked him for his bravery but warned him that the man could have easily had a gun or a knife. 'You could have been in real danger.'

Darryn has always had the instinct to protect others. Maybe it was Troy who inspired him, but it has always been something he cannot ignore. He was born in South Africa and his parents split when he was three and his father left to live in the United Kingdom for two years before coming home. His mum built a family with another man, they had another child together and Darryn was left feeling like he didn't belong anywhere. He found role models away from the family home, in other people's families.

At the age of eleven, he was sent to an all-boys' school – the Jeppe High School – in Johannesburg, South Africa. Darryn says he became a man in that school. At the start, he couldn't look anyone in the eye. He had no self-confidence and no idea what he wanted to do with his life. He had to fend for himself, defend himself when the senior boys would launch night-time raids on the newbies. Shoes were stuffed into pillowcases, rule came via the fist, but Darryn learned that in challenging times, you form strong bonds with others who are going through the same experiences. At Jeppe he learned what it meant to protect others, even if that meant putting yourself in harm's way. The school's motto was, 'For the brave, nothing is too difficult'.

All this prepared Darryn for what happened at Fishmongers' Hall, at the northern end of London Bridge, on 19 November 2019 – a day that changed his life forever.

*　　*　　*

Darryn was a communication's manager with the Prison and Probation Service in London. On that day, he was attending a conference on prisoner rehabilitation which was celebrating the fifth anniversary of Learning Together – a programme run by the Cambridge Institute of Criminology. It was all about re-integrating offenders into society. Jack Merritt, a twenty-five-year-old law and criminology graduate, was at the conference that day. He was working for Learning Together. It was also a significant day for Steve Gallant; a convicted murderer who was serving a life sentence. It was his first day outside a prison in fourteen years. Usman Khan was also at Fishmongers' Hall on that sunny November morning. He had been invited to the conference as a former participant in the Learning Together programme. He had been convicted of trying to launch a terror attack in 2012 and sentenced to eight years in jail. He was allowed to leave Belmarsh prison on a temporary release licence in 2018. One of the conditions of his release was that he was banned from entering London, but he was given special dispensation to attend the rehabilitation conference.

Usman Khan attacked five people with a knife that day. He killed two of them. One of them was Jack Merritt.

Over the course of this chapter, you'll hear from Darryn and Steve, two of the men who took on the terrorist, and from Dave and Anne Merritt, Jack's parents. I don't know if you have experience of the prison system in this country. I don't know how you feel about rehabilitation. I don't know whether you think someone can change. Is there a way back for someone like Usman Khan? Could someone or some sort of programme have convinced him not to do what he did? How do you judge Steve Gallant? Do his actions, which you will read about at Fishmongers' Hall, in any way atone for the murder he committed in 2005? Can he ever be forgiven? Can he change? I hope this chapter, and the accounts of the people involved, help you to answer some of those questions.

'I wasn't meant to be there at all,' remembers Darryn. 'My line manager was meant to be the one attending, but she was in Cardiff, so I went in her place. The event was due to start at 11 a.m. but I got there nice and early at 10. I was taking some photos of Fishmongers' Hall as it's such a beautiful building. I recorded some videos looking at the history on the walls and just the scale of it. I was meant to be writing an article about the day so I took in as much as I could. Little did I know at the time, but I was surveying the battle scene and all that information would become invaluable in the hours to come.'

Just like Darryn, Steve Gallant's attendance was also a surprise. Steve was jailed for seventeen years in 2005 for the murder of ex-firefighter Barrie Jackson. As a convicted murderer, Steve had started his sentence in the most secure facility – a category A prison – but, over the years, had worked his way through the system, and five weeks before the event at Fishmongers' Hall he found out he was going to be moved to an open prison.

Steve picks up the story. 'When I heard the news about the open prison, I put in an application to go to the rehabilitation event at London Bridge. The prison service turned me down, but then, a week before it was meant to go ahead, I found out that I was going and that I would be escorted by a prison officer. It was a big deal for me. That day was the first day I had left prison in fourteen years.'

Steve had been working with Jack Merritt on the Learning Together project and Jack had had a huge impact on him. 'I'd been working with Jack for about two-and-a-half years. He was amazing. He was one of those people who managed to give you a sense of self-worth, no matter what you'd been through. He was passionate. He cared. He would always spend a lot of time with you, and he'd do things like bring in a professor from Cambridge to talk about human rights. Jack was always the first person on the phone when people came out of the prison. I was looking forward to seeing him that day. I walked into the hall, and it was just so beautiful. It was oozing history and opulence,' remembers Steve. 'It was almost magical. It was late November, and the sun was shining and there was this gorgeous blue sky. I remember thinking that I didn't really know what freedom felt like, so I just told myself to enjoy the day. I was meant to be involved in a discussion in the afternoon. That was the only thing I had been asked to do, so I was determined to make sure that I soaked it all in.'

While Steve was soaking in the occasion, Darryn was busy taking pictures. One of them was of the elaborate dining hall where they would all be served fish pie for lunch. When Darryn looks back on that photograph now, he can see one other man, sitting at the table . . . it was Usman Khan, the terrorist.

In the first session of the day, the attendees were asked to think of three negative things to describe themselves, followed by three positive ones. 'I'm never sure if these sessions actually work,' says Darryn. 'I played along, and we were then asked to think about the first time we had felt that negative emotion. For me, like most people I suppose, it all went back to being a kid and the person leading the session made us think about the lesson we would give ourselves as a child. I remember thinking that I would tell myself that parents are not idols, but they are lessons in right and wrong, and they are often wrong.' After that session, there was a break where Steve decided to take the opportunity to go to the toilet.

'I was meant to be involved in the discussion during the afternoon,' recalls Steve. 'I was about to nip downstairs to the toilet, and one of the co-directors from Learning Together pulled me to one side to talk about the question I was going to ask. I found out later that, at that precise moment, Jack (Merritt) was going to the toilet, but Usman Khan was also in there. He was busy preparing himself for what was about to happen and strapping the knives to his hands.'

Steve went back into the hall to re-join the officer who was escorting him for the day for the next session. Darryn was already in there. 'I was at the table,' says Darryn, 'second row from the stage. I was right by the windows at the front of the building. All of a sudden, we could hear some shouting, and someone asked us all to stay in the room. If I'm honest, at first, it sounded like some teenagers or skateboarders had got in the foyer and were causing a bit of a disturbance. Then I heard the scream and the prisoner next to me turned and said, "That's not a teenager messing around!" I stood up and, on the adjacent table, Steve stood up at exactly the same time.'

'I knew it was someone screaming properly,' remembers Steve. 'I knew it was serious and I wanted to investigate, but it was my first day out of prison and my prison officer told me to stay where I was while he went and had a look. A moment later someone from Learning Together shouted, "Everyone stay there . . . it's Usman!" and I knew I had to help.'

Steve and Darryn arrived at the top of the spiral staircase at the same time. 'I tried to survey the scene,' says Darryn. 'There was a woman startled, running up the stairs saying, "Oh my God!" and when I looked over the edge of the banister, I saw Saskia on the stairs.'

Saskia Jones was a volunteer with the Learning Together programme. Two hours before she was stabbed and killed by Khan, she had sat down at his table and chatted to him. Saskia knew him because the Cambridge University Learning Together programme taught students and prisoners side by side. Khan joined when he was in prison and was seen as a success story. They had put him on their promotional leaflets and given him a computer.

'I started to move down the stairs,' says Steve, 'and I saw my prison officer with his hands pressed on Saskia's neck, trying to help her.'

At this point, Khan was attacking people in the foyer of the hall. One of them was a student at Anglia Ruskin University and was working part-time at Learning Together as an office manager. Understandably, for some people the events of the day are still too raw and chapters like this are hard to read. Some individuals have requested that their names be changed, so we'll refer to the part-time office manager as 'Jane'.

Saskia Jones was the second person Khan attacked. Jane later described at the inquest that she had watched as Jack Merritt stumbled out of the toilet after being stabbed twelve times. She screamed, 'No, Usman! Please don't!' before he attacked her. She was one of three people who survived.

Steve was one of those watching on in horror. 'They were on the stairs and there was another girl (Jane) on the floor too. I could see Usman Khan and it was obvious he was responsible. I could see the blood. He had the knives on him, and he was in the middle of a killing spree. My thought processes were working quickly: I knew I needed to slow him down until the police arrived, so I made my way down the stairs.'

Darryn was about to make his way down the other side of the double staircase. 'Steve was on the move. I didn't know what was down there, but I knew I needed to find something to defend people from whatever was attacking them below. I thought about a chair or maybe a big serving lid and a ladle from the dining hall. As I was running back towards the hall to get something, I saw a short corridor with a couple of 2-metre-long tusks hanging each side of the door from the wall. I took one and ran back down the stairs where I could see Steve taking on the terrorist with a chair.'

'I just launched something at his head,' recalls Steve. 'He came towards me and opened his jacket and showed me his bomb.'

'I was looking at Steve holding off the terrorist,' says Darryn, 'and behind them Jane was lying on the floor. This might sound strange, but the room behind was backlit by the sun which was streaming in through the stained-glass windows. The sun is shining off the blood on the floor. As I make my way down there, I meet Usman Khan.' Darryn pauses. 'I don't like saying his name. Do you mind if I don't use his name, Dan? Can I just call him "the terrorist"?' I tell him that's fine and he continues.

'He has thickset eyebrows which I can see just beneath his balaclava. There are two 8-inch kitchen knives strapped to his hands and, just like the blood on the floor, they are glistening. Behind him, I could see Jane on the floor. She looked like an angel who had fallen to the ground. She was motionless. I was convinced she was already dead. There was so much to take in, but I know I had to try and stop him, so I position the tusk at his belly button. As I manoeuvre myself into position, he stops for a moment and looks at me. "I'm not here for you," he says. "I'm here for the police." He was negotiating with me. Behind me on the stairs, one of the course coordinators is also looking after Saskia and says, in disbelief, "Oh my God, he's got a bomb!"

'He hears it too and widens his arms a little to show me what he has strapped to his chest. "I have a bomb," he said. What do I do? What is my next move? There are more than a hundred people in the room directly above him. I have to do something before the police arrive. Steve is propping a door open and throws a chair at the terrorist, hitting him on the shoulder. The terrorist turns towards Steve and starts advancing. I look at Steve, our eyes meet, and I pass him the tusk while trying to keep it pointed at the terrorist's stomach. Now I'm empty-handed and within striking distance of his blades, so I turn and run back up the stairs, passing Saskia and those caring for her, to try and get the second tusk. As I'm trying to get it off the wall without breaking it, my colleague, Tracy, is trying to stop me. She tells me to stay where I am, but I push her away to the wall. "I won't let him hurt anyone else," I tell her and make my way back down the stairs, past another girl who is bleeding from a wound to her arm. I know I have to get back to Steve.'

'There was no need to talk to this guy,' says Steve. 'I just thrust the tusk at his chest. It seemed to bounce off. It almost had no effect at all. I snapped it across his arm and then he runs at me with his knives. I ran back into the foyer and people are throwing things at him and I hit him with another chair. "I'm waiting for the police," he says, but I know I can't let him rest. I can't let him recover. I watch him as he tries to make his way outside and he tries to stab someone on the way. Thankfully, he misses. I follow him out onto London Bridge, and I can see a woman walking towards him, with no idea what has just happened inside. "GET BACK!" I scream at the top of my voice. "HE'S A TERRORIST!" People start to run and panic, and he turns back towards me.' Steve pauses. 'And do you know what, Dan? I have no further memory of the next few minutes. I had to learn it all from the public inquiry. I have just blanked it out.'

Darryn is sprinting down the stairs with the second tusk. 'I can see the shattered tusk on the floor, and I remember thinking that the worst has happened to Steve. He has become the latest victim. I see that the huge front door is closing but I see a foot going out. "LET ME OUT!" I scream. They open the door and I make my way through carefully with the tusk and try and assess the scene from the top of the stairs. For the first time in my life, I go into a state of complete tunnel vision. I can see the terrorist moving towards the bridge. He is running. I make my way down the stairs, and, to my right, a fire extinguisher goes off. It's being held by John Crilly.'

John was another former prisoner who decided to take on the terrorist. 'There is a huge puff of smoke and on the other side of that smoke, is Steve,' recalls Darryn. 'For a moment, I come out of the tunnel vision. He's alive! He's ok.'

Very quickly, the focus returns and all three men are chasing the terrorist onto London Bridge. Darryn is leading the charge. 'He is running towards a crowd of people with knives above his head. It was pure chaos. My focus is completely on the terrorist. Cars are stopping. People are screaming. I thought that Steve and John must have been behind me somewhere so when I approach the terrorist, I think I am on my own. He turns and comes towards me. As he runs, he raises the knives and I see a tiny piece of flesh on his left side, below his clothes. It was over in a heartbeat, but it feels like twenty seconds to me. Everything was in slow motion. I was fighting for my life. I aimed this 2-metre tusk into 1 centimetre of flesh. The impact buckled him over. He didn't cry out and, when I pulled it out, he buckled over again.'

Darryn wasn't on his own. 'John let off his fire extinguisher again and the smoke covered Steve. It worked because the terrorist didn't see Steve running along the bridge. He got past him and behind him and then grabbed his left shoulder and managed to drag or pull him on the floor. I dropped the tusk and jumped on his back and thrust his wrists up as high as I could go to keep his arms up above his head. He had these protective gloves on. I was holding on to him with all the strength I had in my body.'

Just like Darryn, Steve was determined to make sure that the terrorist couldn't get back up off the floor. 'I shouted at Darryn to grab his hands and we are both on top of him on the floor. I remember people shouting, "Give him a kicking!" We thought we had stopped him but, somehow, he gets back on his feet! I landed a few uppercuts to his face and he's back on the ground. I think that's when the police turned up.'

Darryn was still holding the terrorist's hands. 'I was shouting at people to not hit him. I shifted my weight to protect his head. I was screaming at people to get the knives out of his hands, but they were so heavily strapped. He wasn't saying anything at all. I remember someone with tan-coloured boots standing on my hands. It was hurting so much but it was also a relief because it meant I didn't have to apply the same pressure to restrain him. Moments later, the police arrived.'

The problem for Darryn was that he knew the terrorist was waiting for the police to turn up. He knew that this was the moment he was looking for, the moment to detonate the bomb. 'The police are shouting at me to "get back", to "move away". They are tugging at my jumper trying to pull me off, but I won't let go. Steve comes back and says, "Come on, mate, the police are here, let him go." I'm pretty sure that Steve came back to try and save my life. I've still got his hands. I won't let him kill anyone else. Just at that moment, he relaxes his arms. I thought he was giving up, but he looked at the nearest officer and said, "I'VE GOT A BOMB!"'

Darryn pauses, seemingly to reflect on the intensity of the situation. 'The officer screams, "HE'S GOT A BOMB!" and his voice breaks as he does it. My face is 10 centimetres away from this bomb. There was a tiny gap in one of the boxes strapped to the TNT-shaped sticks around his body. I was so close that I could see a 1-millimetre gap and the box looked hollow, but I also saw something that looked like a calculator, or a mobile phone attached. I was wondering, "Is this bomb real? Can I stop it by restraining his hands? Is it remote activated? Or am I going to get shot and we'll all die anyway?" While all this was racing through my head, one of the officers pulls my hands away and I thought that was the moment the bomb was going to go off. I ran off with my hands over my ears. I heard three pops but there was no smoke coming off the device. I thought they must have shot him, but I didn't want him to die. It might sound strange after what he had done but I didn't want him to have the satisfaction of his choice. He wanted to die that day. That was his plan all along, it seemed to me: to kill as many as he could and then blow himself up. I didn't want his plan to work, especially after what he'd done.'

At this point, Darryn's mind went blank for a few minutes. He has no recollection of what happened. The next thing he remembers is being back on the stairs in Fishmongers' Hall looking down on the scene of devastation and still holding a metre section of the tusk in his hand. He called his partner and told her what had happened. While he was on the phone there was another volley of shots and everyone started screaming again. The police had killed the terrorist on the bridge. Darryn was halfway up the staircase standing next to Steve. The pair of them were watching the paramedics trying to resuscitate Saskia. Between them, they'd helped protect hundreds of people. Steve turned to Darryn and shook his hand.

'Hi. I'm Steve Gallant. I'm a prisoner and today is my first day out of prison in fourteen years.'

I remember hearing about the initial incident while I was driving around that day. Like millions of others, I watched the video of the fire extinguisher going off on the bridge and the men fighting with the terrorist. I heard about the casualties and about the Polish chef, Lukasz, who took on Khan after hearing screams when he was down in the kitchen. Lukasz fought him, suffering five wounds to his arm, but giving many others the opportunity to escape. He was one of many heroes that day.

For weeks, details were sketchy, as police continued their investigations. There were rumours that Lukasz was the man with the narwhal tusk and precious little was known about Darryn, Steve and the others who had helped stop the terrorist taking more lives.

I first met Darryn on the *BBC Breakfast* sofa. I remember being fascinated reading about him the day before he came on, because he had hardly spoken to anyone. His account was captivating but, as soon as you start talking to Darryn, you realise it has taken a huge toll on him. Yes, he is a hero. Yes, he saved lives that day. Yes, he could have been killed. Yes, his life will never be the same again.

'I took medication before I spoke to you that morning,' he says, as we meet again. 'Propranolol lowers your heart rate and helps to stop the sweating. I take the drugs to deal with people. Whenever I am in large groups or if I ever have to talk about what happened at Fishmongers' Hall. It helps me to cope with the anxiety.'

Much of that anxiety goes back to the day of the attack and what happened afterwards. While Darryn and Steve were talking on the stairs, the police came in and started shouting and telling everyone to put everything down.

Darryn was taken to the triage centre and separated from everyone else. 'I kept asking about the girl who had been stabbed, Jane. In those early days, she was the one I would have night terrors about. I listened to the news reports, and they said that one man and one woman had been killed and I was convinced they had it wrong. I thought I had watched her die. I thought it might be part of the trauma. The more I asked about her, the fewer answers I got. I kept reliving it time and time again in my head, over and over. It was only the day before Jack Merritt's funeral that I found out that she had survived and then listening to her testimony at the inquiry helped me enormously. I heard Jane say that the attack just felt like a series of dull blows, like punches. That really helped me to know that she wasn't suffering the sort of pain that I thought she was going through at the time. I couldn't bear the idea of her going through that. It was too much.'

Steve also remembers the moment when his brain suddenly clicked back into gear, standing on those steps with Darryn. 'I looked around me and I realised how many people had been injured. The Polish chap (Lukasz) was sitting on the steps and bleeding. I assumed Jane was dead. I can still see the paramedics shaking their heads over the body of Saskia Jones. I asked a friend where Jack was, and he couldn't tell me what had happened; he was too traumatised.' Steve later discovered the truth about Jack visiting the toilet at the same time the terrorist was preparing himself for the attack. It was tragic timing. He was the first victim. Witnesses remember seeing Jack stumbling out of the toilet with his white shirt 'covered in blood'. He tried to take refuge in the nearby reception office but never recovered from his wounds.

Steve found the prison officer who was meant to be looking after him that day. 'There wasn't much to say. We were both just processing information. I was coming to terms with what had happened; with what I had done. My first day of freedom in fourteen years and here I was chasing a terrorist. And, more than that, the first time I'd used violence since the crime which put me in jail. Darryn took me to one side and told me that I'd saved so many lives, but I was thinking about all the opportunities I'd had to use violence in prison and rejected it. Here I was, having to make a snap decision to attack someone to stop them from hurting someone else. I suppose that is rehabilitation. That is what Jack was so passionate about. We spoke about that a lot.'

Steve lost a friend that day. Dave and Anne Merritt lost a son. 'Jack was one of those people who attracted others,' says his dad. 'He was intelligent, he was a thinker, but he was also committed to his work and his friends. He was loyal. It's one of those strange situations where we only found out just how much people loved him, and how much of a difference he made to people, after he'd gone.'

I ask his mum when his interest in rehabilitation started. 'He studied politics at A level,' says Anne. 'He was always interested in social justice; maybe because we discussed that sort of thing as a family. He did some volunteering when he was at university in Manchester and was interested in ethics. He did the Learning Together course at Cambridge University, after his degree, and started to learn alongside prisoners, people who were serving sentences for serious crimes. I think that was a big eye-opener for him. He realised what a privileged upbringing he'd had, and I think he just wanted to help.'

After his Masters, Jack started working for Learning Together. 'He could see how much injustice there was in the justice system,' says Dave. 'He was desperate to have an influence on that but didn't think he could do that if he went into a job as a criminal barrister. A lot of people have said to us that he saw the person rather than the crime and I am proud of him for that.'

'He understood people,' adds Anne. 'He had an understanding of the circumstances that had led them to the choices they had made in their lives and some of the bad decisions they had made. He connected with people, people who most of us would give up on. People like Steve Gallant.'

When you stop and think about it, it's amazing that Darryn and Steve were working in tandem that day. A man who knows that many in society will never forgive him for the crime he committed, face to face with the man who, just like Jack, feels very deeply that people can change.

When Darryn first came to the UK to work, he visited HMP Kirkham, an open prison. 'I was walking in from the front gate and a guy came up to me to escort me through the prison,' recalls Darryn. 'I asked him how long he'd been working there, and he laughed and said, "I'm a prisoner, mate." I never knew that was possible. He was just a normal guy, walking freely around the prison. I thought he was an off-duty officer. It was incredible.

'I met another man later that day who was so keen to engage. He was telling me that he was looking forward to a chance of having what he called a "real life". He had never worked before he was in prison and arrived there after committing a murder at the age of eighteen. It hit me, here I was standing 20 centimetres away from a guy who had murdered someone, and yet he posed no threat to me. He spoke really well and just wanted to live a normal life. As I listened to him, I realised that I had to challenge my preconceptions. I had thought that all murderers were just monsters and would always be that way, but as I spent more time in prison and met more people, I learned there is always more to every story. I was one of those individuals who thought "these people can't change" but I was learning that I was the one who needed to change.'

Ask yourself this question. The same question I have asked

myself as I wrote and read this chapter: what do you think of Steve Gallant? You have met a man who committed a murder and spent, in total, sixteen years and two months behind bars for it. Steve went back to jail after the incident at Fishmongers' Hall and eventually had his seventeen-year sentence reduced by Royal Prerogative of Mercy by ten months after the Secretary of State for Justice, Robert Buckland, went to see the Queen. You have also met a man who put his own life on the line to save others on his first day of freedom.

Do you see Steve as his solicitor, Neil Hudgell, described him? 'When I first met Steve, he struck me as a hugely articulate and reflective person with a wealth of insight into the prison system. He is a shining example of reformation, not only for himself, but others he has helped.'

If you ever get the chance to speak to Steve, you'll find a man who understands what people think of him. He knows there are some opinions he will never change, and he knows there are some who can't, and won't forgive. I find his determination to keep going admirable.

'London Bridge doesn't negate what I did,' he says, in reflective mood. 'I paid the price for what I did. For me, I never wanted to be seen as benefiting from it. I feel guilty about it even now. London Bridge did contradict the narrative that people can't change. I think it might have made some people think. For once we had a story of something happening that people didn't expect. We gave a voice to another side of the system. Humans are far more complex than a single act and that is something I have learned the hard way. My stepdad was violent, you know,

Dan. I'm not making an excuse but, everywhere I looked, I saw aggression and violence as a way to resolve almost every situation. My partner was attacked in my home, and I reacted to that in, at the time, the only way I knew. I went to prison. I was very loyal to my friends. I protected people and the only ones who stood by me in those early days were my family.'

I've visited plenty of prisons through my work but, thankfully, I've never spent a night in one and I hope that remains the case. Steve has spent years behind bars and has learned a lot along the way.

'I realised that violence had actually caused all my problems and that I had become a person that I didn't want to be. Very early in my sentence, I made a decision to change. My problem was, I still had a life sentence to serve. I started studying. I was trying to shatter my previous way of thinking; I suppose you could call it a flawed belief system, a belief system that had led me to murder. Nothing can change you if you don't want to change, but I'd like to think I spent a lot of my time wisely. The system shouldn't be a barrier to rehabilitation. During my time inside, I've seen all sorts of things cause problems for people who genuinely want to change ... staffing issues, resources, gangs, violence, limited access to courses and too much access to drugs. There are often so many things in the way of progress and it's much easier to just stay as you are.'

I ask Steve if people find it hard to trust him. He pauses and carefully considers his answer. 'When I speak to people, Dan, you know, the "hang 'em and flog 'em" brigade, you can sometimes be speaking to a brick wall but, when people see the facts or actually spend time with you, they can see a bit of the real you. I don't think it helps when politicians talk about stiffer sentences all the time and a lack of mercy. I think that adds fuel to the fire and, you know how it works, things get whipped up by the media. It's just incredibly complex. I know there is no easy option but so much of it is about perception. I don't advocate a soft approach to crime. I think there should be a zero-tolerance approach to violence. I should have been behind bars for what I did, but I do think we need to look at the way we treat prisoners. They, we, have got to be dealt with humanely. That is something that Jack understood more than most.'

Jack's parents still find it hard to speak about what happened to their son. It hurts and you can see it when you talk to them. Dave is currently working on a memoir, his account of what happened. He was getting ready to leave work and cycle home on that Friday evening in November 2019. He looked at his Twitter account before he got on his bike and saw a link to the *Guardian* website and a story about a terror attack in London. 'Oh no, not again,' he thought as he read about two people being feared dead. His mind jumped back to the terrorist attacks on Westminster Bridge and around Borough Market two years before.

'My life had already changed forever, but I didn't know it yet,' says Dave. 'In a little over six hours' time, I would be in a windowless room in a hospital in East London, being told by people I didn't know that my son Jack was dead, murdered by a man I had never heard of, at an event I didn't know he was attending.'

When Dave arrived home from work, Anne was frantically asking why he hadn't answered his phone. 'Get in the car!' she shouted. 'We need to go to London now, I will explain on the way.'

Anne told her husband that she'd had a phone call from Jack's girlfriend, Leanne. She had explained that Jack had been injured, possibly stabbed, in an incident at Fishmongers' Hall near London Bridge. Casualties were being taken to the Royal London Hospital in East London. That was all the information they had. They got to Cambridge train station and jumped on a train to the capital. They both started scanning websites for news about their son.

'Almost immediately we saw "Two Dead" on the BBC,' says Dave. 'We thought, "It couldn't be Jack", because we'd have heard about it by now. It was 18.15 and the incident had happened at 13.00. We thought that it must have been someone else, but why hadn't we heard anything from Jack? Maybe he was injured? Why hadn't he called us? We kept checking the websites. Refresh. Refresh. We had no calls from the police or anyone else which we thought was a good sign. We thought that, even if he had been stabbed, he was young and fit and could recover. Our minds were racing so we closed all the websites down and just concentrated on getting to the hospital.'

Dave and Anne did get to the hospital where they met the police family liaison officers and, a few hours later, they were given the worst possible news: their son was dead, killed by a terrorist. Dave's knees gave way when he was told. Jack's girlfriend collapsed on the floor and was sobbing. Everyone was sobbing. No one could believe what they were hearing.

Everyone who loses someone they love speaks of the numbness that invades the body when you're trying to process the enormity of what has happened. Dave and Anne felt that as they travelled home. Where do you even start after hearing that news? How do you rebuild? There are so many things to do. So many people to talk to. So many journalists asking questions. Dave was worried about politicians making capital from the death of his son. He didn't want Jack's murder to be used as justification for draconian sentences.

When you speak to Dave and Anne now, it's clear how incredibly proud of their son they are. When I first reached out to them, Dave sent me an email which told me that, if I wanted to understand who Jack was, I should read the attachment. The attachment was what his mum read out at the start of the inquest into what happened at Fishmonger's Hall.

'Jack Merritt was a good person. Jack was a force for good in the world, someone who made other people's lives better for knowing him. We have said many things about Jack, our son, but we felt the best way to paint a picture of him was through the words of those who knew and loved him.'

What followed was a beautifully powerful testimony from a huge range of people: the landlady at Jack's local, his primary school teacher, his friends, his former housemates, his colleagues, his girlfriend and his brother Joe. They all paint a picture of a remarkable young man and Anne read them all. She also read some of Jack's own words about the importance of the work he was doing and why it meant so much to him.

'When you learn in an atmosphere of mutuality, support

and positive expectation, where the peaks are celebrated and the pains are permitted and shared, it can be transformative, for the individuals involved and for the society they form together. This description of the Learning Together experience rings true of my own experiences on the course and is exactly what I want for all of our students. This is why this work is so important to me.'

Dave and Anne will never recover from what happened to Jack but they take great comfort from the man he became, the principles he lived by and the impact he had on others. Anne's closing words at the inquest remain incredibly powerful: 'We are hugely proud of who Jack was and what he stood for. His death was a tragedy, but his life was a triumph.'

Just like the Merritts, Darryn Frost still struggles with the aftermath of that day. He has bouts of depression and has issues with his short-term memory. He says he has learned to be more accepting of this new version of himself through therapy. To this day, he still takes sleeping tablets. If he doesn't, the night terrors come back. He still finds it hard to talk about.

'I can tell if people just want to know the gory details and I switch off. I feel uncomfortable when people try and make me feel or sound like a hero. We need to remember Saskia and Jack. Saskia was focused on understanding and tackling sexual violence and developing effective, survivor-focused strategies to prevent it. Jack was talking about helping prisoners from minorities and he lived his life trying to make a difference. I've been doing this job for fifteen years and I still don't have the same depth of understanding as they did. We should be celebrating their lives.'

I ask Darryn want he now thinks of the man he calls 'the terrorist'; what he thinks of the man who took the lives of two people who would have defended his rights to the ends of the earth.

'I want to understand him better,' says Darryn, after a moment to reflect. 'I don't believe that people or terrorists are born hateful. There is a journey towards that place. I saw the fear in his eyes. He became almost childlike in his negotiations with me. It was like he was begging, not threatening. I wonder how we lost him. I wonder how he was treated as a child. Then I think about how he was treated in prison and whether we have the resources to tackle terrorist ideology. We all have a duty to stop people becoming what he became. Where does terror come from? That's a question I ask myself a lot. How often are we responsible for planting the seeds of hate? How do we engage? Do we understand that sometimes we are the terrorists? Do we question the wars we have waged and the bombs we have dropped? Are we willing to ask tough questions about our own actions? Do we look at the blood which is on our hands? Learning Together was attempting great things, truly transformative. It allowed people like Jack and Saskia to shine, really helping people like Steve, John and many others. It is a real shame that one horrid man can undo all this and cause so much pain. There should have been more scrutiny about who was allowed to attend the programme and the event that day. I feel this is a joint responsibility between the authorities and Cambridge University who ultimately have a duty of care.'

Darryn feels uncomfortable when people call him a 'hero'. He feels uncomfortable because he has thought long and hard about what prison officers put themselves through every day. He'll accept that he put his own life at risk, but he'll also point towards the landings of prisons all over the country where officers are doing the same thing every single day behind locked doors. Fishmongers' Hall brought that risk into a much sharper focus.

Darryn's primary concern now is the way we treat prisoners in this country. He wants to try and use the events at Fishmongers' Hall to help us all understand a little more about the process of rehabilitation.

'You know, nobody has thanked Steve or John (Crilly) for what they did that day. They prevented a massacre. I was asked how I felt about receiving a Ministry of Justice award for what I did, but I told them that I only wanted it if the men who acted alongside me – the two prisoners – got the same thing. You can imagine how that went down! It is unpalatable to give someone like Steve an award for what he did when I can't think of a better example of bravery. People like Steve are seen as lesser humans. Their lives have less value because of their previous actions. We, as a country, keep judging people without giving them credit for who they are or who they have become. Their criminal records follow them forever. Even shorter stints in prison are a life sentence. They have fewer opportunities and can never overcome the social judgement. The more we punish and stigmatise people, the more likely they are to turn back to crime. Perpetual punishment is proven not to work, but we keep going back to it because it wins votes. It's popular but it's also incredibly expensive and ineffective.'

After Steve's sentence was reduced by ten months for what he did at London Bridge, he was released from jail on 3 August 2021. He spent his first day of freedom with Darryn. They went for a drive and had a McDonalds in Oxford.

Steve still lives with the guilt and regret of the crime he committed that landed him in jail. Barrie Jackson had been enjoying a night out in a pub in Hull in 2005. On his way home, he was attacked and beaten so badly that when the paramedics tried to revive him they could not find his mouth. One of the men who attacked him was Steve Gallant. He believed that Jackson had attacked his girlfriend. Steve knows that some people will never forgive him for what he did and, every time they hear about his bravery at Fishmongers' Hall, it brings back all those painful memories. Can anyone ever really change?

'I refuse to define myself as a convicted murderer,' says Steve. 'I used to see kids come into jail all the time and they'd say, "I'm an armed robber" or "I'm a killer". You can still take responsibility for your actions without being defined by them. I'm not a hero for what I did on London Bridge, but does one horrific act of violence follow me around for the rest of my life? That's not who I am.'

Steve is now a mentor to others. He has a lot of knowledge to share. He and Darryn are working together on an idea called Own Merit which is a housing scheme for those who are released from prison and are trying to find their way back into society.

As a Christian, redemption is fundamental to my faith. I always believe there is a way back. I have seen people change and, speaking to Steve, even though I understand the depth of feeling, it seems clear that he is a different man from the one who took the life of another. Steve has written much more about this in his own book which comes out in 2023. I look forward to reading it. It was people like Jack Merritt who helped him to get where he is now, who helped him to see a little further than he would on his own.

It's incredible to think that Jack made such an impact on Steve, and many others, and he was only twenty-five years old. He was only two years out of university but had already done so much with his life. His parents knew he was a firm believer in life after prison, but they question whether someone like Usman Khan could ever be rehabilitated under our current system.

'We firmly believe that people can change,' says Dave, 'but we don't know enough about de-radicalisation. When you look at what happened to Khan, there were fundamental issues which were never addressed, so he came out of prison more dangerous than when he went in. I can't tell you what Jack would have thought about Khan going through prisoner rehabilitation, but I do know he was a believer in due process. Learning Together was never going to help someone like Khan. The only options we seem to have in this country are custodial sentences and then monitoring afterwards. It's laughably incompetent. If you look at the way they dealt with Usman Khan, they all got it wrong. There were so many mistakes made.'

Both Dave and Anne attended the inquest into the Fishmongers' Hall attack. They were trying to find out not only why their son died but also get some answers about why Usman Khan was allowed to be at the event where he took Jack's life. It was a frustratingly difficult listen.

'In some ways I found it easier that it wasn't just one mistake,' continues Dave. 'If it was one decision that led to Jack's death, then I would find it harder, but all the agencies that dealt with Usman Khan made mistakes. We got fed up with hearing phrases like "I didn't consider that my job" or "I assumed someone else was doing that" or "I assumed someone else was watching him". It was hard, but we found the inquest helpful because people had to step up and accept accountability. They couldn't just hide behind the excuse of national security.'

I ask Anne if she thinks lessons have been learned. 'I'd like to think that's the case, but I'm not convinced,' she says. 'The one witness who really impressed us was the head of the probation service who said measures that they put in place were not fit for purpose. When it came to the work of MAPPA (Multi Agency Public Protection Arrangements), the body responsible for looking after sexual and/or violent offenders like Khan, I don't think I will ever get over some of the incompetence. They manage some of the most dangerous people that we have in this country and I'm not confident that the measures are any better now than they were then. The whole attitude seemed to be one of "there is nothing to see here".'

'You know we have never had an apology,' says Dave. 'Certain individuals have been kind and considerate, but we've also seen staggering levels of arrogance and unwillingness to accept responsibility.'

I ask them how they are now, nearly two-and-a-half years on. They glance at each other, and Dave speaks. 'Birthdays and Christmases will always be hard. The anniversary of the incident, the anniversary of his funeral; October through to Christmas every year remains tough. Daft as it may seem, as horrible as losing Jack has been, there has been an awful lot of publicity for the good work that he was doing, and the person that he was, and that has been a real source of comfort. I often think that if Jack had just been run over by a car, then there would have been none of this, we would never have known or learned so much about him. It's amazing that he was such a help to so many and that continues to help us through.

'People continue to do nice things,' says Dave. 'Cambridge United invited us all along to a football match and did a minute's silence for Jack and they invited us again recently. We have also tried something called Creating With Jack Merritt where we encourage people to do something creative on the anniversary of his death. That certainly makes the day itself a little easier. We find that if you tackle days like that head on, try and fill them with at least something, then the heartache is a little easier to come to terms with. It's lovely that so many people continue to be inspired by what he did. We know that, as time goes by, people's memories of him will fade . . . but ours never will.'

Darryn will continue to wrestle with the demons of that day. He firmly believes, as Jack did, that rehabilitation is possible. The actions of the terrorist he attacked have not changed that. For him, 19 November 2019 is the perfect example of just how blurred the picture is in this country when it comes to issues like race, immigration and rehabilitation.

Speaking to Darryn, Steve and Jack's mum and dad has given me much to think about and I hope it has done the same for you. It has also helped me to frame one of the biggest breaking news stories of the last few years.

The story of that day has so many layers. It's about Lukasz, a Polish immigrant, who put his life at risk. It's about Steve, a convicted murderer, who wants to be part of society again. It's about Saskia and Jack, two brilliant, gifted young people who were convinced that there should and could be life after prison . . . even for the man who took theirs. There are so many elements which make us look at what we believe, what we hold dear and force us to ask ourselves the most difficult questions. I suppose the key to all of this is just how determined we are to find the answers.

JIMI

During my time on television, I have announced a number of deaths and read hundreds of tributes. It is a tough part of the job. Most of those tributes talk about amazing people, great friends and big ambitions. I occasionally wonder how true all those words are and how many are affected by our determination to never speak ill of the dead.

On the morning of 26 April 2021, I remember reading out a series of glowing tributes to Folajimi Olubunmi-Adewole. Jimi, as he was known to his friends, was the young man – twenty years old – who jumped into the River Thames to try and save a woman who had fallen from London Bridge around midnight on Saturday 24 April.

I remember being struck by the depth of feeling from his family and friends. We spoke to the owner of The Cinnamon Club, the restaurant where he worked, and he talked about a young man who inspired all those around him. His parents spoke of his 'precious heart', Jimi's youth pastor at church mentioned the boy who was 'always looking out for others', and his friends, through the tears, paid tribute to someone who they all 'looked up to'.

No one seemed surprised that he jumped into the river. No one seemed surprised that he lost his own life trying to save someone else's. One of his closest friends was with him on the steps at the bottom of London Bridge that night. Bernard Kosia had taken his top off and was ready to jump in. 'No, bro,' said Jimi, preparing himself to hand Bernard his phone. 'You can't swim! Talk to the police.' Jimi jumped into the pitch-black Thames and that was the last Bernard ever saw of him.

The two boys met when they were eleven years old. Jimi had arrived from Nigeria at the age of ten, Bernard from Sierra Leone when he was four. Bernard was doing his usual thing of playing football in the park at 7 o'clock in the morning. He was a trainee at Chelsea at the time, in the same year group as Callum Hudson Odoi and Tariq Lamptey. He was highly fancied. Jimi was also a footballer, but he was out running in the park, as he always did.

Jimi saw Bernard working on his skills and walked over and introduced himself. 'He was so confident,' remembers Bernard. 'He said "hello" and we started talking. He told me about the school he went to and his family. I didn't know it then, but this was the start of the best friendship of my life. We trained together, we laughed together and then we walked home together.'

It was when they got back to their flats that the two lads realised they were neighbours. Bernard lived on the Vauban estate in Bermondsey and Jimi was directly across the road in the Neckinger estate.

'We were best friends from that moment,' says Bernard, 'from that first session in the park. We had a regular routine. We would train at 7 o'clock in the morning and, even at that early age, he was always encouraging me and telling me how far I could go. We went to different schools, but we spent most of our spare time together. As we got older, we just got closer.'

The boys would go to the cinema together. They loved watching films there. If it wasn't the cinema they were down at the local arcade. At the age of sixteen, Bernard was released from Chelsea. It was a crushing blow but there was an opportunity to go to America and play for Columbus Crew.

'Jimi would contact me all the time,' remembers Bernard with a smile. 'That's what he was like, he was confident, but he knew I was shy. We were so tight. I would come back from training late at night and send him a message to ask if he was up and he would come straight back and then we'd be up for hours, on *FIFA*, just chatting. We talked about everything. He was always looking out for me, but it wasn't just me, Jimi looked out for everyone.'

While Bernard was in America, Jimi was back in the UK studying business. He was a young man with big ambitions and big plans. He was the youngest of three brothers but was always telling his family that one day he would be a superstar musician and buy everyone a house.

'He was just different from the rest of us,' says his eldest brother Ayodeji. 'We were all nice boys, but Jimi was special. He was kind and generous. He would give his last penny to someone if they needed it and he would never think of the consequences for himself. I can't really remember him ever saying "no" if someone asked him for something. He was the ultimate servant.'

Jimi's family had arrived from Nigeria in stages. Jimi came to the UK in 2011 and Ayodeji and his middle brother, BJ, arrived much later.

'Jimi loved it when we were together as a family,' says Ayodeji. 'We would sometimes talk about how we could make things better, easier, for our parents. Jimi wanted to buy a big family house where we could all get together at Christmas.' Ayodeji laughs as he remembers his brother's bold promises. '"When I'm rich," he would say, and then tell us all how he would help everyone with his money. I'm the oldest brother but Jimi was a leader. "I will sort this family out," he'd say and we believed him. He was a great footballer, but his real talent was music.' Ayodeji stops for a moment.

'Is everything ok?' I ask tentatively.

'I was just remembering that he passed away a week before the official release of his first single. Did you know that? He had the whole outfit ready for the shoot. We laid him to rest in the brand-new Air Force One trainers he had bought.'

Both his brother and his best friend are full of stories about Jimi. They are bursting with examples of his care and generosity of spirit. 'There was this one time,' says Bernard, 'when we were kids, our parents would give us pocket money for food. We were always hungry after our football training and, one day, we decided to head down to Morley's (the local chicken shop). I only had £1, and Jimi had £2. He took my pound and said, "We are going to share this." He bought five wings and chips and we had a feast. What was his was mine and mine was his. He was always being that guy. He was one of the most welcoming people you will ever meet. His heart was pure, and he would always be loyal and supportive. Jimi also had the talent to make you laugh, however bad you were feeling. You could never be angry with him. I realised that I could talk to him about anything, and he would always give me advice. I would talk about missing home when I was in America. He was the only one who understood, and he would remind me of my purpose for being there and tell me that I just needed to finish things off. "You just need to try your best," he would say, and he was always encouraging me to keep pushing. He believed in me. It's hard for me to explain how much that meant to me. He was just special.'

Bernard came back from the United States because of the Covid pandemic. He needed a job but was really struggling to find one. Guess who came to his aid?

'I was getting desperate. I needed some money to live, and I put it all down in a group chat on WhatsApp. Jimi was working in a restaurant called The Cinnamon Club at the time and called me straightaway and said, "There is a job going here. Come to the restaurant, act like you don't know me, I will open the door so make sure you act professional." I did exactly like he said,' explains Bernard. 'During the interview I spotted Jimi walking past the room to check that it was going well. At the end, he met me on the stairs around the back and I told him the manager had asked for me to come in the next day. He was so happy for

Martin Hibbert and his daughter, Eve, at their favourite restaurant (San Carlo in Manchester) on the night of the bomb. This was four hours before they were injured.

The X-ray showing the lumps of metal in Martin's body after the blast.

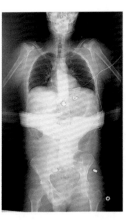

The rehab starts here. It has been an incredibly long road but Martin has had brilliant care throughout.

Sizing up the Kilimanjaro challenge.

The sunrise I told Martin to look out for. I'm so glad he got to see it too.

The summit . . . and the Manchester United flag. Only the second paraplegic to make it to the top of Africa's highest mountain.

Baby Rose with her mum, Donna. Rose was deaf from birth but her mum has always fought for her to have the same opportunities as others.

The nation took her to their hearts and voted her *Strictly* winner alongside Giovanni.

This is the shot I posted the night after the final which went viral. Mum and daughter: they didn't say much but the hug meant everything.

Mike's daughter Beth.

Andy's daughter Sophie.

Tim's daughter Emily.

Mike (left), Andy (middle) and Tim (right). The 3 Dads: ready to start their walk to raise awareness and money for suicide prevention.

It was a long walk but, as Mike, Tim and Andy explain in the book, they met some amazing people along the way and inspired millions.

Start them young! Paul Harvey with his son, Nick, at the piano.

The famous red top, the legendary piano and the genius Paul.

Father and son. Paul's talent was wonderful to watch but so many people were touched by his beautiful relationship with his son.

Darryn Frost (left) and Steve Gallant have remained good friends since the Fishmongers' Hall terrorist attack. What they both did that day was remarkable.

'His death was a tragedy, his life was a triumph'. Dave and Anne Merritt with their son, Jack, who lost his life in the attack.

Jimi (right) continues to inspire his friend Bernard, and many others, after he died jumping into the River Thames to save a drowning woman.

Two-time world champion Nadiya Bychkova with her mum, Larisa.

No piano but this was the rumba with that red backless dress.

Heather Stewart with her husband Stephen. They had been together since they were teenagers but he sadly died from Covid.

Ahsan-ul-Haq Chaudry (second from the right) and his family. Left to right: Saleyha, Saima, Fauzia, Shoaib and Safiyah.

With Shoaib and grandsons Ismaeel and Yusuf.

It's always a pleasure chatting with Maggie Keenan and May Parsons.

As May tells us in the book, the pandemic made her look at nursing in a completely different way.

Giving Tony Foulds a lift. He always makes me laugh. This was the day he told me about his favourite drink – fiddy fiddy – which is half tea and half coffee. Yuck!

He can often be found in Endcliffe Park, blowing the leaves off the path. Apparently, he'll be 'doing the M1' next.

The boat Figen Murray was talking about, with 'Ubuntu' on one side and '#BEMOREMARTYN' on the other.

Figen with her well-deserved OBE. The fight for change continues.

Paula and Tony Hudgell still going strong. You can read an update on them in the 'Still Remarkable' chapter.

Lisa Ashton continues her great work for the Winnie Mabaso Foundation. Palesa is flying at hairdressing college and the kids at Ilamula House were very supportive during *Strictly*.

Tamar Pollard standing next to the memorial to her dad in Hungary.

Jo Pollard (Tamar's mum) with Istvan Dudas – the man she forgave for killing her husband.

me. "I told you you'd get the job," he said. Those are memories you have to keep in your heart.'

Jimi and Bernard were working together at The Cinnamon Club on Saturday 24 April 2021. I ask Bernard to tell me what he can remember about that night and there is a long pause, and he pushes the air out of his mouth.

'It's still hard, you know,' says Bernard. 'I don't like to go over it. I'll see what I can say. I don't like to relive it because it's all so real, but I also want people to see the man he was.' I told Bernard that we could stop whenever he wanted. He said that he finds talking about being on London Bridge that night incredibly painful. 'Let's see how we get on,' he says.

'That day was a normal day in the restaurant,' remembers Bernard. 'The only difference was that we finished early. Normally we would finish work about 1 or 2 o'clock in the morning but, because of Covid restrictions, we got everything done before midnight. "Let's go home, man," Jimi said, so we tidied everything up, cleaned the place and headed out. It was one of those nights where we were just walking and talking.' Bernard laughs ... 'There was never a day you couldn't have a deep conversation with Jimi. He loved to go deep. We talked about life and what we wanted to do. We talked about our families and the sacrifices our parents had made to build us the life that we wanted. Jimi mentioned again that he wanted to move his mum out of the area; to give her a better life. He was telling me about his missus, and we were, you know, bouncing off each other and laughing

'Do you know what?' says Bernard. 'I heard him say "I love

you, bro" and I was so happy he did that. It allowed me to say it back. I started getting deep. I told him that I was so grateful that I could have conversations with him that were so open. I told him I was grateful that he was in my life and that it was great to have such a cool adviser; that is what he was like . . . Jimi the adviser.'

I tell Bernard that it's incredible that the pair of them were talking about sacrifice when you think about what he was about to do. 'It's something we talked about a lot,' says Bernard. 'Both our parents had done so much just to put food on the table. My mum was always working two jobs. She would get up at 4 a.m. to work in a bakery and then do a shift at a shop. Jimi was the same. He had that in him. He was the breadwinner in his family. He would even take some of my shifts sometimes and work double. You could learn so much from his attitude. Let me tell you, when I was in the academy at Chelsea, I felt on top of the world. I had everything at my feet. People look up to you and then, one day, you are released and the dream shatters in front of you. When I got that job at the restaurant, Jimi showed me what it was to be humble and how there is great reward in working hard and serving others. I would watch him clean the spoons. How can anyone clean hundreds of spoons with such a big smile on their face? But Jimi loved it. He had that servant nature built into him.'

I ask Bernard if he feels comfortable to keep talking about the night and what happened after their conversation. He says he does. 'We got to London Bridge around midnight,' he recalls, 'and two people ran up to us. We were around about the halfway point of the bridge. They told us that someone had jumped into the river. They had a video of it. We were looking at the video and Jimi called the police. I ran back and found the steps down to the river. The tide was really high. I could hear a woman screaming but she was already on the other side of the bridge. The current was taking her down the river. We made our way down the stairs on the other side of the bridge, and we could just about see her, right in the middle of the river. Jimi was still on the phone to the police. He was trying to tell them exactly where we were. It was really hard to see anything. It was so dark. We were doing our best to talk to her, and she kept screaming, "I'm going to die! I'm going to die!" I watched Jimi come to life.'

'The only way I can describe it is that he felt the woman's pain,' says Bernard. 'You could see it on his face. I had taken my top off and was ready to go in. There was another guy with us, Joaquin (Garcia) who was also getting ready. Joaquin and Jimi both took off their clothes and Jimi gave me his phone, but I wanted to go too. He said, 'No, bro, you can't swim! You talk to the police.' They both jumped in. They were side by side. I was trying to talk to the police and tell them what was happening and where we were, but I was also trying to listen to Jimi.

'I could just hear his voice echoing around. He was calling my name.

'"BERNZ! BERNZ! BERNZ!" He was desperate.

'I thought I could see something in the shadows, but I was talking and shouting at the river. I couldn't see him, but I knew he was there somewhere. I shouted out to him . . . "HOLD ON

BRO! HOLD ON!" His voice just floated away and then it was gone.'

A few minutes later the police arrived. Joaquin, an Argentinian-born chef, had reached the woman in the Thames and saved her life. I know that this chapter is focusing on Jimi, but Joaquin's actions are also worthy of the highest praise. In a TV interview near the time, he talked about meeting Jimi and being asked by the Londoner if he was ready to 'jump with me'. Joaquin said they counted down from three and leapt into the river. He had just finished his shift at a Mexican restaurant near the Thames and was walking over the bridge at the time. Despite the strong currents, he managed to reach the woman in the middle of the river. As she lay on top of him, struggling for air, Joaquin managed to stay afloat and keep them both alive. They were later rescued from the water by the coastguard and the Metropolitan Police Marine Unit. Jimi never made it to her and never made it back.

'It still haunts me, hearing that voice,' says Bernard. 'I think about that woman a lot. I don't blame her at all. I just hope she is ok. What I remember, more than anything else, is that I just knew Jimi had gone. I could feel it. I was overwhelmed with it all and just in a state of shock. I didn't know what to do. I am not the type to cry but the whole of London heard me that night.'

The police turned up at Jimi's house in the early hours of the morning to break the news to his broken parents.

'My mum called me,' remembers Jimi's brother, Ayodeji. 'My phone went off around 1.30 in the morning. I wasn't in London. I was in the West Midlands. Mum was screaming but not making much sense . . . "THE POLICE!" she said, "THE POLICE ARE HERE!" and she just kept saying his name: "JIMI! JIMI! JIMI!" I could hear the police in the background saying, "We are still searching for him." I knew they wouldn't be there to arrest him because that wasn't Jimi. "JIMI IS IN THE WATER!" Mum was shouting and repeating herself. "What are you talking about?" I said. She was shouting, "LONDON BRIDGE!" Something spoke to me. It was all so confused, but I knew he had gone. Something wasn't right. I think maybe they were trying to give her some hope because she was so emotional. I got the first train down to London in the morning and, just as I got home, the police came round and said they had found his body at Poplar. A few days later we went down, as a family, to identify him.'

What Jimi did that night had a huge impact on so many people. In the days and weeks following, his was a name on so many lips. He was praised by politicians, lauded by community leaders and held up as an example everywhere you looked.

I often think about how I would react in that situation. I appreciate it's hard to know unless you've been there. Are you able to keep your head when everyone is losing theirs? How would you respond if you had to put your own life at risk to help someone else? Would you give it a second thought? Do your actions and words up to that point in your life dictate how you will react or is it just an impulse?

I've never had to think about jumping into a river. The closest I have ever come to something similar was when a friend of mine got hit by a car when we were on mopeds in Benidorm. He didn't look left or right at the final crossroads as we headed out of the city, and he was hit by a car travelling at about 35 mph. I was on the moped behind him and saw it all happen. His bike and body flew into the air and as he landed, he suffered a compound fracture of one of his legs. There was blood and bone everywhere and Stuart was in shock, trying to lift himself off the boiling hot tarmac. One of my mum's jobs was to be a first-aid trainer and it all came flooding back to me. While some of our other friends were being sick on the side of the road, I remembered the basics and looked after Stuart until the ambulance arrived and, on the way to hospital, I rang his mum back in the UK to let her know that he was hurt but he was ok. I am glad I didn't panic. I am glad that I was able to stay calm and think clearly but, the difference is, I was never in danger. There was never any chance of me being hurt or worse. There was no sacrifice. Stuart's mum thanked me for looking after her son and Stuart was happy, he never lost his leg and I know my actions didn't live long in the memory. The difference with Bernard is that, even though he lost a dear friend to the River Thames that night, he lives in the light of Jimi's example and his friend continues to inspire him.

'I still think about what he said to me, Dan,' says Bernard. 'You know, on the steps, when he told me that I couldn't swim and that I shouldn't jump in. Even in his last moments, he still had me, he was looking after me, protecting me. How do you go about replacing a friend like that? There aren't any other Jimi's out there. Let me try and explain. I'm not just saying this because he isn't around anymore, but I never argued with him. I never disagreed with him. The only thing we would ever get heated over was politics!' Bernard giggles remembering some of their conversations. 'We would keep talking about it until we laughed about it.'

When you speak to Bernard, it's obvious that he finds life without Jimi difficult. They were a partnership and Jimi watched out for him, as he seemingly did for everyone. 'Before he died, he sent me some of his music on files,' says Bernard. 'I started playing his songs the day after he died, and it was the story of us. It was the life he lived. It was our life. It meant so much. When I listen to his music, he comes back to me. I just wish he could have lived to drop the songs that he wanted to drop.'

On the first anniversary of Jimi's death, Bernard and some of their mutual friends got together to release one of Jimi's unfinished songs. It was called 'Let You Know'. They enlisted the help of musicians Psychs and C4 and Bernard was so happy with the finished single. I ask him why he is willing to go to such lengths to continue Jimi's legacy.

'The boy still means the world to me,' explains Bernard. 'When someone has been that loyal, all you can do is be loyal in return. I don't live my life for one anymore, I live it for two. I want people to see how much of a heart he had, how he cared about the community. It was an honour to spend time with someone like Jimi and I have to pay him back, pay the world back for the time I had with him. I had someone who taught me life lessons. He motivated me and I like to think I motivated him too. It was a deep friendship and we made sure that nothing would ever come in between us.'

The impact of Jimi's death is felt just as strongly by his family as it is by his friends. His mum, dad and his brothers plan on writing a book about Jimi and their experiences together in 2023, but his eldest brother, Ayodeji, was happy to talk to me about Jimi for *Standing on the Shoulders*. 'I cannot quantify it,' says Ayodeji. 'His loss was huge for our family. We lost our best. Imagine a team losing their best player. My mum and dad have been through therapy, but he leaves a huge hole in all our hearts. I think we would all do anything to bring him back. Anything.'

It was in the months after the incident on London Bridge that Ayodeji realised the extent of Jimi's influence. 'I knew my brother was friendly, but I didn't know he was that popular in London,' says a proud sibling. 'When I say I want to do something for Jimi, thousands of people turn up . . . and I mean thousands. The whole of Southwark and Bermondsey come out for my brother; people even take a day off work for him, even now! I love to hear about the people that he helped. So many people say to me, "Jimi did this for me", "Jimi advised me to go to school", "Jimi helped me at work", "Jimi supported me when no one else would". He would go to any lengths to support people.'

Ayodeji hasn't been through therapy like his parents, but, just like Bernard, he keeps coming back to Jimi's music when he needs a lift. 'I go back to his songs and I still feel his presence,' says his brother. 'I picture myself in a good way. I think about Jimi in the future. I wonder what Jimi would say. When things aren't going well, or I'm having a tough time, I know he would push me forward, I know he would pat me on the back. He's not here anymore but I still feed off his positive energy. I picture him in the future, and he makes me smile. I don't think that will ever change. It's strange because he's my brother, but so many other people know him so well. He has inspired so many. Our house is always open, and it is amazing how many people want to come around and talk about him. We have had so many testimonies. Let me give you an example. We had one event for Jimi and a white lady came up to me and said, "I never knew a black man could have this heart." I know that what she said was clumsy, but all she had ever seen was black kids in gangs. All she knew was stabbings, robberies and crime. Jimi showed her something else, something different. Jimi changed the stereotype.'

This is going to sound strange, but when you hear about Jimi, he doesn't sound real. It's hard to imagine someone so kind, so outgoing, so selfless, so sacrificial, so giving, so caring, and yet there is a familiar thread whenever you ask anyone about him. It's almost other-worldly. I ask his brother if Jimi was a man of faith.

'He was,' says Ayodeji nodding. 'A few days before he died, he called the youth pastor at our church, and they prayed together. I know that he rededicated his life to Jesus Christ in the week of his death. I'm sure that was all in his mind when he jumped in that river to save that woman.'

Sacrifice is one element of the Christian faith that I have always found fascinating. It is a theme throughout the Bible with all the Old Testament practices and sacrifices pointing towards the ultimate example of Jesus' death on the cross. 'Greater love has no one than this, than to lay down one's life for one's friends.' For Christians, sacrifice is at the very heart of the gospel message, a message that Jimi would have known only too well.

And it's a message that evokes such a powerful response wherever you see it. It's no surprise that it has long been used by storytellers and film-makers. Jimi loved going to the cinema with Bernard and I am sure he saw plenty of those examples himself.

I remember my own children all in tears because of the actions of Groot in *Guardians of the Galaxy*. The creators of the Marvel Cinematic Universe were able to make a tree, who only ever speaks the same three words, become one of their most beloved characters. As his friends are about to die, Groot spreads out his branches and covers them in a protective ball of wood. Rocket, his best friend, begs him to stop and Groot simply wipes away his tears and says, 'WE . . . are . . . Groot.' The scene ends, we hear the ship crash and all Groot's branches are shattered, broken and scattered all over the ground.

Cast your mind back to Arnold Schwarzenegger's character in *Terminator 2* muttering, 'I know now why you cry' before lowering himself into the molten metal to save mankind. Tom Hanks as Captain Miller in *Saving Private Ryan* who tells Matt Damon to 'earn' the sacrifice of those who have died so that he would make it back safely. Obi Wan Kenobi in *Star Wars*, Boromir in *Lord of the Rings* and Tony Stark in *Avengers: Endgame* . . . the list is endless. Nothing stirs the heart like sacrifice and that is why I think Jimi's story is so powerful and has made such a lasting impact. There is no Hollywood gloss here. His sacrifice was true and real and pure, and he paid the ultimate price.

When I was thinking about who to put in this book, Folajimi Olubunmi-Adewole was an obvious candidate. Right back at the start, I told you I wanted to write about people who lifted others up. I wanted to write about people who give us a different perspective, help us to see more clearly and encourage us to follow their example. Jimi was all of those things and more and, thankfully, there are many people willing to share his incredible legacy.

'I was so fortunate to have crossed paths with him,' says Bernard. 'Jimi was everybody's favourite person, so I feel blessed to have spent so much time with him. He was adamant that he was going to save that woman; nothing was going to stop him doing what he did to stop her from drowning. Like I said, I am sure he felt her tears and that's why he did what he did. That tells you a lot about Jimi. He brought a light into my life; he brought life into our neighbourhood; he brought energy. There was never any negativity with him. Even if it took a while to find it, Jimi would always get to the good stuff. When I was released by Chelsea, you can imagine I was in a dark place. That was my life. All my dreams were wrapped up in playing football, but Jimi showed me what reality was. I was still living in the past, but he showed me what my future could look like. He was there at the peak of my life, and he was there when I had nothing. That is the sign of a true friend and everyone who shared a path with him would say exactly the same thing.'

It was a real privilege to get to speak to some of those who 'shared a path' with Jimi for this chapter. I caught up with Joseph, Marvellous, David, Adiatu and Yinka after a fitness class, run by Joseph, at a primary school in Peckham. Their words echo much of what Bernard said about his friend, full of life and full of fun.

'We arrived from Nigeria at the same time,' says Joseph. 'We were friends from year seven. We had what I would describe as love fights,' he says, laughing. 'As we got older, we got much closer and we had great talks. He was such a selfless person and he always talked about his family. The timing of everything was just so sad. He had found his passion in music, and it was all about to happen for him. I should tell you, he was annoying too, Dan. I always used to get more attention from the girls when we were younger and then Jimi got taller and more handsome. We always had that banter together.'

Joseph is sat next to David. The pair of them are giggling away as they share stories about their friend. David also came from Nigeria. 'Me and Jimi shared the same skin tone,' he says. 'We had an understanding, brothers in arms. We went to the same sixth form and I could always relate to him. He had so much compassion and was full of the right advice. It sounds strange but, whenever I spoke to Jimi, he would always make me feel calm.'

'Jimi was a flirt,' jumps in Marvellous, as the others erupt in laughter. 'We were always chasing each other, fighting together, struggling together. We shared an immigration story, and he took care of me; of everybody. I used to work in a shop and

Jimi would come and see me on the same day, at the same time, every week, just to check up on me. He would talk to me for thirty minutes; until I was told to get back to work.'

Yinka is the next to join the conversation. 'We were entrepreneurs. Jimi was at the forefront of business. He would go to Morrisons each day before school and buy ice-creams, donuts and cookies. I still don't know how he kept those ice-creams cold until lunchtime . . . but he did. He would sell them all and we would have silly arguments about territory and what we were selling. I loved the fact that he didn't care about negativity . . . about what people said about him. That gave me confidence too. He changed my attitude. I watched him grow so much when he did National Citizen Service (NCS) after GCSEs.' The NCS was set up by the coalition government in 2010 as part of the Big Society initiative. It normally took place in the school holidays and would see teenagers – aged between fifteen and seventeen – go on a residential visit, usually to an activity centre in the countryside. 'If I'm honest with you, he was so annoying,' says Yinka, 'but we all loved him . . . everyone loved him. I admired the fact that, even if he had done nothing wrong, he was always the first to apologise. That is one of the many things I learned from Jimi. He was always teaching us all.'

'And what about you, Adiatu? How were you and Jimi?' I ask.

'Love/hate,' she says through a giant grin. 'I met him in sixth form, and we would always go home together on the same bus. He could be a pain, but he brought light into the whole place. He made everyone laugh and he made everyone happy. You needed his presence to have a good day and there aren't many people like that in the world. Jimi is the reason I continued with sixth form.'

'Really?' says one of the others in amazement.

'Yeah, for real,' replies Adiatu. 'I was down after my exams because I knew I wouldn't see him around much anymore. We would talk on the bus and sometimes he would open up to me. I loved being around him. The sixth form would have been nothing without Jimi.'

'He was the common-room clown,' shouts Marvellous from the back of the group. From this point on, our discussion became much more of a free-for-all with people jumping in and sharing stories of Jimi but also their own lives. We touched on friendship, sacrifice, education, love, government policy, compassion, immigration, racism and everything in between. It was fascinating and, for me, an incredibly educational half an hour.

Marvellous, who also arrived in the UK from Nigeria and first met Jimi in secondary school, continues as the conversation moves to how Jimi changed perceptions of what it was to be young and black. 'When I came here, I knew what I wanted to do. I wanted to do well. So many people helped me along the way: teachers, friends . . . I had years of growth because of those people. It hurts that people don't understand, don't know the heart that we have. Being black . . . I am proud to be black.' The rest of the group nod in agreement. 'We are welcoming and loving. What Jimi did was nothing to do with race. It was just about being a person and looking after your other people.'

'I remember hearing about what happened,' says David. 'Joseph called me, and I thought it was a joke. I heard him crying on the phone. I got a cab down there straightaway. I knew that it was something that Jimi would do, but I was praying that he would somehow survive.'

'David is always the bearer of bad news,' says Marvellous. 'What?' responds David, in mock shock. 'Really?' The rest of the group are laughing. 'You know it,' cackles Marvellous. The conversation settles again as she continues. 'I was in denial at first when he told me but then I thought to myself, "What would Jimi do?" and Jimi would have called everyone, so they heard it from him first. I didn't want them to see it on social media so that's what I did. I called as many people as I could.'

'Bernard was the one who told me,' says Joseph. 'I have thought about this a lot, but I think, if Jimi had another chance, I don't think he would do it again. I think he should have considered the people he left behind. He left his family behind.' He bows his head. 'He left us behind. He had so many plans for the future, he was a hero, he was like my brother. I don't think he was thinking straight. He allowed his heart to take over. I know that I couldn't have done what he did, none of us could,' says Joseph, looking around. 'It breaks me, but I love the way that he died, if you know what I mean . . . trying to save someone else. He died doing the holy thing.'

Yinka hasn't spoken for a while, but I have been watching him carefully listening to his friends. I ask him how he found out. 'Another friend of ours called Princess told me Jimi was dead,' he says. 'My first thought was knife crime. That's what came into my head straightaway. When she told me, I was actually relieved because there wasn't going to be a big discussion about knives and gang culture. Instead, it was all about a celebration of Jimi, who he was and what he did. The next day, we all met up at his house, do you remember?' The rest of the group again nod. 'He was always bringing us together, even in death. Look at us now, here we are again, because of Jimi.'

'Dan,' says Joseph. 'Can I be honest with you?'

'Of course,' I respond. 'What do you want to say?'

'The struggle is real.'

'What do you mean, Joseph?'

'The life of a black immigrant in this country. I don't know if you want me to tell you about it, but it's hard, it was hard for Jimi. It's hard for all of us.'

I tell Joseph I would love for him to tell me about it. He adjusts his position and looks a little unsure for the first time.

'Jimi would still be here if he'd had access to university.' Everyone falls silent for the first time. Bernard, who has been kicking a ball about in the background for much of the conversation, stops and walks in behind Joseph to listen as he continues.

'That's what he wanted to do. He wanted to go to university after sixth form, but he wasn't able to. He didn't have his biometric.'

A 'biometric', or Biometric Residency Permit (BRP), is a card that contains your name, date and place of birth, fingerprints, photograph, immigration status and says whether you have access to public funds.

Joseph continues. 'You can only go to university three years after you get your leave to remain. I arrived here in 2011. I have worked so hard since then. I want to do medicine; I want to be a doctor, but I can't get in the system even though I have the grades. I have just got my biometric but my friends from school are in their third year of medical training. I was robbed of that opportunity.'

'We love this country,' adds Yinka. 'We work hard here, and we pay our taxes, but life is unfair, particularly as an immigrant. None of us have been able to go to university.'

'If feels like we are money-making machines sometimes,' says Joseph as Marvellous joins the conversation too. 'We have to spend thousands of pounds each time we apply for leave to remain,' Marvellous adds. 'We have to do that every two-and-a-half years and, in all that time, you have no access to public funds.'

'That is why Jimi had to set up an empire at school,' interjects Joseph. 'We have to find other ways of making money. It's no surprise that some are working for cash before the legal age. There is pressure to support your family, send money back home to help others. That is what Jimi was doing. We have got to do a lot of things just to survive.'

Yinka jumps in again. 'Education becomes the last thing on your list, even though it should be the most important thing! When you think that you have no prospect of going to university or maybe getting the job you want, you have to change your dreams. You can't really think about the future, you can't look forward because you feel like everything is set up to make it as hard as possible.'

Bernard has never heard his friends talk about this before.

He wants to add something. 'It was different for me, Dan. I was given access to everything because I was a trainee at Chelsea. All this was taken care of. I was ignorant of the struggle. That all changed when I left the football system. I was cast aside, but these guys, and Jimi, had that from the start. That's why Jimi was so important. He made me realise what it was to be a hard worker. That was his way out of poverty. He was already used to it when we worked in that restaurant. He'd watched his parents work every hour and I watched him do the same. He never stopped going, he never stopped working.'

David picks up on Bernard's thoughts. 'And remember, when you clock eighteen, you have to pay more for all the immigration processes because you are then an adult. You can see why people are forced to wash plates at parties when they are underage or pack chairs away for cash. On top of all that, we are all painted as scroungers who are just out for benefits. We want to work; we want to contribute.' He points at his friends. 'Marvellous and Joseph both want to be doctors, but they can't get into the system. Jimi was in that struggle his whole life. There is so much that happened to him that you think would make him hate the world and hate the society that pushed him to the side and is set up against his family . . . but he still jumped in the river. He still tried to save that woman. That is the mark of the man.'

Marvellous is one of those currently lost in the system. 'I applied for my biometric eight months ago,' she says, clearly exasperated. 'I can't apply for a medical course until I get it and it's only after that, that I can apply for student finance. I expect to get the minimum amount and that means I will not be able to go to university anyway. We all know they can process your application quickly because, if you pay them £800, they can do it in a day! That shows you it can be done. We are doing our A levels and doing twelve-hour shifts at the same time! Your life is in limbo. There is complete uncertainty at every turn. You can't plan for anything. Think about the emotional damage and what that does to you, trying to look after your loved ones. My mum hasn't slept for ten years!'

'It feels like we are in a cage, Dan,' says Joseph. 'All we can do is work our backsides off to get out of that cage, but sometimes, no matter what you do, it won't open.'

'There are no excuses,' adds Yinka, 'but, you can see, can't you, why people stop caring about their education. You can see why it's easy just to mess about in school and start mixing with the wrong people. If you rob people of their prospects; if you cancel their future, if you know you can only go so far and there is no help, sometimes you can see why people give up.'

'And that's why we all love Jimi,' says Joseph. 'He never gave up and we are trying to follow his example.'

It was a real pleasure to listen to Jimi's friends. They opened my eyes to a struggle that I had very little knowledge of beyond newspaper headlines. It made me understand a little more of what Jimi was facing in life and, as David said, made me appreciate his sacrifice even more. They spoke to me after all attending one of Joseph's fitness training camps. It's one of the many things Joseph is doing to keep going while he waits to see if he's successful in his attempt to get into medical school. It's all part of the process of trying to get out of the cage.

Before we finish, Marvellous, who one day hopes to join Joseph in the medical profession, has one last thing to say about her friend Jimi. 'He was a good man and could have given so much to so many. That lady in the river, her life came above everything else for Jimi. He was a great friend, a great son. He was great in all that he did, and he left the world in a great way.'

It's not just Jimi's friends that like to talk about Jimi, his family are just the same. They don't really have a choice because everyone talks to them about Jimi.

'The hardest thing is accepting that he's not here anymore,' says Ayodeji, who was nine years older than Jimi. 'Sometimes I like to imagine he is still with us. Every now and again I like to go down to London Bridge and look at the water. That is the last place that he was alive on this earth, and I can just picture him there. It's just a few minutes but it's enough. We would like to get a plaque there on the bridge, to remember him. I'm sure people will keep talking about him, but his music lives on too,' reflects Ayodeji. 'That is my therapy. He gets me back to where I need to be. He has at least left us all with something. I wish he could see how much he is helping me with his music.'

At the end of my conversation with Bernard, I thank him for his time and his openness. We talk about how close he still feels to Jimi, and he tells me that he hopes that never stops. 'Dan,' says Bernard, 'I have a voice note on my phone from Jimi. It's from 8 April 2021.' That was two weeks before Jimi died.

'I had sent him this video of me in a jacket I'd got from Zara. I was pretending to be a model and I finished it with "Bro, what do you think?" Jimi sent me a voice note back and he is laughing so hard in it. "Bernard" he says, "I love you so much. You know how to make me laugh" I do the same with our old conversations on social media. I have saved them all and sometimes I'll just go through them and remind myself of how we used to talk to each other. I miss that and it keeps me close to him.'

At the time of writing this, Bernard is only twenty-one years old. He has his whole life in front of him. A few days after I spoke to him for the first time, he and Joaquin – the other man who jumped in the Thames that night – were going to pick up a bravery award from the Humane Society. The recognition for what Jimi did just keeps coming. Joaquin, who met Jimi on the bridge that night, has always pushed for Jimi to get the same level of recognition that he has received. He too seems like a remarkable individual.

Bernard is currently a freelance camera assistant at ITV. He is studying Sports Management and Sports Media, but his dream job is still to play football. He is looking for a club. I remind him that Ian Wright didn't make it until his mid-twenties and Bernard laughs and says, 'I know. Never stop believing.'

Whatever happens to Bernard, it's quite clear that the time he spent with Jimi will have a lifelong impact on him. When you speak to him about his friend, you notice that he quite often speaks about him in the present tense. I ask him if he knows he does that.

'I feel like he's still here,' says Bernard. 'His mindset and self-motivation, I take all of that onboard every day. Even if something was going wrong, Jimi could find the light in the darkness. That's why I like going around to his mum and dad's house almost every weekend. His mum cooks the best jollof rice but it's also great just to share stories about him. We all loved him deeply and I feel like one of the reasons I am still here is to let people know that good people live among us. His story has touched so many people. Jimi was special. Jimi was a one-off, so that's why I sometimes talk about him like he's still around because I feel like he is. He still walks with me. I am still learning from him every day.'

STRICTLY NADIYA

'Be honest, is this a bit of a disappointment?'

Those were some of the first words I uttered to the two-time World Ten-Dance Champion, Nadiya Bychkova, when we met for the first time at Wembley Stadium in September 2021.

'The thing is,' laughs Nadiya, 'I really wanted to get you. Call it intuition. I didn't know that much about you before I heard you were doing the series, so I looked through all your posts and stories on Instagram and you seemed different from all the other partners I'd had. You were always talking about other people, and I liked that. I knew you were tall so I assumed we'd be put together, but then the production team confused me: they told me I would be driving to the country-side to meet my partner and that I wasn't allowed to wear heels so I thought . . . it can't be you. Then I arrived at Wembley and, when I saw you up in the stands with your hands over your face, I was so happy. We did our filming, and I went off for lunch with my family and I told my mum I was delighted with my new student.'

I am not a dancer. I have avoided dance floors for much of my life. At school discos I was the kid who told jokes and messed about, anything to avoid actually having to move in time to the music. The frustrating thing is, I've always wanted to love it.

I adore music. I feel like I understand music. I love watching other people dance. I love the idea of dancing, but it has always felt like something that other people do. It's actually very hard for me to explain because it makes no sense whatsoever.

I am a confident person. I think you need a bit of that to do the job that I do. When I walk into a TV studio, I feel like I own the place. It's not in an arrogant way, I just love live television. I love that feeling of presenting something that millions of people are watching. I love knowing that everything could go wrong and it's your job to hold it together. I love the rush. Those few seconds before you go live are truly wonderful. It's at that moment that I feel like I reach out and grab the steering wheel.

I love the time just before you go out on stage to host a big event or speak to a live audience. I love it when they call your name and say, 'Ladies and gentlemen, please welcome your host for the evening . . . Dan Walker.' I love the idea of having an audience in the palm of your hand. The pressure, the intensity, the expectation . . . I think I might be addicted to it.

Before *Strictly*, I felt none of these things when it came to dancing. In fact, it's probably the only time in my life when I felt the complete opposite. I had no idea what I was doing. I would cover it with humour, silliness and an endless desire to take the kids to the toilet, get someone a drink or tie a shoelace. Walking onto a dance floor I could also feel my stomach twist and my head would be screaming, 'WHAT ARE YOU DOING?'

I have never sat in a room with a psychologist or a therapist, but I assume they would probably trace it back to my childhood and the fact that I am so huge. In later life, I have learned to embrace my massiveness, but when you are well over 6 feet tall in your early teens, it's hard not to feel like an awkward giant. I would always buy extra-large clothes which would hang around me like a giant blanket. When all your mates are frequenting the trendy shoe shops and you get told, 'Sorry, mate, we only do that size in Hi-Tec Silver Shadow,' it can be a little disconcerting.

I should probably explain that Hi-Tec Silver Shadow were not the coolest trainers when I was growing up. My dad wore them for most of my childhood and, let me put it this way, being seen in a pair of those bad boys didn't add much to your street credibility.

It's much easier to find clothes that fit tall slim men now, but when I was growing up, my mum had to take me to a shop called High and Mighty to find a shirt that fitted my orangutan arms. When you have arms of that length, combined with a 35-inch inside leg, you assume it's impossible to get everything moving in the right direction in time with the music, so I never bothered. Incidentally, one of the first things that Nadiya Bychkova said to me at Wembley was 'Don't worry about being too tall. That is our secret weapon. Your long arms are an advantage'. As you read this chapter, you'll come to understand that Nadiya has a wonderful talent for saying just the right thing at just the right time.

Limb length and concerning degrees of awkwardness were some of the reasons I continually said 'No, thanks' when the lovely team at *Strictly Come Dancing* came knocking. I love the show, lots of my friends have been on it and I've been a regular guest on the spin-off show *It Takes Two* for many years. I had been asked to go on *Strictly* every year since 2017 but always gave a very clear, very early, very resolute 'no'. This time, 2021, was a little different.

My three children approached me just after Christmas and said, 'Dad, can we ask you something?' I thought it was going to be one of their normal complaints about what time they go to bed, me embarrassing them by singing in public or my inability to stop eating their chocolate supplies. Before I go on, I should explain that the chocolate thing is down to the fact that I think that is a legitimate parental tax which I am entitled to collect at any time to level out the amount of time I spend driving them around, the amount of money spent on after-school clubs, clothes and miscellaneous items and the sheer number of nappies I had to change during their early years.

Anyway, it was none of these. They explained that they'd had a tough time of it during the pandemic (like many kids of their age) and we talked about some of the things they would like to do in 2021 to make up for a miserable 2020. The subject matter turned to television and the petition was made for me to cheer them all up by making a commitment to go on two TV shows. The first was *Saturday Mash-Up* and the second was *Strictly Come Dancing*. I could tell from their faces they were deadly serious.

I had already been asked to go on *Saturday Mash-Up* so that part of the request was relatively easy. The second part was a little more tricky. I had a really long think about it, spoke to my wife about it and rang a few people who had done *Strictly* to gauge just how much of your life it devours. Zoe Ball, Carol Kirkwood, Anita Rani, Mike Bushell, Jason Bell, Ranvir Singh and a few others all gave excellent advice and – interestingly – every single one of them said, 'You have to do it. You'd be amazing.' Crucially, none of them had ever seen me dance.

Mike was the only one who had ever seen me anywhere near a dance floor at Louise Minchin's fiftieth birthday party. On that occasion, I decided to disguise my issues by engaging a well-trodden path at large functions of never going on the dance floor without carrying at least one large food item and a drink. Having your hands full allows you to cover all sorts of potential awkwardness and, if all else fails, you can take a bite. On this occasion, Louise's decision to hire in a late-night pancake stall provided the perfect cover.

In addition to the family request, there was also a desire to do something that was just fun after a long slog of covering coronavirus on *BBC Breakfast*. Every morning we were talking about face masks and variants. We were constantly discussing death tolls and predicted infection rates. Every other guest was a virologist, and the only relief came from the occasional ray of light like Captain Tom. I love having fun on TV and *Strictly* began to look like the perfect opportunity to enjoy making a show without having to interview any politicians. The other piece to the puzzle was *Football Focus*. I'd presented the programme for twelve years and, in that time, I'd only ever missed two shows – both for family weddings. I'd finally taken the decision to find a new challenge so, for the first time in a very long time, my Saturdays would be free of football and available for footwork.

In early February 2021, my agent called. It was a request to talk to the team at *Strictly*. For the first time, I agreed. I spoke to Stef Aleksander, who books the guests, and Sarah James, the Executive Producer – both significant cheeses. We had a lovely chat about the programme, what my expectations were, what my dance experience was (a very short part of the discussion) and whether I was a good student. I was given the opportunity to go away and think about it. Within a few weeks, I was signed up and now had about four months of mild panic and regret before the team at *Strictly* made the official announcement.

'When are you doing *Strictly*?' is a question I think I've been asked about 804 times every month for the last few years. Until 2021, I was always able to laugh it off and say 'Never' or 'Have you seen the length of these arms? They'd need a bigger dance floor', but now it was actually happening there were quite a few delicate conversations to navigate.

My wife knew. My agent knew. Zoe Ball knew and that was about it. There was one spectacularly awkward moment when we were all sitting down as a family to watch a film on YouTube. My daughter had the remote control and, as I was making a cup of tea, she said, 'Er, Dad . . . what's this?' My recent search history was on the screen, and top of the list was *Ballroom Dancing For Beginners.* My wife looked at me as if to say, 'You're on your own with this one' and I tried my best to divert attention with some chocolate treats, but our eldest later revealed that that was the moment she started to get excited.

Strictly ended up being one of the greatest experiences of my life but, if I'm totally honest, it started out as one of the worst. Let me explain. I consider myself quite good at putting on a brave face and that's what I was determined to do when we had our first 'studio' day. This is before any of the cast of 2021 had been told about our partners. At this point, we were all still flying solo. We were all invited down to *Strictly* HQ at Elstree Studios in London for our first interview and a full fitting with the wardrobe team.

The fitting came first for me and that was great fun. I basically just had a giggle with Vicky (Gill), Esra (Gungor) and Meg (Sterry) as I tried on various shirts, trousers and shoes while having every inch of my body measured. This was also the day I discovered the magic of 'shants'. Vicky, Esra and Meg explained that, to keep your shirt pulled down when you dance, they sew it into your pants – shirt, into pants . . . 'shants'.

The clothing revelation was quickly followed by a ninety-minute interview in front of various glitter balls and glitter walls. I enjoyed the interview talking about the past, work, family, hopes, the dances I was looking forward to, what I was hoping for from a partner and all the normal stuff. Then came the phrase I had been dreading. 'And now, Dan, we'd love to see you dance.' I felt an uncomfortable chill across my entire body. I went into 'dance mode' and instantly made a joke to try and settle the impending doom. I even looked around to see if they had any large food items I could hold. I was in trouble.

We walked about ten steps across the studio and the lovely producer said, 'All you have to do is stand behind these glitter balls and when you hear the music, walk out and start dancing.' I am a grown man in my forties, and I can honestly tell you that I have never felt more uncomfortable. I knew the show would be primarily conducted in a different postcode to my comfort zone, but I didn't expect my mouth to go so instantly dry at the prospect of being asked to dance. I closed my eyes, told myself that it was going to be ok, and tried to enjoy it. Some ABBA came on and out I came. I can't bring myself to watch the footage back. I think I was smiling, but inside I was melting.

After about thirty seconds of Theresa May-style movement, I decided that I would attempt the old trick of trying to look super confident to cover my awkwardness and embarrassment. For some reason I don't think I will ever be able to explain, I felt it would be a good time in my life to try and moonwalk for the first time. Why not? I had never attempted it before but became convinced that this was the time to give it a go during filming for a clip which would be watched by 10 million people. If we're looking for positives, I definitely moved backwards. The best way to describe it would be if you imagine someone moonwalking with one leg in a welly filled with concrete and the other in a large orthopaedic boot. Thankfully, the whole thing was over in a flash as, two strides in, I collided with a glitter ball and tripped over.

'We'll do some close-ups now, Dan,' said the eternally positive producer. 'Great,' I said in the least convincing fashion ever. It was during the 'close-up' section that I started looking for the exit. There were about five or six people watching me do what some people would describe loosely as 'dance' and about another fifteen or so were viewing the televised carnage on screens behind a black curtain. In my mind, those behind the veil were quickly scouring their list of back-up contestants. Thankfully, one of those producers was Joe Wheatley. Joe made a timely intervention. There was one point during the close-up section when the team were asking me to do something different. I have blanked out much of this time because of the trauma, but apparently, all I produced, for a solid five minutes, was pointing my finger down the camera. I had two options. Either sob gently and tell them I had no idea what I was doing, or run for the fire exit, which I had spotted in the corner of the studio, call my agent, and get him to tell *Strictly* that I'd made a terrible error. At that precise moment, obviously sensing my dancing dilemma, Joe emerged from behind the curtain and said, 'Dan, just wanted to say that the last point looked really cool.'

Now, I know what he said isn't much but, at that point, I was down to my final shred of dignity. The green exit sign was calling my name but that one sentence from Joe brought me back from the brink. I remembered one of the golden rules of TV: it never looks as bad as you think it does when you watch it back. This rule has a 99.9 per cent accuracy rate. The only time I have proved it to be incorrect was when I passed a rugby ball to a child on live television. He wasn't looking. It caught him square in the mouth and he started crying just as the regional news programme finished. I remember thinking, 'It can't have looked that bad' . . . only to watch it back and realise it was in fact at least 500 times worse than I thought it was. There was blood and there were tears.

The *Strictly* studio day was a bruising experience, but it did help to prepare me for what was to come. I felt like I learned an awful lot about the headspace I was going to have to inhabit if it was going to last longer than a couple of weeks. The important thing you have remember about *Strictly* is that you are not alone. The lovely people in charge are kind enough to give you a professional dancer to guide you, teach you and hold your hand through the whole thing. In my case, they decided to give me one of the most amazing humans I have ever met: two-time world champion, Nadiya Bychkova.

'Now remember, Daniel,' she said as we sat down to discuss our *Strictly* experience, 'I can't lie.' She is correct. I have never known anyone so straight-down-the-line as Nadiya. She tells it like it is, with very little fluff attached. She is brilliant but can also be brutal.

'You know there was a reason I asked you to do that little waltz with me when we met at Wembley? I was watching to see how good you were. I was like, ok, he has a little movement. I was wondering why you were so worried. In my head, even that early, I was like . . . ballroom will be great. I wasn't worried about that at all, and I was confident I could teach you Latin. You were worried. I was very happy.'

When I had my initial meeting with the team at *Strictly*, they made it clear that I got no say in who I got as a partner, but they did ask me if there was anything I was worried about. I assumed

I was going to get a tall professional, so I just said I hoped I got someone I was able to get on with. My *Strictly* strategy was quite a simple one: I wanted to enjoy the experience as much as possible. I love being on TV and shows don't come any bigger than *Strictly Come Dancing*. The sheer size of it means it's very easy to become consumed and I've watched it happen to others. You start worrying about all the little things that are going on and forget about enjoying it. I have spoken to people in the past who, once it's all over, say they wish they'd enjoyed it more at the time. I was determined not to be in that position.

After our initial meeting, Nadiya and I sat down in the seats at Wembley and had a chance to chat to each other for about fifteen minutes. I told her when we were sat there that I wanted to make sure that she enjoyed it as much as I did and that, although I had no idea about talent, I wouldn't go out of the competition for lack of effort.

'I knew you were going to work hard from that moment, Daniel. I could see it in your eyes. You know what I am like. I'm a simple person. I can't be friends with anyone who doesn't like food and, within a few minutes, I found it very reassuring that you were already telling me about your favourite biscuits. You promised me I would enjoy it and you were true to your word. I didn't know it then, but we laughed so much, probably I laughed as much in those three months with you as I did in the rest of my life altogether. We talked and cried about important things but, more than anything else, you showed me you were a hard worker and I saw that every week – apart from when you fell asleep while I was talking to you.' A smile cracks across my face. 'You see,' says Nadiya, laughing, 'that's the other thing. You get my jokes! I have to explain to most people that I'm just kidding, but you understood me from day one.'

I could tell from that first meeting that we were going to get on. I love people who work hard to get to the top and Nadiya has always been a grafter. It might not surprise you to learn that the dance world is quite a political one. When it comes to winning championships and top prizes, a lot of it is down to who your teacher is, how well you know the judges (who in some cases can also be the teachers) and which country you are representing. Nadiya does not come from a rich family and there was no dancing pedigree in her genes. Her story is one of dedication. It's a story of hard work, fighting against the odds and overcoming huge obstacles. It is an incredible story of success but, most importantly, it is a love story. It's all about how a five-year-old Ukrainian fell in love with dancing after watching a professional for the very first time. She knew at that moment that she didn't just want to dance, she wanted to be the best dancer. She wanted to be world champion.

Nadiya was born in Luhansk, Ukraine, in 1989 to Larisa and Alexander Bychkov. Her mother was a professional pentathlete but worked on the local market to make ends meet. Her dad trained as a lawyer but, after the collapse of the Soviet Union, he used the family market stall to brings goods in from other places and sell them on.

Nadiya's grandmother, who lived with them in their tiny

house, was a huge part of her life. Babushka Zoya was the one who introduced her to dancing by taking her to a local arts centre as a young girl.

'I loved it from the first moment I saw the dresses,' remembers Nadiya. 'It was all so mesmerising and so beautiful. I wasn't old enough to join in. They said you had to be five, so I waited for a year and spent the whole time stretching to make sure I was ready.'

The following year Nadiya went back, and it wasn't long before she was in her first competition.

'She was incredibly stubborn,' remembers her mum. 'She always wanted to have things a certain way from a very early age. Dancing became everything to her very quickly. She was either at dancing or at school and that was about it. She came home to sleep.'

'I needed a dress, but we had no money for one,' says Nadiya. 'I asked my mum and, in the end, my godmother made it for me. I entered my first competition with a chubby lad called Stasik. He had a bakery in his house, and he was always eating. I think that's why we got on. We won. He celebrated with food!'

Nadiya was spotted even at this tender age and her mum realised she was going to have to start taking things seriously. 'Everyone kept telling her she was talented and gifted, but I knew that from the start,' says Larisa with a smile. 'I watched as she would come alive as soon as she stepped on the dance floor. It was magical to see and very exciting for a parent when a dance teacher takes you to one side and tells you your daughter could be really special. She was very young when her teacher told me that he'd never seen someone with no shyness about performing and who was in their own world as soon as the music started. I could see how much she was enjoying it and, as a parent, I just wanted her to be happy.'

Nadiya started dancing with older boys and got to the final of the Ukrainian championships when she was only seven years old. Her parents wanted to make sure that Nadiya's grades didn't suffer at school, so she was given an ultimatum: she could only go to dance lessons if she got the top grades. She worked harder than ever at both.

'It was getting to that stage where I needed to start making big decisions if I was going to take dancing seriously. At the age of ten, I moved to the city of Harkow. It was about 220 miles from our home, but I needed to be there to dance with my new partner.'

It was that same year that Nadiya came to the UK for the first time to take part in the Blackpool Festival. 'I remember standing in that famous ballroom and just looking around in wonder. What a place. I told my mum while we were standing there that one day I would live in the UK. I think she thought I was a bit mad, but I knew from that moment that I would make it happen. It was just going to be a matter of time.'

At the age of ten, Nadiya and her partner made it to the under-16 final and, wherever she went, success followed success. Her first World Championship title arrived in 2002 in the under-21 competition; she was only twelve years old. The little Ukrainian had arrived on the global stage.

'One of the greatest moments of my young life came in a dance class run by one of the legends of dancing, Espen Salberg,' explains Nadiya. 'He was a teacher that everyone looked up to. There were some really talented dancers in the room, and I was just a kid, twelve years old, not even a teenager. He was trying to teach us all how to do a samba walk. After a few minutes, he stopped the class. "There is only one person in this room who is not doing what I have told you to do . . . but it is a perfect samba walk." He pointed at me, out of everyone. That was an amazing moment. Things like that do make other people jealous, but that is something you just have to accept in dancing.'

Nadiya's growing reputation meant she had to move again, this time to Odessa to train with a new partner. She was now over 600 miles away from her family. Her next stop was Slovenia at the age of fourteen. She was doing all her schoolwork while she was travelling and then, every two months, she would go back to Luhansk to sit exams on what she was learning. She got top marks every time.

The dancing wasn't going quite so smoothly. Nadiya's partner wanted her to be his girlfriend, so she quickly looked for someone else who wanted to compete rather than kiss! When she was sixteen, she met eighteen-year-old Miha Vodicar.

'I could tell from the moment he walked into the room that we could be amazing,' she remembers. 'We had like a perfect dancing connection. I was able to follow him as if we'd been dancing for years without even really thinking about it. We had our first competition after just two weeks, which is almost impossible. We went to the UK and were placed in the top two couples straightaway.'

Nadiya and Miha had the talent to win everything. They

made both the Latin and ballroom finals in Blackpool in their first year together, but with increased notoriety came increased attention and, for the first time, Nadiya saw the power of politics in her sport.

'We simply didn't have enough money to get the right results. You needed to play the game and we didn't have the cash to do it. If you don't have the lessons with the right people, then you can't win the big competitions. We started to struggle with results. We weren't making finals, and you start to question what you love.'

I ask her if she ever thought about giving up. She stares right through me before a huge smile comes across her face. 'Never, Daniel,' she says. 'That little five-year-old didn't dream of just getting good at dancing. That little five-year-old was going to be a world champion and that battle wasn't won. Quitting was never even an option.'

At the same time as the political power games, Nadiya found out that her dad had been living a completely different life with another woman back in Luhansk. He told Nadiya he was going to stop supporting her financially, so the little girl with big dreams had nothing.

During our months together on *Strictly*, I got to spend some time with Nadiya's gorgeous daughter, Mila, and her mum, Larisa. Mila is Nadiya's pride and joy. She wants to give her the same opportunities that her mum gave her. Larisa remains her great inspiration because, throughout her life, her mum made the sacrifices to keep the dancing door open.

'I was determined that nothing would be closed off to my daughter,' says Larisa. 'It wasn't just me making the sacrifices.

She was missing out on parties, friends and a normal childhood. We were both working towards the same goal. I could see that Nadiya had the talent to go to the very top, and all I wanted to do was help her get there.'

Larisa decided to sell everything they had to get her daughter into the right dance school in Italy. She had just five euros remaining when Nadiya left for yet another new start, in another country, even further from home.

'My mum risked everything,' says Nadiya with tears in her eyes. 'Everything. She was selling the dresses she had made me to make ends meet, to pay for rent and food. I saw in her an amazing work ethic, and it was all for me. She inspired me to work hard too. I started teaching when I was twelve years old and, by the time I was eighteen, I was teaching for money. I was modelling part-time; I was training whenever I could, and we were travelling to compete at weekends. It was non-stop.'

Funded by her mum's hard work, Nadiya and Miha got in a car and drove to Italy. She had a bold strategy: Nadiya told the dance teacher – the famous Davide Cacciari – that they could be world champions. Thankfully he agreed, but his dance lessons cost 200 euros a time. Nadiya was earning twenty euros an hour for her teaching, so she had to work for ten hours to pay for one of his lessons. It was worth it. At their first World Championships with Davide as their teacher, they finished second. A year later, in 2013, they were second again. Nadiya and Miha were dancing for Slovenia and, desperate to avoid accusations of bias, it is alleged that the Slovenian judge didn't give them the one extra mark they needed to take the title.

They returned the following year and this time 'everything on the floor was just perfect,' recalls Nadiya. 'I could tell from the first dance that it was going to be our year.' The dreams of that little five-year-old came true. Nadiya was a world champion. The European Championships followed, and in 2015 they were crowned world champions again.

But, even when bathing in success, there was heartache. At the end of 2014, when they were the best dancers on the planet, Miha and Nadiya had a professional falling-out. The dancing relationship came under incredible strain. 'He thought I was the worst person in the world,' explains Nadiya.

There were suspicions of jealousy and rivalry and when they went to the 2015 World Championships, they only saw each other on the dance floor. Miha didn't even want to be in the same room as her.

'I still don't really understand what was behind it all,' says Nadiya, 'but I used to get a lot of attention and I was always in the spotlight. That is often the case with a partnership like ours. It would have been easy to walk away from it all, but my love of dance kept us together. We were brilliant but broken.'

Away from the dance floor, Nadiya was in a relationship with the Slovenian footballer, Matija Skarabot. After her second world title, Nadiya found out she was pregnant. After her daughter was born, she wanted to return to dance together with Miha, but he decided that he would find someone else. 'I told him it wouldn't be easy because, even though we didn't get on, there was no one else like us, but he wouldn't listen.' He went back to the World Championships the following year with a new partner but didn't make the final twenty-four.

The World Championship win in 2015 was to be Nadiya's final competition and it wasn't long before the world of TV came calling. In 2017, she joined the cast of *Strictly Come Dancing*.

Fast forward to 2021 and our meeting at Wembley. Nadiya and I swapped numbers and were warned we had a few more weeks to keep our secret before the launch show. 'I think you'll get Nadiya,' said virtually everyone during those weeks. 'She's the only one tall enough for you.' I perfected the 'you'll have to wait and see' smile.

And while the *Strictly* fans waited, we started on the quickstep. 'Why did no one ever tell me dancing was this much fun?' I told Nadiya on day one.

'I enjoyed week one, Daniel,' remembers Nadiya. 'You surprised everyone. I was trying to teach you quickstep, which is a lot. There is so much to learn but I knew you could be amazing. You were so busy so we couldn't do as much practice as everyone else, but I just loved the way you dealt with it.'

I loved everything about it. The hard work, the technique, the language and the fact that you could eat as much cake as you wanted because of all the exercise. I was learning how to dance and Nadiya was expanding her snack game. She was opening my eyes to the world of dance, and I was teaching her about the powers of flapjack. I think it was a fair trade.

One of the great privileges of my job has been getting to see brilliant people up close and personal. I have stood next to Tiger Woods while he was hitting golf balls. I have watched Cristiano Ronaldo take perfect free-kick after perfect free-kick on a football pitch. I will never forget sitting within a metre of one of the world's great cellists as he played the solo in Karl Jenkins' 'The Armed Man', backed by the London Philharmonic Orchestra. I could feel the notes through my body. I can still feel them now when I close my eyes and listen to that piece of music.

That is what it was like to watch Nadiya. My appreciation of dancers and dance went through the roof in the space of just a few days. I always knew they were talented, but I had never seen the control of the body, the skill, the ability to channel power and feeling through movement. It was all so alien to me at the start. I saw it as a form of communication that I had closed myself off from my whole life. I was desperate to learn it. Thankfully, I was alongside someone who spoke it fluently. Some professional dancers specialise in ballroom and some in Latin, but Nadiya was a 10-Dance World Champion which meant she was a master of both. I couldn't have been in better hands.

'I loved the fact that you understood the work it took to be a professional dancer,' she says. 'Some people think it's easy but, when you have someone who can see it and appreciate it, you just want to teach them everything.'

The most important thing that happened in those early weeks took place at a London hotel and the Borehamwood Accident & Emergency Department. My workload was a little on the hefty side during *Strictly*. I never expected to be in it for more than a month, so I decided to just keep doing all my normal jobs. I was getting up at 3 a.m. on Monday, Tuesday and Wednesday to present *BBC Breakfast*, and then going to London on a Thursday night to film the *NFL Show* on a Friday morning. I would always arrive at Elstree a few hours after everyone else for the Friday run-through, so we were constantly playing catch-up. Looking back now, it was a crazy decision but it worked.

Nadiya told me quite a few times during *Strictly* that she would never complain about being tired again. 'I don't know how it was possible, Daniel. You would wake up at three, travel to work while I was sleeping, and then I'd watch you on TV with a coffee and, an hour later, you were learning something you'd never done before! The more you worked, the better you got.'

But, when you've got too much on, you start to forget things. You leave your wallet on the back seat of a taxi while you're rushing into a hotel and, when you run back out to catch the driver before he leaves, you don't see a giant revolving glass door and nearly knock yourself out. Your teeth go through your lips and the blood pours down your face and a lump forms on your head. The next day you struggle through a TV show trying to tell yourself you're ok as your head throbs and then, when you get to training and meet your partner, she can see how white you are and that you can't stand without swaying.

A medic is called, and you're told there is no way you can train. You're ordered to go to A&E to get a brain scan. Your partner is told she can't go with you because of Covid restrictions, and you can't be seen together because it's meant to be a secret until launch night.

She grabs your hand and says there is no way you're going anywhere without her. You wait for hours at A&E and are eventually told your brain is ok, but you have concussion, and you can't dance for three days. Your partner has waited the whole time for you in the car park and, in the fog of tiredness, a constant headache and mild delirium (mixed with delight that the dancing isn't over before it's begun) you tell her that her actions will never be forgotten and you know that, on that day, in that A&E car park, the friendship has been cemented. That was the day that the bond was sealed. That was the day I decided to throw everything at *Strictly* for as long as it lasted.

'I remember that day well,' laughs Nadiya. 'That was simple for me. I didn't do it for any reason other than that was the only thing I could do. I needed to be there for you even if that meant I would lose my job. I was really worried for you and there was no way I would let you go on your own. We were a team and that wasn't acceptable for me. I think we both learned a lot about each other that day. That was the start of something special.'

The quickstep was our first dance. I surprised myself, my family and most of the watching public with a half-decent, middle of the scoreboard performance. The judges seemed genuinely impressed. Week two was the paso doble and then it was foxtrot in movie week. Each dance required something different. I was loving every minute of it but also expecting it to end every Sunday night. In week four, Nadiya and I went back to my old primary school in Crawley in West Sussex to try and find some school disco inspiration for our cha cha cha to MC Hammer's 'You Can't Touch This'. It was seen by the judges as something of a performance breakthrough. 'You need to start believing you can actually dance,' said Nadiya at the start of the following week. 'I believe in you. I see it every week. You need to start believing in yourself.'

By this stage I was loving the process of learning to dance. It's easy to be crippled with nerves as Saturday night approaches, but I just love being on telly. I knew that I would put the hours in, so the only thing holding me back was the speed at which I could catch the others up in terms of talent. There were so many great dancers in the class of 2021, but we were still determined to enjoy it as much as ever.

Week five was a major turning point. We were doing a Viennese waltz to Billy Joel's 'She's Always A Woman', one of my wife's favourites. 'You were always asking me questions,' recalls Nadiya. 'It was lovely to see how much you wanted to know. Remember the week of Viennese waltz you asked me where the joy came from in ballroom dancing?'

I could see that during some of the Latin dances you could whoop, holler and scream, but during the ballroom, I was struggling to see how you could show that same enjoyment while maintaining your posture and composure. While Nadiya was busy teaching me the practical elements of high elbows, vertical lines and unsplayed fingers, she was also trying to convey the deeper elements of dance: the connection.

'I told you that joy in ballroom comes from two people moving together in harmony. When it works perfectly, it's like two moving as one . . . almost breathing together.'

I had very little idea what Nadiya was on about until one

Thursday afternoon in week five. During our three months on *Strictly* I can honestly tell you that we never had a cross word, an argument or one of those 'toys out, storms out' moments that often happen. But that Thursday afternoon was a frustrating one. We were dancing in a beautiful old hall with stained-glass windows in North London, but nothing was clicking.

'Come with me, Daniel,' said an eternally patient Nadiya. We grabbed our coats and wandered outside into the little garden behind the hall. During that five-minute chat we talked about the importance of me learning to let go a little. We had a laugh about flapjack and the two-time world champion reminded me that I had to trust her and trust myself. I was enjoying *Strictly* so much, but every now and again there were these little moments where I would doubt myself.

'What on earth are you doing?'

'How did you expect to be any good at this?'

'This isn't for you, is it?'

'You look ridiculous, don't you?'

'Everyone is laughing at you, right?'

Nadiya always answered all those questions, but it was frustrating for me not to be better than I was by week five. I think my expectations were writing cheques my talent couldn't afford. I reminded myself of why I signed up to *Strictly* and thanked Nadiya for her wisdom and kindness. We ate some biscuits, cracked a few gags and, when we walked back into that hall, everything was different.

We Viennese waltzed around the room and as we did, the afternoon sun burst through the clouds and streamed through the stained-glass windows at the far end of the hall. It burnt our faces as we turned and spun down the dance floor. It felt, for the first time, just as Nadiya had described. 'I don't want to get ahead of myself, partner,' I said as the music stopped, 'but was that what you were talking about?'

For the first time it didn't feel like Nadiya was dragging me around the floor. For the first time she hadn't put her hand across the small of her back after a run of the dance or had to stretch her neck out. 'That was it, Daniel!' she screamed with a huge smile across her face. 'That was it! Keep that feeling!'

Nadiya was still smiling as we danced it together on that Saturday night with my wife, Sarah, in the live audience. Yes, the judges were a bit picky about my lack of drive and encouraged me to lengthen my stride but, in my head, it was perfect. As we skipped up to see Claudia I waved at my wife and whispered 'thank you' to Nadiya. I tried to explain to Claudia how surreal it was to be watching myself back on the big screen in the 'Clauditorium' and think 'Who is that guy? He's not too bad.' It really didn't feel like I was watching myself.

During our interview, Nadiya said something that I'm not ashamed to say was the closest I came to bursting into tears on *Strictly*.

'Claudia, do you know what, there are two things I really love about this show. I love to teach, and I love to dance, and this week I managed to do both because, as a professional dancer, you are always worried about your celebrity, making sure that they are ok, but tonight, I was able to dance myself. So, thank you very much for this, Daniel.'

I know how much that meant to Nadiya because the one thing you realise about her very quickly is that she just loves dancing. Her face lights up when she talks about technique, performance or just anything to do with something that is so close to her heart. When you spend time with someone who loves something that much, it's impossible for a little of that magic not to rub off on you. She can even convince you to dress up like a giant lobster!

We survived the jive and that was quickly followed by our Couple's Choice of 'Classic' by MKTO. Each week we survived the red lights and avoided the bottom two and the dreaded dance-off. That didn't stop a small section of the press writing the 'how on earth are they still in it?' articles, but brushing them to one side became part of the weekly ritual. Nadiya has always had her fair share of negative headlines to deal with – normally about her private life – and it's interesting to see the way she deals with all the rumours, rubbish and lies. She would walk into training on a Monday and say, 'We take the negative stuff, we laugh, we put it in our hands, and we simply blow it away.' She would then start to teach me another dance. I was very much of the same opinion, so each week it was onwards and upwards.

The week of the American Smooth to 'King Of The Road' was a tricky one. I had picked up a bit of an injury the week before during the Couple's Choice and I couldn't put any weight on my left foot on the Monday, Tuesday or Wednesday. I had physio, acupuncture and was on some heavy-duty prescription painkillers and anti-inflammatories. When I turned up to training on Thursday morning – our final day to get it sorted – I could tell Nadiya was a little concerned.

'How long have we got to learn this dance?' I asked her.

'It's 10 a.m. now and we leave for *It Takes Two* at 4 p.m., so we have six hours,' she said.

'Well, let's learn the dance in six hours then,' I proclaimed. It's amazing what the brain can do when you are all out of alternative options.

'That was a big week, Daniel,' Nadiya recalls as we look back on the series together. 'I remember you promised me that, no matter what, you would learn it and deliver. I saw your brain take over your body and I saw the presenter come out of you. By that stage, you were so much more technically and mechanically aware of your body. I knew we were going to be ok.'

We were struggling with the final lift that week. I had to push Nadiya high above my head and then let her slide down my back before the big finish. Five minutes before we were due on telly, we were practising the lift backstage. Every time we did it, Nadiya's dress went over my head or her heavily beaded sleeves would whack me in the face. There was an emergency call to the brilliant wardrobe department. While they attacked her outfit with a pair of scissors, we just turned to each other and said, 'We don't need to practise this. It's going to be great.' The brain took over the body.

When we walked onto the dance floor a few minutes later, Nadiya noticed something was different and it wasn't just the high-strength painkillers.

'Are you ok?' she said, as we made our way to the stairs at the top of the stage. She was in a gorgeous ballgown – with slightly shorter and less deadly sleeves – and I was in a full tail-suit.

'You've got "TV Dan" from now on, Nadiya,' I said with a smile.

'I like him,' she said. 'What happened to the other fella?'

'He's long gone. "TV Dan" is as comfortable out here as he is in the studio.'

'Is there anything I need to do?' she said as the *Strictly* voice-over king, Alan Dedicoat, started to introduce us.

'Just keep up!' I whispered. The music started and we were off to our first score above 30.

The American Smooth was followed by musicals week, which was so special. It was one of our favourite weeks of the competition and dancing a Charleston to 'Good Morning' will remain one of my enduring memories of being on *Strictly*. Nadiya always said that, if we'd made it to the final, she would have chosen to do that Charleston again. Getting through that week took us to week ten and to a dance with added significance.

One afternoon, early in the competition, I was eating lunch and Nadiya was dancing around the floor on her own. It wasn't a dance I was familiar with, but I could see how much she was enjoying it. She was totally lost in the movement as she floated effortlessly around the room. I asked her what it was. 'That, Daniel . . . is rumba. My favourite dance.'

The following week I played Nadiya a piece of music I said I would love to dance to – 'Desperado' by The Eagles. The story behind it goes back a long way. I always wanted to play the piano growing up, but our house was too small to fit one in. I still want to learn the piano just so I can play 'Desperado'. I told this to Nadiya and, as she listened, she sat upright in the chair in the training room. 'We can dance a rumba to this.' She also explained that she had also always wanted to play the piano and had dreamed of doing it in a red backless dress. It's very peculiar that we have both had the same piano dream with the only difference being the wardrobe choices! I played her the end of the song, where it all gets stripped back to the piano again, and said 'Wouldn't it be great if you started the routine on the piano – in a red backless dress – and I finish it on the piano?'

'Like James Bond in a tuxedo!' she jumped in.

'Yes, a tuxedo sounds great, and we can dance your favourite dance, to one of my favourite songs, wearing a dress you've always dreamed of.'

Nadiya was excited but told me that even the possibility of the rumba was a long way off. Given that it was week two at the time we discussed this, I didn't think there was much chance of it ever happening, but that became my reason to work harder than ever: to stay in *Strictly* long enough to fulfil both our dancing dreams with a rumba, in a red backless dress, to 'Desperado' on a giant piano.

It was week six when Nadiya came skipping into the training room and told me that, if we stayed in until week ten, we'd get to dance a rumba and we'd get to do it to 'Desperado'! That's why we both let out a little squeal when our names were called out at the end of week nine after our Charleston. We knew rumba was next and that 'Desperado' was on the horizon. As we walked off the stage that night, Nadiya had a little sob because I don't think she ever thought it would happen. It was time to dig out the red backless dress.

Rumba week was to become even more special because our film was going to be all about Nadiya's love of dance. I'll come back to that in a minute but, at this point, I'm now going to let you into a *Strictly* secret. I've watched the show for years and have now taken part and I think there are essentially four crucial elements to doing well on *Strictly*.

Obviously, the dance itself is essential. It lasts for ninety seconds every Saturday night, but each couple also gets a ninety-second film (or VT) and another ninety seconds with Claudia. Those are the three key elements, and the fourth is the stuff you do outside the confines of the show, both on social media, and on programmes like *It Takes Two*, the *Strictly* spin-off.

I have always thought that all those elements are just as important as each other and yet most people seem to spend four days learning the dance and hardly put any effort into the VT, the interview or the extra bits. Obviously, viewers want to know if you can dance and are getting better, but the other elements are the only opportunity they get to see who you are, what makes you tick, how well you get on as a couple and whether you're actually someone they want to see dance again. The other elements are just as important as those ninety seconds on the dance floor.

That week, the plan for our VT was for me to speak to Nadiya about how she got into dance and explain her love of rumba. When you hear her talk about it, it's easy to see why it means so much to her. I asked her what makes rumba so special. A huge smile broke out across her face.

She looks up momentarily, as if she is watching one of the great performances from her stellar career . . . 'The rumba is so beautiful, so intense, so feminine. For me, it is the perfect expression of what it is to be a woman. You have the time to express yourself and feel the movement but, not independently or only in certain areas, your whole body is involved. You feel the dance in every part of you. Everything is engaged, every muscle matters, everything is working towards something special, and everything is important. Rumba is the essential Latin discipline, the queen of the dances. The rumba walk is how you warm up your body and it is at the very centre of dancing. If you told me I could only choose one dance for the rest of my life, it would be the rumba.'

She pauses and looks up, back to that perfect routine in her mind. She smiles again and then comes back to me.

'Every step matters, Daniel. Every look, every gesture, every movement, however subtle,' she says rolling her wrists and stretching her fingers. 'Everything has a meaning and a purpose. There is no waste. That, Daniel, is the rumba.'

'And was it always rumba, Nadiya?' I ask her.

'In the beginning it was just dance. I fell in love with it from day one and that fire inside me has never died. As a young girl, I watched a man called Slavik Krykliyvyy performing in Ukraine. I knew then, at that precise moment, that I wanted to dance for the rest of my life. At times, it has been the biggest struggle of my life but also the richest reward. I've had to break down barriers, fight against the system, and dig deeper than I ever thought I could. The journey from the five-year-old, who fell in love with dancing, to the twenty-five-year-old who became world champion, is the hardest, greatest, and most rewarding thing I have done. It was my one dream, and through hard work, sacrifice, dedication, love, perseverance and sheer determination I made it to the top.'

Do you see what I mean? When someone talks about something with such care and affection you can't help but be drawn in and wonder why you've gone your whole life without being able to see it for yourself.

I have another question for the two-time world champion. 'If you love it so much, Nadiya, is it frustrating to be dragging a numptie around the floor who is so far out of your league?'

She laughs. 'That's why I love this show, Daniel. I love to teach you because, when you love something so much, the greatest gift you can give, is to pass that love on to someone else. I love that moment when someone else's eyes light up when something clicks. I love that look in your eyes when you realise that you've done something well and your body is moving in the right way. I love that smile that cracks across your face when you understand the joy that comes from dancing.'

I certainly felt that joy during our week ten rumba. That was a crazy week. It also marked the ten-year anniversary of the death of Gary Speed. I had been asked by his family to film a special piece about the importance of talking to your friends if you were struggling with mental health. Gary, who was a good friend, had taken his own life the night after we'd worked together on *Football Focus* in 2011. I was happy to do the film but, I don't mind admitting to you, I cried for most of the Friday after doing the interview. For some reason, I then foolishly decided to watch it go out live on the Saturday afternoon before our rumba. I also read through some of the incredible messages that people sent me after watching the piece on *Football Focus* and I was a complete wreck for a couple of hours. Nadiya was brilliant that day. She took care of me and helped me get my head back together. We danced our rumba and off we went to the quarter-finals.

During our time on the show, I learned an awful lot from Nadiya. She showed me that I could not only enjoy dancing but that, if I allowed myself to smile as I did it, the world would smile along with me. When I spoke to the publishers of this book, we talked at length about the title *Standing on the Shoulders* and the sort of people I wanted to include within its pages. As we discussed some of the individuals who lift you up, who inspire you, who help you to achieve things you felt were beyond you, I remember thinking that it was the perfect description of how I felt after spending time with Nadiya on *Strictly*.

As I got to know her, I realised that it was also what her mum had done for her in helping her to pursue her dream. Larisa sacrificed everything to allow her daughter to first become a professional dancer, and then rise to the top of the tree. When I spoke to Nadiya's mum, she was also keen to thank me for helping her daughter to be herself for the first time on television.

'You allowed her to blossom,' says Larisa. '*Strictly* is such a big show in this country, much bigger than back home in Ukraine, or anywhere else. I realised that when I came to the studio to watch it for the first time. I had never seen anything like it: the attention to detail, the quality of the dancing and the size of the whole thing. There was my daughter in the middle of it. She has always been a wonderful mover, but you helped to show the world that she is much more than just a beautiful blonde who can dance, and I don't think she will ever forget that.'

When we eventually went out of *Strictly*, we were both gutted. Nadiya had never made it to the final five before, but I was desperate for us to make the semi-finals and get the chance to dance twice in a week. There is not a single doubt in my mind that the best four dancers went through in Rhys, AJ, Rose and John, but having lasted such a long time, and exceeded every expectation, one more week would have been amazing.

On that Monday morning after our Sunday night exit, the alarm went off at 3 a.m. and I picked up the phone to turn it off. There were hundreds of messages on it. After reading my notes for that morning's *BBC Breakfast* I had a quick glance at social media on my way downstairs. If you just count Instagram direct messages and emails that had come through my website, there were more than 8,000 of them! It was mind-blowing that so many people had been moved to write such beautiful messages. It was a reminder of what it's like to be part of a show which means so much to so many people.

There were lots of messages from women telling me that their partners had taken up dancing for the first time. There were messages from men who said they had used me as their inspiration to dance at a wedding. There were fans of Nadiya's who – like her mum – were thankful that they had got to see the real her. There were lots of people worried that they had seen the last of the Yorkshire Barmaid. The barmaid was a little character we had invented for Nadiya during the show. We recorded a sketch each week of her perfecting her Yorkshire accent behind the bar in our training room at City Limits in Sheffield and put it on social media. By the end of the series, they were getting more views than our dances! In among all the Yorkshire Barmaid fans, there were also hundreds of videos from parents of their kids dancing around dressed as lobsters. There aren't many days that pass without someone mentioning the lobster jive or walking past me using their hands as claws.

There was one message which really cut through and that was the message which persuaded me to include Nadiya in this book. It was from a woman called Amy on Instagram.

Dear Dan,

I know you didn't win Strictly *but I hope you realise how special you and Nadiya have been on this series. We all loved watching you learn to dance but, at the same time, it was wonderful to see how much Nadiya was learning from you and how she was growing too. You were blossoming on the dance floor, and she was blossoming on the camera. You were a brilliant partnership. You were great for each other, and we loved watching it every week. That's why we kept voting for you. Keep dancing!*

This was one of the many messages I sent to Nadiya during that horrible week when the show is still on but you're not involved anymore. There is no training, no interviews, no VT to film, no taxis to get in, no trains to catch and no kit to wash. All you have left are the memories of three amazing months on the biggest show on telly.

'I matured a lot during our season on *Strictly*,' says Nadiya, reflecting on our time together while preparing for her next dancing tour of the UK. 'I go into the next series of the show far more confident. I knew I could dance, and I knew I could teach, but being able to work with someone who was so willing and being able to get so far with a complete beginner, it gave me that confirmation that this is what I was meant to do. I see things much more clearly now and you helped me to understand the show from the outside, if that makes sense. I used to only think about the dancing, but it is much more than that. It's the entertainment, it's the fun, it's the excitement. You taught me that if I was willing to give a little bit of myself, to let go a little, I would get so much more back in return. You showed me how much people cared and you helped me to understand how people watch the show and that is going to be so special for me going forward.'

That is why *Strictly* will remain one of the most rewarding things I have ever been involved in. I didn't embarrass my children, I didn't go out in week one, I learned a new skill, I surprised myself, I didn't fall over on TV, we somehow made it all the way to the quarter-finals and, with the help of Nadiya Bychkova, I completely conquered my fear of dancing. It's not just about no longer feeling the glitter-ball-inspired terror either. I feel more confident in general. I have an entirely new walk (which Nadiya taught me in week one) and I think my time on *Strictly* has made me a better TV presenter.

'Do you mind if we use you as an example to recruit men who think they'll be rubbish?' giggled one of the senior producers on the night of the final. 'I bet you wish you'd said "yes" years ago.'

I'm more than happy for *Strictly* to use me as a recruitment tool, but I disagree about wishing I'd said 'yes' earlier. The 2021 season felt like a pretty special season to be part of. Rose, who also features in these pages, was the undoubted superstar, but the whole team of contestants were amazing. We got on so well from day one and encouraged and cheered each other right through to the end, which doesn't happen every year. If I'd done *Strictly* another year, I would have missed out on Friday-night dinners at the Borehamwood Hilton with Adam Peaty, Ugo Monye and the wonderful Sara Davies – founder members of Hotel Club – which later grew to include Judi, AJ and occasionally Rhys. If I'd done *Strictly* another year, I wouldn't have got to know Nina, Katie, John, Tilly, Tom, Robert and Greg. And, without Greg, I wouldn't have been able to talk about falafels to his wife, Emma Thompson. She used to bring them in most weeks. I showed the picture to our youngest and he shouted, 'YOU'RE EATING WITH NANNY MCPHEE!'

Most importantly, if I'd done *Strictly* another year, I might not have had Nadiya as a partner and, above everything else, she was the reason I enjoyed every second of it and put my heart and soul into it. She was the glue that held it all together.

The tango in week eleven was our final time on the *Strictly* dance floor. After the dance-off, you stand there in front of the judges and Tess asks you if there's anything you'd like to say to your partner.

I told Tess that 'sometimes people walk into your life at just the right time and switch some lights on'. I think both Nadiya and I felt that way. She was precisely the person I needed to guide me through the show, and I was precisely who she needed to give her the confidence to be herself and give her the ability to shine on the TV in the same way she always has on the dance floor.

That's why I struggled to find the words to say when we went on *It Takes Two* for our final appearance on the Monday after our tango and Rylan asked Nadiya about our partnership. She thanked me for creating an environment where she felt safe and then said, 'your friendship has given me wings to fly again'. I think that might be one of the nicest things anyone has ever said to me.

I will never forget that. If you can enable someone else to shine, if you can lift someone else up, if you can help someone achieve a little more than they would on their own, then forget the dancing, that's what it's all about.

That's what we managed to do for each other.

That's why two-time world champion, Nadiya Bychkova, is in this book.

That's why I loved my time on *Strictly Come Dancing*.

That's why we'll be friends for life.

BEYOND THE PANDEMIC

My last book, *Remarkable People*, came out right in the middle of the global coronavirus pandemic. I don't know about you, but it seems so strange to remember the sort of restrictions we were all living under for most of 2020 and the huge life and lifestyle changes that were forced upon us all.

I was very thankful to be able to work throughout lockdown, but every day in those first few months on the TV we were talking about death tolls, issues with PPE, a lack of consideration over care homes and the strain our National Health Service was under.

Remarkable People included a whole chapter about people who felt the full force of the pandemic: either surviving, raising money for others, losing a loved one or working on the frontline.

I know the vast majority of us feel that the worst is very much behind us now, but there are still so many people who stick in my mind, so many stories that I still keep coming back to. Sitting on the *BBC Breakfast* sofa, I got to listen to stories of both tragedy and triumph, and I wanted to share some of those with you here. These are the people who I often think about;

some of the people who will never forget life in the pandemic as we all look forward to life after it.

I feel the need to offer a gentle word of warning at this point. This chapter was hard to write and I appreciate it may be hard to read. Coronavirus ripped thousands of families to pieces and that is reflected in the next few pages. I spent hours interviewing the people in this chapter and most of those were spent with tears in my eyes. This is about family, it's about love and loss, but I trust you also see the hope of a brighter tomorrow.

Margaret Keenan was born just outside Enniskillen in Northern Ireland in 1929. Her dad was a butcher, and they had a family smallholding. Margaret, or Maggie as most people call her, used to help her dad every day along with her two brothers and sisters.

'I loved the bright lights of the big city,' says Maggie, 'and I got to go to Belfast for the first time when I was nineteen or twenty – my oldest sister was having a baby and I was to look after her. I met my husband there on Easter Monday 1955. My friend and I had gone to the holiday parade, and we went to the Rainbow café. There was a fiesta going on around the corner, so we popped round, and a fella asked me if I wanted to dance. That fella was Phil Keenan.'

When Maggie met her future husband he was about to go back to Canada, but he had a brother and a brother-in-law in England, so they changed plans and moved to West Bromwich initially and then settled in Coventry when they got married in 1957.

'I was a window dresser, Dan,' says Maggie. 'It was a job that I loved but I stopped when I had children. I worked in a restaurant and then settled into a role as a shop assistant at a jeweller's. I did fifteen years at one jeweller's and then twenty-five years at the next one.'

Maggie first heard about coronavirus, like the rest of us, in those first few months of 2020. 'It frightened me, if I'm honest, from the start. I remembered back to when I was a child and we experienced scarlet fever. I remember it being horrible and, in those days, people died a lot younger than they do now, so I was incredibly cautious. Everyone I knew was cautious. I had a feeling it wasn't going to go away. I was happy to stay at home in a bubble with my daughter Sue. I was on a stool in the hall while Sue and the grandkids would sit on the wall in the garden. That's how careful we were.'

Then things took a turn for Maggie when she became ill with suspected heart failure. 'My breathing was terrible. I don't think I have ever been that ill in my life. I went into hospital (Coventry & Warwickshire) and was being looked after there. Obviously, I was following the news, but I didn't really think too much of it when someone from the hospital came round and asked if I wouldn't mind having the jab.' Maggie starts laughing. 'My daughter Sue said that they asked me because no one else on the ward was really speaking. I've had jabs before, and it didn't bother me. I never considered not having the jab. I didn't really know much about it.'

Maggie was told later that same night that she was going to be the first person in the world to have the coronavirus vaccine.

Maggie starts laughing again. 'I was on a lot of medication at the time, so I didn't really think much about it. I remember thinking that I couldn't really be the first person in the world to have it, there must be someone else having it at the same time elsewhere.

'That next morning, I went into the room and there were cameras and people all over the place. I had no idea it was going to be that big a thing. May Parsons was the nurse who did the jab, and it was all over in a flash. I went back to the ward, and they were all excited. 'You're on TV!' they all said. I rang my daughter Sue and her brother, and they were all watching too. They let me go home from hospital, but I got told to go to Sue's house because there were so many people outside mine, and I couldn't even get near the door. There are a lot of bushes near my house and one of my neighbours told me they were all hiding in there. I didn't want to give the neighbours any problems, so I just stayed at Sue's. She was working from home, and we just kept the lights off because there were people outside the door the whole time.'

Maggie got the jab on Tuesday 8 December 2020. I remember the day well. My boss at *BBC Breakfast* had called a few days before to let us know that it was going to be happening. We didn't know the name of the patient, but we were told it would take place at Coventry & Warwickshire Hospital while we were on air on that Tuesday morning. We had correspondents in place and guests ready to talk about the significance of the start of the vaccine rollout. In the previous weeks there had been so much talk about how many vaccines

242

the UK had bought and whether they would come from Pfizer or Astra Zeneca.

'It's all in the past now,' says Maggie. 'I feel good about it now. I thank God that I came forward and had it. It is a good feeling. I came up the road yesterday and one little boy said, "Excuse me, is it true that you're ninety-four?" I told him I was ninety-two, and ninety at the time of my jab. I'm amazed people are still interested but I suppose it was so important because it was the start of the way out.'

Maggie hits the nail on the head with that one. She may just have been one ninety-year-old lady getting an injection, but she signified something special. I remember listening to various radio stations that day and there was genuine euphoria that there was a little light at the end of a very long tunnel. There had been so much talk about a possible vaccine, and scientists across the world had been working crazy hours to meet demand, and here it was, finally, before our very eyes.

A few months after the vaccine rollout, I got to visit Maggie at the Coventry & Warwickshire Hospital where she'd had the jab. I met the team from the hospital charity who gave her the famous penguin T-shirt she wore for the big moment. They have since sold thousands of them – and are still having them printed even now! Maggie became quite the celebrity.

'Do you know I won an award for that, Dan?' laughs Maggie. 'When I had my latest corona jabs, they gave me a little prize because of all the T-shirts they had sold. It took my mind back to that day. You know, I didn't watch the news that night . . . I was too tired. I kept thinking, I wished I'd brushed my hair. It

wasn't to my liking at all, but I was well looked after by May.'
'May' is May Parsons, the nurse who administered that first-ever
jab. We'll meet May again later in the chapter, but the two of
them now have a very special bond.

'It's lovely to have a friendship with someone that you'd
never met before,' says Maggie. 'I suppose we were thrown
together, and we exchange cards at Christmas too.'

I tell Maggie that she was one of the answers to a question
in the first pub quiz I went to after they reopened. She is dealing
with the attention well. 'I'm having a photograph taken for a
museum in London, which is nice. Whenever people do stop
me, they are very nice and always kind. I still wear a mask when
I go into public places because I'm in my nineties and I think
that's just part of life for some people now. I am so glad that I
did it though. People tell me that I showed them it was safe, and
I have always said that, if I can do it, anyone can. My jab was the
first step. It gave people hope that we could get back to normal
and that there was a way back. I know that so many people have
died, and I remember people being in hospital saying, "Please,
can I have it now?", but it was too late. It's terrible . . . so sad
when you think about the people who have died. I am very
thankful that I am still here to tell the tale.'

I thank Maggie for her time and tell her it's lovely to talk to
her again and she perks up. 'Before you go, Dan, two things I
wanted to tell you. I had a letter last week from a broadcasting
company in Korea. It was handwritten and it was thanking me
and congratulating me. I'm going to write back to them and
say I appreciate it all, but it was nothing to do with me. I just

provided the arm. Everyone else did the work. The other thing, Dan,' says Maggie, 'I loved you on the dancing. Nadiya turned you into such a beautiful dancer. It was lovely to watch. I never miss a single show. I like to watch the dancing but I'm also a keen sewer and I'm always amazed at how those costumes are done so quickly.'

We talk for about ten minutes about Vicky Gill and her wonderful wardrobe team and the magic of sequins.

As Maggie mentioned, there were many people who did lose loved ones during the pandemic. I felt very fortunate to go through the whole period without contracting coronavirus – at least not to my knowledge. I was testing several times a week. I was permanently worried about my elderly relatives, but I'm also very thankful that no one in our family became particularly ill with the virus or required medical attention. My little sister works as a nurse in Derby, and, during the pandemic, she gave our family regular updates on what she and her colleagues were going through. She was moved to intensive care and would send through selfies to our WhatsApp group showing the creases and sores on her face after twelve hours in uncomfortable PPE. She, like many other nursing staff, saw some terrible things during those eighteen months: stretched colleagues, dwindling resources, dying patients and bereaved families. Every single one of those families has a grim story to tell, but there were some that I will never forget. One of them was the story of Heather Stewart and her husband Stephen.

'If anyone in our family was going to struggle with the virus, I thought it would be me,' says Heather. She was meant to start her new job at the Scottish Association for Mental Health on the first day of lockdown.

She and her husband had been together for thirty-two years and married for almost twenty-six. They lived in Motherwell and Stephen worked as a lab technician at the local cement works. He was classed as an essential worker and all he did during those early days of the pandemic was to go to work and then come home. 'He didn't do anything else,' says Heather. 'He was as careful as he could possibly be. We were concerned when it first hit. I could see things happening all over the world. I thought we should be closing our borders and I thought we could have kept ourselves safer. We followed the news closely and followed all the restrictions. My mum lived in a different council area, so we didn't see her for a good nine months. It was just WhatsApp and video calls like the vast majority of people.'

Stephen went to work on Monday 18 January 2021. He'd been back at work after Christmas, and he phoned home and told Heather that he didn't feel 100 per cent. Some colleagues had tested positive, so he did a test and came home.

'Stephen was one of those people who, when he was ill, he'd just go to bed and sleep it off,' says Heather. 'He isolated himself in the bedroom and the test said he was positive. Test and Trace spoke to us, and they said I was also positive after my test. Stephen was being physically sick, and I phoned the NHS, and they sent a car over to take him to the Covid assessment centre on the Thursday of that week. He got an injection, came home and went back upstairs to bed. The first week I wasn't too bad. I was working from home. At the weekend, Stephen asked me to come upstairs. I put the oxygen reading on and it was 71 per cent, which I knew was a long way below what it should be. I called for an ambulance, and they came and took him to the hospital.'

That was the last time Heather spoke to her husband in person.

Stephen went to the University Hospital Wishaw. He was there for ten days and during that time he was too ill to reply to a text message and Heather wasn't able to visit. She would call the hospital for an update on her husband, and they would simply tell her the dose he was on and what his oxygen levels were. Stephen got moved onto a ward but still needed help to breathe. Heather got a call on Valentine's Day from an ICU doctor to say that her husband was struggling, and they were going to monitor him closely and that he was going to go on a ventilator because he had Covid pneumonia. Stephen was on hefty antibiotics but managed to text Heather to let her know that he was hoping to go back to the ward. That sounded like positive news to Heather. That message arrived on the Sunday.

'The following Tuesday, the doctor called again,' says Heather. 'I was told that Stephen was exhausted, and they decided to ventilate him to give him a rest. He said he wanted to "let the machine be his lungs". Again, I wasn't allowed up to the hospital. Stephen was having panic attacks but still I couldn't go up there. Just before he was ventilated, they tried to set up a video call, but it didn't work and we did it on FaceTime instead.

It was all a bit frantic. We had two minutes with him. Stephen was wearing a hooded mask. We couldn't hear each other but at least I got to see him. I told him I loved him, and he mouthed it back and he made a heart with his hands. I told him I would see him on the other side.'

It always seemed to Heather that there was no chance that could be the last goodbye. 'It was always put in a positive light. They phoned me back later that night to say he was responding and was comfortable. On 16 February, the Wednesday, I got a call at lunchtime to say that Stephen hadn't been to the toilet so they had to put him on a dialysis machine, and they had to turn him and they couldn't say if he would survive. I was told I was able to see him for about thirty minutes. He was face down on the bed, ventilated and in an induced coma. There was no communication, but I could touch him and tell him I loved him. I was then sent home and they said they had successfully turned him. They told me that if he crashed or reacted that would have been it because he was already on 100 per cent oxygen. I was able to go back for another thirty minutes. They called me that Wednesday night about 11.30 p.m., and I was told to come back because his blood pressure was all over the place.'

It's clearly emotional for Heather to recall all this. We take a break and talk about something else before returning to that night.

'I was covered in PPE. I sat with him, and he had about twenty pipes and other things coming out of him. They got his blood pressure stabilised, so I went home at 1 a.m. I went back on the Thursday and sat with him playing pieces of music that we enjoyed. He was holding on. I went home again and then I went back to the hospital at about 9 a.m. on Friday 19 February to be told that his organs were shutting down and there was nothing more they could do.' Heather is talking slowly, taking her time, crying. 'I was sitting with Stephen when he passed. I was handed two plastic bags that had all his things in them. His whole life in two plastic bags. I left the hospital in total shock.'

I am speaking to Heather almost eighteen months after the death of her husband and she says her life is still all over the place.

'I was really thankful to see him. I know that so many people weren't even able to do that. I don't think I could have coped with the idea that he was struggling, and I couldn't be there for him. That meant the world to me. It puts things into perspective. There are so many people who didn't get the chance. They couldn't even have the process of grief. The problem is that I feel like we have been together our whole lives. I have no idea how to be on my own. I just miss him. He was such a help, and we did everything together. We were only allowed twenty people at the funeral. There was no wake, no sharing of stories and memories, and then you come back to an empty house, and it hits you . . . this is my new life. A life without him. I still expect him to walk through the doors even now. The world is going about like it's gone, but it still worries me, and I can't shake those memories. I know that we are getting over it, but it's so hard for anyone who has lost someone like Stephen.'

I ask Heather about those people who still claim that the whole pandemic was a hoax and there were empty hospital wards and unused ventilators. She sighs.

'I would tell those people to go and walk along the memorial wall by the Thames in London. We were able to go in August 2021 and visit it. We touched up Stephen's heart and rewrote the words. His heart is on panel 17 and there are now twenty-five panels. He passed away at the height of the second wave and another 70–80,000 people have died since Stephen. I would ask them to go and walk along the Thames and read some of those names and those messages and to think about the devastation that each one leaves behind.'

On the day I spoke to Heather there was another revelation about the parties that went on at Downing Street during the pandemic. She brings it up.

'I don't think you could possibly write down what I feel about that. It is beyond belief that they broke the rules. I don't know any other employer that actively encourages you to drink on the job. Why was it accepted? Why did they smuggle alcohol inside in a suitcase? I want to look up to our leaders. They should be setting the example. I feel like they let us all down. I don't want to be angry though,' says Heather. 'I want to think about Stephen, and I know I need to find a way to live with that but . . . I can't live without him. My life will never be normal. Covid took all that away.'

Heather's story is one which will always stick with me. I remember watching her on *BBC Breakfast* and hearing her powerful testimony. I also have vivid memories of talking to Saleyha and Syira Ahsan. Their father, Ahsan-ul-Haq Chaudry, died from Covid in December 2020 during the second wave, just a few weeks before he was due to get the vaccine.

He lived a remarkable life, and I will never forget the way his two daughters spoke with so much passion and love for their father who had sacrificed so much for them to succeed. His story was made even more remarkable by the fact that all six of his children were working on the NHS frontline during the pandemic. He and his wife, Fauzia, had raised an ITU doctor, two GPs, a junior doctor, a consultant and a pharmacist. A remarkable family mourning the loss of a remarkable dad.

The proud father came to the UK in the 1950s as a nineteen-year-old after fleeing partition violence in India. He was crammed into one of the many trains which left India for Pakistan and his route, through countries like Iran and Turkey, eventually brought him to England.

Syira is his second eldest daughter and still works in the hospital where her dad died at the age of eighty-one. 'My dad was six-foot-two and really overwhelming in stature. All my friends used to think he was really strict, but that was my mum,' she laughs. 'I can only remember my dad shouting at us once in my whole childhood. He was desperate to sleep, and we were making too much noise. He was always laughing. Always having fun. He was like the BFG.'

I ask Syira what her dad did for a living. 'Everything,' she says, 'absolutely everything. Let me see if I can remember. He was trained as a chemical engineer, but he was a civil servant, a maths teacher, a computer science teacher, he worked for the council, and he was a part-time security guard as a second job in the evenings and weekends. He loved teaching and learning. He would always give you a history or a politics lesson when you were with him. He knew so much about the world around him, and he loved to share that with people. He started a lot of his conversations with "Now look here", before launching into something he had observed or picked up. His love of learning never stopped, he even did a degree in Astrophysics in his seventies!'

Syira has one older sister. It's probably worth giving you a little family rundown in age order:

Saleyha: A&E Registrar

Syira: GP and urgent care doctor at Queen's Hospital

Shazlee: Pharmacist

Saima: Consultant Paediatrician

Safiyah: GP and a Sports Physician

Shoaib: ITU doctor

Saleyha also learned so much from her dad's thirst for knowledge. 'He was the man who made me care about news and current affairs. He was all about social justice. He had a hearing problem so he would sit on the floor, watching the news, and we would all sit with him. It was the same every evening – sometimes the BBC and occasionally ITN. We used to love those bongs. We didn't just watch it either. He would talk to us about the stories and the impact it was all having on the world around us. My mum was a royalist, and my dad wasn't quite so supportive of the royal family and we used to have these big differences of opinion, but we all talked about it together. I remember during the war in Bosnia we were watching a report about refugees, and my dad turned to us and said, "I was a refugee once." That was the first time he ever mentioned about coming from India during partition. He saw some truly terrible things, things he never really spoke about to anyone.'

Saleyha got into medicine relatively late after retraining at the age of thirty. Because of what her dad had been through, she was always fascinated by a career in the armed forces. She was the first British Muslim woman to go through the army officer commissioning course at Sandhurst. She knew her dad was incredibly proud of that, particularly because of what the family had faced growing up in Essex.

'We were one of the first Asian families to move into the area of Seven Kings in Ilford,' remembers Syira. 'I remember looking out of the front window one day and asking my dad what "BNP" stood for. He asked me what I meant, and I told him that someone had written it all over our car. It's so strange, because I think Dad was actually teaching the daughter of the leader of the BNP at the time! He said she was a lovely girl. That was him. He was never angry. He would always think that if you can love someone they would come around.'

Her dad was subjected to racism during his earlier years in the UK too when he was first looking for work. Many adverts had the letters 'NCA' on them – No Coloureds Allowed. Saleyha also has clear memories of some of the difficult days. 'I remember being with Mum and our house being pelted,' she says. 'We just stayed inside and waited for Dad to come home. He would always take us for a daily walk around the community in the evening. We would sometimes meet up with another

Asian family and go together. I could sense that, whenever we walked in certain areas, we were prepared for comments or trouble. It's only now that I think about Dad having to shield us from all of that. I will always be thankful for what he did. It can't have been easy.'

Saleyha's dad was also shielding during the pandemic because of his underlying health conditions. The family kept their distance for much of 2020 and visited only to drop off food and supplies to their father, who had lost his wife the year before.

'We don't know how he caught Covid,' says Saleyha. 'Maybe it was one of the shopping drops or when his carer went out on a day off. We don't know, but when he went into hospital, he never came out. I watched a lot of people die from Covid, but it's very different when it is someone you love so much.'

'He was always thinking of other people though,' adds Syira. 'Even when he was lying in his bed, struggling to breathe, he was on the phone to his brother in America, comforting him and telling him that it was going to be ok even though he knew he was deteriorating and that his body was shutting down.'

'Right at the end, Dan,' recalls Saleyha, 'when he was in pain, he had his mask on and he said, "I had six children." He was acknowledging his legacy, I think. He was looking back at his life, all he had come through, and he was thinking about what he had achieved. He was proud of us. I think he also despaired because, you know, we make mistakes and we are far from perfect, but he was happy that we were happy and that he'd lived to see all that.'

After his death, his daughters learned a lot more about their dad from the tributes paid to him and by going through his belongings. 'I remember his teaching and working as a security guard at the same time,' says Saleyha, 'but I never realised how hard he had to fight. Most of it was to pay for our education. He was incredibly highly qualified and yet I found letters in his boxes that he was writing to so many people to get a job as a teacher. He was sending his CV everywhere and begging for any sort of role just so he could support the family. When my dad passed away, some of his former students came forward and contacted us. They are now in their fifties and many of them have successful careers as programmers and they all said they developed their love of the subject in my dad's computer science lessons. He was a pioneer in computer science when the schools didn't even have computers! He would get his pupils to start coding long before it was ever on the curriculum and he would process all that information in his own time, while trying to raise his own six children. He never stopped caring about others. I know he could have been brilliant at anything and that he didn't achieve his full potential because he prioritised us. That is one of the reasons I keep pushing myself . . . I keep trying to achieve more to make his sacrifice worth it.'

'He was just a wonderful man to have around,' says Syira. 'He handled everything really well. He was decent and always held the moral high ground, whatever people threw at him. He could never look at images of war because it always reminded him of what he saw in his childhood in India. My daughter interviewed him about partition for a school project and I think that was the only time he talked about it. He had tears in his eyes that day. I think that's why he was so full of life and always laughing. He was just so thankful that we didn't have to live through what he did.'

Both Saleyha and Syira talk about their dad's love of food. Apparently, before he left India, his mother gave him a week-long cooking course and gave him all the kitchen skills he needed to know for the rest of his life. 'I think he always loved his food because he went through real hunger,' says Syira. 'He appreciated every mouthful and food was the answer to everything. I went through a divorce, and it was getting really hard. I was on the phone to my dad, crying, and he just said, "Enough . . . enough. Come home after work, I am cooking you dinner." He did, and it was lovely. When I was pregnant he decided that he would cook me a gorgeous meal before I went to hospital. He did that and then, while he was in the waiting room, he had a heart attack! The doctors said he was the most dignified patient they had ever met. They asked him if he was having chest pains and he said "Yes" but he just didn't want to make a fuss. That was dad in a nutshell.'

I enjoyed talking to Saleyha and Syira because it was so clear they had learned so much at the feet of their father: watching the news, listening to his impromptu history lessons, sat at his dinner table or just watching the way he treated others.

'My dad was living with us for a while,' remembers Syira, 'and one night we had a takeaway. My daughter came back with the food but also with some change. "What is that?" said Dad. "You never take the change; you always give them extra because you know how hard they work" He sent her outside to give the rest of the money back! He was always buying a McDonald's breakfast for homeless people. We were a poor family ourselves but that never stopped him giving to others. He was a great example to us all.'

It seems that Ahsan-ul-Haq Chaudry had two life rules: study hard and play hard. Syira continues the life lesson.

'He saw from his own example that education was a path to a better life. It wasn't about money; it was about understanding the world that you live in. He also sent us to every sport's club going. I remember him asking me, "When are you going to the Olympics?" and laughing. He just wanted us to love learning new things, to spend time in the library, to love books, to dream big and aim high.' She pauses. I ask if she is ok.

'I'm ok,' says Syira. 'It's just that talking about him now makes me realise that I still haven't really processed the fact that he's gone. I still expect to go around his house and to see him there, cooking food, telling me about politics and making me watch the news with him.'

I thank Saleyha for sharing her dad with the rest of us and ask her what her overriding memory of him will be. She takes her time to answer.

'He was really brave, Dan,' she says eventually. 'He made sacrifices throughout his life so that we could achieve things. He put his own dreams to one side and did what he had to do as a father so that we could fly. He was a talented chef, a great teacher and he was gifted at so many things. He was passionate about education and had such a strong sense of justice. He was always inquisitive, and he had this wonderful, constantly questioning mind. He has left behind six highly qualified children, but it doesn't really matter what letters I have after my name on a piece of paper ... I am staggered by what he achieved. To leave that mess behind in India, to leave his whole life, to come here and then to fight for everything he achieved, against the odds, and to laugh and love the whole time, that is incredible. I'm glad you called your book *Standing on the Shoulders* because that is where I feel I have been my whole life.'

There is another family I want to tell you about too. Josh and Samantha Willis didn't have as many children as Ahsan-ul-Haq Chaudry, but their story is just as compelling. Whenever I think about the impact of the pandemic, my mind skips back to Josh and Samantha.

They met in Northern Ireland back in 2012 on Samantha's birthday, 15 May. Her friends had made her go and Josh was bored. They met up regularly and eventually moved in together and decided to get married in March 2019 in Derry. Their daughter, Lilyanna, was born in April 2017 and Samantha was due to give birth to their second child in August 2021.

'I remember hearing about coronavirus around Christmas time in 2019,' recalls Josh. 'It was all getting hyped up and then, a few months later, it was everywhere. The bars and restaurants in Derry actually closed a week before the rest of the UK. I was working at the Northern Ireland Housing Executive and was off on a week's holiday. I didn't get sent home from work for the first lockdown, I never went back from my break.'

Samantha was working in community care in people's houses and worked right the way through lockdown. 'She had to pass police checkpoints and prove she was an essential worker quite a bit,' remembers Josh.

It was Friday night, 30 July 2021, when Josh got a call from his sister. 'She told me she was positive and we'd been with her that day. We both did the tests, and we came back as positive on the Sunday. Samantha was getting worse with her breathing, and it got to the point that she could barely get out of bed. At this point she was about thirty-six weeks pregnant, so I was a little worried. I called the doctor and told them what was happening, and it took them five hours to come back to me. I got told to bring her over to the hospital, so I did that. They checked her oxygen and then said they wanted to keep her there to get some extra checks done, because of the baby.'

Samantha was put into a wheelchair when Josh dropped her off. He had Covid himself at the time, so it all took place in the ambulance bay outside the hospital. He told his wife he would see her soon.

'There was no kiss and no hug,' says Josh. 'It was a super-quick drop-off. I just left her outside A&E. I went home, finished off packing her baby bag and then went back to the hospital and dropped her bag off at the same place outside the emergency department.'

On Wednesday 4 August, Josh heard that they were going to perform a C-section on his wife for the safety of their child. This was three weeks before the due date.

'I had sent our iPad up in her baby bag so that is what we

used for the birth of our little daughter, Evie Grace. Me and Lilyanna watched it all from our sofa in the house. It was bad, because Samantha never wanted a section. It was one of her fears, and the other one was having to give birth on her own. I'm glad that Lilyanna got to see the birth of her sister, but I knew it was awful for Samantha. That would have been her worst nightmare. She just gave in on the C-section because of the safety of the baby. It was all a bit surreal to be sat watching it on the sofa.'

As soon as Evie Grace was born, she was whipped into the next room. Her mum still had Covid, and she never got the chance to hold, or even touch, her new baby. Samantha went straight to the intensive care unit.

'She was sitting up in bed ok, but she couldn't really finish a sentence. We were FaceTiming her, but she was just exhausted. I would text her and it would take her hours to respond because she had so little energy. I kept asking if she could maybe hold the baby because I thought that would help her, but they just kept saying "no". I understand why. She was out of isolation, but she was still showing symptoms.'

Samantha went back onto the Covid ward, was turned, spent another week in ICU and then, tragically, after sixteen days in hospital, she died in the early hours on Friday 20 August.

'I was ringing twice a day,' says Josh. 'I was worried about her, but I also knew she was only thirty-five years old with no underlying health conditions. At points it looked like she was getting better but, in the end, her body just gave up. She never had the vaccination, because we found out she was pregnant on Boxing Day in 2020 and the advice at the time was for pregnant mums to avoid the jab. She was going to have it after the baby was born.'

Josh recalls getting the call he was dreading on Thursday 19 August. 'They rang and asked if I wanted to come over and see her. They had told me before when I'd asked to go in, that the only way that would happen would be if things got really serious. I knew it wasn't good. I went in to see her with this huge Covid suit on. I was there for about an hour. I was just talking to her. When I left, her oxygen level had gone up a little, which was good news, but she was unresponsive. She was in an induced coma. They called again that night. I was at my manager's house updating him in the garden and I was told I needed to bring my family. There could only be four of us there so I rang her mother, her sisters and her brother and thought, we can decide when we get there. I remember sitting in the office of the hospital and the staff were asking me about a "do not resuscitate" order. I couldn't bring myself to say the words. How can you say that you don't want them to try and save your wife's life?'

In the end, it was decided that Josh would go in to see his wife along with her mum and her two children from a previous relationship – her fourteen-year-old daughter Holly and Shay, who was seventeen.

'I walked into the room,' says Josh, 'and there was a priest there. I looked at the oxygen machine and it was in the sixties. I knew that was bad and I asked the nurse, just checking really, how serious it was, and she looked at me and told me that my wife had just that minute passed away.' Josh is recounting the events at a much slower rate now. He is understandably taking his time.

'I was glad I was there; I was glad I got to see her earlier that day. I hope she heard me when I was talking to her. I asked if she could hear, and I just talked about our family and I told her to keep fighting. For most of it I just held her hand. It sounds stupid, but I remember, while I was there, thinking about the people saying that Covid was a hoax. Here I was, saying goodbye to my wife.'

Josh went home in the early hours of Friday 20 August to collect some clothes to put Samantha in. He went back with a lock of Evie Grace's hair and Lilyanna's hair, and the nurses dressed her.

'I brought some photographs with me, to go in the coffin. I had some of the girls' toys and I brought the perfume that she had for our wedding. Normally, we would have had an open coffin in the house for a few days but, because of Covid, that wouldn't be happening, so I knew this was the last time I would ever see her face. I sprayed her with the perfume. I told her kids to tell her whatever they needed to tell her, and I said to them that all they could do now was make her proud of them. I kissed her through my visor and tried to leave. I knew they needed her bed for another patient, but I just couldn't walk away. I knew that I was never going to see her again. I tried to go about five times but just kept circling back to her side. I knew that as soon as I walked past that curtain . . . that was it. As I drove away in the car, I remember thinking that we should have been together for the best part of fifty years. I thought we would have all the time in the world to do the things we wanted to do. We were in the process of buying a house, I had just had a job interview for a promotion and, if I'd got that job, we were hoping that she wouldn't have to go back to work. There was so much to look forward to.'

Josh's uncle, Joe Clifford, was a priest in America. He was the one who had married them, and he was coming over for the funeral. He arrived at the house on the Sunday after Samantha's death and Josh asked him if he would be able to christen Evie Grace in the short time he'd be in the country.

'He looked at me,' remembers Josh, 'and said, "I don't know if you're allowed to do this, but do you think we could christen her at Samantha's funeral?" I just said "yes" straightaway without thinking about it. I wanted her to be there. I know she had gone, but I didn't want her to miss it. The chapel said it was ok, so we decided we would do it.'

Josh hasn't watched the funeral back. He doesn't think he ever will. 'It wasn't a big thing,' says Josh. 'We didn't publicise it to the people who were there. It was just something we wanted to do, so it just happened at the side of the church. I think it brightened things up a little bit. Evie Grace was christened because I wanted them to feel close to each other. I wasn't really thinking about what I was doing, but I just wanted Samantha to be there. It felt special to have them both together.'

Life remains hard for Josh and his two daughters. The enormity of the loss still hasn't really set in. He is so busy with the girls, and he still visits the cemetery every day. 'I just tell her what is happening,' says Josh, 'you know, the date, the weather, any news, what the girls are up to. They are always up to something. It's hard to know what Lilyanna will remember. There is endless information on Google which I can't really protect her from forever. I have put pictures up of her mum everywhere, so she remembers her. I have kept newspapers, pictures, and put them all in a box. One day she can read them all and see what an amazing person her mum was.'

Josh put a post about his wife on Facebook on the Friday of her death. That weekend was a big vaccine weekend in Ireland and the circumstances of Samantha's last few days had a huge impact on people.

'It took off,' remembers Josh. 'I wasn't making a political point. I don't think I even said "Get the vaccine" . . . I just told our story. There were people queuing for hours to get the jab. It's strange to think about it now because hardly anyone talks about Covid anymore. I don't blame anybody. I am just sad. I can't change it. I wish it hadn't happened, but I can't do anything to bring her back.'

I ask Josh how he will remember his wife. He tells me about a video on his phone.

'We were together for just over nine years, and I've got loads of videos and photos but there is one that stands out,' he smiles. 'She was out dancing, blowing me kisses, you know . . . laughing. She was happy, she cared, she loved people, she had goodness in her. She was my best friend as well as my wife.' Josh laughs before telling the next part . . .

'I've got to tell you, Dan, when she got into bed at night it was like her feet had been in the freezer but . . . I miss all that . . . you know, the annoying stuff. I miss all the stuff we never got to do, the stuff we were planning. The two little ones keep me going so I'll just keep going forward, one day at a time. One of the last things she texted me was from hospital. She was talking about cutting the drama out of her life. She wanted no negativity. She wanted to keep moving, to keep being positive, so that's what I need to keep doing for her. I know that now, she is just a number. One of thousands of people who died with Covid. I just hope her story lives on, and kids can read about her. To me, she will never be a number. I would rather her be named than just a pregnant person who had a baby. She would have hated every part of that, but I want people to know who she was, and how special she was. She was great at what she did, and everybody loved her.'

I thank Josh for his time. He is round at his sister's house, and I've made him late for a fried breakfast.

'Don't you worry, Dan,' he says. 'This is important. Can I just tell you one more thing?' he asks, almost whispering.

'I feel that she's around a lot of the time. There was one night, back in November, I felt like she walked me down to her graveside. I could feel the weight of her arm on mine. I know it sounds daft and maybe it's in my head but, believe me, I felt it. She was with me as I walked back up the hill and then, as I stepped out of the graveyard, it was like she stayed inside, and I left. It's one of the weirdest things I have ever felt. I don't know if my mind is playing with me, but there are little things that I feel, like she is trying to send me a message sometimes.

I hope she's happy with what I am trying to do with the kids. I hope she knows I'm trying to stay positive and keep going. She always said that if she went first, she would haunt me. Maybe that's what is happening. I just hope she stays around for as long as possible.'

Earlier in the chapter, we met Maggie Keenan who received the end of the needle containing the first coronavirus vaccine in the world. As promised, it's time to introduce the person who was on the other end of that syringe: May Parsons.

May's official title is Modern Matron for Respiratory. She trained as a nurse in the Philippines, graduated in 2000 and arrived in the UK in 2003. She has been working at Coventry & Warwickshire Hospital ever since.

I caught up with her the morning after another long shift. May has always been brutally honest about what it was like to work in a hospital during the pandemic and she paints a pretty grim picture of those early months of 2020.

'From the very start of it all, I volunteered to go into the intensive care unit. That was a time when we didn't have anything to protect ourselves. We were just catching people who needed ventilation. There were days when you had a group of people none of whom would be there the next day, they had all passed away. I can still remember the youngest person we saw; she was only twenty-two years old. There were young, fit, muscular men from the BAME community who would come into the ward and die overnight. It felt like our job was just sending people off, you know, making their deaths as comfortable as we could. It was hard to call a family member and tell someone that their loved one is going to die, and it just kept happening, day after day, after day.'

I ask her how she coped with that.

'I just don't know. You can see that people are scared, they are terrified of dying, worried about going on a ventilator and never coming off it. I was dealing with health workers terrified of catching the virus themselves and taking it home to their families and loved ones. I remember I told my husband and my kids that I would live in a hotel, but I just couldn't do it. I couldn't have survived without them. I would shower after work and scrub all my stuff before I went home. I was getting undressed in the garden to protect them and then, in the house, I would sit in the same chair. I couldn't hug my own son. He was crying, I was crying. It was awful.'

Did she ever think about her own mortality when she was surrounded by so much death?

'I tried not to think about it, you know, "What if I get it?", "What if I die?" I think that would have stopped me from doing my job properly. I've never thought about that in my twenty-four years of nursing before Covid. I was just trying to keep myself safe, keep my family safe and keep people alive. That was my motivation every day but, the longer it went on, the more you realised that we were losing the battle time after time. I felt a sense of helplessness for months. I knew that I couldn't save someone, but I could make sure that they didn't die on their own. It wasn't why I signed up to be a nurse. Have you ever tried holding someone's hand when they are dying? My colleagues were terrified. We just felt like sitting ducks with no protection from what we saw all around us.'

I ask May whether she and her colleagues spoke about what they were seeing and what they were going through, or was it just a case of ploughing on? May starts to cry. She doesn't stop. She apologises and tells me that it is still so raw and her colleagues are still so deeply affected by it.

She continues, 'There were a lot of conversations with colleagues about death. As a senior nurse, I just wanted to make sure that people knew that there was help when they needed it. We had what we called a "wobble room" – if you needed five or ten minutes to cry or scream then that was available for everyone. Some people chose to speak to the hospital chaplain. He was a busy man, but he did a great job for so many people. You can imagine that we formed a close bond and we became very protective of each other. That was the one real benefit from all of this . . . that bond between us became such a strong one. We had to rely on each other and help one another. I could see that some people were really struggling. There was a lot of trying to keep people's heads above the water.' May is still crying and takes a deep breath before continuing.

'I couldn't even tell my family what I was going through at work. How do you even begin to talk about that? All I know is that I am not prepared to do it again in this lifetime.'

'Did you ever think of leaving, May?' I ask. She replies immediately.

'Never. I never thought of leaving. I just wanted to focus

on the job in hand and fulfil my nursing duties. As a leader, I needed to show my colleagues how to be a nurse even when the job seems impossible. How can you ask people to risk their lives when you are not doing it yourself? I had no other option than to just carry on. I remember when I did my oath in nursing school. We promised to do our best for our patients. It didn't matter what I needed because someone else needed me more.'

May is keen to talk about the everyday stresses of working through a pandemic.

'You have to imagine what is going through the heads of a workforce that is under more pressure than they have ever faced before. Every day there are more patients dying and more patients arriving. At the start, there was not enough PPE and there was a race to get the equipment to treat patients. Every day you are thinking, "Is today the day that I get it?" You are under intense strain, people are dying around you, you are calling relatives, trying to look after yourself and others, you are all thinking about PTSD, and you are scared to go to work. If you cough at work, you are stared at by everyone and you're asked to test, test, test all the time. That is why I still wear a mask now,' says May. 'I think it's the legacy of everything that we went through. That was the one piece of protection that we felt we had.'

It's when you consider all that, you begin to realise why that morning with Maggie Keenan was such a big one for people like May. It marked what she hoped would be the beginning of the end of the nightmare.

'I gave Maggie the jab on a Tuesday morning, and they asked me about it at the end of the week before, I seem to remember,' says May. 'I had been part of the steering group for the delivery of the vaccination. I remember I was told that there "might be a few cameras" but I had no idea it would be as huge as it turned out. There were fifty NHS trusts rolling it out on the same day and I didn't know ours was the first. I met Maggie on the Monday before the jab. We talked about the fact that she didn't want to wear her hospital gown, so I went to buy her some clothes and I think that is where the famous T-shirt came from. I came and woke her up at 5 a.m. so that she would have plenty of time to prepare. I know it was hectic and there were TV crews everywhere, but I wasn't really looking at the cameras. I was just focused on Maggie. I knew she was ninety and I just wanted her to be ok.'

The significance of that day was certainly not lost on May and the rest of the staff at the hospital.

'I know that the pictures were important, but that day felt like a big one. I have done thousands of injections and I never thought that just one of them would cause such a stir. Covid had made us all feel like we were in the firing line, but the vaccine was our way of fighting back. It felt like a big step forward. Until then, we were feeling hopeless. We were looking after people with our hands tied behind our backs. I will never forget that day.'

I don't know if you lost someone close during the pandemic, but I do know that whatever you went through, it is something we will never forget.

And I hope that it stays that way but I wonder how society will look back on it all in ten, fifteen, fifty years. What will our children tell their children? How will history remember the death of so many? How many pages will it get in a textbook? As time passes I imagine it will be more about numbers and less about names. The individual stories will quickly fade.

That's why I'm so thankful to have had the chance to meet the people in this chapter and to learn from their experiences, sacrifices and heartache. I trust that you have been able to learn something too, and that you won't forget them.

STILL REMARKABLE

When the publishers of this tome first approached me to write a book in 2018, they wanted me to write an autobiography. I really didn't want to go down that road, because there are only so many copies my mum can buy. I asked if I could write about other people and that was the start of *Remarkable People*. I loved writing about some of the individuals who have made a lasting impact on me and I am still amazed by not only the number of people who wanted to read it, but the amount who still want to talk about the people in it.

There isn't a week that goes by that I'm not asked about Tony, Terrence or the orphanage in South Africa. I am often being asked how Ilse is, or whether I'm still in contact with John Sutherland.

When the opportunity arose to write another book, I wanted to revisit some of those individuals and see how they are getting on. They were 'remarkable' a few years ago and they remain just as impressive now.

Figen Murray is one of the people I get asked about all the time. She was the mother of Martyn Hett, one of the victims of the Manchester Arena bomb. It was a real pleasure to catch up with Figen again, although she doesn't appear in this chapter. You'll be able to find her in 'The Truth About Monsters', a chapter about forgiveness, which is such a central element to her story.

You might also remember Maria, the wonderful Brazilian I met on that beach in Rio de Janeiro back in 2016 during the Olympics. Well Maria, her husband and her beautiful daughter Joanna are still going strong in Portugal and we remain in close contact.

Let's start with John Sutherland, the former police officer, turned author, who remains one of the wisest people I have ever met. I didn't need to catch up with John for this book because we speak regularly. He is doing wonderfully well and, if you're interested in books, John published his first novel in 2022. It's a thriller called *The Siege* and it's brilliant.

I've also managed to keep in regular contact with Paula and Tony Hudgell. Tony is the amazing young lad who had his legs amputated after being abused by his birth parents. He was adopted by Paula and she has seen him grow into a gorgeous boy who, inspired by Captain Tom, walked 10 kilometres during lockdown on his prosthetic legs and raised more than a million pounds for the Evelina Children's Hospital in London – the hospital where he has all his treatment.

'Life has been pretty hectic,' says Paula. 'Tony went on to win a Pride of Britain award, which was amazing. Ant and Dec gave him his prize in Hamleys, but it was in the middle of the pandemic so they couldn't touch each other. His walking is improving all the time and his profile is growing too. One of the most amazing things that happened was when his photo popped up during the Queen's speech at Christmas. It was one of the 100 Photos Of Lockdown. It was so strange. I was late putting the telly on, as usual. It had just gone 3 p.m., she had started and the first thing I saw was a photo of Tony! I thought it must be a mistake but then my phone started going berserk. All my friends were contacting me. I had to rewind it to make sure it was actually happening. It just made me think of how many people he has been able to reach. How remarkable is that? We only set out to raise £500 for the Evelina and I think he's near enough £1.7 million now.'

'How are his legs?' I ask. 'Has he got new ones?'

'Yes,' says his mum. 'He has kept improving his prosthetic legs – he can walk unaided to a certain extent and he has knee bends put into his legs now. He is a lot more independent and able to interact with his peers. He is the same height as his friends now, which might not sound that important, but it's a huge thing for Tony just to be on the same eyeline as them. Some days he has to spend time in his wheelchair, but being able to stand next to his peers and look them in the eye, has changed his whole outlook on life. You wouldn't recognise him, Dan,' says Paula, oozing pride. 'He is so much more confident. For the first time, he can reach the surfaces in the kitchen, so he's making his own toast and hot chocolate. His whole world has opened up. He is a normal seven-year-old. He's even able to kick a ball around with his friends.'

Tony's issues run much deeper than his prosthetic legs. There are a number of ongoing health concerns and the emotional damage will always be there too. 'He is always going to have challenges,' says Paula. 'He will always need surgery on his legs, his hip permanently dislocates and his face will need looking at soon because his jaw is very small from the blunt-force trauma. He's had surgery on his wrist because so many of his bones were broken by the abuse, and his arms are deformed from all the injuries. That is the reality of the life away from the smiles you see on TV. You know I love him to bits, but he is a troubled young man.'

One of Paula's concerns when we spoke last time was the answers she would need to give Tony when he grew up a little and started asking about his birth parents. 'He asks more questions,' she says, with something of a heavy heart. 'He thinks his issues are due to being poorly from infection. It's heart-breaking sometimes. Recently he asked me, "When I'm older, Mum, will I have my legs?" He seems to think his legs might grow back. He has seen photos of how his legs were before they were amputated. We are always honest with him. If he asks the question about his parents, I won't lie to him. The last thing I want to do is for him not to hear the truth. I owe him that. They (his abusers) are both due to be released this year. That's always going to be there. I don't know how to deal with all that really.'

I ask Paula how she feels about Tony's abusers being back in society. Paula considers her answer for a moment. 'You know, she actually sent him a couple of letters via the charity Barnardo's? They are not appropriate for Tony now. When do we give him those? All we can do is do what we feel is right at the time. It's a massive parental conundrum – when do you show him? When do we open him up to all that? What is right for one child isn't right for another – people are always saying, "you should do this". Mark and I want to do the best for Tony. That is all we have ever wanted. It was strange for me. I do wonder how much remorse and understanding there is. I'm assuming that the letter was sent as part of her rehabilitation programme, but the real test will be when they come out in August. There are probation restrictions and there are limits and they can't make contact with him or any of us. If they break any of that they go back to prison. After five years on licence, they can do whatever they want. I do worry if she goes on to have another child. I worry about them changing their names and getting lost in the system.'

All this was the inspiration for Tony's Law, an attempt to see child abusers in England and Wales spending a lifetime behind bars. Under those changes, campaigned for by Paula, if a child survives, their abusers will spend fourteen years behind bars instead of ten and, if a child dies, the maximum sentence can be life imprisonment. Under the old system, the maximum sentence was fourteen years.

'It has been a struggle for us,' says Paula. 'Finally, Dominic Raab got it (Raab was the Justice Minister at the time). We went to his office to discuss Tony's Law and, to be fair to them, they have been really good at staying in contact. There are other things we want to do too. We want a Child Cruelty Register so that you are on there for life, even if you change your name, just like they do with sex offenders. The police can keep tabs on them then. It's about accountability. I'm also having meetings about a dedicated Child Cruelty Department within the Crown Prosecution Service. There is one for rape, one for murder, but nothing for one of the most complicated areas . . . child cruelty. Only 3 per cent of child cruelty cases actually make it to court and that has to change.'

Paula is formidable. She is a fearless campaigner who gets things done time and time again, but it has taken its toll on her health.

'I tried to get a GP appointment at the end of 2020, but we all know what that is like. I thought it was a flare-up of my IBS (Irritable Bowel Syndrome). I've suffered with it for thirty years. When it's one of our children, I just demand to see a doctor, but I'm not as pushy when it's me. I tried again in early January because it was getting much worse. I finally got to see a GP and was told I was probably alright because there were no lumps, but my blood tests were not right. I had a colonoscopy in mid-February and the doctor called me in and said he'd found a large tumour in my colon and it was cancerous. That was the biggest shock of my life. I was young at fifty-four and it had been there a long time so they needed more tests to see if it had spread. You fear the worst. I walked out thinking that my time was up. My biggest fear wasn't death but for my children and for Tony: I am his world, I do everything for him. I take him everywhere and I am his number one. If I am no longer around, who will look after him? It's not easy bringing up a disabled child. Everything moved really quickly. I had CT scans and an MRI and they found that the tumour had been there for ten years but it hadn't spread. I had it removed in March and it was far worse than giving birth to seven children. I woke up with a stoma bag and now I need a six-month course of chemotherapy because it was in my veins.'

I ask Paula how the family reacted.

'All the older children know. It's been a crazy two years with some real highs and deep lows. I lost my mum in 2019 and then my dad in 2020; both to lung cancer. The kids lost two grandparents in a short space of time and I felt a responsibility to show them that not everyone dies of cancer. I need to be around for my children. I need to be here for Tony. I am convinced he can do whatever he wants in life. There are no boundaries for this boy. He will have so many opportunities. He is bright and confident, loving and caring, and has a great sense of humour. Because of the surgery, I haven't been able to pick him up for months, but I've told him the world is his oyster. The one thing I want for him is to be happy, and he knows how to do that now.'

I remind Paula of the first time we spoke to each other for *Remarkable People* and we both cried as she told me about the consultant who was assessing all of Tony's injuries and said, 'Who would want this kid?'

'I am so grateful the consultant said that,' says Paula. 'That was the kick I needed. He made me see it. I was just doing my job and that day . . . Tony became my life and he has brightened all our lives. I don't think I would be as strong mentally if I didn't have Tony in my life. He is so positive about everything and that has made me try and take that onboard. When I had my cancer diagnosis, I was incredibly low for a while and Mark and Jess, who is sixteen, were a real mess. I remember saying, "We have to be like Tony," and that has pulled me, all of us, through so far. Tony never complains. His whole life is an uphill struggle and he just keeps on walking.'

There must be something about Tonys because we are going to move from a young superstar to a slightly older one. I am writing this chapter on a day when I have seen Tony Foulds again, back in the park where we first met in 2019.

Tony was in Endcliffe Park in Sheffield in 1944 when an American bomber called *Mi Amigo* crashed into the trees behind the current café to avoid children playing in the open field. All ten of the airmen onboard died. Tony was eight years old at the time and was one of those playing in the park. He says he has always felt guilt over their deaths and has spent many years tending the memorial in the park: sweeping leaves, planting flowers and telling anyone who will stop about the ten men he calls his 'lads'.

I met him and listened to his story just six weeks before the 75th anniversary and, with a little help from social media and a lot of help from the US Air Force, we managed to organise a flypast on the day of the anniversary and there were over 15,000 people in the park to see it as Tony stood alongside the family of some of those who had been onboard. It was a magical bit of TV watched by millions of people all over the UK and around the world. I wrote all about Tony in *Remarkable People*.

'I've had so many people come up, Dan,' says a very cheery Tony. I catch him on one of the many days he is blowing leaves off the paths around the memorial. The council have had to resurface the walkways behind the café because so many people are visiting Tony these days.

'They all tell me that they've read your book. I reckon I'm due some royalties,' he laughs. 'I hope this next one is even better. University!' he shouts at me. 'I've had people come from all these universities today. It's been lovely. There was a time that nobody walked down this side of the river. I'll have to blow all the way to the M1 soon. I can't have it dirty.'

I watch as Tony breaks off to speak to a family who have turned up with a family member who is 101 years old. They still remember the war well and Tony relives his own memories and talks about visiting the graves of the men who died in the park in 1944. Once he's finished chatting, and retold his joke about the M1 again, he returns to talk to me and give our dog Winnie a little stroke.

'You and this dog have changed my life, Dan.' I had promised my wife I would walk Winnie in the park on that day in 2019, but I was late for work, so we went a different way to normal which took us past the memorial. That led to the meeting with Tony.

'I am invited to all these events,' he says. 'The US Air Force have been great. I go and visit memorials all over the country now. I have been to, let me see, Norfolk, Bedworth, Derby, Nottingham . . . I even got invited to Edinburgh! Do you remember Dan, a few year ago, when I asked you if you thought it would all go away? You said that we'd have to wait and see, but you thought that people would always be interested. Well, you were right. It's gone mad.'

Tony has picked up a number of awards and is a regular visitor to US air bases around the UK where everyone knows his name. There was a trip to America planned to visit the home cities of the men of *Mi Amigo* but it was another casualty of lockdown.

'I was thinking of writing to (President) Biden,' says Tony. 'I wanted to ask him to look after them properly, you know, the graves. I have seen some of them on pictures. They are just a little stone, same size as two house-bricks. I would want to go and visit all the graves. I thought when we first started that they were all in the Arlington Cemetery, but they are all over the USA. I just feel so happy that so many people know about the lads now. They teach about them in schools and I get people from South Africa, Australia . . . all over the place, who come here just to see it on their trip to England. I had one last Monday from Winnipeg, in Canada. "We've come to see you, Tony," they said. Can you believe that? From Canada!'

We walk back to the memorial together. 'I want it to be the best-looking one in the country, Dan,' he says, bending down to pick up a leaf which has fallen on the path since his latest blowing session.

'If you look,' he says, pointing at the memorial, 'we now have ten vases for each lad and I buy the flowers for the vases. At the front we are full of flowers and full of colour. The shrubs are fully grown; there are ten tubs with shrubs and flowers, ten pots full of pansies and ten vases full of fresh flowers. I don't accept money and if anyone insists I send it all to Duxford where the last *Sally B* is – to look after that.' (*Mi Amigo* was a B-17 Flying

Fortress and *Sally B* is the last remaining Flying Fortress in Europe and is stationed at Duxford.)

'I've even been invited to other memorials to help people look after them,' says Tony, puffing out his cheeks. 'I can't get round them all, Dan, but these last three years have been the best ever. I'm too busy down there to get poorly. The Park Run goes past the memorial now; twice every single Saturday. The organisers have given me a proper tunic so I'm now a marshall for the run. They all wished me "Happy Birthday" this year. It were great.' He pauses and looks me straight in the eye. 'April the second, by the way.'

Tony says his connection to the story and to the men who died in Endcliffe Park feels stronger than ever. 'I do feel much closer to these lads,' he says, resting his hands on some of the pictures at the memorial. 'When I come down here now, my son and my daughter say, "Are you going home?" I hate leaving them and I hate going away, but I've got a good friend who checks in on them when I'm not around.'

One thing that has changed is the Stars and Stripes that flutters in the wind above the memorial. The flagpole was erected after the flypast and was part-funded by a local school in Sheffield and the rest came from Boeing. Every time I walk past, it reminds me of just how far the story reached, touching everyone from a primary school around the corner from the park, to a multinational company. Tony loves it too.

'As far as I know, we are the only place allowed to fly the flag in the UK,' he says, with an understandable degree of pride. 'It actually came from Omaha beach in Normandy. It were flown on the anniversary of D-Day and it were flown specifically for the *Mi Amigo*. It were given to me by RAF Mildenhall and I were given permission to fly it outside a military base, which never normally happens. We only ever used to be able to fly it on the day of the anniversary (22 February), but now I just bring it down to clean it.' Tony looks up at it and the tears start to well in his eyes. 'Doesn't it look beautiful?'

One of the questions I often get asked about Tony is how he is doing healthwise. His essential tremor is slowly getting worse but he continues to look after himself.

'I am eighty-six now, Dan. There isn't much I can do. I've been told that the Chinese are making a bracelet and it does stop the tremors, but it's a bit chunky. I have now joined an essential tremor association that meets in Sheffield. That's been great, but I can't have a shirt with buttons; I can't have shoes or coats without that sticky stuff, you know . . .'

'Velcro?' I suggest.

'That's the stuff,' says Tony. 'I love that stuff. I can't use knives or hot things and it's worse in the morning and it's worse when I'm stressed. The only thing that helps is whiskey but, as you know, I don't drink. Although, I do think my milk and egg helps.'

'You what, Tony? Milk and egg?' I reply.

'Yep. When I used to be a bodybuilder, and enter competitions, I would mix raw eggs into milk and drink it all down. I have that every now and again, but most of the time I just drink fiddy fiddy.'

'You'll have to help me out with that one, Tony,' I say, laughing. 'Is that fifty fifty, as in half tea and half milk?'

'No, Dan, fiddy fiddy is half tea and half coffee. Every morning on our estate, I pop into Steve's Café for a mug of fiddy fiddy. I'm not allowed to make any hot drinks myself because of the shakes, but Steve brews one up every morning. It used to be the old toilets, you know.'

'What did?' I ask.

'Steve's Café. They turned the toilets into a café. It's great. Fiddy fiddy every day.' Tony laughs and slaps me on the back. 'He says I am the only one who drinks it.'

I tell Tony I'm not overly surprised and tell him I'll see him soon.

'You'll still come and see me, won't you, Dan?' he says.

'Of course. What do you mean?'

'Well, you're one of my best mates, and I keep being told that you've left the BBC and you've gone to Channel 5. You won't forget about me, will you?'

I give Tony a hug, assure him that I'll still see him in the park each week and tell him that, just for him, I'll try out a mug of fiddy fiddy. I did. It was awful.

Of all the interviews I have ever done, I still think that the one with Ilse Fieldsend is the one that keeps coming back to me. I spoke to her during a show on BBC Radio 5 Live in 2015. It was a special show, based at the Queen Elizabeth Hospital in Birmingham, looking at the issue of donors and transplants. Ilse came on to talk about her daughter, Georgia. In 2013, they had been on a family holiday to Egypt when Georgia collapsed with a ruptured brain aneurysm on a beach. She was rushed to hospital and eventually back to the UK where her parents had to make a decision about donating the organs of their dying child. Georgia died that night but she saved four lives with her kidney, her liver and her heart valves. There are two young men who can see because her parents took the heart-breaking decision to donate her eyes too.

Ilse's life was torn apart that night and she still lives in the shadow of that loss. She is broken but brilliant and, for all those who ask me how she is doing, that's where I started when we caught up with each other again.

'We are ok,' says Ilse. 'We are surviving. We are happy, our son Joshua is getting on with life and I am a professional dog walker.'

Ilse's son Josh is turning eleven this year. Georgia would have been twelve on 10 May 2022.

'Josh is talking to a counsellor at school which has been really helpful. He finds it hard to see happy families and he is talking to her about loss. I think he finds it hard to come to terms with why we lost Georgia and why it happened to us. We are still working through it all. In the past, I have done a proper party and invited all of Georgia's friends on her birthday. I make a rainbow cake, we crank the music up and have balloons but, on other occasions, we just keep it quiet. I am worried. I feel quite nervous, like I can't be Georgia's mum in the way I used to. People forget, which is totally understandable, but I can never forget. Once or twice a year I talk about organ donation and I go on radio stations and I think that helps me as much as it helps others. I still want people to ask me about her. That's why I was happy, sad and a bit worried when you asked me to talk to you for your new book, because I don't talk about her that much anymore. Life does go on. You have to be happy, you have to try and fit in. I have to be a happy parent for Joshua.'

The pain is still very much on the surface with Ilse. She still feels like a mother of two even though Georgia has been gone for almost a decade.

'Losing a child is like losing a limb,' she says. 'It's a part of your heart that will never be repaired. Her bedroom is still the same as it always was and I still sleep in her bed. I'm better, but it's still hard to move on. I see her friends becoming young girls and I wish I could be there for her to guide her through as a mum. I'm much better at coping with comments like "You are so lucky you don't have a girl, boys are so much easier". I never have a go at anybody, but my heart breaks every time. I have become far more tolerant with time. I used to react if someone said, "I can't wait to get rid of the kids after the holiday", but now I just smile.'

I ask her if she feels she'll ever not need to sleep in Georgia's bed.

'I know that people will read this and think that I am doing the wrong thing, but this is my way of getting through the days. I don't think I can ever get rid of her things. I still take a few of her dresses away with me when we go on holiday. I just want to feel her presence. She goes on holiday with us too. I can't see that changing any time soon. We take her ashes with us. That is how I cope. I am sure it will change. I just feel that when I wake up I can't breathe because I don't feel as close to her. I think one of the main reasons is that I can do less for her. When I did the charity song, or the coffee mornings to raise awareness, I still felt like her mum, but sometimes I feel like she is disappearing. I have to hold on to her. I know I won't love her any less if I didn't sleep in there, but I want her to know that I am still with her.'

Ilse is right, it is very easy to judge her, but it's also impossible to know how you would act if you found yourself in that situation.

'When we go out for a meal it's hard when people say, "Is it just the three of you?" My head says, "What are you doing?" I know deep down it is all too much but, at the moment, this is where I am. I have done therapy but it hasn't really worked for me. There is only so much you can say about how sad you are. It doesn't help, because nobody can bring her back. I don't tend to bother too many people with Georgia because I know I become too much to cope with. That's why I sent you so many messages when you asked me about my daughter again, because not many people want to talk about her.'

Ilse still gives talks about the importance of organ donation and, occasionally, her son asks her about where his sister's organs went. Ilse would love to be in contact with all the people who were helped or saved by Georgia, but she knows that is a choice that the recipients have to make for themselves.

'I know that one of her kidneys went to a young boy and he is now healthy. Every now and again, we get letters to say that he has gone from being in hospital all the time to being young and healthy. That is great to hear and the point I always make is just encouraging people to talk to their loved ones. We have an opt-out donation system now, but it's still essential to discuss plans because, as we found out, nobody wants to have to make those death-bed decisions.'

Ilse often speaks to her auntie and uncle who lost their daughter, Sandy, when she was nineteen in a car accident. Her cousin's death had a huge impact on the then fourteen-year-old Ilse, who still asks her auntie and uncle how they cope, how they move on and how they managed to move house but still hold on to the memories. There are many people who have contacted her since reading about her story in *Remarkable People*.

'There was one woman,' says Ilse, 'who said that she hadn't spoken to anyone until she read the chapter about Georgia in your book. She told me that the only way she could feel close to her dead son was to sit in the bath and pour his ashes over her. It's so easy to judge, but she was completely lost. When you've been through something like that, and feel it so deeply, you inevitably lose friends. I am sure she has and I know I have. It's just part of life. I'll keep going. I'll keep loving and supporting Joshua and hopefully, the next time we speak, Dan, I'll be able to tell you that things are improving.'

I know we are all trying to move on from the pandemic, but the next person I wanted to catch up with was one of those who put a big smile on many faces while we were all worrying about coronavirus. Kia Tobin was the care-home worker whose video was watched by millions when she presented resident, and veteran, Ken Benbow, with a cushion with his late wife's photograph on it.

Kia is a fascinating woman with big plans for the future and quite a bit has changed since she went viral during a virus.

'I left the care home last year,' says Kia. 'It was a really hard decision for me but, because we had to live there at the same time, it got to the point where there was no separation from my work and home life.'

Kia now works as a healthcare assistant at The Harbour, a mental health hospital in Blackpool. 'It's weird because I always wanted to work there. It opened in 2016 and I was about fourteen or fifteen and mental health has always been something that has interested me. My goal in life is always to work with people, all different sorts of people. I find it so rewarding to help so many different individuals with different issues and I'm able to work with all sorts of different conditions. We are a hospital, so we get patients who need rehab. They are dealing with things like bi-polar, personality disorder and schizophrenia and my job is to build up good relationships with them. I don't expect them all to like me, but there is something amazing about trying to get to the bottom of people's problems and seeing them progress.'

I ask if she misses the care home where, like many employees during the pandemic, she moved in to try and keep the residents safe.

'Of course I miss aspects of the care home. I miss the residents, I miss Ken. It was a big thing for me to leave but quite a few people left. I miss that family vibe, but things change. I got myself in a place where I wasn't able to not take work home with me. I was trapped and I don't think it would be the same now. I think he found me leaving quite hard to understand, but I have to remember that it's a job and I've grown up a lot in the last two years.'

Kia turns twenty this year and still wants to eventually work in Africa. 'I would love to keep going to work, get all the qualifications I can, and then I can go to Africa when I am twenty-five with the funds, the means and the knowledge. I want to make a difference in the world and I think I can really help people there. I'm enjoying life here at the moment, though. I am managing to help a lot of my friends with their issues too and I've had problems of my own as well, but I feel like I am learning all the time.'

Kia has moved on, but does she still think back to the madness around that video which sent social media into a spin and saw her and Ken appear on TV stations around the world? 'I was on a training course the other week and the first thing someone said was "Were you on TV?" It all seems like a bit of a blur if I'm honest. It just happened, I rode it out and I look back on it with fond memories. It's more important to me that people saw what it was like for carers during the pandemic. We all did the clapping for carers and it was lovely to get a bit of recognition for people working outside the NHS too, because there are thousands of us, and it was brilliant that so many young carers progressed and saw value in their jobs even though we were all going through something that was so horrible.'

*   *   *

If you have an amazing memory you might recall that the first chapter in my last book was centred on the work of two women. One of them, Winnie Mabaso, is sadly no longer with us, and the other, Lisa Ashton, is the woman who was inspired by Winnie and is trying to continue her legacy.

Lisa runs the Winnie Mabaso Foundation which currently funds an orphanage in South Africa and, as she told me when we caught up with each other, they have big plans going forward.

'I actually had a cheque this morning,' says Lisa with her customary bubbliness and enthusiasm. 'A £1,200 donation from a group down in East Sussex who read about us in your book. We get so many encouraging messages and so many people who are now supporting us on a regular basis.'

Lisa takes time out every week to write back and thank the charity supporters. It's one of the many things that mark her out. When I last spoke to her, there were plans for a second home, a forever home, for girls who were moving from the main house at Ilamula into full-time employment. Lisa has some exciting news.

'We are busy preparing our new property, Tropic House. We bought it in 2020 and it was completely dilapidated. It has taken us an age to do it up because of the pandemic, but two of our staff are living there at the moment and Palesa (who we met in the last book and is now twenty-one) will be one of the first to move over there.'

Palesa was one of the shining stars in *Remarkable People*. She was from an abusive home and found love and hope at the Winnie Mabaso Foundation. When she first moved there, her sisters were still stuck in the family home, but eventually they were able to join her and the three of them have thrived under the same roof.

'Palesa is now at college studying hairdressing,' says Lisa. 'She got 88 per cent in her latest creative assignment and is doing really well. My dream is to bring her to the UK one day . . . then you can get to meet her in person.'

Palesa's two sisters, Maki and Lerato, are still at Ilamula and loving their time at high school.

'We have two new little girls in our family now,' says Lisa. 'They are our first two Muslim children so we've had to introduce halal food to Ilamula. They are both sisters, only two and four years old and they take us up to twenty-three girls in all.'

The plan, eventually, is to have twelve older girls based at Tropic House. As the numbers continue to grow, so does the size of the job for Lisa.

'I think, like all charities, the last few years have been a real struggle. A lot of people who would normally have donated have found it tough during the pandemic, but we have just about managed to ride out the storm. The joy for me is for all the girls to have the opportunities to better themselves, but it's hard to be hands-on when you're stuck here in the UK. Before Covid, I was able to spend a month here and a month in South Africa but, like everyone else, we had to rely on video calls. I was back out there in March of 2022 for the first time in two years and it was incredible to see them all again and to see them all maturing. They were safe and loved and cared for by an extraordinary team in South Africa. By the way,' asks Lisa, 'did you get to see all our videos and pictures during *Strictly*, Dan?'

I did. The girls at Ilamula sent through regular good luck messages and cards and I showed them all to Nadiya throughout our time on the show.

'They loved doing them,' says Lisa, 'and it's just one of the ways we try and keep them connected to their international family. They definitely feel it and it makes a difference to them all. They were so excited when you made it to the quarter-finals! I think this is part of what makes the Winnie Mabaso Foundation so special . . . it has always been about family.'

In that 'family', many of the girls call Lisa their mum. She provides the love and care of a mother and what I have always found so inspiring about her is the fact that she goes further than most of us. Most of us have an ability to see a need but we rarely get to the 'what am I going to do about it?' stage. Lisa is already there. She spoke so powerfully in *Remarkable People* about how she was driven to help by looking through the back window of a charity food bus to see children chasing the vehicle holding an empty bowl. That image has stayed with her because, in her mind, there is always another child somewhere who needs food, who needs help, who needs lifting up. She is managing to teach that attitude to the girls at Ilamula.

'Let me tell you about Forgiveness who is twenty-one,' says Lisa. 'This year, she has started studying law at university. She wants to be an attorney because she says she wants to be a voice to the voiceless. How cool is that? She wants to help people who haven't had the same start as her. I am always impressed by how children are so remarkably resilient; you want them to thrive but you also need to help them repair their broken lives. These girls have been through so much, but they are so happy and so positive and they are so filled with joy. Our charity house is not a place of sadness. You've seen that, Dan, for yourself. It is a place of joy.'

I first visited the orphanage, on its old site, in 2010 during the football World Cup in South Africa. It was an amazing day where we showed the children a football match for the first time on a giant TV screen. In those twelve years since that visit, the charity has been able to do so much and, even though they were slowed down by the pandemic, Lisa says they have been able to re-start all their additional activities on a nearby squatter camp.

'We are back in business,' she says with a smile. 'We did have to rethink what we did on the camp during the pandemic. All the clubs had to stop but we could still deliver food parcels. Our focus shifted from face-to-face work to practical care with basics like sanitiser and toiletries. Everyone was telling them that they needed to wash their hands for twenty seconds, but it's hard to do that when you have no soap and no running water.'

I ask Lisa to run me through all the things they are currently running for the local community. 'This may take a while,' she says laughing. 'Ok, we have a pre-school, an organic gardening scheme where one hundred families have been trained to grow their own vegetables, a library, a mobile clinic where we do smear tests, blood tests and injections, a granny club, a mother and baby group, a homework club, meals on wheels and we are still doing the basic food delivery drops too. I think that is everything.'

The workload is exhausting. In an attempt to run the charity without any overheads, Lisa remains the only employee in the UK and there are forty-three people working in South Africa.

I ask her if she ever thinks she needs to take a break from it all and she replies in typical Lisa fashion. 'You can't take a break from life, can you? It's not a job. I can't take a holiday. This is what I do!' She laughs . . . 'I know I look one hundred and four years old at the moment, but my focus at the minute is on getting Tropic House up and running as soon as possible. I want to support the girls as best we can. We invest a lot of money in their education, but we just want them to grow up and be thoughtful and loving in life too. Many of them have been through so much trauma and have missed huge chunks of their childhood. We are trying to restore all that. You can't take a break from that. They are never going to stop being my girls. They will never stop being my family.'

From Lisa, with her massive extended family, to a man who spent twenty Christmases on his own.

I first met Terrence on the *BBC Breakfast* sofa in December 2019. He was taking part in a loneliness campaign for the charity Age UK and, during our chat, he talked about the fact that he'd spent every Christmas Day on his own since the death of his mother two decades before and he didn't even have a Christmas tree.

I said we would try and help him out, and a local college in his home town of Oldham got involved and we turned up at his house that night with a tree and a choir to sing his favourite carol, 'Silent Night'. He was very teary on the doorstep and the piece that we made about our visit went around the world and was watched millions of times.

Terrence's life changed dramatically. He became something of a local celebrity and has kept his friendship going with Oldham College. The best news is, he no longer spends Christmas on his own.

He did promise me that he was going to celebrate his eightieth birthday by doing a skydive, and that's where we started our catch-up.

'My doctor wouldn't allow me to do it at all,' says Terrence. 'He told me straight. He said I was a diabetic with asthma and he also mentioned that I'd had a heart attack. I said, "When you put it like that . . ." He told me there was no way he would sign a form to let me do it. I can't skydive, but I can still help people and that's what I love doing. I've been in the caring profession all my life. I left school at fourteen with no qualifications whatsoever but, when I eventually got into nursing when I was twenty, I took to it like a duck to water.'

Terrence has always fought for the downtrodden. When he was younger he was brutally bullied and never fought back. His father was particularly cruel about his dyslexia and Terrence has struggled with confidence his whole life. He retired at the age of fifty to become a full-time carer for his mum, but his life changed immeasurably after that appearance on *BBC Breakfast*.

'After talking to you, people started recognising me. I had a funny experience last Sunday. I was serving teas and coffees for a charity and a ninety-two-year-old said to me, "I know you from somewhere . . . you were on television!" If I was to tell you the number of people who have stopped me, you would never believe it, Dan. I couldn't understand the impact at first. It changed me a great deal. It hasn't made me a different person, but it has made me appreciate things a lot more and it has also brought the struggle of loneliness and isolation to a lot of people's minds. I was alone at Christmas, but loneliness is a 365 days a year problem. I know you won't put this in your book, Dan, but it's all down to you really; you are a very kind and caring man. It's always about more than just the story, you are interested in the people involved and you don't forget them.' (If this quote is still in the book, it's because the publisher wanted it kept in.)

Terrence still loves talking to other people. Nancy, the woman he spoke to every week through Age UK, died last year and Terrence really misses her. In the last two months, he has lost three good friends to cancer.

'I get my joy from volunteering and staying busy. My mother has been gone for twenty-one years and I still miss her every day. I had Christmas dinner with my friends Andrew and Simon this year and I will never forget my Christmas in 2019. I am still in contact with the kids at Oldham College. I am so thankful for their friendship. I know a lot of people out there are still struggling and need help, but I am no longer a lonely old man. Friendship has changed my life.'

*   *   *

It was a real treat to catch up with Terrence and with the rest of the people in this chapter who all featured in *Remarkable People*. I love the fact that they are all still carrying on quietly being amazing in their different corners of the world.

When I left *BBC Breakfast* in 2022, the production team made a wonderful leaving film which included getting Tony and Terrence together. They spent a lovely day with each other. Terrence remembers watching the flypast and told Tony it was one of his 'favourite ever bits of TV'. Tony said it was a real pleasure to meet Terrence. When I last met up with him I asked him if they got on, and Tony answered as only a Yorkshireman can . . . 'Me and Terrence? Aye, we got on. He were a reyt lad.'

THE TRUTH ABOUT MONSTERS

How do you see forgiveness? I have always thought that it is a quality which is easy to admire in others but becomes a lot more complicated when it arrives at our own doorstep.

If you look at the clinical definition, the websites and self-help manuals will tell you that forgiveness means different things to different people. Generally, it involves letting go of resentment and thoughts of revenge. The act of forgiveness doesn't entirely remove the pain, but it helps to free you from the control of the person who you feel has wronged you. It can even lead to feelings of understanding, empathy and compassion for the person or people who hurt you in the first place.

I did a search online and found a list of eight benefits that forgiveness can lead to:

Healthier relationships

Improved mental health

Less anxiety, stress and hostility

Lower blood pressure

Fewer symptoms of depression

A stronger immune system

Improved heart health

Improved self-esteem

The manuals also speak of all the potential complications which centre around how the person you forgive reacts. What if they don't change or are repeat offenders? What if forgiveness doesn't lead to reconciliation?

As a Christian, forgiveness is a fundamental part of my relationship with God. A simple search of the word will produce verse after verse encouraging us to forgive others because God has forgiven us. The Christian's understanding is that God's forgiveness flows from Jesus' sacrifice on the cross for the sins of all of us. Forgiveness is at the heart of God's character and Christians are called to be 'loving' and 'good' and to follow that example.

That is one of the many reasons I have great admiration for people who are able to forgive others. They are the sort of people who show us all that forgiveness is not a theory, it is something that you have to practise. It's hard sometimes to get our heads around, particularly when you see it in others and you try and put yourself in their shoes. I want to focus on three women in this chapter who have all found it in their heart to forgive. I have learned so much from talking to them and they have certainly challenged some of my preconceptions.

The first of them is someone we met in my last book, *Remarkable People*. I have no idea in which order you have read the chapters of this one but, if you've read the 'Still Remarkable' chapter before this one, you'll know that I didn't include Figen in there, but I did promise to catch up with her as part of this chapter.

Figen Murray is the mother of Martyn Hett, one of those who lost their lives in the Manchester Arena bombing in 2017. Despite suffering immeasurable loss, Figen took it upon herself to try and learn about why the terrorist chose to do that to her son. It also started her on the road to forgiveness. She began studying counterterrorism and has been pushing for legislation in her son's name – Martyn's Law – to make sure venues are better prepared in the event of another attack. When I caught up with her, she had just completed her Masters.

'I must have been mad undertaking the whole thing,' she says. 'When I look back now, I had started the Masters when I was attending the trial of Hashem Abedi in London.' Hashem Abedi is the brother of Salman Abedi who actually carried out the attack. Hashem Abedi helped organise the bombing and is serving a life sentence.

'I would go to attend my Masters in Preston in the morning and then get a train to London – writing essays on trains and in hotel lobbies. I didn't want to be a special case. I just wanted to be like everyone else. I just stayed up all night sometimes with my laptop and a pizza. It's strange how you get motivation for things like that. I got through it and got it done. I was writing my dissertation in a corner of the family room of the Old Bailey, but I managed to get a distinction.'

Figen now spreads her time between speaking at conferences, going into schools, reading the occasional novel and working on the implementation of Martyn's Law.

'I am still having regular meetings with those in government. The final details are being put together. It might still take some time. I am impatient, but I also want it to be right. I have worked on it for such a long time and people need to be able to use the law properly, so I want to make sure we have thought of everything. It won't be about his name, it has always been about making sure that no one had to go through what I went through. I also thought that once Martyn's Law comes in, I could disappear but I realise I can't do that now. I expect plenty of teething problems and there are going to be a lot of issues and chaos and people wondering what they should and shouldn't do. I have embraced that role and I don't mind going and talking about security. The UK is at the forefront of good modelling and I have to keep pushing that through. I look a little bit different to the bald men in tattoos that you normally associate with the security industry . . . but I can be just as persuasive,' she says with a glint in her eye.

On the day after the anniversary of Martyn's death in 2022, Figen was going to Washington to speak at an international security conference. Her work has spread far and wide. Her guiding principle is that she wants us to be more resilient as a nation. She wants adults and young people to take part in counterterrorism training programmes. She is convinced that she can change the world around her and, while she is doing that, she is also a mother who misses her son.

'It doesn't get any easier. I don't enjoy doing all these talks, but I know it's my job even though I just feel like I'm a mum to Martyn and the rest of the family. I always feel like he is at my side and it's teamwork between him and me. I am doing it in his memory and he drives me on. I love him so much. It's hard for me to explain, because I miss him more than ever and yet I find it hard to look at photos of him sometimes. I still cannot look at his photo on the windowsill.'

Whenever I think about Figen's story, I think about the bear. One of the ways she copes with grief is to spend her time making them. She gives them names and a backstory and sells them for charity. She mentioned in *Remarkable People* that she wanted to make one very special bear using the pieces of metal that were left in her son's body after the blast. The police had always told her that she would be able to get the pieces back once the inquiry had been completed. In the early days after Martyn's death, Figen also started collecting screws and nails off the floor. Her plan was to melt all of them down and mould them into the shape of a bear with its arms outstretched. In those outstretched arms, the bear would be holding a heart shape, made out of the pieces of metal that killed her son. It would be a permanent reminder to Figen that out of the depths of hatred and pain, she could find love.

'I have everything back from the police now,' says an emotional Figen. 'It still feels very raw and the days before the anniversary are always the hardest. I find it helpful when another anniversary is over. It's almost as though a fresh year of grieving starts. The whole of May is a tough one for me. As each day approaches, it gets more and more uncomfortable. There is too much to think about. I don't want to be consumed by grief. It is there in the background and then, as soon as the anniversary goes, I have a fresh drive to carry on living and to get on with life again. I remember the day after the first anniversary I told Stuart, my husband, that I could breathe again. There are a lot of things I am doing now that I could never have done in the first twelve months, but I have fresh energy every year.'

Figen is still making the bears. 'They help me on the bad days. There are some days, Dan, when I know it's going to be a tough one, and what I tend to do is get myself a cup of tea, put on a TV show and surround myself with ribbons, wool and buttons and that is my happy place where I can recharge. I keep things very basic. I don't run away from days like that anymore. I know I have to work through them. I know those days are important for self-care. I am better at looking after myself. I knew I was talking about Martyn to you today, so I am going for a walk with my friend after this. All of that helps.'

I ask Figen if she still has plans for the bear holding the metal heart. She takes a long pause before answering. 'I do,' she says hesitantly. 'Some of my children are struggling with having too many things about Martyn around the house and I understand that. When I do get it done, I don't think I will be displaying it in the house. It will probably go in there,' she says, pointing to a cupboard. 'I will get it done because, whether I look at it or not, that is my "up yours" to terrorism. I can turn what killed my son into a heart and that is how I try and make sure that I am not eaten up by the bitterness and the hatred. I don't need to look at it every day. It is part of the whole process for me. Grieving is a journey and it's something that is so precious and important to me. It would be the end of a chapter for me, and the bear will be a symbol of love for me going forward. I can't wait for it to be done. It's on my mind a lot.'

As I prepare to ask Figen about another topic, she raises her hand. 'There is something else, Dan. You won't believe this,' she says as her eyes widen. 'I have stopped collecting screws and nuts and bolts and, ever since I made that decision, I haven't found any. For years I have just found them everywhere, without ever really looking for them. I sit down, and there would be one next to me. I cross a road, and there would be one there on the floor by the kerb. They used to just appear in front of me but, ever since I decided to stop collecting them, I haven't come across a single one.'

The bear is all part of the continuing grieving process for Figen. As a trained psychotherapist, she can see the stages she is moving through very clearly.

'The bear will complete something,' she says confidently. 'It will free up time for me to do other things. It will give me more head space. I don't need the screws anymore. I don't need that crutch. The next task for me will be to really step up the number of talks I give to school children.'

Figen tells me that the day after we talk, she is going to speak to 1,000 children about her experience. That means she has personally addressed nearly 20,000 kids since Martyn's death. I ask her what she tells them.

'The first thing I talk about is Martyn and the others who died that night. I talk about my visit to the morgue. The last thing I talk about is the power of online radicalisation. I admit that my generation has made a mess of things and remind them that theirs can sort it out. I ask them how many of them want to become parents in the future and I remind them that they have a huge responsibility to teach their children the right values. In between those two things, Dan, I talk about Ubuntu.'

Feeling a little ignorant, I ask Figen what 'Ubuntu' is all about. 'I love explaining this,' she says. 'A few months after Martyn died, a woman sent me a message on Twitter. She said that she had read all about him and it made her so upset and reminded her that life was too short. She said that it had given her the motivation to fulfil her lifetime dream of moving to the Gambia. She had made the move and, once she was there, she asked a man to build her a boat. She asked him to put some words on both sides of it. On one side there was the hashtag *#BeMoreMartyn* and on the other was this word, "Ubuntu". The woman explained to me that it is an African concept that means "I am because you are". As soon as I heard it, I told my husband that I had found the name for our house. You see,' explains Figen, 'all the houses on our street have a name except ours and I knew that one day I would find the right name for it; a name that summed up all the things I felt about Martyn; something that encapsulated his kindness, his empathy and his compassion, and there it was: "Ubuntu" – I am because he was. He inspires me every day. That's why I talk about Ubuntu. It is the one word that brings it all together.'

Figen remains a remarkable woman. I find her attitude to life and loss incredible. I love the way she quietly works things through at her own pace and how she is aware of her fragility and limitations at the same time as recognising her strength. I'm glad she is taking care of herself and, when we spoke, I told her I was going to write about the subject of forgiveness. One of the schools she is going to speak at is the school where the

Abedi brothers went. How does she feel about Salman Abedi, the young man who killed her son? How does she feel about forgiveness?

'His name is just a name,' she says. 'I forgave him very early on.' I am reminded of the story Figen told about seeing the face of the bomber on the front page of a newspaper for the first time a few days after the explosion. She froze on the spot and was struck by how young he was. 'He was in his early twenties. What on earth would you know about the consequences of your actions at that age? I remember wondering why he would choose to throw his life away.'

Figen also recalls the incident four weeks after Martyn's death which had a significant impact on her. 'My family had all gone home. My husband had gone back to work and the doorbell and phone stopped ringing. I suddenly found myself at home on my own. I went across to the Co-op and I bought some newspapers. I opened the front page and there was a picture of five men linking arms and a guy on the floor. It was a picture from the Finsbury Park Mosque attack in London. The guy on the floor had tried to kill them and they were there protecting him, telling people to get back until the police arrived. I had the whole day to think about that picture and it had a big impact on me. When my husband came home from work that night, I told him that I was going to go on the BBC the next morning and publicly forgive the terrorist for what he did. My husband thought I was completely mad, but I told him that when there was so much hate and anger around, it was really important for me to try and rebalance things.'

I ask Figen if that act of forgiveness has allowed her to get to where she is today. 'When you are a therapist you learn a lot of skills. I think I have told you before that I used to tell my clients to imagine a helicopter when they face what they think is an impossible situation. I tell them not to worry about not being able to fly it but to imagine getting inside and looking at what they face from as high above as possible. That's what I did for myself because, from that perspective, you can also see solutions. You will see things much more clearly. You can see people who can help you. You are also further away from the pain, the suffering and the anger. I could see the terrorist as a baby. I remember thinking, "You were not born a terrorist". My overriding emotion was always sadness that I had lost Martyn. I was never angry with the terrorist. That was helpful on my road to forgiveness.'

The other thing that helps Figen is speaking to others. She wants to reach as many people as she can with Martyn's message.

'I want us to be kinder to each other. I want to live in the UK where most adults have skills to help others because they've had the training and I want to live in a world where it's safer to go out to the theatre, to the cinema and we know that our children are safe. We talk a lot about post-traumatic stress but I firmly believe there can also be post-traumatic growth and that is what I am experiencing. I am convinced that, if I wasn't trained as a psychotherapist, I would have gone under after Martyn died. I am not spiritual, but I do believe that everything happens for a reason and I am convinced that I was given the tools, the years of training to deal with what landed in my life.' Figen stops talking. This is clearly something she has thought about a lot.

'Maybe Martyn needed to die for this law to happen. There are questions I cannot answer. There are roads I dare not even turn down. There are bridges I will never cross. I have come to the point where, even though it has broken every part of me, I can accept what happened. I will never be able to explain it, but I have learned to live with it . . . to live without him.'

I am not sure 'enjoy' is the right word, but I do enjoy every conversation with Figen. She always gives you something to think about, something to take away and use in your own life.

'Can I leave you with a poem, Dan?' she says, before we say goodbye. 'You asked me about forgiveness and, when I was studying for my Masters, I used to sit next to another mature student because, as you know, the older ones tend to stick together. He was a former police officer and we would often share our experiences. He sent me a poem one day and said, "I don't know if this will help you but, when I read it, I thought of you." It's called "The Truth About Monsters" and it has helped me because it has reminded me that my enemy is not Salman or Hashem Abedi . . . my enemy is terrorism. I don't hate those young men, I hate what they became, what they did to my son and to others and what turned them into that. The best way to defeat your enemies is to learn about them. Those are the first few steps on the road to forgiveness.'

'The Truth About Monsters' by Nikita Gill

> *The truth is this:*
> *every monster*
> *you have met*
> *or will ever meet*
> *was once a human being*
> *with a soul*
> *that was as soft*
> *and light*
> *as silk*
> *Someone stole*
> *that silk from their soul*
> *and turned them*
> *into this*
> *So when you see*
> *a monster next*
> *always remember*
> *do not fear*
> *the thing before you*
> *fear the thing*
> *that created it*
> *instead.*

I have always wanted to talk to Mina Smallman. The first time
I heard her speak was when I watched her on television saying

that she had forgiven the man who had brutally murdered her daughters.

Mina was the Church of England's first female archdeacon from a black and minority ethnic background. She also used to be a schoolteacher.

On 6 June 2020, her life was ripped apart when two of her daughters were murdered by a stranger at Fryent Country Park in Wembley, north London. Bibaa Henry was a social worker and Nicole Smallman was a photographer. They were celebrating Bibaa's birthday in the park with friends. In the early hours of the morning, Nicole sent a message to her boyfriend saying she and her sister were still dancing. Soon after, the girls were dead, stabbed to death by Danyal Hussein, a nineteen-year-old satanist who was determined to make sacrifices which he thought would enable him to win a lottery jackpot. He stabbed the two women nearly forty times.

It was Nicole's boyfriend who discovered the bodies after the police did not search the park. To make an awful tragedy even worse, Mina was later informed that the two police officers who were guarding the crime scene, Deniz Jaffer and Jamie Lewis, took photographs of her daughters' dead bodies and posted them on WhatsApp groups where they referred to Bibaa and Nicole as 'dead birds'. Mina decided to take on the Metropolitan Police because she was convinced there was a racial element to the treatment of her daughters. She firmly felt that if they had been white women, the park would have been searched and the two officers would not have taken the photographs.

'Forgiveness is an interesting concept,' says an eternally

thoughtful Mina. 'I have spent a lifetime forgiving injustices that have been done to me. I have had to fight hard for most of my life. As a black woman you spend a lot of your life being over-looked. Sometimes it makes you angry and then you become the "angry, black woman". I have made mistakes too and I hope people can forgive me for those. I don't believe you can forgive alone. I see it as a gift of grace from God. The Lord blessed me by allowing me to let Danyal Hussein go. He is not my respon-sibility. As soon as I heard about his satanic motivation I knew it was not my job to judge him. It was at the point that I heard about his pact with the devil that I can say the Holy Spirit came down and filled me with peace and strength. I knew I was equipped with what I needed to forgive him. It was a feeling that I was being held and it is so hard to explain to anyone who hasn't had that experience. I released that burden. If I'm honest, I don't think about him at all. Forgiveness is a gift, but you have to be open to that gift. The gift I was given was the load being taken away from me. That is what I feel. I turned to God and asked Him to help me. "I need you," I said, and He was there.'

Mina is dual heritage. Her mother was white and Scottish, her father a black Nigerian. 'When you are from that back-ground, you have to battle just to be heard,' says Mina. 'I went through the education system when there was a whole issue of treating black children as if they were educationally subnormal. There were individual teachers who gave me so much support and went out of their way to help me, but the system was built against me. As I got a bit older, people I was with would talk about black students in a derogatory way and say, "Present company excepted" and I would be like, "What do you mean?" They would say, "Not you, you're different, Mina". The level of ignorance was staggering at times. I remember being told that "someone like me" wasn't clever enough to do Shakespeare at school! Maybe that's what drove me on to become a teacher of English Literature and Drama. Drama was my passion.'

Teaching is where it started for Mina. She taught drama for fifteen years before feeling the call to join the church. She was ordained as a priest in 2007, served as a curate in Harrow and Stanmore and was then appointed as the Archdeacon of Southend in 2013 where she served for three years until her retirement in 2016. During her time in the church she had to take many funerals, preparing people to remember their loved ones once they had gone; skills she had to use herself. The death of her daughters was one thing, but the actions of the officers at the crime scene made her feel like she had lost them twice.

'Bibaa was a lot like me,' says Mina. 'She was "Marmite". Loud, proud and a real dynamo. She was a brilliant social worker and really streetwise. Nicole was a talented musician and super cool. She had gone to performing arts school and, even though there were a lot of years between them (Bibaa was forty-six and Nicole was twenty-seven) they were best friends. It was devastating to lose them and I hadn't even thought about what they looked like until I was told that those two officers had been taking photos. You start thinking about it, you start picturing it all in your head. You're trying to do the everyday normal things like getting up, getting dressed, but it's all you can think about. You've been robbed of normality. All you're trying to do is hold yourself together to function, but you just keep going back to why they chose to do that to my girls.'

Mina found it in her heart to forgive the killer, but it has been much harder when it comes to the police officers. She agreed to meet with them as part of a restorative justice process but that offer was withdrawn after the two officers decided to appeal against their thirty-three-month sentence for misconduct in a public office and Mina attended the hearing.

'I don't hold any malice or hatred, but I haven't forgiven them,' says Mina. 'When I was listening to their unsuccessful appeal I thought I was going to pass out from the stress. I could feel my heart pounding in my chest. I was having this incredible physical reaction to what their advocates were saying. Jaffer's defence lawyer was arguing that the photographs were only shared with close friends and didn't go any further than that. He said things like, "It was part of the culture to share photos from work" and compared it to saying, "Look at what I'm doing today." It got even worse when the barrister asked us to think about how his two teenage daughters would cope while he was in prison! That's when I thought the stress of it all was going to kill me. What about the impact his actions had had on others, on me and my family? Part of me wants to meet with them and talk to them about their attitude to women and how destructive it is, but I'm not sure I could do that at the moment.'

When you think about what Mina had to endure, you can see why it might be hard to ever think about a resolution, but she still comes back to the issue of forgiveness.

'Maybe I will be able to forgive them one day. I'm not ruling it out, because Jesus Christ is my ultimate example and perhaps I just need a little more time. I don't hate them. I feel . . .' she pauses, 'let me think . . . neutral. I am still cross about what they did and why they did it. The good thing is, I don't think about them. I wish we would focus on the victims more. Look at the Prince Andrew situation,' she says. 'You have the Archbishop of Canterbury talking about forgiveness for him, but why is our gaze on him? What we need to focus on is not the suggested, or alleged, perpetrators, but the victims. We need to concentrate on helping them to put their lives back together and helping them to find peace in this life. To my mind a lot of these cases come back to that issue of white privilege: men of a certain age feeling that they have the power to do whatever they want, to whoever they want, wherever they want. It's the same when it comes to women's safety at the moment, which is something I am passionate about. So often the people discussing it are old, grey, white men; people who have no lived experience. I don't think that only women can speak for women but representation is essential and, now I'm retired, I love the freedom to say whatever I want. It's quite liberating.'

I ask Mina what she would say to her daughters' killer now if she had the chance. 'That is a great question,' she says. 'If you'd found me ten years ago and said to me, your daughters are going to be killed by a satanist who thinks he's a member of the Aryan race, I would think I would struggle to forgive him for doing that. I think about the sort of mum I am. I would do anything for my girls. When Nikki said she wanted to go to Thailand, I told her that if anything happened to her there I would go full

Liam Neeson and come and find her. Nothing would stop me, like in those films. What are they called, Dan?'

'*Taken*,' I suggest.

'That's it! That would be me. But now, when I think about him, I don't think I would have any words for their killer. I don't know if he'd be able to hear it. I really upset him at the trial, because I think he thought he could intimidate me. I just smiled and winked at him and I think that really annoyed him. There is nothing I could say to him that would make a difference. I just hope that one day he sees the impact of what he has done. There is a verse in the Bible, in the book of Ezekiel (chapter 36, verse 26), which talks about God giving someone a new heart. It says that God can turn a "heart of stone" into a "heart of flesh" and that is my prayer for him, that God would do that for him. I hope he experiences that one day. There is nothing more powerful than God's forgiveness, than realising that the world doesn't revolve around you, that you are not at the centre of the universe, that God is in control and he has a plan for your life.'

It has been fascinating to talk to Mina. She is so open about her experiences and, just like Figen, has no issue when it comes to the things that she struggles with. Her husband deals with loss very differently. He keeps himself active and their different approaches have actually brought them closer together. They don't judge each other for the way they have chosen to grieve. Mina finds that talking about her struggles makes her stronger and those 'struggles' are not just mental. She suffers with Chronic Fatigue Syndrome and Fibromyalgia. On three separate occasions she had to postpone our chat because her energy levels were so low.

'This has all taken its toll on my body,' she says with a sigh. 'I have to balance my energies really well. I can't sign up to things because I don't want to let people down. I was diagnosed with it before, but all the stress and anxiety has definitely made it worse. I wasn't in a great place. I shy away from promising more than I can do, but I know I have a purpose and I know I can still do good in this world.'

I ask Mina what is next for her, where she wants to be in five or ten years' time.

'I just want to still be here,' she laughs. 'If I'm still here at seventy, I'll be celebrating.' Mina is currently sixty-five but worries about her family history. 'I come from a weak gene pool, Dan. I am the only one left and I shouldn't really be here. My dad died from a stroke when I was sixteen and my mum was born with cardiomyopathy (heart disease) and was always struggling. Talking about forgiveness, I'm not sure my mum could have forgiven the killer for what he did. She was of good tartan stock,' laughs Mina. 'She would be baying for blood. My brother has gone as well. He was seven years younger than me but also died from cardiomyopathy and my older sister passed away after a five-year battle with cancer. I think the murders finished my sister off. Anne was very close to Bibaa and I found it really hard to talk to her at the end of her life because she only ever wanted to talk about the girls and I couldn't bring myself to do it. It's too hard for me. I couldn't even go to Anne's funeral because it was at the same place the girls had theirs. It was too soon to go back.'

Mina says sometimes she feels like she is two different people: the campaigner who challenges bias and prejudice and who took on the Metropolitan Police, and the mother of two murdered girls. Anyone who watched Stacey Dooley's recent documentary about Mina will have seen them both: the activist and the mum. The activist, empowered and ready to take on the world; and the broken mum, who feels like she can't leave the house to go to the shops because she doesn't want to be seen. Grief is a powerful master. Mina is as fierce as she is fragile.

I tell her it's amazing that, despite all she has been through, she has been able to forgive the man who has had such a devastating impact on her family.

'Remember, I have found the strength to forgive from God. I couldn't have done it on my own. Forget about the health issues; the hatred and the anger would have killed me by now otherwise. I was able to let go of that and I am so thankful that I did.'

Does she have any advice for someone else thinking about forgiveness?

'If you have lost someone like me, the most important thing is to remind yourself that you are not letting your loved one down by letting go. If you let the anger eat you up then the murderer wins. Try, with everything you have, to let that anger go. It still hurts. I still miss my daughters more than anything, but forgiveness has given me the chance to live the rest of my life, however long that is, without the weight of bitterness.'

*　　*　　*

The final person I want to tell you about is Tamar Pollard. Just like Figen and Mina, Tamar lost a family member in horrific circumstances.

'Mum and Dad were in Prague in 1968. They were on a youth hostel holiday and they woke to the news that the Russians had invaded. They knew that people's lives would change overnight. They were both Christians and they thought about what it says in the Bible's 1 John chapter 3 verse 17: "If anyone has material possessions and sees a brother or sister in need but has no pity on them, how can the love of God be in that person?" They were both challenged by that and a friend said to them that they were both teachers, with long holidays, so why didn't they use them to come back each year and bring humanitarian aid? So that's what they did. That's what we all did as a family.'

From the age of seven months old, Tamar travelled around Europe with her parents. They would spend one summer in northern countries like East Germany, Czechoslovakia and Poland and the next a little more south in places like Romania, Yugoslavia and Hungary.

'We rarely spent more than a day in one place,' says Tamar. 'Our van was always loaded with basic foods like flour, sugar, coffee and tea and we would give out toys, clothes, sweets and we would sometimes take prescription glasses too. Every year we went, sometimes at Christmas, but every single summer. We started off in a Skoda; I had to sleep in a hammock pulled across the back of the car! We had camper vans, and in 1990 we had one with a shower! I remember we thought it was the height of luxury but Mum and Dad just used it for storage.'

Tamar was one of three children. She has an older sister, Rebecca, and Andrew is her younger brother. They all have some incredible stories to tell and Tamar just drops them casually into the conversation.

'The Romanian revolution was on my thirteenth birthday,' she says, very matter-of-fact. 'I remember that one. I know I stopped going on the trips in 1993 when I stayed in the UK to do my GCSEs, and we were once stuck in Yugoslavia during a war, and there was another time that there was a military coup in Kiev and we had to rush to get out of Ukraine as quickly as possible.'

Tamar was marched at gunpoint when she was eight years old on the Hungarian-Romanian border. 'My sister was twelve and Andrew was six. I remember they searched our vehicle and they found that we had food, clothing but also some Bibles which had been translated into Romanian and Bulgarian. They said it was illegal and they wanted more than £3,500 to let us go free. We went to the toilets on the border and I tore up the addresses of the people we were going to visit and flushed them away and my sister hid money in her pants. The guards said that we had to give them the camper van and they took Mum as hostage! We were marched back to the nearest town in Hungary and Dad had to spend the next few days at the local post office. He organised a loan to pay for Mum to be released, and we did get the van back but we were banned from Romania for five years. When we got Mum back, she joked that it had been the most peaceful part of her holiday. We all laughed but we also knew how serious it could have been. Lots of people back home thought Mum and Dad were mad taking us on their travels, but it was just something we did as a family. It was a bit different to a fortnight in Tenerife!'

Tamar started out resenting the long summer trips but eventually enjoyed them. 'I saw them like a *Famous Five* adventure. In some places we weren't allowed to talk in the street, we could never stay in one place for long but I saw some amazing things. I went to orphanages in Romania at the age of thirteen and I realised how much I had back home. I started to see how big a sacrifice my mum and dad were making for others. I was amazed at how much they cared and my eyes were opened to what it meant to love your neighbours without question. They saw their job as serving other people.'

From 1996 onwards, things changed. Tamar, Rebecca and Andrew would stay in the UK for their education or work and their parents travelled alone. The kids were given a rough itinerary and they would get a phone call every now and again to say the van had broken down, but there wasn't ever day-to-day contact. One night in 1997 changed everything.

'Mum and Dad were going through Slovakia and then Hungary on their way to Romania,' recalls Tamar. 'As they drove, the lights on the camper van failed. They used to try going through border crossings at night because they were much quieter, but the roads were poorly lit and really bumpy so they pulled into a lay-by. It is something they did quite regularly. It was a Monday night, 4 August. They were woken up by two men who said they were police officers. They were trying to fine them fourteen pounds for staying in the lay-by. Mum and Dad knew they weren't proper police, but they paid the fine and the officers left them alone. The problem was, they had seen inside the van and it was packed with stuff for Mum and Dad to give away. The two men came back and Dad jumped into the cab and tried to drive off. One of them got through the driver's window and beat Dad to death with an iron bar. They left again, but Mum knew they would soon be back. She tried to resuscitate Dad but he was gone and she couldn't drive away because he was slumped over the steering wheel. She hid everything valuable she could think of and she just had to wait there for them to return. They came back with someone else and beat her, strangled her and left her for dead. She woke up on the Tuesday morning and couldn't see because they had sprayed something in her eyes. Eventually, someone stopped by the side of the road and took her to hospital. She looked awful, so bad that the police translator collapsed at the sight of her. Mum's jaw had been shattered and she couldn't speak.'

The news of Michael Pollard's death was broken on Sky News on Wednesday 6 August at 6 o'clock in the morning. At the time, none of his children had been informed. Rebecca was working in Leeds in IT and she was the first to hear. Andrew was woken up by the *Daily Mail* at the family house and Tamar was doing voluntary work with children in Broadstairs in Kent.

'Someone came and got me but I wasn't told anything,' remembers Tamar. 'I was walking up the hill back to the main building thinking, "Maybe I have to take over the cooking for the day." I wondered what I had done wrong, especially when I saw there was a policeman waiting for me. He took off his helmet, which is never a good sign. In my head, I remember thinking, "Dad's dead," but he was just talking about Mum. It was like an out-of-body experience. I knew he was talking to me, but I was in total shock.'

Tamar had to call the foreign office. Tamar's mum, Jo, was in a bad way. The children all met at Heathrow and on the plane they got complimentary copies of the *Evening Standard* newspaper. Their parents were on the front page. 'I just hadn't processed it at all,' says Tamar. 'We were upgraded to business class and I was looking around watching people reading the news while they were drinking a glass of champagne. I felt like shouting at them, "THIS IS MY DAD YOU'RE ALL READING ABOUT."'

When they arrived in Hungary it was late. The next morning they had a three-hour drive to the hospital and, upon arrival, they heard that the three men who killed their dad had been arrested. One of the things their mum had successfully hidden in the van was the receipt the criminals gave them for the traffic violation. Jo had put it behind the cutlery drawer. She had planted £50 in a purse near the door in an attempt to distract them and it worked. It really was amazing clarity of thought when her husband had just been brutally murdered and she was convinced they were coming back to finish her off.

I asked Tamar why her mum didn't run away from the van to try and escape.

'My mum was raped when she was nine years old,' says Tamar. She took a deep breath. 'Ever since she has been terrified of the dark. She knew they were coming back for her, she was wondering what they were going to do with her, but she couldn't even think of walking the streets because, as a child, she was attacked when she was walking home from school. The man grabbed her off the street and, later in court, admitted that he'd planned to kill her and dispose of her body. Her whole life, you could never put your hand near her nose or mouth because it freaked her out. That's why she stayed in the van . . . she was more afraid of walking around outside so she waited for them to come back.'

The men who attacked her were arrested on the Thursday morning. One was eighteen years old and the other two were twenty-two. That morning, the children walked in on their mum as she was doing a live interview with the local news back in Yorkshire.

'I was listening carefully to what she was saying, but it wasn't sounding like Mum at all. Her jaw was still broken and she was so battered and bruised. I remember that it was the first time in my life I felt proper hatred in my heart. I was in a rage and it got even worse because, at the end of the interview, she told the TV station that she didn't bear any malice and she said, "If there are any Christians listening, can I ask them to pray that these men just didn't know my forgiveness, but God's forgiveness." I could have exploded. How could she say that when they'd tried to kill her and killed my dad? How dare she forgive them! I stormed out of the room and just stood on the balcony. I was angry with my mum, angry with God. The reality of my dad's death really kicked in and with that came all sorts of questions. I stood fuming on the balcony thinking, "Do I believe God is real?

Do I believe God is good? Is he kind?" I was wrestling with all this, but I knew the answer was "yes" to those questions. I had seen that from my own life. I was convinced that God was not just big and powerful but that he was interested in the small, tiny details.'

This was all racing through Tamar's brain during that thirty minutes on the hospital balcony. 'I was out there thinking, if this is all true, how am I meant to act? I knew I was meant to forgive because I had been forgiven but, at the time, it was just too big an ask. I was in the depths of despair. That is a lot to think about on a hospital balcony, but I firmly believe that God gave me the ability to forgive. As I prayed to him, I asked him to turn hatred to forgiveness, to turn anger to peace. I walked back into the room and told my mum that I could be with her in this. I have found that forgiveness is a daily choice. I am still working it through. It didn't reduce the grief. I was twenty and my dad had been murdered.'

Tamar's mum was in hospital for a week. The family needed to get back home for Andrew's A level results. The fact that Jo had forgiven Michael's murderers made the story even bigger. They arrived home the following Wednesday to a press conference at Leeds Bradford airport.

'I didn't know how I should look,' says Tamar. 'Did I need to look sad? Should I smile? What should I wear? People were staggered by the forgiveness thing. They couldn't get their heads around it. What Mum had done went against everything in human nature. She kept getting asked about revenge and she was asked why she wasn't angry after all the people they had helped, over so many years, across Eastern Europe. She was on the front pages of magazines. It was discussed on *Kilroy* and there were double-page spreads in the newspapers. She got a bravery award from the Queen and Tony Blair. Andrew got his A level results the next day.'

Jo Pollard seems like a remarkable woman. What she went through was truly tragic and the strength she showed in those first few days after the murder is hard to get your head around. Her ability to forgive baffled many of those who heard about it, but what she did next didn't make as many headlines but is arguably even more impressive.

Jo went back to Hungary in January 1998 with Rebecca for the trial. She wanted to look her husband's murderers in the eyes. The judge gave her the opportunity to say something at the end. She told them to their faces that she had forgiven them and gave them all a care package to help during their time in prison. It included toiletries, stationery, sweets, biscuits and a Bible. She asked to stay in contact with all of them and two out of the three said they would like that. For years they exchanged letters.

'I think about it a lot,' says Tamar, 'the way she treated those men after what they did to her. They nearly took her life away and she wanted them to have theirs back. The local mayor erected a memorial on the first anniversary of Dad's death. Mum kept going back too. She visited the two of them in prison, and one day she received a letter from the eighteen-year-old. His name was Istvan Dudas and he was the one who had beaten Dad to death with the iron bar. It said, "I caused death but I found life". He said in the letter that he just couldn't get over how she could forgive him. He said that whenever they met, Mum was always "banging on about God" but he had become convinced that he had to look into whether the Bible was true because Mum's faith was so real and there was no human explanation for it. The man who killed my dad had become a Christian.'

Jo Pollard got early Alzheimer's and died in 2008. In 2017, Tamar went back to Hungary on the twentieth anniversary of her father's death.

'Dad's killers were sentenced to six, seven and eleven years in jail so they are all out now,' says Tamar. 'I have tried to find them through Google and Facebook a few times, but the only photos I have are from 1997. I couldn't recognise any of their faces on social media as their names were quite common, so I didn't want to message the wrong stranger. I don't know what I would say to them if I met them . . . "Hi, you killed my dad!" I would love to know what they are doing. I would like to tell them that I forgive them too, just like my mum did. It is easy to say that when you are not in the room with them, but face to face it would be an incredible challenge. I would love to hear how their life is and, after being shown so much kindness by my mum, I want to know what they did with that.'

Tamar, just like Figen and Mina, is at peace with her decision to forgive and it has enabled her to continue to live her life. When you speak to her about what forgiveness looks like, she's honest and says sometimes you have to re-forgive and sometimes you have to remind yourself that it's ok to feel like that. She talks about the freedom that comes from letting go of your right to justice and fairness. We can all feel like we are entitled to get something first and, when we are wronged, we want people to know. Forgiveness means letting go of that sense of entitlement and, as Tamar told me time and time again, trusting God.

'What happened in 1997,' says Tamar, 'of course that shapes who I am, but it doesn't define me and, if I hadn't forgiven them, it would have defined me. I am shaped by what happened, but I am not defined by it.'

Tamar's brother and sister have been on their own journey. Rebecca found it hard for years and Andrew graduated in 2001 but then moved back home to become his mum's main carer when she was diagnosed with Alzheimer's.

'For a long time we didn't talk about it,' says Tamar. 'Forgiveness is one thing but tragedy and guilt leave deep scars. We don't do what normal families do and discuss memories from childhood and we all process it differently. I buried myself in work, I still do.'

I'll be honest with you. I've been sitting here and I haven't written a single word for about twenty-five minutes. I'm thinking about how I would react if I had a loved one stolen from me like Tamar, Figen and Mina. Would I be able to find a path to forgiveness? Having spent hours talking to these three incredible women, one thing that links them all together is that they would all say they are in a better place because they were able to forgive. They also all have something in their lives to keep them going. Figen has her passion for teaching the next generation about counterterrorism, Mina remains half-activist, half-mum and Tamar has a passion for working with children and is about to move to Australia to start a new job. She takes huge inspiration from the way her parents cared for others.

'The more I think about it, the more I am staggered by what Mum and Dad did together. They were models of faith in action. They trusted in God's goodness and they taught me to be thankful for what I had and gave me a deep appreciation of other cultures, other ways of thinking, other ways of doing things. They spent their lives trying to understand others and they didn't see the boundaries that most of us see. They used all their time, all their money, all their holidays to help other people. I often think about them and, in the light of their actions, I ask myself what I'm doing. What am I investing in? How effectively am I spending my time? As I've got older, I think a lot about how we look after people who struggle. When Dad died, lots of people didn't know how to support me, and that has made me really aware of others who find themselves in that position and how I walk with them and care for them. I am much better equipped to help because of what my parents showed me, because of what they taught me. That is their legacy. I know it cost my dad his life and I know my mum's Alzheimer's was accelerated by her head trauma but, even though I wouldn't have chosen my life to go that way, I wouldn't change it. My mum and dad trusted in God above everything else and their love for Jesus shone out in their lives. She'll never know it but, when Mum forgave those men, just a couple of days after they killed Dad, she changed their lives and my life forever. I miss them both but my world is so much bigger because of what they showed me.'

ACKNOWLEDGEMENTS

I am never entirely sure what to put at the end of a book. I know I have to write a few thank yous and I'll get to those.

I really hope you have enjoyed reading about the people in this book. I have loved speaking to them and writing about them even though this all happened at the busiest time of my entire life.

I had just finished *Strictly Come Dancing* and then I started doing most of the interviews for *Standing on the Shoulders*, just at the time when I was having discussions about leaving *BBC Breakfast* to go to Channel 5. It was all happening at the same time!

What kept me going were the incredible people I was talking to. With each one of the chapters in this book, I have felt a deep responsibility to tell the stories with great care. Many of the people in here have either not spoken before or have trusted me with their deepest and most personal feelings.

So, the most important thing is to thank them all for their time and their trust.

Thank you to all those who were happy for me to pester them again after already appearing in *Remarkable People*. Paula

Hudgell, Lisa Ashton, Ilse Fieldsend, Terrence, Kia Tobin, John Sutherland and Tony Foulds . . . you are all amazing individuals, and my suggestion is we all get together for a cup of Tony's famous fiddy fiddy.

Thank you to the wonderful Rose Ayling-Ellis and her mum Donna. Rose mesmerised the nation during *Strictly* and learning more about her relationship with her mum and how she made such an impact on all of us, and Giovanni, was a real treat. I loved writing that chapter and I'm absolutely delighted that Rose agreed to write the foreword for this book too. She is officially the best!

A special thank you to my professional partner and two-time world champion, Nadiya Bychkova. Most of the people in this book have made me think about others in a different way; she changed the way I look at myself. With her mix of skill, style and serious hard work, she showed that I could enjoy something that I thought was completely beyond my capabilities. She also taught me how to eat a chocolate biscuit properly (chocolate side facing down). If you've never tried it, get involved. Believe me, it is a game changer.

My deepest appreciation also goes out to those who were willing to talk about loss. Figen Murray will never stop amazing me and Mina Smallman and Tamar Pollard were willing to tell their incredible stories of forgiveness in the face of such brutality. There is so much to take from their testimonies.

Tim, Mike and Andy – known collectively as the 3 Dads – continue to inspire millions of people out there, including Hollywood superstars like Nicole Kidman, who I still can't quite believe was happy to be part of this book. Thank you to Nicole, and to Kate Morley for helping to set that up.

The chapter about the 3 Dads was actually the first one that I wrote for this book. I don't mind telling you that, once I had finished it, I was in a bit of an emotional state for a while. I couldn't come back to the writing for another six weeks because I couldn't stop thinking about what they had been through and how heart-breaking it was. They have all been wonderful to deal with, as was Sandy, the man who found Sophie's body, and, to my mind, is a pretty incredible man. We could all do with a Sandy in our lives.

The chapter that took me the longest to complete was the one about the terrorist attack on Fishmongers' Hall. The interviews with Darryn Frost and Steve Gallant lasted for hours and I was so careful in trying to thread their stories into the chapter in a way that didn't glorify the violence. The event is still so raw for Darryn, for Dave and Anne Merritt and everyone touched and damaged by the actions of Usman Khan that day. I often think about the final words that Jack Merritt's mum uttered at the inquiry when she read out some of the tributes to her son: 'His death was a tragedy but his life was a triumph.'

One of my favourite chapters to write was the one about Jimi Olubunmi-Adewole. I was so struck by the love that his friends and family had for him. I learned so much about the life of someone who comes to the UK from talking to his old school friends David, Joseph, Marvellous, Adiatu and Yinka, and I thought that Bernard displayed a wonderful gift in being able to describe the beauty of real friendship and what it means to live in the light of that. My love goes out to Jimi's family, and thank you to his older brother, Ayodeji, for agreeing to be such an important part of that chapter.

The two people that made me laugh out loud on numerous occasions over the past few months are Paul and Nick Harvey. I've loved their relationship ever since I first met them on *BBC Breakfast* and it was a real delight to talk to them at length and to see the pure talent that Paul possesses in his fingers when he sits at a piano. It was lovely to hear from Nick, Alix and Dominic – his old students – Pete his former colleague, Grace from the dementia charity and Sir Tom Hunter who was one of those inspired by their appearance on the TV in the middle of lockdown.

Which brings us to the chapter 'Beyond the Pandemic'. I don't think any of us will ever forget those eighteen months from March 2020 onwards and coronavirus leaves a deep legacy, particularly for the people who feature in that chapter. The names of Maggie Keenan and May Parsons will always be associated with the way out of the hole the world was in, and Heather, Saleyha, Syira and Josh represent some of the thousands of families ripped apart by the loss of a loved one. I really appreciate the fact that they gave me the opportunity to tell their stories.

The final interview I did for the book was with the amazing Martin Hibbert. When I first spoke to him for this, we finished our chat by saying we would catch up after he'd climbed Kilimanjaro. Having done it myself for Comic Relief, I was aware of the scale of the challenge but there was no doubt in Martin's mind that he was going to get to the top just over five years after he was left without the use of his legs after the Manchester Arena bomb. I am part of a WhatsApp group that Martin used to update people on his climb and, in the video he posted on the day he reached the summit, he said, 'Don't write someone off just because they are in a wheelchair.' I get the feeling we will be hearing a lot more from Martin.

There are a few other people I need to mention. I want to thank my wonderful wife Sarah for being a constant support and encouragement. She remains a regular source of wisdom and I know how frustrating it must have been to see me come home from work and then disappear off to write this for the rest of the day. She is amazing, as are our three gorgeous children Susanna, Jessica and Joe. I hope they get to read this book one day and get an insight into some of the incredible people their dad gets to meet at work.

Many of these chapters came from conversations that started on the *BBC Breakfast* sofa. I loved my time on there, first with Louise Minchin and then Sally Nugent, and the team behind the camera remain some of the very best I have worked with. A significant thank you to my old boss Richard Frediani and, in particular, to Liam Blyth and Charlotte Simpson for their help and support – even though Liam ignored one of my texts for eight weeks.

I must also sprinkle a little love in the direction of the team at my publishers, Headline, led by Jonathan Taylor, who has once again been a delight to work with and a real encouragement along the way; and to my agent Jonny McWilliams for being a permanently present sounding board. Jonny was also the man who persuaded me that it was a great time to write another book.

I'm really glad he did, but this book has taken a long time to write and also a long time to think about. I have often found myself staring into the distance for vast amounts of time thinking about how I would respond to some of the situations in here. I have mentioned my faith in a few chapters and I kept coming back to the same thought: there is no way I could have dealt with some of the things detailed here without my faith in God.

When I was in the depths of writing one of the chapters, I could hear my kids playing a song downstairs. It's called 'Christ Is Mine Forevermore' by CityAlight and it includes lyrics I have kept coming back to:

> *Mine are tears in time of sorrow*
> *Darkness not yet understood*
> *Through the valley I must travel*
> *Where I see no earthly good*
> *But mine is peace that flows from heaven*
> *And the strength in times of need*
> *I know my pain will not be wasted*
> *Christ completes his work in me*
> *Come rejoice now, O my soul*
> *For His love is my reward*
> *Fear is gone and hope is sure*
> *Christ is mine forevermore*

My final thank you goes to all of you who, for the last few years, have asked me when the next book was coming out after enjoying the first one so much. I hope you have found the people in here just as inspiring and I look forward to talking to you about it all at either a book-signing, an event somewhere or wherever we happen to bump into each other.

I'll be happy to talk about anyone in here because I think they are all amazing. Many of them have come face to face with some of the most destructive waves that the sea of life can throw at us. 'Don't make it too sad,' said my wife when I started writing this and I hope it isn't. There is certainly sadness in here but there is also hope. I trust you can see that hope alongside the love, the encouragement, the determination, the struggle, the fight and the light at the end of the sometimes very long tunnel. What I wrote at the end of *Remarkable People* remains just as true a few years on . . . life can be a struggle and, as Joseph said in the chapter about Jimi, 'the struggle is real'. It arrives at our doorsteps in many different shapes and sizes. For some of us the battleground is grief, illness, persecution, stress, family breakdown, death, abuse, injury, but what I hope you've seen in these pages is that the people here are trying to find a way to cope with some of the horrors they have faced.

I don't know what trials you are currently facing in your own life, but I truly hope you have found something or someone in this book to inspire you. The people I have written about are those who, I think, help to give us a clearer picture. They are the people who enable us to think differently, to see further than we would on our own and sometimes change our perspectives. The people in here might not know it but, to me, they are 'giants' and I hope you've enjoyed spending some time on their shoulders. It has been an incredible honour to write about them all.

I am off to celebrate with a giant slice of cake.

INDEX

3 Dads
  background 79–91
  fundraising 91–5, 102
  poem for 109–11
  relationship 109
  suicide prevention awareness 83,
    101–3
  walk 95–101
3 Dads Walking 91–5
  JustGiving notifications 95
  the walk 95–101
100 Photos Of Lockdown 273–4

Abedi, Hashem 301
Adiatu (friend of Jimi) 190–8
Age UK 295, 297
Ahsan, Saleyha 250
Ahsan, Syira 250–8
Ahsan-ul-Haq Chaudry 250–8
Aleksander, Stef 56, 205
Andy (Sophie's father)
  death of Sophie 72–3, 88–90
  drive to Edinburgh 89
  fundraising 91–5
  grief 88–91
  half-marathon 90
  meets Mike 83
  meets Tim 83
  and Papyrus 83, 90
  relationship with Sophie 71–3
  and Sandy 103–7
  void 90
  the walk 95–101
Annabel (Emily's sister) 79–80
Arch, Dave 53
Ariana Grande concert bombing 1–8,
  301–10
  memorial service 20
Arlington Cemetery 281
Ashton, Lisa 290–5
Atkinson, Ron 19
attitudes, changing 67
autism 70
Ayling-Ellis, Donna
  acting weekend 36–7
  the final 61
  impact of *Strictly* experience
    62–8
  on the moment of silence 55
  pride 36, 43, 56, 57
  Rose's acting career 38
  and *Strictly* 45–6, 49–50
  Strictly announcement 42
  and *Strictly* trial 41–2
  support for Rose 32–4
  World Cup dream 57–8

Ayling-Ellis, Rose 32–68
  acting career 38
  acting weekend 36–7
  battles 39
  childhood 37
  confidence 37, 65
  Couple's Choice 50–5, 58
  on dancing 47–8
  drawing 36
  DW first meets 33
  exhaustion 59
  the final 59–63
  first job 37
  four '10's 49
  impact 56
  impact of *Strictly* experience 62–8
  importance of *Strictly* to 55–6
  as inspiration 34–5, 62
  likes surprising people 33
  moment of silence 50–5
  moment of silence achievement 54–5
  movie week 47–9
  Mum's support 32–4
  and music 47
  pain 45–6
  partner 54–5
  paso doble 58–9
  performance 48
  positive about being deaf 51
  responsibility 56–7, 66
  Spotify playlist 48
  Strictly achievement 55–6
  Strictly announcement 42–3
  Strictly appearance 32, 33, 35
  Strictly Day one 43–4, 44–5
  Strictly training 35
  Strictly trial 39–41
  supermarket job 37–8
  tango 49
  team support 56–7
  Trafalgar Square BSL rally 67
  week one 46–7

Bags for Strife 96
Ball, Zoe 205
BBC Breakfast x, xi, 7–22, 220–1, 239, 242, 250, 296–7
BBC Radio 5 Live 284
#BeMoreMartyn 306
Benbow, Ken 288, 289, 290
Bertoncello, Arduino 51
Beth
  background 70
  beautiful voice 77
  death 76–9
  poem for 109–11
Biden, Joe 281
Biometric Residency Permits 194–5, 196
Birmingham, Queen Elizabeth Hospital 284
black immigrants, life of 194–7
Blackpool Festival 214, 215–16
Borehamwood Accident & Emergency Department 220–2
Bosnian War 252–3
brain injury patients, music therapy 136
British Muslims 250–8
British Sign Language 35, 56, 65–6, 66–7
Broadcasting House 112–13
Brown, Helen 100
Buckland, Robert 161
Buxton 97
Bychkova, Larisa 212, 213, 216–17, 232–3
Bychkova, Mila 216, 218
Bychkova, Nadiya 201–38, 245
  American smooth week 226–8
  background 212–13

birth of daughter 218
can't lie 210
Couple's Choice 226
dance partnership breaks up 218
dancing career 213–19
DW's first dance 222
DW's *Strictly* experience with 219–34
first meets DW 201, 211–12
first World Championship title 214
as inspiration 232
joins *Strictly* 218
love of dancing 225–6
love of *Strictly* 232
mum risks everything for 217, 232–3
musicals week 228
partnered with DW 210–12, 219
reflection on *Strictly* 236
rumba interview 230–1
Rumba week 228–33
Strictly exit 234
Tango week 236–7
Ukrainian championships final 214
week one 219
week five 223–6
wisdom and kindness 224
Yorkshire Barmaid 234–5

Cacciari, Davide 217
Cambridge United 93
cancer 277–8
Caruana, Pete 123
Casualty 38
Channel 5 x
charities 291–5
child abuse 273–8
Child Cruelty Register 276

Chris (security guard Manchester Arena) 3–4
Chronic Fatigue Syndrome 316
Cinnamon Club, The 174, 178
Clifford, Joe 263
Comic Relief 28
companionship 75–6
confidence 37, 296
cost-of-living crisis x
counselling 6
courage 143–4, 257
Coventry & Warwickshire Hospital 241–3, 266–71
COVID 19 pandemic 30, 73–6, 76, 86, 178, 203, 239–71, 280, 291, 293
  100 Photos Of Lockdown 273–4
  Ahsan family story 250–8
  bereaved families 245–50, 258–66
  births 258–66
  deaths 250, 266–8
  Downing Street parties 250
  FaceTiming 260
  fear 241, 267–8
  first person to have vaccine 241–3
  frontline workers 245, 251, 259, 266–71, 288–90
  funerals 249, 262–3
  grief 249, 262–6
  Heather's story 245–50
  hoax claims 249–50
  hospital experience 74–5
  last goodbyes 247–8, 261–2
  lockdown 246–50, 258–66
  Maggie's story 240–5
  Margaret's story 266–71
  memorial wall 250
  nursing staff 245, 266–71
  penguin T-shirt 243
  PTSD 269
  second wave 250, 251
  sense of helplessness 267

shielding 254
testing 245
track and trace 246
vaccine rollout 242–3, 264, 269–70
Willis family story 258–66
Craig, Daniel 92–3, 95
Crilly, John 154
criminal records 168–9
Crouch, Peter 93

Daily Mail 322
David (friend of Jimi) 190–8
deaf awareness training 57
deafness 33
death, acceptance of 7
death bed decisions 287
Dedicoat, Alan 228
dementia 112–42
    coping mechanism 113
    day to day impacts 118
    dealing with 119
    decline 117–19
    disappearance of person 132
    medication 117–18
    memory loss 119, 132, 137–40
    memory theft 140
    moments 130
    music therapy 133–7
    perception of 137
    recall 127
determination 16
disabled rights 8
discrimination 37–8
Dooley, Stacey 318
Downing Street parties, COVID 19 pandemic 250
Dyer, Danny 41, 42
dyslexia 296

East Grinstead, Imberhorne School 123

EastEnders 38, 41
Edinburgh 71, 89
Elinson, Iso 115
Emily
    ashes scattered 86
    autism 70
    background 70–1
    death 73–6
    funeral 75
    note 87–8
    poem for 109–11
    siblings 75
Emily (Beth's sister) 79
Endcliffe Park, Sheffield 279–84
essential tremor association 283
Everest, Mount 30

Fibromyalgia 316
Fieldsend, Georgia 284–8
Fieldsend, Ilse 284–8
Fieldsend, Josh 285
Finsbury Mosque attack 307
Fishmongers' Hall terrorist attack 144, 145–56
    aftermath 155–6, 156–73
    attack starts 149
    bomb 150, 151, 154–5
    casualties 145, 150, 157, 158, 164
    Darryn enters 151–2
    inquest 150, 171
    Learning Together conference 145–7
    on London Bridge 152–5
    police arrive 154–5
    Steve holds off the terrorist 150–2
Flynn, Ged 92
Football Focus 204–5, 232
forgiveness 299–329
    benefits 299–300
    complications 300
    definition 299

difficulty 314–15
Figen's story 300–10, 328
and freedom 327–8
Mina's story 310–18, 328
Tamar's story 319–29
Forgiveness (law student) 293
Foulds, Tony 279–84, 297–8
'Four Notes: Paul's Tune' 121–2
Freeman, Alison 89–90
friendship 295–8
Frost, Darryn 143–73
 aftermath of attack 155–6, 156–7,
  166–8, 171–2
 anxiety 157
 background 144
 BBC Breakfast appearance 156–7
 demons 171–2
 depression 166
 early courage 143–4
 enters hall 151–2
 Fishmongers' Hall terrorist attack
  145–56
 gets narwhale tusk 150
 immobilises terrorist 153–4
 Learning Together conference
  145–7
 on London Bridge 152–5
 medication 157
 primary concern now 168
 visit to HMP Kirkham 160
fundraising 7–9, 21, 30, 91–5, 102,
 140, 273–4, 291

Gallant, Steve
 aftermath of attack 158, 161–3,
  169–70
 background 146, 161–2
 courage 168
 decision to change 162
 guilt and regret 169
 holds off the terrorist 150–2

immobilises terrorist 153–4
Learning Together conference
 145–7
on London Bridge 152–5
perception of 161
rehabilitation 146
release 169
return to jail 161
on self 161–2
sentence reduced 161
on violence 162–3
Gilkison, Jason 51
Gill, Nikita, 'The Truth About
 Monsters' 309–10
Gill, Vicky 245
Glennie, Evelyn 35
Glynn, Dominic 125–6, 127–8
Grande, Ariana 2
Gregor (Sophie's brother) 83, 88
grief 79, 164–5
 anger 85
 bad days 304
 complexity 81–2
 COVID 19 pandemic 249, 262–6
 dealing with 79–82, 284–8, 303–5
 despair 89
 emotion 107–9
 emotional switch 96–7
 experience of 84–91
 and forgiveness 85
 getting beyond today 88
 guilt 91
 keeping going 265
 loneliness 84
 memories 86–7
 pain 91, 97–8
 Papyrus 82–3
 power of 318
 professional help 81
 safe space 95–6
 struggles 316–17

support 81, 84, 165–6
and tributes 99–101
trying to stay positive 265–6
understanding 96
the void 90
way out 80
and what ifs 85–6
grief counselling 80
growing up 288–90
guilt 78

happiness 285
Harvey, John Augustus 114
Harvey, Louise 6, 18
Harvey, Nick 112–17, 138
  BBC Breakfast appearance 113
  coping mechanism 113
  and dads decline 117–19
  favourite memories 116
  moments 130
  relationship with father 122, 136,
    137–41
  support role 129
Harvey, Paul (ambulance driver) 21
  accident 20
  Ariana Grande concert bombing
    5–8
  bee tattoo 19
  friendship with Martin 6–8, 18–21
  shock and trauma 6
Harvey, Paul (dementia sufferer)
  112–42
  background 114–16
  BBC Breakfast appearance 113
  book 138
  brought back to life 118–19
  conversation jumps 138
  coping mechanism 113
  decline 117–19
  Dyson vacuum trick 140–1
  four notes 112, 118–19

'Four Notes: Paul's Tune' 121–2
frustration 139–40
full of life 113
fundraising 140
honesty 116
as inspiration 122–31, 137
living in the moment 137–41
magic of 122–30
medication 117–18
memory loss 119, 137–40
moments 130
music 112–17, 118–19, 127, 141
musical genius 119–21
performance 127–8
recall 127
relationship with Nick 122, 136,
  137–41
self image 122
strength 142
students on 123–30
support from Nick 129
talent 134
teaching career 115–16, 123–30,
  137
hatred 324
haunting 265–6
Helen (Beth's mum) 79
Henry, Bibaa 311, 313
Henry, Thierry 93
Hett, Martyn 301–10
Hibbert, Eve
  Ariana Grande concert bombing
    1–5
  condition 13
  first speaks again 15
  injury 3, 13
  lies unconscious 4–5
  Martin first sees again 12–14,
    14–15, 16
  progress 15, 25–6
  PTSD 26

taken to Manchester Children's
Hospital 7
Hibbert, Gabby 9
Hibbert, Martin 1–31
  accepts death 7
  Ariana Grande concert bombing
    1–8
  background 14
  BBC Breakfast appearance 7–22
  bee tattoo 19
  desire to see Eve 11–12
  determination 16
  determination to stay awake 4–5
  and disability 24–5
  enthusiasm 8
  Everest plan 30
  the explosion 3
  on feeling disabled 17–18
  first sees Eve again 12–14, 14–15,
    16
  flashbacks 22
  friendship with Paul Harvey 6–8,
    18–21
  fundraising 7–9, 21, 30
  gift 7–9, 25
  injuries 3–4
  as inspiration 29, 31
  journey to hospital 6–8
  Kilimanjaro climb 27–30
  Kilimanjaro climb plan 7–9, 20–2
  last memory from the night 7
  mindset 18
  motivation 16–17, 23–4
  neck injury 3–4, 7
  nicknamed Lion 29
  operation 9
  outlook 14
  perspective 26–7
  PTSD 22–3
  recovery 9–11
  reflection 30–1
  shaves 11
  spinal cord severed 3
  sprinkles mother's ashes on
    Kilimanjaro 29
  strength 14
  on survival 23
  survivors' guilt 24
  told never walk again 10
  walks past terrorist 2
Hillsborough Disaster 89
Hi-Tec Silver Shadow trainers 202
hope, loss of 76
Hudgell, Neil 161
Hudgell, Paula 273–8
Hudgell, Tony 273–8
Humane Society 199
Hungary 323, 326–7, 327
Hunter, Ash-Leigh 51
Hunter, Sir Tom 130–3

Imberhorne School, East Grinstead
  123
Include.org 124
isolation 295–8
It Takes Two 203, 230, 237

James, Sarah 40, 50–1, 51, 52–3, 54,
  56, 57, 205
Jane (Fishmongers' Hall survivor)
  149–50, 151, 157, 158
Jane (part-time office manager) 150
Jenas, Jermaine 93
Joaquin (Garcia) 181, 199
  jumps into Thames 182
Jones, Saskia, killing of 149, 149–50,
  151–2, 166
Joseph (friend of Jimi) 190–8

Keenan, Margaret 240–5, 266,
  269–70
Keller, Helen 35

Kendal 69, 72

Khan, Usman
  bomb 150, 151, 154–5
  conviction 145
  Fishmongers' Hall terrorist attack
    145–56
  immobilised 153–4
  Learning Together conference
    145–7
  on London Bridge 152–5
  preparations 148
  target 151

Kidman, Nicole 93–5, 95

Kilimanjaro, Mount 7–9, 20–2,
  27–30

kindness 308, 327

Kirkby Lonsdale 98

Kirkham, HMP 160

Kosia, Bernard
  background 195–6
  first anniversary of Jimi's death
    185
  friendship with Jimi 175–6, 177–
    80, 184–6, 189, 198–200
  future 199
  Jimi jumps into Thames 175,
    180–3, 184–5
  voice note from Jimi 198–9
  walk to London Bridge 179–80
  and the women in the Thames 182

leadership 269

Learning Together 145–7

Lewer, Alix 124–5, 126, 128–9

Lloyd, Steve 28

loneliness 295–8

Louisa (home help) 120–1

low moments 79

Lukasz (Fishmongers' Hall hero) 156,
  158, 172

Mabaso, Winnie 290–5

Macari, Lou 95

Manchester, Ariana Grande concert
  bombing 1–8, 301–10

Manchester Royal Infirmary 5

MAPPA 171

Marham, RAF 96

Martyn's Law 301–2

Marvellous (friend of Jimi) 190–8

Meadows, Grace 133–7

memorialisation 273–8, 303–4

mental strength 278

Merritt, Dave and Anne 145, 158–9
  aftermath of attack 163–6, 170–2

Merritt, Jack 147, 150, 158, 158–60,
  163–6, 166, 170

Metropolitan Police 311, 314, 318

Metropolitan Police Marine Unit 182

Mi Amigo 273–8

Mike (Beth's dad)
  3 Dads relationship 109
  anger 85
  death of Beth 76–9
  desperation 84
  first conversation with Tim 79–82
  and forgiveness 85
  fundraising 91–5
  future 84
  grief 79–82, 84, 108–9
  guilt 78, 91
  meets Andy 83
  PTSD 109
  suicide prevention awareness
    102–3
  support 84
  the walk 95–101

Mildenhall, RAF 282

Minchin, Louise 132–3, 204

mindset 18, 65

moments 130

Motherwell 246

motivation 16–17, 23–4
Murray, Figen 272–3, 300–10, 328
    act of forgiveness 307–8
    coping mechanism 303–5
    Martyn's Law campaign 301–2
    post-traumatic growth 308–9
    talks to school children 305–6
    Ubuntu 306
music, power of 127–30, 133, 186–7
Music For Dementia 133
music therapy 133–7

National Citizen Service 191
Newcastle University 69
Newton, Isaac xi
NFL Show 221
normality, robbed of 313–14

O'Connell, Paddy 113
Odessa 215
Oldham College 295–8, 296
Olubunmi-Adewole, Ayodeji 177,
    182–3, 186–7, 198
Olubunmi-Adewole, BJ 177
Olubunmi-Adewole, Folajimi (Jimi)
    174–200
    background 175
    body found 183
    calls to Bernard 181–2
    family background 176–8
    first anniversary of death 185
    friends on 190–8
    friendship with Bernard 175–6,
        177–80, 184–6, 189, 198–200
    generosity 176, 177–8
    impact of death 183–200
    importance 196
    as inspiration 187, 196
    jumps into Thames 174–5, 180–3,
        184–5
    last moments 184–5

legacy 189
    National Citizen Service 191
    passion in music 190
    plans 179
    recognition 199
    struggles facing 194–7
    tributes 174–5, 183, 185–6
    university aspirations 194–5, 197
    voice just floated away 182
    voice note 198–200
    walk to London Bridge 179–80
organ donation 284–8
Own Merit 170

Palesa (abuse survivor) 291–2
Papyrus 82–3, 90, 92, 108
Parsons, May 242, 244, 266–71
Paton, Chris 28
Pernice, Giovanni 32, 56
    best ever dance 49
    Couple's Choice 50–5, 58
    Day one 43–4
    the final 59–63
    forgets Rose deaf 58
    impact of *Strictly* experience
        63–5
    moment of silence 50–5
    movie week 47–9
    paso doble 58–9
    Strictly trial with Rose 39–41
    tango 49
    week one 46–7
Poliakov, Stephen 38
Pollard, Andrew 320–1, 322, 325,
    326, 328
Pollard, Jo 321–7, 328, 329
    act of forgiveness 326
    rape 323–4
Pollard, Rebecca 320–1, 328
Pollard, Tamar 319–29
    act of forgiveness 324–6, 327–8

background 319–21
death of dad 321–4, 329
Hungarian-Romanian border
    incident 320
inspiration of parents 329
mother's rape 323–4
press conference 325–6
travels 321
positivity 278
post-traumatic growth 308–9
Power, Jason 135
Pride of Britain award 273–4
PTSD 22–3, 26, 106, 109, 269, 308

Queen Elizabeth Hospital,
    Birmingham 284

Raab, Dominic 276
racism 253–4, 311
recognition 199
redemption 170
refugees 252–3
rehabilitation 145–6, 162, 172
Remarkable People (Walker) ix–x,
    xi, 239
    catch ups 272–98
    Figen Murray 300–10
    Ilse Fieldsend 284–8
    John, Sutherland 273
    Kia Tobin 288–90
    Lisa Ashton 290–5
    Palesa 291–2
    Paula and Tony Hudgell 273–8
    Terrence 295–8
    Tony Foulds 279–84, 297–8
    Winnie Mabaso 290–5
remorse 79
restorative justice 314
Romania 321
Romanian revolution 320
Ronaldo, Cristiano 219–20

Rose, Danny 93
Roussos, Saffie 24
#RunForSophie 90

sacrifice 179–80, 187–9, 257, 266–71.
    see also Olubunmi-Adewole,
    Folajimi (Jimi)
Salberg, Espen 214–15
Salford Royal 7
Sam (Rose's partner) 54–5
Sandy, friendship with Andy 103–7
Saskia, Anglia 149
Saturday Mash-Up 203
Saxena, Mr 9
Scottish Association for Mental
    Health 246
Second World War 279–80
security industry 302
sex offenders 276
shants 207
shared experience 79
Skarabot, Matija 218
Slovenia 215, 217
Smallman, Mina 310–18, 328
    act of forgiveness 310–11, 312
    background 312–13
    campaigner and mother 318
    daughters murder 311
    goals 317
    ordination 313
    struggles 316–17
    at trial 316
Smallman, Nicole 311, 313, 315–16
Sophie
    background 69
    death 88–90
    final purchase 106–7
    first anniversary of death 106
    funeral 104–5
    poem for 109–11
    relationship with father 71–3

Sandy and 103–7
struggle 71
suicide 72–3
South Africa 291–5
Southgate, Gareth 93
Speed, Gary 78, 82, 99–101, 232
Spinal Injuries Association 7, 21, 22
Sports Division 130–1
Stewart, Heather 245–50
Stewart, Stephen 245–50
Strictly Come Dancing vii, x
American smooth week 226–8
announcements 42–3
costume fitting 207
Couple's Choice 50–5, 58, 226
day 53
Day one 43–4
DW partnered with Nadia 210–12, 219
DW's decision to appear on 201–7
DW's exit 228–33
DW's experience 219–38
DW's first dance 222
early weeks 222–3
the final 59–63
first interview 207–9
four '10's 49
the horrible week 235
impact 62–8
importance to Rose 55–6
moment of silence 50–5
movie week 47–9
musicals week 228
Nadiya joins 219
paso doble 58–9
Rose appears on 32, 33, 35
Rumba week 228–33
shants 207
studio day 210
subtitles 56–7
tango 49

Tango week 236–7
team support 56–7
training 35
trial 39–41
week one 46–7, 218
week five 223–6
workload 221–2
Stuart (friend) 184
Sue (Emily's mum) 87
suicide
mess 90
power of word 99
see also 3 Dads
suicide prevention awareness 83, 101–3
Summer of Rockets 38
survivors' guilt 24
Sutherland, John 272, 273

Talman, Pete 123, 126–7
Taylor, Helen 97, 109–11
Terrence (loneliness campaigner) 295–8
Thames, River 174–5, 180–3
Thompson, Emma 236–7
Tim (Emily's dad)
death of Emily 73–6
first conversation with Mike 79–82
fundraising 91–5
grief 85–8, 107–9
meets Andy 83
memories 86–7
the walk 95–101
what ifs 85–6
title xi
Tobin, Kia 288–90
Tom, Captain 273
Tony's Law 276
Trafalgar Square BSL rally 67
tributes 174, 183, 185–6

Tropic House 291–2, 295
Twitter 118–19

Ubuntu 306
Ukraine x
University Hospital Wishaw 247
US Air Force 279, 280

Van Eede, Nick 123–4, 126, 129–30
Variety Playhouse 115
Vodicar, Miha 215–16, 217–18
volunteering 295–8

Walker, Dan viii
 American smooth week 226–8
 confidence 202
 Couple's Choice 226
 and dancing 201–2
 decision to appear on *Strictly*
  201–7
 first dance 222
 first meets Nadiya 201, 211–12
 Hi-Tec Silver Shadow trainers 202
 injury 226–8
 musicals week 228
 partnered with Nadia 210–12, 219
 post *Strictly* messages 234–5
 reflection on *Strictly* 236–8
 Rumba week 228–33
 Strictly exit 234
 on *Strictly* experience 207

Strictly experience 219–38
Strictly fitting 207
Strictly interview 207–9
 as *Strictly* recruitment tool
  236–7
Strictly strategy 210–11
Strictly week one 219
 Tango week 236–7
 TV Dan 227–8
 week five 223–6
Walker, Mike 204
Walker, Sarah 225
Walsh, Tony 20
Wheatley, Joe 209
white privilege 315
Wildman, Stuart 9, 11, 15–17, 17–18,
 21–2
William, Prince 93
Willis, Evie Grace 258–66
Willis, Josh 258–66
Willis, Samantha 258–66
Winnie Mabaso Foundation 291–5
Winterburn, Anna 53
Woods, Tiger 219
World Doctor's Orchestra 133
Wright, Ian 199
Wythenshawe Hospital 7

Yinka (friend of Jimi) 190–8

Zoya, Babushka 212

Praise for *Stop, Ask*

Excellent leaders create conditions that advance and empower those around them, especially in times of uncertainty. In *Stop, Ask, Explore*, Joan P. Ball offers a field-tested framework and practical tools and approaches to help leaders—from first-time managers to C-suite executives—navigate change and equip their teams to overcome challenges in their presence, as well as their absence. FRANCES FREI, HARVARD BUSINESS SCHOOL PROFESSOR, THINKERS50 AWARD WINNER, AND CO-AUTHOR OF *UNLEASHED: THE UNAPOLOGETIC LEADER'S GUIDE TO EMPOWERING EVERYONE AROUND YOU*

So many books simply suggest that change is something we cope with, adjust to, or survive. This book does far more. Rather, in a wonderfully clear and gracious way, Joan P. Ball empowers us to find the power in flux. Once we've understood that possibility, we don't just cope. We're transformed. CAIT LAMBERTON, MBA, PHD, ALBERTO I. DURAN PRESIDENTIAL DISTINGUISHED PROFESSOR OF MARKETING AT THE WHARTON SCHOOL, UNIVERSITY OF PENNSYLVANIA

Creating a workplace where women of color can thrive requires a commitment to transformation in every part of the organization—and getting there means rethinking everything. In *Stop, Ask, Explore*, Joan P. Ball provides a framework that favors action and experimentation to navigate the messiness and uncertainty on the journey to genuine change. MINDA HARTS, WORKPLACE AND EQUITY CONSULTANT, PROFESSOR, AND AUTHOR OF *THE MEMO: WHAT WOMEN OF COLOR NEED TO KNOW TO SECURE A SEAT AT THE TABLE* AND *RIGHT WITHIN: HOW TO HEAL FROM RACIAL TRAUMA IN THE WORKPLACE*

A wonderful book asking profound, vital questions that will help propel us all to a better, more secure, more interesting, and successful life. TOM GOODWIN, CEO OF ALL WE HAVE IS NOW AND AUTHOR OF *DIGITAL DARWINISM: SURVIVAL OF THE FITTEST IN THE AGE OF BUSINESS DISRUPTION*

Joan P. Ball lit up a room of skeptical, hard-nosed engineers who aren't normally comfortable delving into soft skills. She used her authenticity, her wonderful energy, and her sense of humor to really reach them. I watched everyone's posture change during her presentation. Instead of sitting back with arms crossed, they were leaning forward and interacting with Joan as well as their peers. She gave them rich content that convinced them of the value of arming their teams with resilience, tools, and hope during a period that she so aptly described as "active waiting". KIM FURZER, CHIEF OF STAFF TO CIO, VERIZON MEDIA

All too often, disruption can drive one of two extreme reactions: either a deer in the headlights paralysis or knee-jerk response. *Stop, Ask, Explore* is the structured set of principles and fresh, practical tools that can finally equip leaders to take action that's truly effective in the face of disruption. It's the missing link in the path to get to the best "next". ANDREA KATES, PARTNER AT SUMA VENTURES AND AUTHOR OF *FIND YOUR NEXT: USING THE BUSINESS GENOME APPROACH TO FIND YOUR COMPANY'S NEXT COMPETITIVE EDGE* AND GET TO NEXT MASTERCLASS SERIES

Leadership of the recent past required unquestioned experts to drive productivity top-down through execution of well under-stood tasks in relative certainty. Leadership of the current requires humble, curious learners to inspire their people bottom-up to explore, to find, and to frame new challenges in a world of continuous change and uncertainty. *Stop, Ask, Explore* is not a "how to" book, because it acknowledges that we will not go back and our path forward is unclear. Since our path forward is

yet to be forged, we need "learn to" guides that help us become comfortable with not knowing, exploring, and wayfinding. *Stop, Ask, Explore* is a book that clearly understands all this. From Joan P. Ball's deep research, we learn the power of self-reflection and self-awareness in establishing a new breed of leaders who can help lead us through ambiguity towards a better, more inclusive, and equitable future for all. HEATHER E. MCGOWAN, FUTURE OF WORK STRATEGIST, KEYNOTE SPEAKER, AND AUTHOR OF *THE ADAPTATION ADVANTAGE: LET GO, LEARN FAST, AND THRIVE IN THE FUTURE OF WORK*

Everybody has experienced the challenge of getting from "What now?" to "What's next?" In this wonderful book, told through compelling stories and backed by years of rigorous research, Joan P. Ball will help you do just that. This is so much more than a book to enhance your career. It will animate your life! I couldn't recommend it more highly. GREG SATELL, TRANSFORMATION AND CHANGE EXPERT, INTERNATIONAL KEYNOTE SPEAKER, AND BESTSELLING AUTHOR OF *CASCADES: HOW TO CREATE A MOVEMENT THAT DRIVES TRANSFORMATIONAL CHANGE*

STOP, ASK, EXPLORE

Learn to Navigate Change
in Times of Uncertainty

Joan P. Ball

KoganPage

Publisher's note

Every possible effort has been made to ensure that the information contained in this book is accurate at the time of going to press, and the publishers and authors cannot accept responsibility for any errors or omissions, however caused. No responsibility for loss or damage occasioned to any person acting, or refraining from action, as a result of the material in this publication can be accepted by the editor, the publisher or the author.

First published in Great Britain and the United States in 2022 by Kogan Page Limited

Apart from any fair dealing for the purposes of research or private study, or criticism or review, as permitted under the Copyright, Designs and Patents Act 1988, this publication may only be reproduced, stored or transmitted, in any form or by any means, with the prior permission in writing of the publishers, or in the case of reprographic reproduction in accordance with the terms and licences issued by the CLA. Enquiries concerning reproduction outside these terms should be sent to the publishers at the undermentioned addresses:

2nd Floor, 45 Gee Street	8 W 38th Street, Suite 902	4737/23 Ansari Road
London	New York, NY 10018	Daryaganj
EC1V 3RS	USA	New Delhi 110002
United Kingdom		India

www.koganpage.com

Kogan Page books are printed on paper from sustainable forests.

© Joan P. Ball, 2022

The right of Joan P. Ball to be identified as the author of this work has been asserted by her in accordance with the Copyright, Designs and Patents Act 1988.

ISBNs

Hardback	978 1 3986 0562 6
Paperback	978 1 3986 0560 2
Ebook	978 1 3986 0561 9

British Library Cataloguing-in-Publication Data
A CIP record for this book is available from the British Library.

Library of Congress Control Number
2022002940

Typeset by Integra Software Services, Pondicherry
Print production managed by Jellyfish
Printed and bound by CPI Group (UK) Ltd, Croydon CR0 4YY

For Martin, Kelsey, Ian and Andrew—my partners
in wayfinding

"Explanations establish islands, even continents, of order and predictability. But these regions were first charted by adventurers whose lives are narratives of exploration and risk. They found them only by mythic journeys into the wayless open." — James P. Carse

Contents

Introduction 1

01 What Now? Moments and navigating uncharted territory 11

Too many tools, not enough practice 14
The space between What Now? and what comes next 17
Interruptions, disruptions and the What Now? Moment 18
Stop, drop and roll 20
Stop, ask and explore 22

PART ONE
Stop 27

02 Don't follow your passion: Dispassionate curiosity and active resilience 29

Practicing stop in a world that wants go 32
That time I got fired (kinda) 36
Follow your dispassion 37
Building active resilience 38
Equipping for active resilience 40
The resilience wheel 41

03 Don't pivot: Active waiting and minding our metaphors 49

Pivot, persevere... or inquire? 50
What's a pivot anyway? 51
Metaphors (and why they matter) 52
Opening space for active waiting 54
Time horizons and active waiting 56
Metaphors and the What Now? Moment 57
Metaphors in practice 58

04 Lost in transition: Creating learning space to get your bearings 65

The psychology of lost 67
Creating transitional learning space 68
Learning in liminal space 69
Getting our bearings: the myth of true north 70
Marking points of transition 74

PART TWO
Ask 79

05 Zoom in: Rigorous self-awareness and making sense of new terrain 81

Isn't this just common sense? 85
Wayfinding and the self-world fit 86
Why start with rigorous self-awareness? 88
Rigorous self-awareness in practice 90
Start making sense 94
Sensemaking wayfinding and wayfinding as sensemaking 96

06 Zoom out: Wayfinding from the outside in 99

Wayfinding fundamentals 101
Unaided wayfinding 102
Wayfinding is a practice, not a product 104
The role of hope in getting your bearings 105
The problem with problem solving 108
A few notes 113

07 What's possible? Identify possibilities and put everything on the altar 115

Pause and gather your pieces 116
Don't create categories—at least not yet! 118

Identify the locus of possibilities 120
Everything on the altar 122

PART THREE
Explore 127

08 Learn by doing: The art and science of experimentation 129

Learning in action 130
Making space to explore 133
Experiment design canvas 133
I wonder... 137
From "I wonder" to "let's find out" 137
Research questions and time-boxed activities 140
Observations, analysis and accountability 140
Experiments are not decisions 142
Figuring it out or sussing it out 144
Experiment in practice 144

09 Now pivot! From exploration to execution 147

Wait, I thought you said don't pivot 149
Moving from wayfinding to waymaking 150
Discernment at points of inflection 150
Sensemaking, discernment and moving into execution 151
Learn 153
Discern 155
Choose 155
Confirm 157
Execution to exploration and back again 158

10 Now follow your passion! 159

How much is enough? 161
Pursuing your passions and making an impact 162
Hope and impact 165

11   What Now? Moments and life in uncharted territory 167

Walking in circles 169
What Now? Moments are inevitable—so prepare 171
Every What Now? Moment is novel—and similar 172
Approaching uncertainty takes confidence and
    humility 173
Wayfinding is an art—no one size fits all 174
Helping others to face What Now? Moments 176
Living in the liminal 177
Parting words 179

Conclusion 181

Appendices 191
    A Emotion regulation 193
    B Resilience 196
    C Conceptual metaphor 199
    D Transformative learning and threshold concepts 203
    E Sensemaking 208
    F Wayfinding and navigation 213
    G Participatory action research 218
    H Stop, ask and further exploration 220
References 221
Acknowledgments 225
About the author 227
Disclosures 229
Index 231

Introduction

My father was thrilled the day I told him I had accepted an offer to be a communications manager at Consolidated Edison in New York City. It was 1994. I was a 28-year-old college graduate and a single mother with two kids aged five and six. He was sure accepting this job meant I'd finally get "back on track" in the wake of an unpredictable personal and professional journey through my early 20s.

"ConEd is a solid company with great benefits," he told me with a combination of celebration and relief. "You'll have this job for life."

Looking at this scene through 20th-century eyes, it's not surprising that he—a New York City fireman born in 1940 and raised in a working-class neighborhood in Brooklyn—believed that a position at a regulated utility company in New York City meant a stable and predictable path forward for me and my kids.

I did too.

None of us knew in the mid-1990s what changes were waiting just around the corner. Deregulation of industries, the dotcom boom (and bust), globalization, personal computing and the internet, mobile technology, social media, the rise of LGBTQ+ rights, 9/11, school shootings, the 2008 recession,

Ferguson, Black Lives Matter, MeToo, the Covid-19 pandemic. Despite the upheaval of the 1960s and '70s, many Americans in the late 20th century still embraced a collective naïveté about where a single mom with a degree in economics from a State university could go if she just worked hard, found the right job, the right partner, the right house, and lived the right kind of life. Many of us still embraced the hope (or the collective delusion) that things would get "back to normal" and that the post-WW2 American Dream was still ours to lose.

Despite starting our careers in a recession, those of us who came of age in the 1980s and '90s (Gen Xers if generations are your thing) benefited from that idealism. It kept us busy. It helped us focus. It provided a guiding framework for action—even when we chose to push up against it. We were like a group of passengers who survived a plane crash and landed in the middle of a dense forest. A ton of uncertainty, a dash of fear and despair, but still holding on to the hope that we would stumble upon a remote town or a search and rescue team.

But what happens when the rescue doesn't come—or to the people who never got a seat on the plane in the first place? What happens when the passengers are forced to accept that going back is not an option and the way forward is unclear? Xers were the first modern generational cohort to face that question, followed by the Millennials, and now Gens Z and A. Together with those who came before us, we're all now charged with learning new ways of being and doing work and life, on the fly in a shifting landscape. For me that's meant a half dozen jobs, two graduate degrees, a small business, and a (very!) surprising shift from traditional industry to academia—all since that "job for life" conversation with my father in 1994. And, while I've since gained some career stability as a tenured professor, researcher, writer and consultant, I'm confident that there are more surprises, opportunities and challenges in store as we all learn to adapt to new ideas and technologies that have yet to be imagined.

Learning to survive—and eventually flourish—in this new terrain will require us to accept that many of the strategies, tools and tactics that once provided comfort and guidance may no longer be relevant or helpful in this new environment. The 2020s are proving to be a time of wrestling and reckoning and renegotiation of what it means to live a good life, treat one another with dignity, share resources and influence, and collaborate with people who think, act and live differently than we do. We need to keep up with the compressed life cycle of skills and embrace lifelong learning or become obsolete. These are liminal times, and the future is uncharted territory. And learning to navigate uncharted territory requires a new relationship with uncertainty and change.

That's why the subtitle of the book says "learn to" rather than "how to." Exploring new ways to live, learn and lead in times of constant change is both exciting and daunting. It requires asking hard questions and a willingness to go beyond the familiar to find new, and sometimes surprising, answers. A committment to inquiry and discernment is necessary if we are to discover which frameworks, models and tools hold up in practice and what needs to be modified or adapted to meet the moment. The capacities, skills and practices we need to maintain our composure and thrive in changing circumstances are not developed from lists of how-tos or what-tos. Moreover, since every person and context is different, we need to train for many possible scenarios and develop our capacity to apply them (or get reinforcements) on the scene and in the moment. This is especially important in times when many of us feel overwhelmed with choices and change—real or perceived.

In the following pages I invite you to reimagine your relationship with uncertainty and change—even when it is frightening or frustrating. Not because it is comfortable, but because it is inevitable.

Rather than offering a prescriptive approach to navigating change, *Stop, Ask, Explore* invites you to consider the benefits of learning to *stop* in order to gather the resources you need to acknowledge and accept when change feels threatening and make space for learning. Then, once settled into a dispassionate curiosity, we are more able to *ask* how best to engage these questions for yourself by considering the particular resources you need to respond (rather than react) to life in this environment, and then *explore* new possibilities in a way that takes into consideration who you are, where you are, and where you hope to go. It is a book about growing capacity to face uncertainty head on and learning to flourish when interruptions and disruptions throw us for a loop.

This book evolved from nearly a decade of research into one simple (but not so simple) question: what prevents talented, ambitious and change-minded people from responding well to uncertainty and finding new ways to live meaningful and impactful lives? My curiosity about these questions was piqued about 10 years ago, when I noticed a viral "stuckness" among my business students as they sought to cross the threshold from school to work. It was the early 2010s, when the generational cohort we call Millennials (or Gen Y) was coming of age and 20-somethings entering the workforce at the time were routinely portrayed as lacking the skills and motivation to move into adulthood. Research reports with titles like *Failure to Launch: Structural shift and the new lost generation* (Carnevale et al, 2013) and *A Rising Share of Adults Live in Their Parents' Home* (Fry, 2013) described the challenges that both blue- and white-collar workers faced as they attempted to start their careers in the wake of the 2008 financial crisis. The theory of emerging adulthood, a relatively new research stream in developmental psychology at the time, called for acknowledgment of the 20s as a new life stage in industrialized countries due to a variety of factors, including shifting cultural norms regarding marriage, family, and other traditional markers of "growing up" (Arnett, 2000).

At the time, many people scoffed at the idea of emerging adulthood, preferring to embrace a narrative that young people were simply lazy, entitled and content to live off their parents. This tension was fueled by hundreds—if not thousands—of click-bait titles that blamed hover-parenting and trophy culture for a generation lost on the road to adulthood, more than happy to benefit from the comforts of their parents' homes and enjoy a delayed start. While this stereotype was born in a critique of young people in the upper socioeconomic classes, it settled into the public imagination as a Millennial phenomenon that crossed class, ethnic, racial and national boundaries.

But I observed something very different in my undergraduate and graduate business students. Many were ambitious and hard working. They were more than eager to set out on their own, but felt hamstrung by debt, a tight job market and the rising cost of housing in many cities across the globe. This made sense on one level. The early 2010s economy was still reeling from the 2008 economic crisis, and the transition into the workforce was not easy. Yet, Millennials were not the first cohort of young people to enter adulthood in trying times—and events like the Covid-19 pandemic make it clear that they will not be the last. But something about the experience facing this group of graduates felt different.

I recall sitting in my office across the desk from a young man as he told me how trapped (but grateful) he felt living with his parents. "I want to go out on my own," he told me through tears, "but I just can't see a way forward from here." The more I poked and prodded and gathered the stories of these young people, the more I began to suspect that there was something about this stuckness and the resulting "failure to launch" that the existing analysis was missing.

And it wasn't just my students.

As I expanded the inquiry to more established professionals and their teams in their 20s, 30s, 40s and beyond, I noted a similar stuckness in people of different age cohorts, life stages,

socioeconomic and cultural circumstances. I saw it in emerging leaders charting new career paths and seeking new ways to integrate rather than balance their work and life. I observed it in my work with the Center for Social Innovation in New York City where more than 300 small- to medium-size social enterprises were reimagining the social contract and exploring the intersection of commerce and human connection worldwide. I saw it in the teams and departments I worked with in legacy business organizations as they sought innovative ways to adapt to changes sparked by the effect of new technologies and an increasingly uncertain future of work. I saw it in professional women in my field from across the globe.

Rather than study these challenges from a distance, I facilitated transition workshops, which led to more formal participatory action research with multi-year cohorts and one-on-one engagements in established organizations and startups. This led to multi-day retreats for emerging and established leaders, small business owners, community leaders and educators, where I learned more about the challenges people faced as they wrestled with change and uncertainty in their professional and personal lives. In every setting, despite the variety of contexts, educational backgrounds and socioeconomic resources, these engagements led me to smart, ambitious and talented people who searched for words to describe this... something... they couldn't put their fingers on that kept getting in their way or holding them back.

As I continued to explore, I noticed new language emerging in popular culture to describe people having trouble finding their way at points of transition. Among the early career cohorts, terms like "quarter-life crisis" and "adulting" were coined to describe a shift in how people in their 20s and 30s were approaching professional and personal aspirations and commitments (Robinson, 2015). In mid-life, "sandwich" or "panini" generation were used to describe the pressures facing families in their 40s raising young children while caring for aging parents (Williams, 2004). The term "third act" emerged to describe

elders exploring what it takes to live and thrive for decades past traditional retirement age (Black, 2020). The challenges of moving through life stages is nothing new, of course. So why are so many people having so much trouble navigating them? Robert Frost's 1915 poem, *The Road Not Taken*, hints at an answer.

Picture Frost standing at a turning point, sorry that he has to choose one of two roads before him rather than take them both. "And be one traveler, long I stood," Frost (1915) writes as he peers down the two roads hoping to see something that might help him to decide which road he wants to take. He eventually makes a choice, but the turning point offers him both a sense of opportunity and uncertainty that points to a quaint early 20th-century version of FOMO.

But what if Frost were writing in the 2020s?

Equipped with groundbreaking technology, shifting cultural norms, new and evolving community and family structures, and emerging ways of living and working, the 21st-century traveler faces countless possible roads to enter a shape-shifting wood. The sheer quantity of choices about where to live, how to live and why we do it means we're often paving our own roads while we're traveling on them. More like bushwhacking into uncharted territory than choosing a road more or less traveled. This new terrain offers countless exciting new opportunities for people from all backgrounds to chart new paths that were once impossible to imagine. At the same time, this freedom to work, and live, in new ways can be destabilizing, disorienting and overwhelming. If standing on the threshold of two possible options gave Frost's traveler pause in the early 20th century, it's no wonder we feel stuck, lost and confused when we face ours. I've come to believe that this is the piece we're missing about the Millennial failure to launch and other examples of stuckness when facing uncertain transitions. We've underestimated what it takes to equip ourselves and others to navigate in uncharted territory and the emotional, physical and social toll it takes when we feel under-equipped to do it.

It is through this lens that I offer *Stop, Ask, Explore.* Not as a solution, but as a call to inquiry, exploration and the equipping of a community of wayfinders who can navigate without a map or compass. This is a practical book that is rooted in theory and research conducted with individuals, teams and organizations in transition. The content is presented in three main sections that are bookended by two chapters that set the stage for readers to embark on a wayfinding journey, individually or with a team.

Part One draws from self-regulation, resilience, curiosity and conceptual metaphor theories and presents frameworks, principles and practices drawn from ongoing participatory action research. New concepts including dispassionate curiosity and active resilience are introduced as routes to help temper the threat response and open transitional learning space in the face of uncertain transitions.

Part Two introduces frameworks built upon hope theory designed to prompt self-awareness, self-direction and sensemaking as routes to inquiry in transitional learning spaces.

Part Three introduces the experiment design canvas, and the learn, discern, choose, confirm framework for transitioning out of liminal learning spaces. Detailed lists of resources and references are provided at the end of the book for readers who are interesting in reading more about the theory behind the practice. Stories and anecdotes are based upon real people who have engaged with the frameworks, principles and practices in a variety of settings and contexts. Some go by their given names. Others are pseudonyms and their stories have been amended to protect their anonymity.

In any case, the book is designed to be a practical guide to learning to flourish when living in the liminal, whether that means changes at the society level or the uncertainty that comes from a change in your family, your job, your health or your business. It is my hope that the work will provide an artifact to support further participatory action research with new

communities and a support for people to help one another to learn to navigate change in uncertain times.

In the beginning of his seminal book *Story*, Robert McKee writes, "A rule says, 'You must do it this way.' A principle says, 'This works... and has through all remembered time'." (McKee, 1999). In the pages that follow, you will find no rules for what it takes to learn to navigate change in uncertain times. To offer a prescription for adapting to an unfolding reality that is beyond our imagining would be at best unhelpful and at worst malpractice. Instead, I invite you to consider the value of pausing, asking good questions, and exploring possibilities to help you to make sense of how you can learn to the changing terrain of 21st-century life. I invite you to recognize that quick decisions are not always good decisions, and to see the value of opening up space and time for reflection, sensemaking, discernment and wayfinding for you and those your serve. Here's hoping you will find your way—or, as my friend and colleague a.m. Bhatt likes to say, for your way to find you.

What Now? Moments and navigating uncharted territory

It is time now to explore the creative potential of interrupted and conflicted lives, where energies are not narrowly focused or permanently pointed toward a single ambition. These are not lives without commitments, but lives in which commitments are continually refocused and redefined.

MARY CATHERINE BATESON

I met Ashley Rigby at a mentoring event in New York City. We found each other at the refreshment table in the impeccably designed offices of a 100+-year-old furniture design firm with showrooms across the globe. Ashley filled a small plate with fruit and cheese and poured a sparkling water as she told me that she was a regional sales manager with the company and a mentor co-hosting the event. Over the 10-minute break between sessions I learned that she was a rising star at the company who had captured the attention of senior leadership. I also learned

that, despite having ample opportunity for promotion and professional development, she was thinking about leaving to follow a dream.

"I started something with my mother and my sister," she told me. "A side gig really, but I'd love it to become something more." She went on to describe a community-based organization called Jam Program that they had designed together to provide space for women to network and share resources. Pilot events in Brooklyn, NY and Hartford, CT were already gaining momentum with cross-generational cohorts of professional women, and Ashley was confident that leaving her position and focusing on Jam Program full-time was necessary to take the project to the next level. It was apparent even in the short time we had together that Ashley and her partners had the vision, skills and capacity to make the new venture work. Perhaps even more importantly, the ambition and motivation were there. She was clearly hungry to do something meaningful, something with purpose, something that fulfilled her desire to be of service to others and to herself.

But she was also conflicted.

I watched the expression on her face toggle between excitement and hesitation as she described competing priorities and commitments at the intersection of a promising career, a high-potential passion project, and a very active family life with her husband and two young children. While she was more than capable of making tough decisions and following through on them, she was struggling to find a way to bring her best in three domains at once. Despite feeling stuck, Ashley was confident that she'd figure something out eventually. In the meantime, the plan was to keep her head down and juggle the job, the side hustle and family responsibilities until she could see a path forward—even though she knew her current pace was not sustainable. We set a time to grab a coffee the following week.

I've heard stories like Ashley's hundreds of times, in different forms and for as many reasons, as an educator and in my research and consulting practice. Whether I'm working with

college students, helping early- to mid-career professionals to integrate their professional and personal priorities, or equipping established leaders and their teams to imagine the future of work, a common thread runs through their varied experiences. Regardless of the particulars, even the most educated, talented and experienced people can (and often do) get stuck when they stand on the threshold of a professional or personal transition.

Who among us hasn't, like Ashley, found ourselves operating at an unsustainable pace without a clear sense of how to lighten the load? Or received that text, call or email with news—good or bad—that upends our plans and forces us to reconsider the path we're on? From high-stakes disruptions like job transitions, to the daily challenges of dealing with a difficult co-worker, situations that scuttle our plans or challenge our intentions are an inevitable part of professional and personal life. And, while many of us may feel we have a gift for avoiding unwelcome surprises, even the most foreseeable life changes—like graduations, marriages, children and job promotions—can ignite the need to rethink how we live and work. Yet, even if we acknowledge that "the only constant is change" and accept that we need to "get comfortable being uncomfortable," most of us devote very little time or attention to the practice of preparing ourselves to navigate uncertain transitions. Though it's not for a lack of trying.

Regardless of the particulars, even the most educated, talented and experienced people can (and often do) get stuck when they stand on the threshold of an uncertain professional or personal transition.

Visit any large bookstore in person or online and you'll find thousands of titles, that have sold millions of copies, on the topic of change. In the same way that most people know they should eat well and exercise to keep in shape, it's not news to anyone reading this book that the world is changing, and we need to build new capacities and skills to keep up. Perhaps you've

already committed to having a growth mindset, building new skills and capacities, improving your EQ and becoming more empathetic, vulnerable and adaptive in your professional and personal life. Unfortunately, if you're like most people, you live somewhere in the gap between these ideals and reality—and the distance between can feel like a chasm. Add an interruption or disruption to the mix and we find ourselves in an all-too-common conundrum: drowning in ideals, frameworks and change management approaches yet feeling perpetually under-equipped when we face uncertain transitions.

Too many tools, not enough practice

In an era where we've decided that more data and information is better, the sheer quantity of change-related tools and tactics can actually hinder efforts to navigate change, especially in times of uncertainty. In fact, attempts to apply one-size-fits-all solutions to nuanced challenges in shifting contexts can actually contribute to rather than alleviate the destabilization, disorientation and stuckness we feel when we face disruption. This is not as counterintuitive as it may seem. In the same way that a building contractor doesn't use every tool in the truck for every job, we don't need *all of the tools* at our disposal to navigate every part of every uncertain transition. Identifying the *appropriate tools* for the circumstances and engaging them in helpful ways, when they're needed, is a skill we rarely discuss or practice. As a result, we often confuse having a tool with knowing how to use it in practice.

I see this principle in action every time a person shakes a mobile phone at someone and says, "You have all of the world's information at your fingertips, why don't you know how to _____?" Assuming that access to technology means knowing how to apply the information you find there in context is like stepping into the lobby of The Library of Congress in

Washington, DC (the largest in the world) and expecting to be able to apply the content in the 170 million items in your day-to-day life. Unfortunately, much of our education, training and professional development operates on this assumption. That having access to information about change and uncertainty means that we actually know how to make sense of it and are able to draw useful insights that we can apply easily in dynamic circumstances.

As a result, we spend tons of time, energy and money on *learning about* change rather than developing consistent and sustainable practices and approaches to help us *apply what we learn* in context.

Our relationship with speed and decisiveness may be partially to blame for this. In a world where faster frequently means better and efficiency is glorified, intentionally making time and space to stop, ask good questions and explore possible routes forward when we face uncertain transitions is viewed as a luxury at best, and indecision at worst. As a result, we often make quick decisions with partial information about situations that are new and emerging—then wonder why we feel lost in transition or wind up in places we never wanted to go as people we never expected (or wanted) to be. Ashley and her decision about whether to remain at her job or leave and focus on her startup provides a perfect example.

We spend tons of time, energy and money on learning about change rather than developing consistent and sustainable practices and approaches to help us apply what we learn in context.

We had a long coffee a week after that event, and it was clear that Ashley would likely benefit from carving out time to reflect on her work situation more deeply. I invited her to join me for a solo retreat. The experience involves a few days of completely unstructured time alone in a comfortable loft space. No mealtimes. No workshops. No massages or meditation classes. No alarms. No agenda. Just space, time and

two three-hour conversations—one at the beginning and one at the end to help retreat participants to enter and exit the space with some intention (or not). There is no prescription for what people discuss in these conversations or how they spend their time between them. My only request (and it is only a request) is that visitors set aside their usual work and make space to step out of their normal routines. Most report that it is the first unscheduled time they've spent in years—and, for some, the first in their adult life.

Ashley, like so many others, arrived for her visit ready for a highly productive weekend. We laughed together as I pointed out the irony of showing up with an open canvas bag filled with more than a dozen leadership and personal development books. Over the course of our first three-hour conversation, it became clear that she had read everything there was to read about change, transition and building a successful career. Yet, when faced with the challenge of deciding how best to apply that learning to make sense of her particular situation, the "how to" and "what to" models fell short. I listened closely as she described her happy home, her love for her work at the design company, a growing dissatisfaction with her role there, and her deep desire to build Jam Program into something more. When she finished, I asked a clarifying question.

"Are leaving your job or staying at the company your only choices?"

She responded like most people do when I pose this sort of question: with a list of constraints and issues that completely justified her working theory that there were only two paths forward. She could stay at her primary job and keep the new business small or leave her job and focus on the passion project full-time. "Perhaps you're right," I pressed. "Tell me about how you identified those two options."

Despite having thought about it deeply, she could not articulate how she'd arrived at these two choices. She talked about

logic and common sense as she described the unconscious process she'd used to consider what was possible. We discussed the importance of considering less obvious potential choices, and I invited her to consider using her time on retreat to better understand her current context before deciding what might come next. I left her with large sketch pads, a white board, sticky notes, markers and a few prompts to help her get whatever was on her mind out of her head and in front of her. "Forget the books," I suggested. "Acknowledge that you stand at the threshold of a space between What Now? and whatever comes next that is ripe with creative possibility if you allow it to be."

The space between What Now? and what comes next

It's important to note here that I didn't know Ashley very well at the time and I had little context for what she wanted and what might be best for her career, her family or her life. I had no insight into whether leaving her job was the right move for her and, to be quite candid, I didn't care. Guiding her in a particular direction—toward greater success or a higher salary or greater wellbeing and slowing down—was not my aim. My hope for her, and for anyone reading this book, is to build upon what Mary Catherine Bateson wrote so elegantly in the quote at the beginning of the chapter and help people at every life stage to recognize that the uncertain transitions we face across the span of our interrupted and conflicted lives offer tremendous creative potential to refocus and redefine our commitments.

The uncertain transitions we face across the span of our interrupted and conflicted lives offer tremendous creative potential to reflect, refocus and redefine our commitments.

And yet, rather than respond to that creative potential as an invitation, we often view interruptions and disruptions as a threat. These What Now? Moments, which I define as *any interruption or disruption that causes a person to feel lost, uncertain, disoriented or stuck in the face of an uncertain transition*, can spark uncomfortable thoughts, incendiary emotions and knee-jerk reactions, especially if we don't have a clear and immediate sense of how best to respond. That's why I believe that acknowledging the inevitability of What Now? Moments, and developing the practices we need to prepare ourselves to navigate them in professional and personal contexts, is a 21st-century imperative. So, what gets in the way?

Interruptions, disruptions and the What Now? Moment

Interruptions and disruptions come in many shapes and sizes. Internally in the form of our thoughts, feelings or aspirations—or exernally in the form of expected and unexpected situations that keep us from doing what we plan, when and how we plan it. As illustrated in Figure 1.1, they can have a spiky side, like when we lose a job unexpectedly or are forced to deal with a chronic illness. But they can also emerge when things go our way, like when we're offered a big promotion or get engaged to the love of our life. In any case, interruptions and disruptions capture our attention and can be destabilizing.

Of course, not all interruptions and disruptions are destabilizing. Sometimes the way forward is clear and we are able to recover easily and move on quickly. When a way forward is less clear, however, we can feel lost or unsettled. This can compound feelings of uncertainty, disorientation, distraction and despair and result in intense, incendiary emotions.

There is ample research to suggest that it is possible to temper our incendiary emotions if we are properly resourced, and that doing so can be beneficial in a variety of ways. (see Appendix A).

So, why don't we do it?

FIGURE 1.1   What Now? Moments

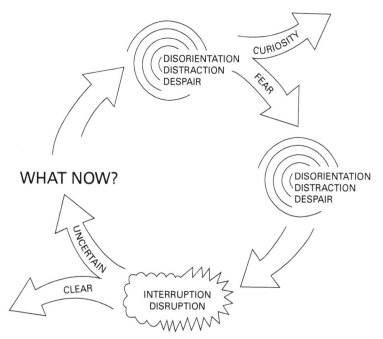

QUESTIONS FOR REFLECTION

When is the last time you faced a What Now? Moment?

What was your initial response?

Did you take immediate action? Avoid? Other?

If you had paused and taken more time before acting—whether it be a week, a day or even just an hour—how might you have responded differently to the situation?

"There is no time!" and "You don't understand what we're up against!" are two of the most common reasons people give to justify succumbing to threat reactions with quick decisions and bold responses rather than making time and space for inquiry in the face of a What Now? Moment. Inquiry requires shifting from a *knowing orientation* to a *learning orientation*, which is counterintuitive in environments where decisiveness is rewarded. Navigating the uncharted territory that emerges from a What Now? Moment requires a willingness to adapt to the needs of the context—with or without ample data—which can feel risky when applied in systems where certainty and clarity are considered leadership virtues. Fortunately, we can draw upon other contexts, such as emergency services, to model how inquiry and exploration can co-exist with precision and expertise in the face of uncertainty, even when we feel time compressed.

Stop, drop and roll

As the child of a New York City firefighter, I was raised with fire safety as a front-of-mind priority. I knew which route I would take if the house went up in flames, how to best evacuate from my second-floor bedroom, to crawl on the floor to avoid smoke, and to "stop, drop and roll" if my clothing were ever on fire. I was also taught that whatever I learned would need to be abandoned if the route I chose was blocked or if I found myself in an unexpected situation. "Fire is unpredictable," my father would tell us. "The best you can do is create a plan, but also be ready for anything." Years later I worked for Consolidated Edison, a large electric utility company in New York City, and was deeply involved in emergency planning efforts at the Indian Point Nuclear Power Plant. Like those childhood exercises, we developed elaborate emergency management plans for the plant and surrounding 50 miles. We held days-long drills with detailed scenarios for evacuating millions of people if there were an event at the plant. My

father's words were true in that case as well. The best you can do is create a plan, but also be ready for anything.

The more I learn about how people respond to What Now? Moments, the more I think about my father's words and my experiences with emergency planning. There is an uncanny similarity between the ways people respond to incendiary emotions when a What Now? Moment throws them into uncharted territory, and how people respond to other types of emergencies. Fear. Panic. Fight. Flight. Freeze. That's why, whether it's a fire drill or learning to stop, drop and roll, we practice *before* the fire starts so we're as well equipped as we can be in the heat of the moment.

What is stop, drop and roll?

For those who are not familiar with what I mean when I say *"stop, drop and roll"*, the term was introduced in the 1970s as a fire safety public service announcement in the United States. The reason for the campaign is terrifying. A cutting-edge fabric technology—polyester—was used in a popular nightshirt that would catch fire easily. Despite a 1953 regulation to ban the fabric, polyester stayed on the market and a public service announcement became necessary to help people know what to do when their clothing caught on fire. Non-flammable fabric is now a thing, but this simple framework is still taught in schools in many countries across the globe, so kids are prepared to respond well in the face of a fire emergency of this sort. Without it, people are more likely to follow the impulse to run than they are to stop and drop to the ground to put out the flames. The same can be true in the context of preparing to navigate change in times of uncertainty.

When a What Now? Moment sparks our threat response, a similar mantra can remind us that we can stop to self-regulate, ask relevant questions and explore possibilities rather than react impulsively to unfamiliar or threatening circumstances. In doing

so, we have a greater likelihood of moving from a fear-based, knee-jerk reaction to a curious and thoughtful response to changing circumstances. It stands to reason that, in the same way that we prepare ourselves in early childhood for how best to respond to fire and other emergencies, we can prepare ourselves for life's inevitable What Now? Moments. Enter *stop, ask, explore.*

Stop, ask and explore

The nature of any given What Now? Moment varies widely, but one thing is common among them—when they spark our threat response, everyone panics. Even emergency responders and others who are trained to operate well in danger. In fact, professionals who operate in dangerous environments learn to temper the threat response as part of their training. No matter our level of experience, we are all subject to physical and emotional responses to uncertainty that we perceive to be threatening. This may land uncomfortably—especially for people who are used to putting out "fires" at home and at work on a regular basis. But even the most seasoned among us can get caught up in our own incendiary emotional and physical responses at the point of impact of a What Now? Moment. In this way, our initial reaction to a What Now? Moment is like reacting to a house on fire. If we can condition ourselves to *stop, ask and explore*, we can find more creative and context-appropriate responses to uncertain transitions.

Stop: settle incendiary emotions

If we succumb to our incendiary emotions, we may enter a *fear loop* (see Figure 1.1), which is *when the incendiary emotions compound feelings of threat, disorientation, distraction and despair, leading to further interruption and disruption in the face of uncertainty and change.* By pausing to acknowledge and accept when we are reacting to threat rather than responding to the

---

disruption, we can make space to understand what has changed and how best to respond. This might involve not reacting immediately to the excitement of being offered a promotion or the concern about losing a job and creating space to consider the implications before choosing a path forward.

Ask: practice dispassionate curiosity and open transitional learning space

If we intentionally inquire about our new circumstances and open space for learning, we may enter a *curiosity loop,* which is *when tempering the threat response at a point of interruption or disruption is followed by intentional inquiry that leads to increased feelings of agency, hope and motivation.* This *dispassionate curiosity* can be a countermeasure to falling into the fear loop when we face a What Now? Moment (more on this in Chapter 2). This might involve considering new questions, like: What will the promotion mean beyond money and title? What about the level of responsibility? Does it work with other areas in your life? Will it lead in the direction you hope your career might go?

Explore: create opportunities for learning in action

If the inquiry suggests the position is right for you or leads to a clear path forward after the job loss, take the position or move on to a new one, and good luck! No need to explore beyond that return to clarity. If the inquiry raises new and important questions, there are many ways to explore new possibilities. This may involve taking the position on a trial basis to determine if it is the right fit or considering a new industry or cross-training in the wake of a job loss. More on exploration in later chapters.

In any case, the prompt to stop, ask, explore reminds us that we are capable of more than an incendiary reaction when we face What Now? Moments. In Ashley's case, she confirmed by the end of her retreat that she loved the company where she worked and valued the time she'd spent there. She also recognized that she could only stay there long-term if she was involved in work

that was more aligned with her desire to engage in community building through her startup. She left at the end of the weekend not having chosen either of the two paths she had believed to be the only ones before her at the outset of the retreat. Instead, she decided to propose a new role for herself that would serve both the needs of the company and her desire to pursue her passion project. By the end of that same week, she called me. "This is why we hired you," her boss had told her at the end of a fruitful discussion about her future at the company. "To come up with ideas like this." By making space and taking time to consider new possibilities beyond the binary stay or go, Ashley opened new doors for herself that continue to create exciting opportunities at the design firm and beyond.

Of course, it could have gone the other way for Ashley. Pausing to temper incendiary emotions and to make space between What Now? and what comes next is not a magic bullet. Pursuing new possibilities does not always result in the answers we want—but it does give us what we need to make more informed choices rather than speeding through interruptions and disruptions without consideration. This creates room to reflect on the implications of the change or how it might affect who we are, where we are and where we hope to be. It is also a way to acknowledge that, despite all of the "rethink," "reimagine" and "innovate" rhetoric that is popular today, most of us (I include myself in this category) remain novices in the art of finding our way when the way forward is unclear. *Stop, ask, explore* is not a cure for that ailment. Instead, it is a prompt for all of us to acknowledge that What Now? Moments are inevitable, and that we can develop practices and approaches to help us learn to carve new paths forward when navigating uncharted territory in response to change.

So, please don't engage this work to find your superpowers or add another checklist of activities to your already busy schedule. Instead, consider this an invitation for you, your team, your organization or even your family to consider how you deal with change and what it might take to gather the resources you need

to be better prepared to respond well to your next What Now? Moment. Or, if you're facing a What Now? Moment right now, it is an opportunity to engage with change in new ways and to develop new practices that make sense for you and your situation. And finally, it is an invitation for all of us to get better at helping one another to navigate the uncertain transitions we will face together as we reimagine and reshape our organizations, communities and lives built for the pursuit of human flourishing in the 21st century.

So, as you engage with the content of this book, I ask nothing more of you than to become willing to enter the unknown and learn what opportunities exist there—even when we have no true north, compass or maps upon which to rely. Then, as we enter this transitional learning space, let's acknowledge that we are neither doomed nor can we rely on the magic of positive thinking to navigate change in uncertain times. Instead, we can learn to accept that operating in uncharted territory may feel uncomfortable and that the terrain might not feel accommodating. But this is the straw we've pulled as human beings born in this time in the place where we find ourselves. So, like other humans born before us to uncertain times, we need to examine ourselves and determine how we want to live, what meaning we hope to bring to bear on the circumstances we're facing, and what it will mean to live well together in uncertain times.

So, What Now?

TAKEAWAYS

- What Now? Moments are inevitable, so we need to prepare ourselves to navigate in the uncharted territory between What Now? and what comes next.

- Learning to orient ourselves when we feel lost in uncharted territory is a 21st-century imperative.

- We can improve our relationship with change and uncertainty, but it takes willingness to learn, attention and practice.

PART ONE

Stop

A note to the reader as you begin 'Stop'

If you are skeptical of stopping in the face of change and uncertainty, then you are entering into this section of the book with just the right attitude. For a variety of conscious and unconscious reasons, pausing in the face of uncertainty and change can feel counterintuitive—even dangerous. In this section I invite you to explore the relationship that you and those you engage with professionally and personally have with uncertainty, transitions and change. These What Now? Moments are inevitable, so understanding who we are and where we hope to go at points of inflection is a practice we need to cultivate in ourselves and others in times of persistent change. I hope you will take advantage of the prompts, mark up the book, and engage with the work in a way that allows you to be challenged and to challenge back. This is your journey—and I'm honored to be part of it.

Here's to a healthy pause,

Joan

Don't follow your passion

Dispassionate curiosity and active resilience

"Imagine you're sitting on this beach." I'm standing beneath a floor-to-ceiling video screen projecting a loop of an empty beach and the blue sky on a beautiful sunny day. The sound of waves lapping on clean white sand fills the room where a group of social enterprise leaders are gathered for a workshop at the Centre for Social Innovation in New York City. I offer a series of prompts—pausing briefly between each to make space for the participants to imagine themselves in the scenario.

"What do you see?" I ask them.

"Is anyone there with you?"

"How do you feel?"

Whether it's due to the calming sound of the waves, the clear blue sky on the horizon, or their desire to place themselves in the relaxing scene, the responses start slowly and gradually pick up steam. Some participants imagine beaches filled with colorful umbrellas, cool drinks and island music. Others a quiet place

where they can enjoy some solitude. As the stories become more detailed and personal, people loosen up and begin to have a little fun with it. They smile and laugh together, comparing notes about hanging out with friends and family or much-needed rest and relaxation. Despite being strangers only minutes earlier, momentum builds, and ideas start to flow effortlessly. Individuals come together to combine experiences and weave stories of larger beach parties.

I give them some time to enjoy each other and their faux beach vacations before I change the image on the screen. The horizon is the same, but in the second scenario a nearly capsized sailboat can be seen at the center of the image. The sea is calm, and the boat appears to be recently abandoned. "Now," I say. "Imagine you're sitting on the same beach, but you just survived a boating accident. You're soaking wet, full of sand and feeling winded after swimming to shore. What Now?"

I've run this exercise with hundreds of people—from students to leaders and their teams—and the results are remarkably similar. The transition from playful imagining to hard-nosed problem solving happens in an instant. People who were laughing together a moment earlier shift their tone and body language to postures that say, "Let's get down to business."

Unlike the generative, upbeat conversations that tend to bubble up from the first beach fantasy prompt, the shipwreck conversations generally provoke the creation of small subgroups who develop concrete plans with surprising speed. Some even take on a mildly combative tone as they debate which approach to take in the face of a fictional What Now? Moment.

Without any guidance beyond the initial prompts, two primary groups tend to emerge in the shipwreck scenario. I call them the rescuers and the survivalists. The rescuers favor taking immediate steps to get off the island. "We should draw a big SOS in the sand or swim out to the boat to see if there are flares, or start a

signal fire," they say, as they consider how best to connect with a passing ship or plane passing overhead. "No, no," the survivalists tell them. "We need to build a shelter and find food and water before the sun goes down." The more time I allow for this part of the exercise, the more assured the two factions become that their approach is the right one and the more animated they are in their defense of their chosen position. As individual and group confidence grows, the sense that the others simply don't see the (completely fictional) situation clearly tends to emerge.

As the debate continues, a third, less cohesive, group of people emerges organically—the disengaged. These people quietly pick up their phones, excuse themselves to go to the bathroom, or otherwise pull out of the exercise. Some chat together, while others sit alone doing other work or watching the scene unfold from across the room. I walk around and ask them individually or in small groups how they would respond to the scenario. Most say that they'd wait to see how things played out and follow the group decision. Others say they would have already left the beach by themselves or with a small group to explore the rest of the island. Eventually, I break into the debate between the rescuers and survivalists to ask a clarifying question:

"What if there's a resort on the other side of the island?"

The humble pause that follows is simply delightful. People who were certain of their view of the situation a moment before smile sheepishly as they look around at one another. Most are quick to admit that in their haste they jumped to solution-finding before thinking through the problem (although, a few always blame the scenario and my "unclear instructions"). The disengaged crowd finally speaks up—often glibly—saying they would have already found the resort and been on the deck with a cool drink waiting for the others to figure it out.

QUESTION FOR REFLECTION

What was your first thought about the best response to the beach scenario?

The point of the exercise becomes clear as the larger groups admit that they jumped the gun. Most smile and say I "got" them. Wherever they land, the group is now primed to discuss the potential perils of reacting to disruption quickly, without thinking. We discuss how we often perceive What Now? Moments as a threat that can prompt a fight (take steps to survive), flight (seek rescue) or freeze (opt out) reaction. The "stop" in *stop, ask, explore* prompts us to acknowledge that initial reaction, and points to the value of developing a practice that helps to create space between our first, often emotional, reaction to threat and a response that is informed by both our emotions AND our circumstances—even when time is of the essence.

Of course, that can be easier said than done.

Practicing stop in a world that wants go

"I don't have time to stop!"

"I don't need to stop!"

"I'm already stuck and you're asking me to stop—I need to figure out how to get going!"

These are three of the most common reactions I observe when I invite people to consider intentionally stopping at the point of impact of a What Now? Moment. The exclamation points are

not for effect. The call to stop is alarming for many people. It sparks reactions that lead people to wonder if I'm either naive or delusional by even hinting at the suggestion. How could I possibly think that to stop could be the right option for their situation? Implied (and sometimes stated) in this response is that I have no idea what I'm talking about or what they are going through. If I did, they tell me, I wouldn't dare to think they have the option, interest, or necessity to stop.

You may be thinking the same thing yourself as you read this.

Neuroscientists, psychologists, and others who plumb the depths of the human brain to understand how we tick are making remarkable strides in learning about what happens in our minds and bodies when we face a perceived threat. We know more than ever about the brain: which parts are active, what responses lead to more or less activity, the involvement of the nervous system, and the ways our bodies drive our thoughts, and our thoughts drive our bodies (Hartley et al, 2010). Yet, this emerging understanding of the physiology and psychology of perceived threat does little to help us with the practical matter of acknowledging that, when we're presented with uncertain circumstances, even the most experienced and well-trained among us can default to knee-jerk reactions.

When we're presented with uncertain circumstances, even the most experienced and well-trained among us can default to knee-jerk reactions.

These instinctive reactions can be helpful sometimes. Like when we pull our hand away when it gets too close to a hot stove, or we rush a child to the hospital when they break their arm playing on the playground. It makes sense to take these actions because we know that burns are worth avoiding and that broken bones need to be set. But what happens when our past experiences don't fully inform our understanding of future challenges and we need to adapt to an uncertain environment? How can we act quickly to bring both our past experience and the

emerging reality of a changing situation to bear in a way that moves from reaction to response? Let's consider these questions through the lens of our firefighter example.

Through intense scenario planning and hard-lived experience, firefighters develop a deep understanding of how fires work. They know what makes them spread and how changing temperatures and different fuel sources influence smoke and potential for backdrafts and explosions. They are trained to determine the best time of day or night to hand off from one team to another without losing ground on a rapidly spreading blaze. There are few individuals or teams who are more time-compressed than firefighters. Yet, despite all of their individual and collective talent and experience—and in spite of all of that time pressure— no firefighter rolls onto the scene, jumps out of the truck and immediately starts fighting the fire.

Even with lives and property on the line, first responders and others who work in high-threat environments know that they need to ground themselves and gain an understanding of the situation before deciding how best to respond. They know that each scene has nuances that inform how best to approach the emergency. They are trained to know that their bodies and minds are operating in high alert and recognize that they need to draw on a balance of confidence in their own abilities and the humility to understand that, while they *know* about fire, they do not know the particulars about this fire. A gas fire is not the same as a forest fire which is not the same as an oil fire. Every scene is different, so learning to stop and assess the contours of an emerging situation is fundamental to an effective response to a fire emergency.

While not every What Now? Moment is a house on fire, there is a lot we can learn from emergency responders about dealing with change and uncertain transitions. Each one is different, so learning to stop and assess the contours of an emerging professional or personal disruption or interruption is fundamental to an effective response. We need to consider a combination of expertise and prior understanding and ground it in the humility

to accept that our experience and expertise may be more or less relevant to inform our actions in the new environment. Getting there requires us to bust a few myths about change that are repeated so often that it's easy to believe they are true.

Change Myth #1: Change and uncertainty are scary

From the moment you open your eyes in the morning until the moment you close them again at night you are constantly changing and adapting to uncertain situations. The vast majority of those changes come so easily that you don't even register them in your conscious mind. The changes and transitions that register as scary are the ones we perceive as a threat to ourselves or others, which means it's the threat, not the change that prompts fear and discomfort.

Change Myth #2: Some changes are good, and others are bad

We all react differently to change, depending upon who we are and the context in which we find ourselves. A change that one person might perceive to be threatening is someone else's adventure. While we might be more vulnerable to viewing certain kinds of changes as difficult or threatening, to characterize change as good or bad outside of its context can be unhelpful and limiting.

Change Myth #3: I can't deal with uncertainty, so I'm not good at change

If you have stepped into a car, onto a bus or crossed a street, you have proved you can deal with uncertainty and change. Human beings are built for change and adaptation. We are born for it and spend our lives doing it. Learning to apply those fundamental skills to other situations—even threatening ones—is possible with attention, resources, and practice. There is no "normal" when it comes to our response to change, and everyone can get better at navigating it.

These myths point to the critical role that context plays in our perception of change and whether or not we view it as a threat. Let's use that time I got fired (kinda) as an example.

That time I got fired (kinda)

At first blush, getting fired might seem like the type of What Now? Moment that anyone would dread. It taps into fear of losing security and can call into question who we are, what is possible and where we go from here. I came about as close as one could come to experiencing it in the mid-1990s while working for a small, but growing, software startup. I'd taken the position as an attempt to move from the highly regulated and structured electric utility industry into what was then a rapidly emerging tech sector. The position involved supporting the CEO and COO with communications strategy, media relations and crisis planning. A perfect fit given my most recent experience. Or so it seemed.

It became abundantly clear within days of taking the job that the position the company had hired for was not the one they needed to fill. The goals and objectives I was tasked with required fundamentally different skills and experience than we'd discussed during the interview process. I did what I could to adapt, but the gap between their expectations and my experience was too wide to close at the pace required for me to succeed in the position. It only took a few weeks for me to see the handwriting on the wall.

The market for people with my skills was strong at the time, especially among startups, but leaving a job after less than two months was still frowned upon in my industry. To add another layer of stress to the mix, my husband had recently launched a small business that was just starting to gather some steam. That meant my income and benefits were critical to keeping our family of five afloat. This was my What Now? Moment—and, as you might imagine, incendiary emotions were running high.

DON'T FOLLOW YOUR PASSION

Follow your dispassion

In a world where following our passion is touted as a useful navigation tool for professional growth and personal fulfillment, I'll admit that the concept of dispassion can seem out of place. Let me be clear, I'm not advocating against finding inspiration and motivation in passion, which is defined in the Oxford English dictionary simply as a strong and barely controllable emotion. In fact, incendiary emotional responses—both positive and negative—can prompt us to pay attention and stay motivated when we need inspiration (more on this in Chapter 10). That said, making sense of our passionate responses at the point of impact of a What Now? Moment can get tricky, especially when we're unsure what's next. So, while following our passion can provide wind at our backs when the way forward is clear, it can also be unhelpful when it creates emotional noise that clouds our judgment or leads us astray when we face uncertain transitions.

In the case of my What Now? Moment, putting my incendiary emotions aside briefly allowed me to take some initiative and begin looking for a new position, despite the possible fallout that might come my way for leaving quickly. Fortunately, I was able to secure a new position rather quickly with an online learning company. I remember sitting at my desk in the warehouse of a not-so-sexy open office, breathing a sigh of relief when I received the news. I had planned to give my two weeks' notice on my way out at the end of the day, when the COO came by my office to tell me they were giving me two weeks to get my house in order, but they had to let me go.

A month earlier, that same conversation would have sent me into a tailspin. I can just imagine how it would have felt to have a two-week clock ticking on a salary and benefits that were critical to keeping the lights on for me and my family. Not only that, but I'm also sure that the misstep would have led me to question my decision to leave a more stable industry for a burgeoning

one, and that I may have come to doubt my suitability for work in the emerging tech sector. Undoubtedly, my threat response would have engaged—and a call home may have prompted the same for my husband, Martin. Instead, because I had faxed (yes, faxed) my signed contract to my new employer earlier that day, the same news held no threat. Same scenario, different perspective, different response.

This example raises some interesting questions about how we can prepare for What Now? Moments and equip ourselves to better navigate uncertain transitions that feel threatening. In my case, preparing for what felt like (and eventually proved to be) an inevitable parting of ways, allowed me to find a new way forward before the spark of a threat became an inferno. As a result, I was able to reorient myself within the space between What Now? and what comes next in a way that both served my needs and made space in the organization for someone who was a better fit. On both sides of the equation—mine and my employers'—this anecdote illustrates a helpful practice I call *active resilience*.

Building active resilience

When most people hear the word resilience, they think about emotional resilience and what it takes to "bounce back" from adversity. More recently, the concept has been expanded to include concepts such as post-traumatic growth and anti-fragility (Taleb, 2014) that suggest we can do more than bounce back when we face a disruption; we can actually be better for it (see Appendix B for resources). My exploration of stuckness led me to the question of how, like emergency services professionals, we might prepare ourselves to be resilient before we encounter adversity rather than hoping to bounce back after the fact. At the time I was particularly interested in how we design services for transformation and wellbeing and what resources people need to keep from getting stuck in the face of uncertainty and

change. That's when I first encountered the work of Dr Michael Ungar and his robust view of resilience.

Michael Ungar is the principal investigator for the Resilience Research Centre at Dalhousie University in Halifax, Canada, where he is a professor in the school of social work. His research and practice in the fields of social and psychological resilience spans decades, continents and contexts—from children to adults to organizations and communities. He defines resilience in adversity as "both the capacity of individuals to navigate their way to the psychological, social, cultural, and physical resources that sustain their wellbeing, and their capacity individually and collectively to negotiate for these resources to be provided in culturally meaningful ways" (Ungar, 2019). What I love about Ungar's view of resilience is the emphasis on resource gathering, community building and the cultural context in which these elements come together. This points to the value of developing a practice of "active resilience" that we can pursue—individually, communally, and organizationally—before, during and after we face What Now? Moments.

Ungar's definition focuses less on resilience as a trait or the passive act of waiting to "bounce back," and more on the agency that we have to pursue resources (or to seek assistance finding them). As a result, we have something to focus on when we don't know what to do. This simple act of having agency, which refers to having some control over the circumstance in which we find ourselves when we feel like we have none, can help us to temper our initial reaction to threat and engage in *dispassionate curiosity*, directed toward identifying the resources we have, the resources we need and how we might connect with them. This helps us to focus more on what might be possible in the face of uncertainty rather than ruminate on incendiary emotions and fear of what may go wrong. It also offers a powerful way to support others who are facing What Now? Moments by pointing them in the direction of identifying and gathering the

resources they need rather than offering uniform and overly simplistic advice.

But where do we begin? Identifying where we are more or less vulnerable to perceive change as a threat can be a very helpful starting point for understanding what kinds of resources to gather before we encounter a disruption. This helps us to be as prepared as we can be when a What Now? Moment pushes those buttons.

Identifying where we are more or less vulnerable to perceive change as a threat can be a very helpful starting point for understanding what kinds of resources to gather before we encounter a disruption.

Equipping for active resilience

If you're like most of the people I encounter in this work, you've already begun the process of connecting with emotional, material, physical and social resources through professional and personal development practices like coaching, psychotherapy, exercise, meditation, and mindfulness practices, playing games, socializing with friends, interacting with family, and connecting with community resources. Whether it's filled to the brim or has just one or two items in it, this is the active resilience toolbox you're starting with today. As I share some new tools and tactics with you in the coming pages and chapters, I encourage you to use them to complement what is already working and help you to connect with relevant resources when emotions are running high. Rather than advocate for a new way of addressing change, I'm encouraging you to stick with what works, supplement where necessary, and practice using the tools you already have in ways that will make you better equipped to face What Now? Moments now and in the future. I'm also encouraging you to clarify where you are more or less resourced psychologically, socially, culturally, or physically when you encounter What Now? Moments so you can

begin to think about how you might access relevant resources before, during and after you're feeling lost in transition.

The resilience wheel

Recognizing where we are more or less likely to be resilient can help us to be better prepared the next time a What Now? Moment throws a potentially distracting spark on our emotions. The resilience wheel in Figure 2.1 provides a fast (and fun) way

FIGURE 2.1 Resilience wheel

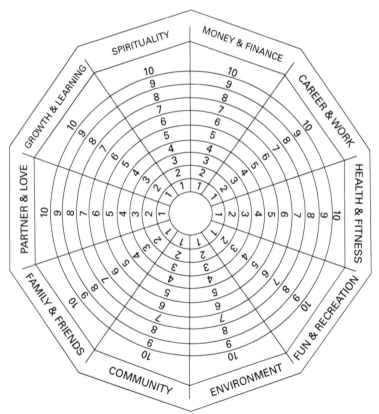

to think about our perceived resilience across some common domains. Here's how it works. Start by grabbing two different-colored pens, because you'll complete two self-assessments on the same wheel. You can do the exercise right here in the book, or visit my website and print a free pdf.

Choose one of your colored pens and rate yourself on a scale of 1 (least resilient) to 10 (most resilient) if you encountered a *huge disruption* in each of these 10 domains. I'll give you an example from my own experience to illustrate. I love my work and value my position teaching at St. John's University in New York. I would be very disappointed if something happened, and I could no longer serve there. That said, I have a rather high risk tolerance when it comes to finances. I've had times in my life that I lived on very little and others where I had more than I needed. Yes, I am a college professor, a writer, and a consultant—but I've also supported myself waiting tables and cleaning other people's houses. Since I am willing to do either kind of work to keep me afloat financially, I feel confident that I would navigate to the resources I need if I had a huge disruption and needed to adjust to pay the bills. Given that, I might place a line on the number 9 or 10 in the money and finance space in the wheel or in the career and work category to represent a high self-perception of resilience in this area.

When it comes to family and friends, it's a different story. Close human interactions are not my strong suit, and I can be very hurt when they go wrong. That makes me more vulnerable to a threat response in that area, so I might fill in the 4 or 5 for that category. Taking each category on the resilience wheel one by one (alone, with a group or with a professional), you can identify your unique spectrum of potential strengths and weaknesses when you encounter What Now? Moments. The completed wheel will look something like what you see in Figure 2.2.

Once you've completed the wheel with a huge disruption in mind, complete it again on the same wheel with a different-colored pen. This time, rather than focus on a major disruption, think about how you might respond to a *daily interruption*.

FIGURE 2.2   Resilience wheel

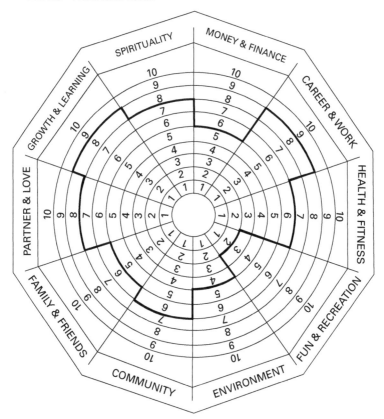

Nothing catastrophic. Just the day-to-day issues of annoying co-workers, meetings that go over schedule and other minor frustrations that get under our skin. Since we often see threat differently in the same domain when the stakes change, your final wheel might look something like Figure 2.3.

Once you've completed both self-assessments on the resilience wheel, you'll have a deeper insight into where you have ample resources to respond to What Now? Moments and where you might want to identify the resources you might need to prepare in the event that you face pressure in one or more of these domains.

FIGURE 2.3 Resilience wheel

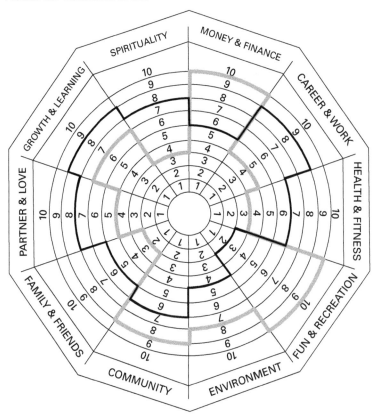

You can use this tool in a variety of ways to reflect on your overall resilience or in different contexts and at different scales. Some people choose to layer their self-assessment across life domains (i.e. at work, at home, on a team, etc.). Doing so can help you to get a better sense of how you might be likely to respond when the stakes are high and if that is different to how you might respond when the stakes are low.

Using my example above, I might be quite resilient if I had a catastrophic financial setback—but when I forget my phone and

wallet on the way to work and don't have money to buy coffee and lunch, that type of a minor annoyance can get under my skin. If you are unsure or wonder about how you come across to others, you can even ask your partner, your therapist, or a trusted friend to share their observations about times they've seen you face What Now? Moments and whether they see places where you tend to be actively resilient and places where you might need more resources. At work, you can run this exercise with a group or team to see where the team is or is not resilient as a means to identify places where resources are needed.

It's important to note that this is not a contest—nor is the goal to be a 10 across the board. Despite how we often talk about resilience, no one is resilient in all things or lacking resilience in all things. Resilience is not a binary all or nothing. Instead, it is about recognizing that we are all resilient in some areas of our life and less resilient in others.

Overall, we can take steps to become more resilient through an engaged practice to focus on a specific domain of our wheel and choose to gather resources to better equip ourselves in that area. The point is to use the wheel to shine a light on places where you might view change or transition as a threat. This can help you to avoid the fear loop and access the curiosity loop when change inevitably comes your way. Once you become more familiar with your perceived vulnerabilities with respect to resilience, you might have a better sense of what types of situations might require you to gather extra resources when under pressure—not as a matter of weakness or failure, but as a way to have what you need in your metaphorical backpack to make your way through uncharted territory. It can also provide a way to make sense of the information you've gathered in all of the books, resources, courses, and professional/personal development materials you've engaged with over the years!

It's important to recognize that, like responding to What Now? Moments, practicing dispassionate curiosity and building active resilience are very context- and resource-dependent endeavors. We all start in different places and under different constraints. Practicing active resilience involves a commitment to humbly accept that, regardless of our background, training, or experience, gathering resources for our professional and personal journeys is a lifelong practice that each of us will approach in our own way—individually, in community, and in and outside of the institutions where we work and engage with the world.

As we learn to engage uncertain transitions more like emergency services professionals, with confidence and humility, we can then develop practices and approaches to help us to gather the resources and fundamental skills we need to thrive in uncertain times. This invites us to accept that we are all equally subject to the threat response, and that there is value in learning to, as Ungar suggests, navigate to the resources we need in ways that are culturally and contextually relevant to us.

For some, this might mean developing a mindfulness practice. For others, that might feel out of reach. For some, it will be faith or spirituality. For others, that may feel abstract or off-putting. Some will dance or sing or engage with the arts. Others will use exercise or community or therapy or an executive coach as resources for active resilience. I am agnostic about your approach to this. I only advocate that you consider the benefits to you and those you serve if you develop your own methods and approaches to make space for you or your team to face your next What Now? Moment with dispassionate curiosity and active resilience rather than fear and trepidation. Of course, that's not easy if we're constantly expected to move fast and pivot.

TAKEAWAYS

- Learning to stop during What Now? Moments can be easier said than done—especially when change feels like a threat.

- Shifting from incendiary reaction to a dispassionate and curious response can transform our relationship with change.

- Practicing active resilience can help us to gather the resources we need to gain stability as we navigate uncertain transitions.

Don't pivot

Active waiting and minding our metaphors

"How do I know whether or not I should pivot?" I couldn't help but smile to myself as this question was posed by a breakout author under contract for two books (while promoting a third!). The earnest question came during one of my weekly public conversations about the philosophy and practice of finding our way when the way isn't clear. "The issue is that I am a person with interdisciplinary interests who is not much of a multitasker," she continued, "and I'm not sure if I should integrate, remove things from my plate or…" Like so many others who find themselves on the threshold of uncharted territory, her voice trailed off toward an elusive choice she was not yet able to articulate.

I knew from previous conversations that the stumbling block was about more than an incapacity to multitask. Like so many of us who are living complex lives that span multiple domains, making sense of competing professional and personal pressures and commitments requires something more than a quick choice.

"Whether or not to pivot is a concrete decision," I told her. "It sounds like you're not there yet."

Pivot, persevere... or inquire?

The pivot metaphor became popular in Silicon Valley startup circles in the early to mid-2000s with the release of several books about entrepreneurship. One of the most popular among them, *The Lean Startup* by Eric Ries, outlines an approach to innovation designed to bring new products and services to market as quickly as possible, in a very systematic way (Ries, 2011). The idea is simple... and effective. Learn what works (or what doesn't) by getting new products into the hands of customers as quickly as possible. Ries's "build, measure, learn" framework has proved to be an effective way to use customer feedback to determine whether to change strategic and tactical direction (pivot) or remain on the current course (persevere). This systematic approach to building fast while mitigating risk has been the darling of startup founders and venture investors, so it's no surprise that many people have embraced the pivot metaphor in other contexts. I hear it now in conversations with students who are thinking about changing majors, individuals thinking about a career change, and in conversations about the future of work, education and learning.

So, what's my problem with a pivot?

Let me start by saying that the pivot has its place. When we stand at a turning point and the choices we face are distinct, viewing next steps through the lens of a pivot metaphor may keep us from getting lost or stalled in indecision and inspire us to act (see Chapter 10 for more on this). But, when we face What Now? Moments, the binary choice to either pivot or persevere can force a decision before we have time to gather resources and orient ourselves in what is effectively new terrain.

Author and psychiatrist Owen Muir, M.D. said it best when we discussed my hesitation about the pivot metaphor. "The pivot makes sense if you're a VC-backed startup trying to find a better product-market fit," he told me. "Finding a better self-world fit is much harder to do." I thought long and hard about the notion of a self-world fit after that conversation, and how important this distinction between what works for a business and what works for people finding their way in the world is when we consider adopting business principles like pivoting to guide our thinking about the human aspects of navigating uncertainty and change.

The binary choice to either pivot or persevere can force a decision before we have time to gather resources and orient ourselves in what is effectively new terrain.

What's a pivot anyway?

In its most simple definition, to pivot is to turn or rotate around a point. Many examples apply, like a hinge on a door or a player's foot on the basketball court. The pressure we feel (real or perceived) to move through uncertain transitions faster than is truly necessary can sometimes make us feel like that basketball player, stuck with one foot in place, turning around in circles hoping to find an open route to make a pass or take a shot. That's why when the author at the opening of this chapter—or anyone else who is facing an uncertain transition at work or at home—asks, "How do you know when to pivot?" I remind them that, despite the accelerating pace of business and life, most What Now? Moments don't require us to pivot. We get to lift our foot off the ground, put the basketball down and create our own, less limiting metaphors to guide our thinking about where we are, where we're going in the space between What Now? and what comes next.

Metaphors (and why they matter)

When we think of metaphors (if we think of metaphors at all!) it tends to be as a vehicle for telling a good story. We know we can bring a pitch, a speech, or a written communication to life by describing a goal as a *mountain to climb*, a challenge as *a river to cross,* or a competitor as an *enemy to vanquish.* When issues run deep we see the *tip of the iceberg.* Our vision for the future sits *on the horizon* and, as we've discussed, a change of direction is *a pivot.* But there is more to metaphor than good storytelling. Whether or not we are aware of it, the way we use metaphor shapes our perceptions of the world and how we operate in it (Lakoff, 2006).

Let's take the way we think about the human brain as an example.

We know exactly what someone means when they say that a particular way of thinking, being or doing is "not how I'm wired." But what are the implications of thinking about being or not being "wired" to do something? Conceptually, "wired" is rooted in a metaphor that casts humans as a computer or other electronic device. In this view, we are "wired" to do things or think things or be a particular way. We may or may not be able to be "rewired" to do things or think things or be a different way. How does this framing influence the way we approach learning? Motivation? Identity? Ability? If I'm not wired for something, why would I apply myself to pursue it? Why would I rely on you to collaborate with me on something that requires it? What does it mean about how I learn? How I interact with others? How I navigate uncertainty?

Let's play with this idea for a bit.

Since we are moving rapidly toward an increasingly wireless world, it is interesting to think about how we might view being "wired" 100 years from now. A time when plugging something into a wall or weaving hundreds and thousands of wires together

to connect things will seem quaint, old-fashioned and remarkably static. Brain *plasticity* already provides a more dynamic metaphor for how the brain develops and changes over time, which is arguably more inspiring from a learning perspective. And who knows what metaphors we will use in the future to make the abstract notion of how our brains work more concrete? The point here is that humans use metaphors to make sense of the world around us—and the ones we choose can both help and hinder the way we approach change.

QUESTION FOR REFLECTION

What are some metaphors you use to think about transitions and change?

There is a rich and diverse stream of research focused on understanding how metaphor shapes and influences human thought and action (see Appendix C). Authors Lakoff and Johnson, for instance, have devoted much of their professional lives to exploring how humans engage with metaphor. Their ground-breaking research on the topic suggests that our use of conceptual metaphor to think and communicate is fundamental to how we make sense of the world in a way that is unavoidable and mostly unconscious (Lakoff and Johnson, 1980). Harvard Business School professor and metaphor elicitation expert Gerald Zaltman made the same observation in his work with tens of thousands of people using his patented metaphor elicitation technique, ZMET™ (Zaltman, 2008). According to Zaltman and his colleagues, deep metaphors exist across cultures and "capture what anthropologists, psychologists, and sociologists call human universals, or near universals, the traits and behaviors found in nearly all societies."

Zaltman and his colleagues describe seven deep metaphors (balance, transformation, journey, container, connection, resource, and control). While every one of these universal metaphor types can be useful for understanding our thoughts and actions when we face uncertain transitions, journey and container metaphors can be especially helpful when we think about alternatives to the pivot metaphor and contemplate the potential benefits of opening up space for inquiry and exploration when the way forward is unclear.

Opening space for active waiting

Carving out space and time to make sense of changing circumstances before choosing how best to move forward is neither a luxury nor a waste of time—it is a necessity. Even when time is short, moving away from the "foot on the court" basketball mentality to opening up dedicated space and time to acclimate to new circumstances can help reduce the sense of urgency (and threat) we feel when we face a What Now? Moment. This is not about creating space to sit on your hands or getting lost in analysis. It is about developing a practice of pausing our journey to create space for what I call active waiting. Active waiting is the intentional process of creating time and space to gather resources, reorient to new surroundings and engage in inquiry and exploration when faced with uncertain transitions.

A mountain climbing metaphor provides a useful way to think about this.

Climbing Mt. Everest or another of the world's largest mountains is not a straight shot to the summit. Climbers move from periods of trekking to time spent in base camps as they make their way up the mountain. Trekking to base camp requires certain skills, capacities, resources, and approaches. The journey may be difficult, but the direction and intention are clear. The climber has a clear goal and knows where they are headed.

Trekking to base camp is a helpful metaphor for thinking about how we execute on a clear goal. We know where we are, we know where we are going, we gather the resources we need and make the trek. We may hit barriers to progress, but the objective is clear until we reach our goal or encounter a What Now? Moment along the way.

Active waiting is the intentional process of creating time and space to gather resources, reorient to new surroundings and engage in inquiry and exploration when faced with uncertain transitions.

Once a climber reaches base camp, there is a pause in the *journey* up the mountain. Activities and objectives change from pressing forward to reflecting on the trek and equipping for the next legs of the climb. Base camp provides a *container* within the larger journey that is about much more than stopping to take a rest. In stark contrast to Reis's quick pivot, climbers and their teams spend an average of one to two months at Everest base camp. Days in base camp are spent focusing on what they and their teams need to replenish, reorient and reacclimate to be sure climbers are physically and mentally prepared to reach the summit. This period of *active waiting* requires different skills, capacities and resources than are necessary for the trek to base camp or the climb to the summit. While not focused on pressing forward, activities in the container of base camp are as important as what takes place on the journey to the summit. Leaving base camp too soon or without the resources the climbers and their teams need can have deadly consequences. So, to spend time in the nurturing, exploratory space of the base camp before returning to the climb increases the likelihood of reaching the summit safely.

The successful climber recognizes both the value of the trek and the time of recalibration and replenishment at base camp— the journey and the container. As a result, they are practiced and adept at moving between them (or working under the advice

FIGURE 3.1 Base camp

and support of someone who does!). This mountain climbing metaphor not only provides a useful illustration of the process of moving from execution to exploration on a project or endeavor, but it is also a wonderful example of why metaphor is such a powerful tool for making sense of What Now? Moments. Too often we favor execution over exploration, when both are critical parts of any journey. As a result, we press (or pivot) through uncertain transitions rather than making time to recalibrate, reorient and tease out new possibilities that emerge when our plans are disrupted or interrupted. By consciously shifting from execution to exploration—from the trek to basecamp—we get the best of ourselves and our teams in both domains.

Time horizons and active waiting

When we open up space for active waiting, it is helpful to consider the time horizon we're operating on and ask ourselves if it is real or perceived. A *time horizon* is *a point in the future that is determined to measure or complete a task*. It can be as precise as a fixed deadline, or as loose as a date on the calendar to reflect on your chosen trajectory. In any case, how we think about time

horizons influences our expectations and the pace at which we work and live. When a person decides that they need to build a successful business by the time they're 30, for instance, they are setting a time horizon that will guide their steps through their 20s. When we (or people in our lives) set expectations that we should be married or have children at a certain age or before or after we reach a career milestone, we are setting out time horizons. Some time horizons are fixed—you can't win a 30 under 30 award when you are 45. Others have the potential to be fluid, whether or not we perceive them to be. Creating time for active waiting at points of transition provides us with an opportunity to pause and discover just how flexible our time horizons can be.

Metaphors and the What Now? Moment

While the mountain climbing metaphor is useful to think about creating time and space for active waiting, there is no single metaphor or framework that encapsulates all that goes into finding our way when the way isn't clear. Sure, the mountain encapsulates the resource gathering, direction finding and movement toward an aspiration or goal that some people find inspiring. But it might not land for someone who has a multitude of interests and is not setting out on a singular quest to reach a particular goal. For them a metaphor of exploring a galaxy or planting a garden might be more resonant.

And that's just fine.

Our focus on metaphor is not about choosing a single way to think about uncertain transitions and learning to adapt to it. Instead, understanding the metaphors that guide our thinking is about acknowledging that people naturally make sense of the world in terms of metaphors, and that understanding that the ones we rely upon can be helpful (or unhelpful) when we consider them in practice. Let's ground this with a few examples.

Metaphors in practice

My research into stuckness and what it takes to navigate uncertain transitions sparked a What Now? Moment for me. I'd made a shift from a 17-year professional communications career into academia in the early 2000s, and the transition from viewing myself as a communications professional to a university professor was clear and unambiguous. There were some detours and surprises along the way, but from an identity perspective, it was a textbook pivot. That changed when my research expanded into professional engagements with individual leaders, teams, and organizations. People close to me knew I was primarily an educator, but bringing my work into the field meant others began referring to me as a coach, a consultant, or a facilitator. On the face of it, none of these roles fit my work—especially when viewed outside of a job description with a metaphor lens. My approach to professional and personal development did not fit the way a coach works. Consulting came closer, and it suggested an expertise dynamic that I could have sold if I cared to, but did not describe the way I engage with my clients and research participants—especially since my work transcends commerce and is applied at school, with individuals, with teams, etc. I decided to contemplate my own metaphors and concluded that neither coach nor consultant made sense for me. Facilitator came even closer, but still lacked the depth and breadth of my engagements. As I continued to consider possible ways to think about how I worked, I expanded my inquiry to consider how people outside of my field approached their work. Doing so led me to a surprising, but apt metaphor. I approach my work like a midwife.

Midwives have expertise, but they don't call the shots. They engage with expectant mothers as equals, acknowledging that they are there to support based upon the needs, desires and unique circumstances of the expectant mother and their family. They recognize that all pregnancies are different—from the resource

perspective, the social perspective and the manner in which people want to make their own choices about how, where and with whom they want to approach the birth experience. They adapt themselves to particular rituals, traditions, and cultures where they engage. And, perhaps most importantly, they recognize that they are partners in bringing the baby to life—not in raising it!

Once I saw myself in this way it became much easier for me to organize my work in a way that makes sense to me. It also helped me to shake some unhelpful expectations that came with some other ways of framing my work. People I work with still like to think of me as a coach, a consultant, a facilitator, or an educator—and that's fine by me. The midwife metaphor is an organizing principle that helps me to understand my place in a world, not a communication or marketing tool (although I nod to it with the name of my company, WOMBLab). Considering my work in this way helped me to see the power of intentionally using metaphor to orient myself in times of uncertainty and was instrumental in my exploration of its use as a tool to help others to make sense of their uncertain transitions.

I worked with a building contractor, as an example, who decided to go to college in his 40s to explore new career options. He was committed to the process and more than willing to do the schoolwork, but battled self-doubt and anxiety with regard to his ability to complete the program and actually make something out of it. I asked him to tell me more about what he was going through, but he wasn't able to articulate an answer beyond saying that he was skeptical about his capacity to make a successful transition to a new career upon graduation. I gave him a brief overview of conceptual metaphors and how they shape our view of the world, and asked him to share his situation, placing himself as a character in a movie. Without hesitation, he described a scene in detail. "You know those huge ships, the freighters with curved sides that are four or five stories above the ocean?" he asked. "Well," he continued. "I'm the guy who jumped off the side of the boat who's stranded in the ocean with no way to get

back in. Graduation and a new job are beyond the horizon that I can't see—or maybe they're not there at all." We sat quietly for a moment while he reflected on the metaphor. Eventually he started to laugh, and I joined him when he said, "and I barely know how to swim!" No wonder he was feeling stressed!

In the space of less than an hour we were able to come up with several new possible transition narratives grounded in less threatening metaphors. Although he still had his fears and concerns about what was ahead of him, he described the process of reframing the uncharted territory between where he was and an unknown future as a relief and continued to use both the old metaphor and the new ones to gauge his thoughts and actions in the weeks and months that followed. He told me later that, whenever he found himself stressed out about school or stuck in transition, he thought about himself flailing in the middle of the ocean and started laughing.

The beauty of exploring the use of metaphor as a tool for understanding is that it can be used in team and client environments as well. In an online conversation with a group of people who were new to the concept of using metaphor in this way, I asked for an example from participants. A woman who was having some challenges with workflow, communication and interaction with a new client volunteered to share her challenge and frustratedly described her interaction with the team as "too many cooks in the kitchen." Rather than rely on me to help her to come up with an alternative, other participants in the session, all of whom were new to using metaphors in this way, chimed in with wonderful ideas about alternate ways this individual might view the situation as she prepared for a meeting with the client scheduled for later that day. Together, this group of mostly strangers considered what might happen if the individual were to shift from viewing the members of the team as "cooks in the kitchen" to "a variety of ingredients" that, when combined together in the right order, right measure and right timing, could create a delicious recipe. She took both metaphors to the meeting that

afternoon and used them as the stepping-off point for what she had feared might be a contentious encounter with her client. Instead, she later told me, the metaphors paved the way for some clarifying conversations that not only got things unstuck in the moment but provided a useful language for the future.

Rebecca Taylor, a world-renowned strategist and consultant for museums, galleries, art fairs and luxury brands found value in exploring metaphor when her world was disrupted in a positive way. New opportunities in an adjacent field opened surprising and unexpected doors that expanded her influence and placed her in the spotlight, a role she valued for her clients, but not for herself. After she shared this sentiment in an online session about the use of metaphor for wayfinding, another participant reached out and offered an alternative view: to step into the sunshine, not the spotlight. "I'm writing that down," she told him. "It resonates so much because I love the sunshine but loathe the spotlight. One is full of joy and warmth, the other ego, so the framing is really poignant for me."

As you can see from these examples and the many others I draw upon to discuss change in this book, What Now? Moments may present as a river to be crossed, a garden to be planted and tended to, a switching yard, the space between conception and birth, and so many

We can choose to create personal metaphors to guide sensemaking in our day-to-day lives and can play with metaphor as a tool to make sense of how we navigate in the world.

others. There are countless metaphors we can use to make sense of uncertain transitions and the challenges and opportunities they provide for us. This means that we can choose to create personal metaphors to guide sensemaking in our day-to-day lives and can play with metaphor as a tool to help make sense of how we navigate in the world.

This can involve developing a practice of observing how we use metaphor in thought and action and intentionally adapting and shifting metaphors in context as a way to understand how we view change. Here are some prompts if you'd like to try it out. Keep in mind that, as mentioned previously, the goal of this exercise is not to find the perfect metaphor. Instead, it is to get a deeper understanding of how metaphor is already guiding our thoughts and how we might become more aware of where metaphor helps and hinders our approach to What Now? Moments.

EXERCISE Playing with metaphor

Spend one day observing how you and those around you use metaphor—especially in the context of change, transition, and uncertainty. You may choose to focus on work or home or online. Collect as many metaphors as you can and observe how they help or hinder understanding and communication.

- Which metaphors resonate with you?

- Which metaphors create barriers to understanding?

- What is the most helpful change metaphor you observed?

- How might you use it to guide your thinking in the future?

- What is the least helpful change metaphor you observed?

- How might you use it to guide your thinking in the future?

Identifying your own metaphors is useful to get a conscious and unconscious sense of where we are when we're feeling lost or unmoored. When working in groups, the process of comparing and contrasting where metaphors align or clash can help to capture unspoken similarities and differences among group members and get a deeper understanding of where barriers to progress and misunderstandings might arise. In either case, I often ask participants to draw pictures, make collages, play with LEGO—anything that helps them to surface the metaphors they use—consciously and unconsciously—to make sense of change and points of intersection.

As you continue to play with your own change metaphors you will see that even the most helpful metaphor breaks down in some contexts. That is fine. We learn as much from where a metaphor fails as where it works. If you have to convince yourself or your team too that MY metaphor is the correct one for YOUR circumstance, then the metaphor you're using is unhelpful. The goal is not to identify a single perfect metaphor and adapt ourselves to its use. Instead, we hope to identify multiple—maybe even mixed—metaphors as a tool to understand where we are and where we hope to go from here.

So, if climbing the corporate ladder or finding your "true north" is helpful—stick with that and use it as a tool to guide you on your journey. If those metaphors cause confusion or leave you feeling stuck, then consider others. All in all, I'm not interested in advocating a single new, "better" metaphor to describe how we approach our competing professional and personal commitments in the new terrain of work in the 2020s and beyond. Instead, I invite you to add metaphor to your sense-making toolbox, so you are better equipped when What Now? Moments leave you feeling lost or disoriented.

TAKEAWAYS

- Business concepts like the pivot can be helpful to guide strategy and growth in tech companies but are less helpful when we face What Now? Moments in other contexts.

- Making time and space for *active waiting* allows us to pause our journey and create a container for inquiry and exploration when we face uncertain transitions.

- Reconsidering the metaphors that guide our thoughts and actions can help us to reframe our thinking and reduce perceptions of threat.

Lost in transition

Creating learning space to get your bearings

"I don't want to pick a lane." Erica wasn't the first person to say that to me, but she is certainly one of the most remarkable. She's a CEO and founder of Langston League, a published novelist, and an educator and former school administrator whose Cardi B cover-turned-geography lesson went viral online and in television and print media. Not entirely surprising, since Erica was a rapper and HBO Def Poet in her teens. Now she is expanding into educational entertainment, television writing and has other high-profile projects on the near horizon.

Oh, and she is only 33.

When we first connected, Erica was trying to make sense of her varied expertise and wrestling with the advice she'd received countless times. "You're doing too much," her mentors, teachers, family and leadership experts told her, "You need to pick a lane." As the gig economy mindset spills over into even the most traditional career paths, more and more people find themselves

challenging 20th-century paradigms and engaging in a constellation of activities rather than a singular career goal or focus. Unfortunately, our systems and even our greatest supporters haven't all gotten the memo.

It was clear to Erica that her confidants had her best interests in mind. She *was* burning the candle at more than both ends, and she *did* need to pace herself. But she had a deep sense that doubling down on just one of her many talents was not the only way to sustain herself and bring her aspirations to life. Despite her ongoing successes, she felt exhausted, overwhelmed and unclear about how to reconcile her commitment to her work while maintaining her own health and wellbeing in the face of competing priorities and limited resources. She perceived herself to be at the junction of two less than desirable paths forward— to give up some of these thriving initiatives or to continue grinding down her current path and suffer the inevitable burnout. Neither choice felt right. In our conversations and chats she often described herself as feeling both inspired and lost at the prospect of charting a less traditional and focused career and life course. And she is not alone.

Words like lost and disoriented come up frequently in my discussions with people who find themselves on the threshold of uncertainty and change. This may explain why uncertain transitions spark incendiary emotions that throw us into the fear loop. Just the thought of being lost in the woods, the jungle, the desert, or any remote place without a means of finding a way out leaves most people feeling physically and emotionally vulnerable. Being lost causes fear and anxiety, which makes a lot of sense, since losing our sense of direction in the wild can quickly become a matter of life and death.

Remarkably, it doesn't take being in the wilderness to conjure equivalent fear and anxiety of being lost in physical spaces. Learners experience a similar sense of being lost or stuck, sometimes called a disjunction or a disorienting dilemma, when they encounter concepts that cause them to question prior ideas,

beliefs and values in ways that challenge their self-concept (see Appendix D). Thus, when people find themselves lost in transition, we encounter a one-two punch. The ill-defined space between What Now? and what comes next taxes both our self-concept (who am I?) *and* our self-direction (where do I go from here?) (Oldham, 2015). Stopping to acknowledge feeling lost and understanding how it affects us is fundamental to reorienting ourselves in uncharted territory.

The psychology of lost

Kenneth Hill, professor emeritus of psychology at St. Mary's University in Halifax, Nova Scotia has been thinking about how people behave when they are lost since the mid-1980s. Professor Hill's interest in the subject was born in tragedy when he joined the search and rescue efforts to find a lost nine-year-old boy who was found deceased nine days after he went missing near his home in Canada. According to Hill, there was no rhyme or reason to the way the search was conducted because, at that time, there was a fundamental lack of understanding of how people think and behave when they are lost in the woods. His pioneering work has since led to a rich and now expansive field of research into the emotional and behavioral ways that people respond to being lost.

According to Hill, being lost involves two simple but distinct components—experiencing disorientation and a lack of an effective means to reorient oneself (Hill, 2011). While his work is focused on the experiences of backwoods travelers, hunters, hikers and others who find themselves lost in the wilderness, the parallels are evident in stories like Erica's. She had many possible paths in front of her but could not see an obvious or effective means of orienting herself in a way that honored her broad talents and varied ambitions. Despite being highly successful in each of several professional and personal domains, she found

herself without a clear sense of direction, feeling stuck and unsure how to proceed. Rather than choose, I invited her to stop and create a transitional space for inquiry as a means to consider other possibilities and explore new options.

Creating transitional learning space

Rather than ruminate on feelings of being stuck or unsure, uncertain transitions can be an invitation to ask new questions and explore opportunities we may not have considered *before* we make firm choices or commitments. Think of it as creating an ad hoc personal learning lab. A creative space to develop your practice of active waiting and dispassionate curiosity that is designed by you, for you, and aligned to your needs, context, and resources. Emergency services professionals do this when they create an emergency operations center on the site of an event or at another location. The climbers we discussed earlier have it at base camp. For an individual like Erica, it can be in a journal, on a white board, in the corner of a home office, or coordinated online with software or an app.

If you're working with a team, you can create shared space in the office or in a collaborative space online. None of it needs to be fancy. It can be a fixed spot or created on the fly. The context, time constraints and available resources will guide what's appropriate and possible. All that matters is that it be a space where questions, new ideas and an exploratory mindset are valued and supported. A space where fears and threats are voiced as areas inviting creative attention rather than a reactive response. The point is not to create an extra step in your process, but to intentionally create a third space between where you were before the What Now? Moment and where you will be when you reorient around a new course of action (or recommit to the course you're on). Sometimes called a neutral zone or liminal space in anthropology (Van Gennep, 2019), this transitional learning space is

both distinct and ill-defined. It is uncharted territory where we acknowledge that we have more questions than answers. It's the container where we have space to recognize that we are not ready to decide until we make sense of the situation we're in, and take active steps to gain a deeper understanding of what potential routes forward exist outside of our first thoughts (and our comfort zones).

It is important to note here that creating a transitional learning space is not about finding the answer. It is about accepting that there is rarely a single right or wrong answer in the wake of a What Now? Moment. That's what makes them so difficult. Choosing between A and B is much easier than making sense of abundant possibilities in a world where there is no single route to building a successful company or career and living a good life. So, if you've embraced the call to stop and are eager to move on to the part of the book that offers immediate solutions or quick fixes, you picked up the wrong book. Instead, now that we've begun to settle the threat response and gather resources (active resilience), pause (active waiting), and commit to a process of reflection, inquiry and learning, we're ready to think about learning in the liminal space between What Now? and what comes next.

Learning in liminal space

Liminal learning involves creating a container for creative problem solving where learners intentionally reorient themselves around new information and possibilities in times of uncertainty and change. According to education expert Maggie Savin-Baden, that can lead to a "shift in identity or role perception, so that issues and concerns are seen and heard in new and different ways" (Savin-Baden, 2008). So, the very shift of identity and self-concept that sparks our incendiary emotions and throws us into a threat response is just what we need to tap into new ideas and

consider alternative possibilities. This is what makes learning in the liminal so exciting—and so terrifying! This may seem obvious, but identity shifts are no small matter when it comes to our sense of who we are, where we are, and where we are going.

Whether we are in professional or personal settings, changes to our work or life status can lead to deeper, meaningful questions like: Who will I be if I make this change? What will I have to sacrifice? Will my reputation take a hit if I fail? This can raise the stakes of what can appear to be a minor change—like moving to a new team—and elevate our perception of the potential consequences if things don't go as expected. As a result, transitions and change are about more than simply accepting new ideas, approaches or circumstances, as many leaders mistakenly believe. Instead, organizational changes and work and life transitions outside of organizations can challenge identities and shift personal and professional trajectories in ways that lead to deep, existential questions about who we are and where we're meant to be. Until we settle these questions, the threat to identity and self-direction can lead to avoidance, push back, or unwarranted certainty that can create barriers to progress as we approach the task of finding our way when we feel lost or displaced. That's why developing practices that help us to get our bearings when we face interruptions and disruptions is so important.

Getting our bearings: the myth of true north

When Erica's loved ones encouraged her to pick a lane they were working on a common and well-worn 20th-century paradigm: the way to get ahead in life is to set goals and focus all of your attention, resources and time on bringing them to life. In that view, What Now? Moments and uncertain transitions simply become bumps on the road that may cause angst or require a detour, but the objective remains clear. Become a doctor, lawyer, firefighter or small business owner. Get married. Have children. Participate in

the life of your community. In this paradigm we approach work and life as many people would a cross-country drive. Pick a destination. Map out a route to get there. Even if you take the scenic route, the destination is clear—even if the particulars are not.

Most professional and personal development tools are designed to accommodate this approach. You find your "true north," whether it be a specific vision of success, or purpose, or "why?" and set off with a map in one hand and a compass in the other to reach that destination. This framework is so ingrained in Western education and professional and personal development circles that we have come to believe that a person with many interests and talents cannot succeed unless they know where they are going before they begin and pick a lane to get there as quickly as possible—preferably at scale. Thank goodness Leonardo da Vinci didn't take that advice!

Yet, as the demands and expectations of professional and personal life shift in ways that require all of us to adapt to persistent changes and reimagine what it means to live a good life, even people who would love to pick a lane are finding that they need to diversify their practices and approaches to meet the needs of a changing environment. This means expanding beyond old paradigms and reflecting upon what it means to flourish in a world where much is unknown, challenges abound, and what is possible is yet to be imagined. It also requires us to consider new—and perhaps return to old—ways of being, learning and knowing. Unfortunately, we rarely think about how we learn and what practices we need to develop to create effective learning spaces for ourselves. This is not surprising, since most of us were raised in learning environments where what we learn and how we learn it was prescribed by a teacher, a syllabus, or a program. As a result, we do what Ashley did—gather

Unfortunately, we rarely think about how we learn and what practices we need to develop to create effective learning spaces for ourselves.

books and resources only to find ourselves overwhelmed with knowledge without a clear sense of how to apply it in practice.

"Can I read more on your website?" students, clients, mentees and others ask me once they embrace the notion that a What Now? Moment is an invitation to deeper inquiry. "Is there a course I can take?" I understand the desire to have a roadmap when the way forward is unclear, and a guide to show us the way. But finding the *right* product or service will not clear away the fog of uncertainty and light our path forward when we're navigating change. Of course we've been conditioned to believe differently. Whether in the slick offerings of a "success industrial complex" that promises bigger, better, faster ways to shape our careers and find success, or a "wellbeing industrial complex" that claims to hold the secret to a healthy and happy life, finding our way is contextual—and learning is personal.

Unfortunately, no matter how many tools, approaches and frameworks these multi-billion-dollar industries have to offer, there's no roadmap for exploring uncharted territory—it's mysterious, wild and a little bit risky. Despite the marketing promises, there is no single, cleanly packaged, off-the-shelf approach designed for mass appeal at scale that will fit all, or even most, people in the vastly varied circumstances you or your team or your family or your community face in your individual context on a day-to-day basis. Even the most well-researched model or framework can't do that work for us or offer us a turn-key solution.

That's why, rather than espouse a particular way of navigating, I encourage you to develop your own approach, built on your own principles, trusted resources, exploration, and circumstances. That means engaging in a process of rigorous self-awareness and observation of the world around you in order to explore where your aspirations and ambitions intersect with the needs of others at work, at home, in your community and across the globe. It also points to a collection of skills and capacities that we rarely discuss that are imperative for navigating

uncharted territory—sensemaking, wayfinding and discernment, which we will discuss in the next two sections.

For now, as we consider what we've learned from allowing ourselves to stop, temper our incendiary emotions, gather the resources we need, and intentionally open up a liminal learning space where we can inquire further, it is important to acknowledge that we stand on a threshold between where we were and where we hope to be. Moving across this uncharted territory it involves a commitment to thinking differently and a willingness to be intentional about developing an approach to learning that is aligned with the resources at our disposal and the way we approach gathering and processing information. This is a good news/bad news situation. The good news? Learning is a creative act that can be approached in a variety of ways. The bad news? Folding new information into existing frameworks and paradigms can be more troublesome than we think. That's why having the humility to acknowledge that we have something to learn and the willingness to become teachable when we choose to meet uncertainty with curiosity and an exploratory mindset is fundamental to learning to flourish in the face of What Now? Moments.

It is important to note here that being teachable does not mean a willingness to accept new ideas and frameworks at face value. Instead, teachability is simply a willingness to believe that new circumstances, information and contexts may require us to shift our perspective and consider new ways of being and doing to meet the moment. It involves a readiness to consider that our view is not fully formed. That there is always more to learn. That we know what we know today but are not so firm in our knowledge that we close ourselves off to new information that might allow us to see things differently. This is a bold and courageous choice because accepting "I don't know" and entering liminal learning space can be its own threat. That means you stand on a threshold with a choice to make. How will you mark the occasion?

Marking points of transition

In some cultures—current and past—the creation of rituals, rites of passage and traditions were and are commonplace ways of marking and moving over thresholds and into transition. There are so many examples that could be used here. Rites of movement into adulthood, marriage rituals, rites for grief, death and dying. But also for the changing of the seasons, hunting celebrations and others.

Unfortunately, many such traditions have been lost in the modern era. For many people, marriage is viewed as "just a piece of paper" and the equivalent of a successful hunt is a promotion from manager to director that may or may not be followed by a celebratory drink. More and more, the combination of the pace of living and the devaluing of tradition is resulting in perpetual motion and the assumption that moving forward to more, bigger and scaling, is more important than creating and participating in rituals to be more intentional about life's planned and unplanned changes. Marking our entry into and out of transitional learning spaces helps to define our container and ground us in a third space. Human beings have engaged in such rites of passage for millennia—and we might learn from the rituals of the past to understand how to create new ones that help to inform how we engage with an uncertain future.

Understanding the contours of what we know and what we don't as we move into a transition is an important factor in change that is overlooked when we stand on the threshold of liminal space. This is especially true when we are thrust into transition or find ourselves lost in a transition we did not choose. Rites of passage and milestone markers are guideposts we can rely on when passing into and through transitional learning spaces. Being clear about how we approach the liminal learning space can make or break how we navigate them. Every What Now? Moment offers the opportunity to consider whether we're

on the cusp of big moves and grand changes or a time for reflection and remaining on the same path. Developing rituals to mark transitions gives us a chance to ask—do I want to bloom where I'm planted now? Should I return to a place where things were more aligned with where I want to be?

This is not a common chapter in most professional and personal development books. The chapter that says: if you are not ready, then wait. If you are not sure, then contemplate. If your dream is not a dream for now, then make it a dream for later. Authors like me are "supposed to" inspire and motivate readers to do it all and do it now.

That is not my role.

I don't want to inspire you to do more or do things differently. Instead, I'm inviting you to consider that thresholds to change are important milestones that are worthy of attention and remembrance. This is not a call to return to past rituals—although some people may choose to look to the past to find ideas. It is a call to create new ones. To create your own traditions in professional and personal spaces where you mark spaces of transition and change— even troublesome ones. These moments of reflection, action or practice provide entry points into the unknown that can lead us to places and possibilities that we might not have considered had our paths not been disrupted.

QUESTIONS FOR REFLECTION

As you consider entering liminal learning space, reflect on the following questions and find a way to capture your reflections in a way that is right for you. Write some notes, take photos, draw pictures, make a spreadsheet, record your voice or a video, start a new journal—whatever allows you to remember what you were thinking as you cross the threshold into inquiry. This can be a helpful way to create a ritual for transitions and change that you can draw upon now and in the future.

Do you feel ready, eager, and equipped?

Do you feel curious?

What is it that we are committing to?

How might you mark this place?

How might you return to it in the future?

Is there some sort of action or ritual you want to do to mark the space?

What if you decide not to proceed?

What inquiry do you need to embark upon to find out whether you are choosing to move forward or avoiding moving forward as a point of procrastination?

Are you being driven by fear or are there good and substantial reasons why you should not press forward?

Whose voice is in your head?

Do we need to resource ourselves to understand if we are embarking on our own journey or the journey that we *think* we are expected to be on?

So, as we shift from a reflective pause into inquiry—from stop to ask—be ready for anything. You may recommit to the path you are on with a reinvigorated sense of what is possible within a familiar terrain like Ashley, or consider possibilities you never imagined like Erica. By entering intentionally into inquiry, we can consider where challenges that might seem insurmountable are actually prompts to creative problem solving that can lead us in new directions. Or we may find that things we thought would be easy or quick actually require more effort and longer-term commitment than we first expected. Wherever it leads, inquiry creates space to pursue at least a cursory understanding of new terrain before driving to decide, so we can consider new possibilities and make sense of them.

This applies to changes that we choose, and those that are thrust upon us, although the latter—the three-alarm fires—can present some of the most tangled uncharted territory of all.

Inquiry creates space to pursue at least a cursory understanding of new terrain before driving to decide so we can consider new possibilities and make sense of them.

In any of these cases, moving from stop to ask is a turning point. We stand at a threshold. Think of it like a train switching yard. Many different paths forward—or sideward, or even backward to move forward. Entering liminal requires some intention and a sense of what it is that you are and are not committing to. Whether you choose to take a big step or just dip your toe in the water, making space and time to ask new questions will give you a better sense of where you are and where you hope to go.

TAKEAWAYS

- Being lost is a psychological state that is steeped in our perception of where we are and what pathways we might take to find new ways forward.

- Learning to get our bearings when we face uncharted territory is a critical threshold into transitional learning space.

- Creating rituals or rites of passage can be a helpful way of marking entry into the liminal space between What Now? and what comes next.

PART TWO

Ask

A note to the reader as you begin to 'Ask'

If you've reached this point in the *stop, ask, explore* journey you've slowed things down enough to acknowledge that What Now? Moments can be a threshold to uncharted territory. Like a hiker standing at the edge of the meadow preparing to enter a thick forest, you stand at the turning point. Do you have the will to consider new ways forward and to explore the uncertain space between What Now? and what comes next? If the answer is yes, there are three core questions to examine in order to begin making sense of the new terrain we find ourselves in and to discern how best to navigate it. The chapters in this section provide some frameworks and practices to consider as you contemplate where you are, who you are and what is possible in the wake of any What Now? Moment.

Joan

CHAPTER FIVE

Zoom in

*Rigorous self-awareness and making sense
of new terrain*

Have you ever walked into a restaurant and wondered: "Do we seat ourselves or wait to be seated?"

We've all experienced it in one context or another. The low-stakes yet awkward moment when you enter an unfamiliar space and aren't quite sure what to do next. It may not be a restaurant. The same happens in the lobby of a building. A hospital. A school. In fact, the purpose of a lobby and all of the signage we typically find there is to invite people into a space and help them understand how best to navigate it. The placement of those signs and other signals of where to go and what to do when we enter a space is the little-known but important purview of wayfinding professionals. In this context, wayfinding refers to "the spatial organization of a setting" (Passini, 1996). These unsung heroes are the people who create the flow we follow in physical spaces— say when we enter a park or land at an airport.

When wayfinders do their job well, we don't notice it. We turn the corner in the labyrinth of hospital hallways and take for granted that there is a sign on the wall or hanging from the ceiling, right where we need it, telling us what step to take next. We come over a rise while hiking and see the white spray-painted strike on a tree or other mark just before we would have started to wonder if we'd missed something or were off track. Whether or not we would use that term for it, we also rely on organizational and cultural wayfinders to guide us on our professional and personal journeys. Onboarding processes, training programs, handbooks and other guidance help people to orient themselves and find pathways forward in their careers. Advisors, administrators and educators provide wayfinding services for learners. Cultural norms, traditions and rituals provide wayfinding clues for how we engage with our friends, families and in our communities.

Or do they?

As new technologies, processes and approaches to working, living and learning change, these imperfect, yet consistent sources of wayfinding cues are shifting from top down to bottom up. Rather than rely on employers, institutions or systems to tell us where to go and what to do, people increasingly view the trajectory of their careers and lifestyles as theirs to imagine and bring to life. This is great news, especially for people who were marginalized or otherwise not well served by the systems that defined the 20th century. It also shifts the role of wayfinder somewhere between individuals and organizations, leaving fundamental gaps in vision and practices that make sense on both sides of the equation.

As a result, individuals can no longer take for granted that there will be a sign or a signal around the corner to guide their way—or that we can plan the journey of one domain of our life without considering the implications for another. At the same time, leaders need to reimagine what it means to partner with the people who they rely on to sustain their organizations by

focusing on their needs and aspirations in and outside of work. This is uncharted territory, which means we all need to learn to become our own wayfinders in and out of work—especially when we find ourselves in the liminal space between clear-cut career paths and the abstraction we frequently refer to as the "future of work."

As we move further away from long-term relationships between employees and organizations toward a more nomadic workforce, people can no longer take for granted that there will be a sign or a blaze to show them which way to turn on the path toward their own professional and personal flourishing. Unfortunately, since the hand of the wayfinder in modern life is intentionally invisible, many people credit their own sense of direction rather than the skillful placement of signs and markers for the ability to find their way. This leaves us vulnerable to disorientation and confusion when we find ourselves outside the domain of well-defined pathways to find the best way into, through, and beyond this uncharted territory.

As we move from top-down, hierarchical systems to ones where individuals, teams and groups have more autonomy to find their own way with the support of the organization rather than at the direction of the organization, the need to develop wayfinding skills and support others as they do the same is a 21st-century imperative. Thus, it is more important than ever for people to understand where the signs and signals we see are coming from and what it takes to make sense of them—especially in the context of how we choose to navigate our professional and personal lives.

As we reimagine and renegotiate the systems, structures and norms that drive culture across the globe, and employ new technology and approaches to guide our paths at work and at home, the onus of finding our way falls increasingly on us as individuals and communities. This is compounded in consumer-based cultures where the spirit of creating personalized experiences that meet our unique and particular needs in context means we have a constant stream of new options and are tasked with making sense

of complex sets of choices that can be overwhelming, even when we welcome them. In formal and informal education and training settings in particular, learners are encouraged to develop their own pathways and follow them in their own way at their own pace. Family and community cultures have shifted, allowing multiple acceptable pathways for partnering, child-rearing and living arrangements. Ideas about what it means to be successful or the ways of pursuing a career trajectory have moved from particular paths driven by family expectations or a "corporate ladder" and allow for freedom to traverse a corporate lattice as we gather skills from in and outside of companies and develop personal narratives on how they come together and why our disparate skills apply in varied circumstances. Even in a grocery store, customers can choose to order online, engage with a cashier, or do self-checkout.

All of this freedom to pave our own way of being and doing in this new world is very exciting. It can also be disorienting, especially since most of us were educated in systems that not only didn't teach wayfinding skills—they discouraged them. As a result, this increasingly popular, "if you build it, they will find their way" mentality ignores the invisible role that wayfinding traditionally played in helping us to find our bearings and stay oriented. It also misses the lack of training and skill building we've done individually, among leaders and in our learning organizations in this regard. Because so much of that direction came from the invisible hand of the structures and rule-makers, we miss that wayfinding is not "human nature" but is a capacity that we need to develop in ourselves and support in those we hope to serve in our organizations, families and communities.

Unfortunately, even if we are committed to finding or helping others to find a helpful route to education, training and retraining, the wayfinding tools to do so are woefully lacking. Too often we rely on a Google search that spits back a million results, the first few pages of which are populated by the offerings of skillful marketers selling learning programs. In a conversation

with an HR leader for a global media firm during a several-day leadership retreat I facilitated several years ago they admitted that, while they were quite proud of all the training and development content they'd curated in their intranet, their people weren't using it at all. When I asked some of the attendees if they used it and why, they said they were not sure where to start. There were too many choices. They were busy. And making sense of it felt like a chore, so they left it alone.

Isn't this just common sense?

"Wait a minute," readers over 40 may be thinking. "Nobody taught me how to do this. Wayfinding is just common sense."

According to Webster's dictionary, common sense consists of knowledge, judgment and taste, which is more or less universal and which is held more or less without reflection or argument. So, if you find yourself in a homogeneous environment where most people agree upon the way things are done (the most simplified definition of culture) and you embrace the hand of the invisible wayfinders to guide your steps, it's easy to believe that what's popular and familiar to you is "common sense." In the 20th century, what was popular and familiar in many Western cultures was aspiring to have a good job, a "traditional" family, a nice house, and to live a nice life. Moving up in a company was not about choosing multiple paths upward—it was climbing a prescribed ladder. Moving from position to position across firms or industries was "job hopping," not skill and experience gathering. Choosing alternative family arrangements and making decisions about fertility was uncomplicated, not freezing eggs and IVF. We didn't see the guidance of cultural wayfinders because they were simply the system in which we had been born and were conditioned to operate within. We don't always see it now in the form of algorithms, influencers and technologies built to nudge us in one direction or another.

As the cultural norms that once guided our professional and personal paths are dismantled and reimagined, the task of finding our way through a company, a career, a community, a life involves unlearning identities, reconsidering old habits, rethinking existing power structures, reimagining what work means to us, and reflecting upon what it means to live a good life—all while keeping up with the abstract but much-discussed "lifelong learning." Unfortunately, many of the people I've worked with over the past decade report that they feel ill-equipped for this complex task. That's because reflecting on who we are, what we hope for and exploring how we might bring those hopes to life involves more than identifying your strengths, finding your "why?" or building a particular set of skills. It involves developing practices, principles and frameworks that can help us to know who we are and how we fit across different contexts and circumstances as those contexts and circumstances are constantly shifting and changing. I think this is what Owen Muir, M.D. was talking about when we discussed the pivot metaphor and he nodded to the challenge people face as we try to find our self-world fit.

Wayfinding and the self-world fit

Understanding who we are (identity) and where we hope to go (self-direction) are key orientation points when we engage in wayfinding in the context of navigating uncertain transitions. Despite how helpful it can be to draw upon stories and principles of navigating in physical spaces to understand being lost in transition, finding tangible markers and guideposts to help navigate liminal learning spaces is more elusive.

Employing tactics like developing rites and rituals or engaging with metaphors can help us to construct guideposts to orient ourselves as we move in and out of liminal spaces and seek to find *alignment between our perception of self and our environment— our self-world fit.* When that alignment is off it can contribute to

feelings of being lost and disoriented, which can prevent us from entering liminal learning spaces. When our self-world fit feels more in alignment, we can be more adventurous, learning, exploring and experimenting, and less likely to view change as a threat.

Unfortunately, our self-world fit can come ajar when we encounter What Now? Moments. That's what happened to Andrea Bussell. Andrea left her position as a successful communications professional at a high-profile cultural institution in New York City to take a job she knew wasn't right for her from the day she accepted it. She told me, "They recruited me and made such a strong offer that it seemed like an interesting next step. But almost immediately, it became clear to me that I'd landed in a toxic and chaotic startup culture that was unaligned with my values and left me little room to perform to the best of my skills and expertise." She knew she was a creative spirit at heart with a deep desire to find work that aligned with her love of nature, but as the Covid-19 pandemic intensified, she found herself living alone in a tiny Brooklyn studio apartment working

Understanding who we are (identity) and where we hope to go (self-direction) are key orientation points when we engage in wayfinding in the context of navigating uncertain transitions.

FIGURE 5.1 Self-world fit

from home 16 hours a day on projects that didn't inspire her. "I just kept dreaming of being in the forest somewhere and was trying to come up with a way to make that happen realistically. I knew I wanted to leave New York, but I was conflicted because I'd built a life there for 17 years." On top of that, her relationship with her partner was imploding, so she was experiencing a What Now? Moment across professional and personal domains.

Once we temper the threat response that this sort of complex, multi-dimensional What Now? Moment often sparks, deeper questions emerge. For Andrea, that meant opening an inquiry into broader possibilities than she'd considered previously. For others it involves questioning who they are and what matters to them after being "downsized" or wondering what their place is in an organization where their team or department is merged with another. In each case and countless others, rigorous self-awareness is a helpful stepping-off point for getting as clear a picture as possible of the "self" in self-world fit.

Why start with rigorous self-awareness?

Self-awareness is a critical part of orienting ourselves in the world. How we identify ourselves and how we are viewed by others can play a big part in how we make sense of the world and place ourselves in it. We've talked about how destabilizing and disorienting interruptions and disruptions can be and how they can call our identity into question. Who am I if I don't get a good job when I graduate? Who am I if my skills are no longer vital in a changing economy? Who am I if I have this child? Who am I if I decide to go back to school or close my business? Too often we ask these kinds of questions on rotation in our heads rather than actually address them as creative prompts. As a result, they become ruminations rather than invitations to inquiry. This is a missed opportunity to gather helpful information that can contribute to our wayfinding efforts.

Organizational psychologist Tasha Eurich calls self-awareness the meta-skill of the 21st century, and defines it as "the ability to see ourselves clearly—to understand who we are, how others see us, and how we fit into the world around us." Of course, the pursuit of self-understanding goes much deeper and further back than a 21st-century thought leader. As a species, human beings have spent millennia trying to understand how we fit in the world and what it means to live a good life. This is not surprising since, as Eurich suggests, "when we see ourselves clearly, we are more confident and more creative. We make sounder decisions, build stronger relationships, and communicate more effectively" (Eurich, 2017). Moreover, there are moral implications, such as decreased likelihood that we will lie, cheat and steal, and we are "more effective leaders with more satisfied employees and more profitable companies" (Eurich, 2017).

Seeing ourselves as clearly as possible with the information and insight we have at our disposal is particularly important when we enter liminal space and engage in liminal learning. Like someone lost in the wilderness, finding what direction to walk is only part of the information you need to reorient yourself and find your way. Your approach to finding your way is as much built on who you are in the moment as it is where you are. Are you injured? Are you in shock? Can you trust your judgment? Do you have any impediments you need to consider before you walk on? You might approach the task of finding your way out of the wilderness differently if you had a twisted knee. You wouldn't take a route across a river if you don't know how to swim. You might make poor decisions if you're in shock. Understanding your own strengths, weaknesses and vulnerabilities in the moment helps to determine the best way over, under or around the barriers to progress that come your way.

Research suggests that most of us don't know ourselves very well, even though we think we do. This leaves us in the dark to strengths we can maximize and vulnerabilities we can gather resources to support. By taking what some call a fearless and

searching look at who we are and what we hope for, we have information with which to orient ourselves and set course. We began this process in Chapter 2 with the resilience wheel by reflecting on what potential points of resistance might help us to temper our incendiary emotions and knee-jerk reactions when we face What Now? Moments. Knowing what kind of situations and circumstances tend to get under our skin and spark the threat response gives us a better chance of recognizing incendiary emotions, tempering them, gaining our composure, and moving from reaction to a dispassionately curious response. But self-awareness is about more than where we are vulnerable to threat. What matters to us, what professional and personal roles we hope to play, how our aspirations intersect with the needs of others in our lives, communities, workplaces, and the world at large—these are more complex questions that invite deeper reflection and integration across the domains of our professional and personal lives.

Rigorous self-awareness in practice

Whether we embrace the promise of uncharted territory as an opportunity or a challenge (or maybe a little bit of both), understanding the terrain we're in and choosing the path we want to take involves developing guiding principles from the inside out rather than relying solely on cultural norms and societal dreams to guide the way. That is why zooming in and committing to a practice of rigorous, honest self-awareness is a key capacity for 21st-century life. So, how do we move from trite calls to follow our passion or ideals of living meaningfully to opening an intentional inquiry into what makes us tick? What resources do we need to do so in ways that are both healthy and productive?

As mentioned previously, there is no shortage of books, blogs, podcasts, personality tests and other assessment tools we can use to learn more about ourselves. We can also connect with therapists, coaches, educators and others dedicated to professional

and personal development. We have created industries around tools, frameworks and resources designed to help us identify strengths, clarify our identities, manage our time and build new capacities to deal with change. Some of them are wonderful. Others are less helpful. Rather than add another tool to the mix, I suggest you consider using what you've already done to make sense of what you know, what you don't know, and how you might fill in the gaps.

This helps keep us from zig-zagging from solution to solution in search of the "right" tool to "answer" the question of who we are, as if we are doing market research. Instead, we can develop a practice of self-inquiry, built on approaches that align with our capacities, interests and aspirations. It places us in an orientation of discovery rather than problem solving. Engaging with self-inquiry in this way liberates us from moving from tool to tool looking for a quick fix. It also alleviates the guilt and frustration many people experience when we feel forced or obligated to engage with practices and tools that do not resonate. If you are a leader or an educator, it may also be helpful to encourage those you serve to go beyond simply accumulating certificates and taking courses and provide them with resources to make sense of what they've actually learned about, who they are, and how they hope to show up at work and beyond. You might even bring a practice of inquiry and sensemaking into your development practices and reviews as a means to encourage people to think about what matters to them and how they can bring those values, ambitions and motivations to bear in the organization.

Where to start?

Whether you are working on your own or with others, inquiry begins with an intentional exploration of our inner terrain, and there is no single "right way" to approach it. Many readers will come to this book having spent years developing practices to explore who they are and what makes them tick. Others will be new to it. Either way, the focus here is less on how we respond

when things are going our way. In this context, we're focusing on how you respond to the What Now? Moment in front of you—and that response can be surprising. Disruptions and interruptions can bring out the best, the worst or the unexpected in all of us. Timid people can be uncharacteristically brave—and otherwise courageous people can become timid in the face of one sort of uncertain transition. Those same people can go the other way when the transition context and risk factors change. That's why it is can be helpful to take a clear-eyed snapshot of your current state whenever you face a What Now? Moment, without making assumptions based upon previous responses to change. This prompts an inquiry into the now and into ourselves as we relate to the world around us in a particular context. No aspiration. No ideals. No "I wish I was." A simple, but rigorous, examination of where you are today—with all the warts, scars and half-baked parts of the cake we bring to where we stand. This can help you to identify a grounding point for navigation. The current state mapping exercise below can be a helpful tool to get you started.

EXERCISE Current state mapping

Mapping where we are at the beginning of our inquiry can help to ground us in the current reality before we wander too far in uncharted territory. This doesn't need to take long, nor does it need to be "complete." This is just an opportunity to capture a snapshot of the transition terrain as you see it from the vantage point of where you begin your exploration. There are no right or wrong answers—and identifying what you don't know is as important as capturing what you do know. You can return to this exercise again and again as you proceed with your inquiry. You can then use some of these reflections, insights from the resilience wheel, your metaphors and other observations and information you have to make sense of where you are and where you hope to go. Keep in

mind that you can collect these reflections in any form—analog or digital. Make it your own. Also, please resist the urge to categorize or understand (more on that in Chapter 7). Simply reflect, capture and create, and you'll have a great place to start.

- **Activity Map**: Reflect on your current activities and create a visual representation that reflects how you currently spend your time (at work, outside of work, online, etc.). Use your calendar, diary, or any other tools to capture as thoroughly as possible how you currently spend your time.

- **Skills Map**: Reflect on your current skills and create a skills map. These may be professional skills, personal skills, or things you can do that have seemingly no relationship to what we are doing here. Think about times you have been proud of an outcome and what you were doing, whether or not it seems relevant to our work together. Again, please don't censor yourself.

- **Influence Map**: Reflect on your current sphere(s) of influence and create a visual representation that shows all individuals, groups, organizations, online communities, etc. where you hold any amount of influence—large or small. These may be areas where you love having influence, or ones where you wish you didn't. Please do not censor yourself. Include them all.

- **Impact Map**: Reflect on your current sense of things. What do you hope to know, do, change, impact in the world? Your life? For yourself? For others? What legacy do you hope to leave? What needle do you want to move in your home, your community, at work, in the world? Identify these boldly (think big picture!) without censoring yourself.

- **Barriers Map**: Reflect on your current sense of what is in your way. What is missing? Where are you under-resourced? What isn't working? What are the stress points? The pain points?

- **Resource Map**: Reflect on your current sense of the resources available to you. What is working? Where are you well-resourced? What are the strong points? The points of joy?

Start making sense

As we populate these maps, the terrain of our transitional learning space begins to take shape. Looking at the maps you'll begin to see what resources you have, whether or not they feel complete. Aspirations for where you want to go may emerge, whether or not you have clarity of what is ahead of you. You may have the impulse to quickly assess the content of the maps and move forward, but the purpose of this exercise is to understand the new terrain and acknowledge that we have entered uncharted territory. Here's where I begin. X marks this spot. I can choose to go forward. I can choose to go back. I can stay right here where I am—or I need to find another possibility. This is my best understanding and estimation of my circumstances, and I am ready to commit to a deeper inquiry and process of sensemaking before I decide my next move.

There is a deep rabbit hole you can go down if you want to learn more about sensemaking in theory and practice. Researchers and practitioners deliberate and debate about what sensemaking is and how it can be applied to understand where we are and where we are heading in changing times. I find these perspectives fascinating, and highly encourage anyone to avail themselves of the sensemaking resources at the end of the book to learn more

about how to take your interest further (see Appendix E). For our purposes, in the context of using these skills to find our way day-to-day in professional and personal life, we draw upon a combination of natural sensemaking skills we already rely on to navigate the spaces we inhabit, and build upon them through observation, inquiry, and trial and error.

Let's begin with an important point. All of us already have the fundamental capacity to be sensemakers and wayfinders. These are innate human skills that come so naturally to us in some domains that we take them for granted. This is a missed opportunity to recognize an inherent strength we all share and engage that strength intentionally in circumstances and contexts where it does not come naturally by default. It takes attention and practice and a dispassionate curiosity about what it means to make sense of things and how a sensemaking practice might support your wayfinding efforts. Thankfully, there is no single way to make sense of things. Sensemaking is much more of an art than a science, so, rather than focus on a single definition of sensemaking, I invite you to think about sensemaking as one of many practices we can engage when a What Now? Moment throws us off course. In that moment of threat, we can practice the art of intentional inquiry. "I don't know what to do!" can shift to questions like, "How am I doing?" "Where am I stuck?" and "How might I connect to the emotional, physical, material and social resources I need to get my bearings and reorient myself?" In doing so, we move from saccharine calls to "get curious" to an engaged inquiry — dispassionate curiosity in action.

This approach invites you or your team to develop your own capacity to make sense of the unfamiliar and navigate it based upon your own constellation of aspirations, values, resources, relationships, and other considerations that are unique to you and the situation in which you find yourself. You have the capacity for sensemaking in you. We all do. But you can also build your sensemaking capacity and develop a practice of gathering observations and seeking to make sense of them as a vehicle to sensemaking.

Sensemaking wayfinding and wayfinding as sensemaking

As we've discussed throughout this book, we know we are living in a tumultuous age marked by persistent and enduring change. On the one hand, everything is different from previous generations. Opportunities have increased tenfold thanks to technology and other advancements, and along with those new opportunities come a myriad of complex situations and decisions we might not have faced in different times. Yet on the other hand, the ways in which we form communities, grow, change and learn, seek meaning and purpose, and share wisdom with those who come next are remarkably similar to those who came before us. Ultimately, despite the shifts that require us to rethink everything, we humans are born, grow, change, become—and then we go. Just like our ancestors did. For all the answers we've found about the world around us, the core questions of what it means to be human—what it means to live a good life, how we're meant to be—remain equally interesting and largely unanswered. With all the technology and advancements of the past few centuries, we are engaging with ancient questions in new contexts.

Rather than seek to answer these kinds of questions in a deep or profound way, however, we often work them out through mundane and practical questions, like what we should do for a living. So, finding our purpose or seeking meaning becomes something that is in service to professional or personal wayfinding. When we face professional and personal turning points, we are not only called to reconsider where we should go and how we should get there (direction), we are also called to consider who we are (identity) and how we choose to live (presence). This is true of us as individuals and in community, at work and beyond. Making sense of these aspects of life and how they relate to our self-world fit—or having a confidence that we can develop approaches to learn—is not only a fundamental part of being

human, but is also at the core of developing a wayfinding practice that is grounded in sensemaking.

We observed this on a global scale during the Covid-19 pandemic, when challenging circumstances were coupled with a deep and prolonged pause. All but the front-line workers among us were prevented from distracting ourselves with typical day-to-day activities and found ourselves asking deeper questions than we might have done otherwise. But we don't have to wait for these kinds of massive existential events to engage with deep inquiry. Even the most mundane What Now? Moments can, if we let them, become more than points of decision. These milestones along our journey can become catalysts of our own becoming and the becoming of the organizations, projects, and endeavors we have set out to create.

So, if you enter into liminal learning spaces with an eye on learning to make sense of who you are and what is possible in your unique and complex circumstances—you can identify a broad set of options that can help you maintain a sense of direction.

But it doesn't stop there. We need to consider what we learn in our practice of rigorous self-awareness in the contexts we share with others and recognize that where we bring our aspirations to life also offer clues and insights that are useful for wayfinding. That is why wayfinding is not a set of steps we follow. As with the wilderness explorers we've discussed throughout the text, it is a continual process of learning in action and a willingness to continually calibrate and recalibrate as we gather new information and fold what we learn in times of inquiry and exploration into times of execution. We do this by wayfinding

If you enter into liminal learning spaces with an eye on learning to make sense of who you are and what is possible in your unique and complex circumstances— you can identify a broad set of options that can help you maintain a sense of direction.

from the inside out (zooming in) and bringing what we learn into context, so we are also wayfinding from the outside in (zooming out).

TAKEAWAYS

- Rigorous self-awareness provides a grounding point for our wayfinding journey as we enter uncharted territory.

- Finding our self-world fit can be a point of orientation as we engage in a process of sensemaking and wayfinding.

- Mapping our current state is a helpful stepping-off point for inquiry.

Zoom out

Wayfinding from the outside in

"So, what do you hope for?" I ask this question frequently of my students, clients, and research participants when they're feeling lost or unsettled.

"I just want to be happy."

"I want to do something meaningful."

"I want to follow my passion."

"I want to be famous."

"I want to make money."

"I want to change the world."

All perfectly reasonable, but not very helpful when it comes to orienting or reorienting ourselves in uncertain transitions. That becomes crystal clear when I follow up with the second set of questions.

"What makes you happy and what route do you plan to take to pursue it?'

"What do you find meaningful and how might you bring meaning into your life both professionally and personally?"

"What are you passionate about and how does that relate to the way you walk through the world on a daily basis?"

"How much money and fame are enough and how will you know when you've arrived?"

"What change do you want to bring to the world and what makes you think you are the right person to bring it?"

Shifting from ideal outcomes to specific, grounded questions about how we intend to bring our ideals to life on a day-to-day basis moves the wayfinding question from theory to practice, and it is a place where many people get stuck. Hoping to find our way back to the car when we're lost in the woods, or to find an oasis in the desert, is very different than knowing what route to take to get there. That's why zooming in to focus on rigorous self-awareness *and* zooming out to develop a deep understanding of the context in which we are operating are both crucial parts to finding our way.

When we move from ideals to action in the context of an uncertain transition, we quickly see that there are many ways to pursue joy or happiness, to do meaningful work or to make a good living—even when we feel constrained by limited time, resources or opportunity. If we rely solely on self-awareness to guide our way, we can risk making ourselves and our own needs, wants and desires the central point of orientation for wayfinding. If we overcorrect in the other direction, we can make more worldly concerns our central point of orientation for wayfinding and become too focused on the expectations or needs of others, which can throw us off course. By looking both inside and out, we can avoid the trap that so many good-hearted people fall into—focusing on ourselves to the detriment of others or focusing

on others to the detriment of ourselves. Finding and maintaining a sustainable balance between the two is like a dance where one partner moves with the other and anticipates where the other is headed—sometimes before they know themselves. When it flows, it can be magical. When it doesn't, we may step on some toes and need to try again. In either case, this is at the heart and soul of our pursuit of wayfinding.

Wayfinding fundamentals

In Chapter 5 I described wayfinding as the system of signs, maps and other navigation systems that guide us through spaces (see Appendix F for more on wayfinding). In the navigation of physical spaces, that is called *aided wayfinding* and it includes tools like GPS and other navigation assistants that help make finding our way less ambiguous (see Figure 6.1). Despite the changing shape of work, there are still fields and firms where aided wayfinding still exists in the form of prescribed paths and roadmaps to "climb the corporate ladder." The military, law enforcement, emergency services and government service are some good examples. Some areas of healthcare, teaching and professional services are some others. In each of these industries, there remain some prescribed routes for advancement that follow a particular path or trajectory—at least for now.

FIGURE 6.1 Aided wayfinding

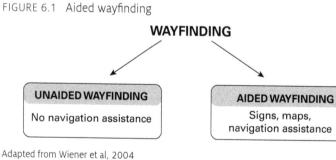

Adapted from Wiener et al, 2004

People in these fields encounter What Now? Moments along the way, but they are more likely to be potholes or detours. When people operate in systems that have retained those 20th-century models, uncharted territory still exists, but it typically comes when we enter or leave the organization, rather than from inside it. The year I accepted the position my father was so thrilled about at Con Edison, the average tenure of a person at the company was 34 years. The people I worked with made one career decision in their late teens or early twenties and received their paycheck from one organization until the day they retired. Career paths were set by human resources departments, union contracts and organization charts that were fixed and predictable for people who got their foot through the door, and major life events were driven by cultural norms and traditions. The point of orientation and desired outcome remained clear, even when things went wrong in the day-to-day. It is increasingly rare for 21st-century work and life trajectories to unfold in that way.

Unaided wayfinding

In unaided wayfinding there is no navigation assistance. No maps, signs or GPS. This is the empty beach, the gig economy career trajectory we've discussed previously (see Figure 6.2). When we step outside the signs, systems and structures that prescribe a set trajectory for our work, our life, our business or our strategy, we have the freedom to go our own way. Like a person who enters the woods for a hike and chooses to step off the trail and explore outside of what's already been blazed. There is freedom in this approach, of course, but also greater uncertainty and potential to become lost or turned around because we are finding our own way. We can view that distinction as a reason to stick to set paths, which can feel like the safe bet until we hit a barrier to progress and face a What Now? Moment. In these cases, the way forward is ours to discern. As a result, clarifying

FIGURE 6.2 Unaided wayfinding

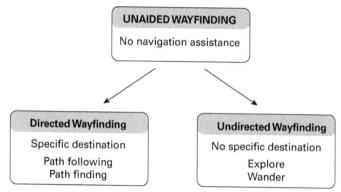

Adapted from Wiener et al, 2004

what we do or don't know about where we hope to go and possible routes to get us there can illuminate possible next steps, even if we are unsure of the specific outcome we seek. Unfortunately, despite an increasing need for unaided wayfinding skills in our personal and professional lives, most people have received little instruction in the topic.

Directed wayfinding

There are two types of unaided wayfinding: directed and undirected. When we engage in *directed wayfinding* we have a specific destination in mind and the primary task at hand is to find (or create) a path that leads to the intended destination. Sometimes we know where we hope to go, but don't have an established path or milestone markers to guide us. Maybe we were thrown off course or we're just entering the workforce and have not yet discovered how best to bring the specific aspiration we have to life. Navigators call that directed wayfinding and it involves searching for what we hope for, following when a path shows up in front of us, and seeking new paths to arrive at a chosen destination. In practice this can involve connecting with people who have arrived where we hope to go and learning about their paths to getting there. Or familiarizing ourselves with the terrain by

immersing ourselves in it or connecting with and observing the experiences of people who are where we hope to go. We might find a job or an internship to place us in closer proximity to where we hope to be, or we can gain insights through other experiences that provide a window into a terrain we have yet to travel within.

Undirected wayfinding

Undirected wayfinding is different. This is for people like Erica, Ashley, and others who don't have a specific destination in mind. It involves exploration and roaming, which we will discuss more in Part Three. In either case, whether we have a set destination or are learning as we go, being and doing in a technology-driven world that is less hierarchical and prescriptive means we are more frequently operating in unfamiliar terrain that invites us to develop a wayfinding practice.

Wayfinding is a practice, not a product

Even though we know that the days of finding a good company and staying there for three or four decades are gone, many people—even students in their late teens and early twenties—are nostalgic for a time when career and life paths were clearer from the onset. People embrace the ideal of gaining new skills, experiences and networks, and becoming willing to learn, grow, adapt and be a good problem solver, but we fall short when we face the question of how to prepare ourselves and others to bring those ideals to bear in the day-to-day. This hesitation—which can sometimes overwhelm—raises questions about how we can develop our self-direction skills and what kind of wayfinding supports and services are necessary to help people get their bearings and find their way forward in rapidly changing environments.

Before we move into deeper inquiry about what it means to engage wayfinding in this task, it is important to acknowledge

that any of the wayfinding frameworks, tools or tactics I present here were created in the field with individuals and teams to equip them as they engaged with their own uncharted territory. While they have been tried and tested in a variety of contexts and scenarios, they are meant to be interacted with experimentally and adapted to meet the needs of the contexts in which they are applied. Play. Engage. Test them out and adapt them to your context—then take what works and leave what doesn't. Let's start with the hope compass, a tool that was created to help people get their bearings as they cross the threshold into uncharted territory. It has proven to be a helpful tool for grounding individuals and teams in liminal space.

And yes, I am using the H-word.

The role of hope in getting your bearings

Before the "hope is not a strategy" and "hope is wishful thinking" folks get up in arms, let's make some space for a more robust view of hope. I draw on the research of Luthans and colleagues and their conceptualization of hope as part of their psychological capital model to demonstrate a positive relationship between hope and performance (Luthans et al, 2015). In areas as varied as athletics, academia and coping for individuals, and profitability of business units and employee satisfaction and organizational commitment in organizations, finding the will and the motivation to search for new pathways forward has been demonstrated to lead to increased energy and a sense of control that often results in an upward spiral of hope (Rand et al, 2009). While I am sure there are philosophers, theologians and social scientists who might balk at the practicality of this view of an ancient concept, for our purposes, commanding our own agency and pointing it in the direction of a pathway to change provides a very helpful framework for thinking about hope in the context of feeling stuck or lost on the threshold of an

uncertain transition. In particular, their characterization of hope as *willfinding* and *wayfinding* speaks to what it takes to set off on a journey into uncharted territory.

Hope compass

It is important to note that the hope compass I present here (see Figure 6.3) is not designed to point you to true north. Nor is it designed to be a sure-fire way of finding yourself, your purpose, or your "why?". In fact, while we've used navigation references throughout this book, this compass is more like the primitive compasses that appeared in China around the 4th century BC than those we picture today. Those early compasses were less geared toward navigation in physical spaces (although they could be used for that purpose). Instead, they are said to have been used to help people uncover insights into how they might order and harmonize their environments and their lives (Merrill et al, 1983). While the hope compass is not a tool that promises to help you find success or wellbeing, it can be a useful orienting tool in the face of uncertainty.

The first and most important thing to remember as you engage with the hope compass is that, like any compass, there is no single way to use it—and it won't tell you where to go. It won't lead you in a specific direction and it doesn't have an ideal destination in mind for you.

And neither do I.

The tool simply provides a place to begin to get your bearings when the way forward is unclear and you are unsure how to begin thinking about it. This can be applied to big questions, like "should I change careers?", or mundane ones, like "should we take this new client?". Unlike tools designed to drive progress and growth, this is particularly suited to liminal spaces and What Now? Moments, because it prompts reflection across domains.

FIGURE 6.3 Hope compass

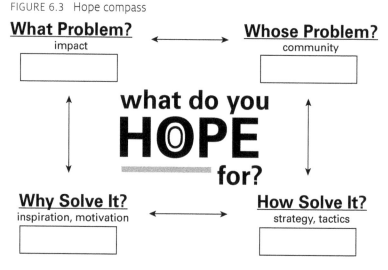

What do you hope for?

There is something very provocative about pondering the question of what we hope for. It feels lofty and abstract, neither of which are typically valued or rewarded in professional settings. Perhaps it's a little more acceptable in personal settings, but it's still a less than concrete starting place for execution and planning. That's what makes it so useful in liminal space. Pondering what we hope for and how we might move toward it allows us to zoom out and consider a direction without fully defining a precise outcome. It is a point of orientation rather than a point of execution. It also serves as a very helpful guidepost for reflecting on what matters and grounding ourselves and our teams in inquiry when we stand on the threshold of a new project or are tentative about how to approach a new challenge.

QUESTION FOR REFLECTION

Think about a challenge or turning point you are facing now. Reflect on the before, during and after and consider the question: what do you hope for?

The problem with problem solving

Before we dig further into the hope compass, I offer a cautionary critique of its problem-solving orientation. If we are not careful, viewing wayfinding as a problem to solve can lead us to a mindset that everything is a problem and we can miss opportunities. The old "if you're a hammer, everything is a nail" adage. That said, when people find themselves entering liminal space (or lost in it) they tend to view the initial inquiry as a problem to solve, which means that many people find the problem-solving orientation to be helpful. So, in the same way that a good carpenter creates their own tools, I encourage you to change the words in the framework to better match your metaphors or your circumstances if it makes it more useful to you. Like any wayfinding tool—from maps and compasses to GPS—it is imperfect. But it also provides a prompt for gaining clarity and identifying gaps in knowledge and understanding. Reflecting on these prompts provides us with a sense of who and where we are within the evolving context, before we move to solution finding and decision making. Again, we are not looking for a specific answer here. The key is to allow the hope compass to help spark reflection and inquiry, rather than get bogged down in specifics. It is another sensemaking tool that can provide us with further insight into where we are, how we are, and where we might proceed from here. It can also help identify the resources we need to engage with the challenge (or opportunity) at hand.

Another note. While I will walk you through the compass to help you become familiar with it, this is not a one-off exercise. You will likely return to this tool over and over again, in the same way you might pull a more modern compass or your GPS out of your pocket as you move in and out of orientation and disorientation on a long journey. As such, it is better understood in use than it is as described. I hope you will take it off the page and learn from it rather than learn about it. That said, here goes...

What's your problem and how do you solve it?

Whether we're dealing with professional or personal challenges, most of us have been trained to view a swift move from problem to solution as the most efficient way to respond. It is certainly how most people I work with come to wayfinding. They arrive in liminal space convinced that they know what the problem is—the job they need to leave or the work/life balance conundrum they need to address—and they want answers. Preferably as quickly as possible. While the hope compass can be quite effective at prompting new thinking about problem solving, the route from problem to solution is not direct.

While the hope compass can be quite effective at prompting new thinking about problem solving, the route from problem to solution is not direct.

Instead, by asking a variety of questions and gathering insights across domains of inquiry, new questions and surprising insights can emerge. Often, rather than moving straight from problem to solution, the inquiry leads to clarification of the problem itself. So, rather than instinctively starting in one place, I invite you to enter the compass beginning with whichever question makes you feel most grounded in your inquiry.

Some people (you may be among them) are very clear about a particular problem they aspire to solve. This can be a manager who is having trouble with team dynamics or a graduating student who hopes to make a difference or a mid-career leader who aspires to become a top-level executive. For these people, beginning in the top left corner of the model makes sense. Don't worry if you are not clear yet. You are simply grounding yourself in your best first thought. The key to using this tool effectively is to concern yourself less with the specific answer to any one of the questions, and more with how the questions relate to one another to help to define your best thinking about your circumstance in the moment. As I mentioned earlier, these questions

and how they relate to one another will raise more questions than they answer. That is fine. In the space in Figure 6.4, capture your best sense of what the problem is that you are facing.

FIGURE 6.4 What problem?

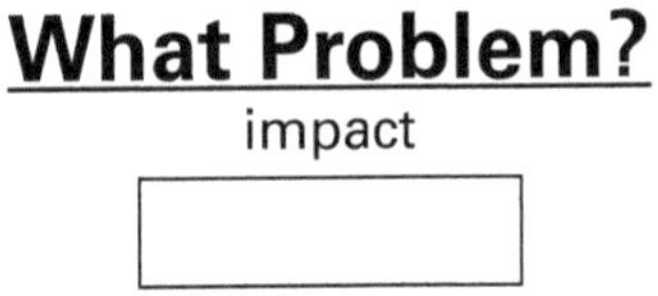

What Problem?
impact

Next, with that problem in mind, think about whose problem you seek to solve. For instance, if the problem you hope to solve is to increase sales, whose problem do you care to address? The customer's problem? The salesperson's challenge? The manager or leader who is tasked with creating strategy and tactics? As you can see from these simple prompts, the way you might go about solving that sales challenge might be very different depending upon whose problem you seek to solve. This question prompts a deeper reflection, which can help to home in on the specifics of both the problem and possible solutions. Place your thoughts on whose problem you hope to solve in the box in Figure 6.5.

FIGURE 6.5 Whose problem?

Whose Problem?
community

Contemplating why you are the right person or team to solve a problem can be a very helpful and grounding step in contemplating whether the problem we're focused on is actually ours to solve. It may seem counterintuitive at first or prompt responses like, "because it's my job" or "because I said so." It is a more nuanced and thought-provoking question than that. We all face

many challenges in our professional and personal lives, so there is no shortage of directions we can turn our attention toward, especially in liminal spaces. But how do you know that you or your team are the best resources to address the challenge? How do you determine which problems are your problems to solve? Contemplating this can help us to deploy the right resources to the right problems at the right time. Be sure to think about this question in the context of your answers to other questions in the compass. As I mentioned previously, this tool is most effective when it is used as a prompt for comparing and contrasting across prompts rather than coming up with "right" answers in any single domain. Using the problem you identified above, reflect on why you or your team are meant to solve it. Place your thoughts on whose problem you hope to solve in the box in Figure 6.6.

FIGURE 6.6 Why solve it?

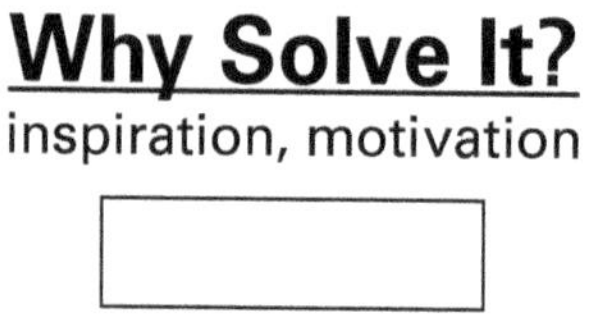

Why Solve It?
inspiration, motivation

Most teams and individuals are used to beginning by asking how to solve the problem. In fact, in some settings, we are instructed to not present a problem to the team unless we have a solution and are ready to take on the task of solving it. The hope compass offers an alternative approach that points the user to zoom out and consider the bigger picture. By considering the problem through the lens of the people doing the solving as well as those whose problem is being solved, we have a greater likelihood of making connections across the whole solutions ecosystem. Doing so through the lens of what relevant stakeholders hope for provides another layer that will shift thinking from simplified responses to a more context-based approach to creative problem solving. Now that you've considered your example across each of the prompts, think about how you might solve it and place your response in Figure 6.7.

FIGURE 6.7 How do you solve it?

How Solve It?
strategy, tactics

[   ]

HOPE COMPASS IN ACTION

Tim Gilligan, a design leader at a large international financial services company, has embraced the use of the hope compass and other wayfinding tools for himself and with his team. "When we're asked to lead in design and innovation, there is no roadmap," he told me. "There are a million paths that you can take at any point of inflection. This work has really helped me coach my team on what they hope to accomplish, what they hope to be able to give or leave the team or the project with."

According to Gilligan, the value proposition of leaders tasked with leading change is not to apply best practices or rigid frameworks, but an invitation to change the system:

"The hope compass and the wayfinding mindset have helped me to coach myself and my team in a time of great change and nuance. It gives us a way to hold the adversity the business throws our way and the joy of delivering great experiences for our colleagues and customers at once. It helped create a language of experimentation, patience and curiosity in times when best practices do not apply."

The ability to focus on outcome and then navigate to that outcome using the unique values, perspectives and approaches each member of the team brings to the table has been both unsettling and liberating, Gilligan stated. "Once we got over the initial unbalancing of accepting that there is no roadmap, we were able to accept our role as the map makers. The wayfinders. And that was liberating."

A few notes

Like any other process of inquiry, the prompts in the hope compass will raise as many questions as they answer. It is designed to help you or your team to uncover what you do and don't know about your orientation (or disorientation) in this moment and where you stand against the challenges you face—whether they are major disruptions or minor interruptions. It is important to understand that, in the same way that each *What Now?* Moment is different, who we are when we encounter each of them is also different. We are growing, changing and evolving creatures with values, motivations, aspirations and commitments that change over time. Our circumstances, priorities and values may shift as we learn new things and consider new ways of being in the world—as individuals and together.

I walked through the hope compass here in a particular order, simply to give you some fundamental insight into the reasoning behind each of the prompts. As you play with the tool in your own context, be sure to remember that where you begin with the compass will completely depend upon what seems most clear to you—and that will change depending on the circumstances. "What do you hope for?" may feel like a big question you are not ready to answer at the beginning of your inquiry. You may have a deep sense of who you hope to serve, but not how you might want to serve them. You may have a deep sense of what problem you want to solve, but have never interrogated why you are the right person to solve it. Start wherever you have the most clarity. If you get stuck, choose another prompt. Whatever it takes to begin asking questions across domains and clarifying who you want to serve and how you want to serve them.

TAKEAWAYS

- Wayfinding is a nuanced process that is approached differently depending upon how clear we are on our destination and whether or not we have the tools we need to orient ourselves in uncertain spaces.

- Grounding ourselves as we move into and through inquiry is a fundamental wayfinding skill that requires a well-curated toolbox.

- The hope compass is one useful tool to help get our bearings as we navigate into and through the unknown.

What's possible?

*Identify possibilities and put
everything on the altar*

"If I handed you a 2,000-piece puzzle, how would you take it on?"
When I ask this question, most people respond in one of three
ways. "I would start with the edges," is the most common,
followed by "I sort by color" and "I look at the picture and
collect pieces related to the image."

It is rare that people give the answer I'm prompting with the
question—that nearly 100 percent of people who do a large
puzzle first dump out the pieces, spread them out on the table,
turn the pieces over and look through them before they employ
their chosen strategy to put them all together.

"Now what if the puzzle had no edges?" I ask. "Or if it were
a single color or didn't have a predetermined picture on the box
to use as a reference? How would you approach the puzzle
then?"

We rely on old or standardized processes and fail to recognize that we, our families, our organizations are evolving and changing as the context around us changes. This simple exercise is a helpful stepping-off point for taking our discussion of sensemaking in the context of wayfinding from theory to practice.

We rely on old or standardized processes and fail to recognize that we, our families, our organizations are evolving and changing as the context around us changes.

Every puzzle is a new shape—and every *What Now?* Moment is unique. When we face uncertain transitions, we often skip the fundamental step of dumping the pieces, spreading them out, turning them over and looking at them collectively to see how we want to approach the puzzle. We may like to start with the corners and edges or sort the pieces by color, but the nature of the puzzle often dictates the approach. Applied to wayfinding, the way we like to do things or feel best suited to do things does not always translate to the most effective way to approach sensemaking in a liminal context.

Pause and gather your pieces

Over the past six chapters, you've been prompted to reflect on many things related to identity, self-direction and wayfinding when we face uncertain transitions. First, your relationship with the threat response. How you react when a What Now? Moment comes your way and the importance of gathering resources to equip ourselves to navigate uncertainty. Then we considered how we reframe our thinking about points of transition through metaphor—moving from a journey metaphor to a container metaphor (basecamp), in order to define transitional learning space and, where appropriate, the time horizon for the inquiry we are opening. Once we use this reflection to compose ourselves

and get our bearings we begin to inquire: where am I and who am I in this space at this time? I shared some mapping and reflective exercises that might be helpful, but also encourage you to use any tools that have worked well for you in the past to examine these questions. These can be books and other individual resources, social resources, or time with a coach or therapist or teacher or other people you know that you can rely on to get a clear picture of your current state—inside and out—whether or not you like what you see.

I return to this not as a simple wrap up of where we've been, but to underscore that all of this reflection—the bits and pieces of what we've learned as well as the gaps and holes that raise questions or point to the need for more resourcing and deeper inquiry—are the pieces of the puzzle of inquiry that we are considering in the *ask* of the *stop, ask, explore*. There is something quite important about gathering these pieces, getting them outside of our heads and having them in one place where we can see everything at once—across domains. Skipping this can compound the confusion we feel when we face uncertain transitions. Keeping all of the pieces in our heads is like trying to do a 2,000-piece puzzle without taking any of the pieces out of the box. It is possible—but it is more difficult to make sense of things and develop an approach that makes the process enjoyable rather than overwhelming and frustrating.

There are a variety of ways to approach this practice, which is less about organizing information and more about making space for sensemaking. For those of you who are used to making lists or gathering information in spreadsheets, I invite you to consider a different approach. Lists and spreadsheets have their place, of course, but they are more helpful when the objective is to manage information and drive production. In the sensemaking context, however, production-oriented tools can be limiting, in the same way that taping multiple pieces to one another would hamper completing a puzzle. Instead of organizing and categorizing, sensemaking begins with creating space to get disparate thoughts,

ideas and concerns out of our heads and into a place where we can visualize them, move them around and consider different, possibly surprising, combinations and configurations. Like creating an external hard drive for recurring thoughts and concerns.

If you like to work in analog, sticky notes, index cards or other small, distinct items can be useful materials. Perhaps clear a wall somewhere in your home or office where you are willing to make a mess for a period of time. Let the ideas linger in the space in the same way you might keep a puzzle on a table. Add new thoughts and ideas as you have them. Organize and reorganize them. Let the ideas speak. You might want to carry your materials with you so you can gather new insights and ideas as they emerge. If you're using sticky notes or index cards, you can carry them in your pocket or in your bag, put some on your end table in the bedroom and have them handy in other places. This will prompt you to remain reflective and provide a convenient way to capture thoughts to add to your sensemaking space in the flow of the day, not just when you're brainstorming. For people who prefer to work digitally, there are a number of tools that can be useful for visual sensemaking. I'm particularly fond of online whiteboards like Miro and Mural as a place to easily gather and play with ideas.

Don't create categories—at least not yet!

Gathering information without categorizing is really difficult for many people because it is the polar opposite of what many of us have been taught to do. Instead, we approach our ideas in a way that is the equivalent of picking through the puzzle box to find the "right" one, as quickly and efficiently as possible, usually by narrowing it down to two or three options and choosing from among them, and often without looking at all the choices in the box. In sensemaking, we do the opposite. First, we gather all of our ideas, thoughts and other pieces in one place without

compartmentalizing. This gets messy when we gather the professional and personal in one place. But the mess is worth the cost when we are able to zoom out and observe our situation holistically. It allows us to see our competing commitments clearly across and between domains.

Of course, even when I encourage people to stay away from creating themes, they laugh as they tell me that they can't help it. In part, because it's how we're trained, but also because visualizing all of the items we keep track of in lists and in our heads in one place can feel overwhelming at first. But, as you begin to see the benefits that come from capturing ideas and thoughts outside of our head before we decide how best to put them back together, the value becomes clear and the process becomes less overwhelming. Many people I work with view this part of the work as a game changer. They feel liberated from constant ruminating. As I guide people through this process, they consistently look at their sticky notes or index cards or online whiteboards and are surprised by how much information about stakeholders, stressors, dreams and fears they carry across their professional and personal worlds —and how much of a relief it can be to get it out of their heads and into a space where they can consider it in a more structured way.

When Yvette Owo, a former business strategy lead at Accenture who now owns a strategy and coaching firm, began using Miro, she called it an aha moment. "I had been at base camp for a few years. Most people around me were telling me to climb, but what I needed was to organize resources, to rest, refuel, and develop a game plan." Owo had experienced a number of high-stakes What Now? Moments, from career changes and launching a business to dealing with the aftermath of being hit by a car and mental health issues. Posting recurring thoughts on her digital whiteboard allowed her to release mental and emotional space and freed her to focus on other things. "There's something in the brain called the reticular activating system (RAS)," she told me. "It helps us keep things top of mind

so we don't forget them, and also tells us what to ignore." According to Yvette, she had *tons* of things top of mind, and she found it mentally draining. "I was constantly thinking about the business. About my health. About family and personal life," she said. "From day one it was clear that my RAS was letting me release the thoughts once they were captured on the board."

Unlike others who like to have a wall or whiteboard filled with sticky notes for their ideas, Owo prefers to keep her ideas out of sight until she is ready to consider them. "I don't want to put hundreds of notes all over a wall in my home, which would then be screaming at me to do something with them," she continued. "And a list leaves me with the impression that I must do something." Instead, she puts a thought on the board and returns to it when she is ready to make sense of it. She was so pleased with the approach that she now uses it with her team to make sense of priorities, drive collaboration and identify new possibilities.

Placing all of our puzzle pieces on the table, turning them over and looking at them in all of their messy glory allows us to develop new, context-specific approaches that are more likely to carry us through.

Identify the locus of possibilities

Once the puzzle pieces you've gathered (so far) are in one place, then exploring them at once, across domains, can help us to identify surprising opportunities that might not be immediately obvious if we only explore within a single domain. It raises interesting questions about how we might create a life, organization or community of practice that not only leads to traditional variables of success, but also creates time or space for flourishing and service to others. That's what happened to Andrea, whose What Now? Moment we

discussed in Chapter 5. She knew she needed and wanted to leave New York and find a career that was closer to nature, or at least a life that allowed for a deeper connection with it, but was lost in a transition she hadn't yet defined. She'd considered a few options—forestry, botany, environmental science, even becoming a park ranger—but hadn't yet watered the seeds of consideration with a wholehearted inquiry. This left her wanting, but stuck. I encouraged her to take a step in the direction of possibility by learning about all of the options that came to mind, no matter how impractical.

What would it take to be a forest ranger? What other career opportunities exist in those spaces? Do you have the skills you need, or would you need to go back to school? What resources do you have at your disposal to open up a space for active waiting? By opening up to a broad set of possibilities, Andrea began to untangle which aspects of these possibilities appealed to her in practice, and which seemed outside of her desired self-world fit.

Eventually, that initial inquiry allowed her to take some incremental steps toward her desired outcome, first by visiting family and friends for a few months in the forests of Colorado and Washington, and then to a longer stay in the Kerry mountains of Ireland. She's since moved to Stockholm and is exploring her ongoing transition from a life that was not working for her to one that feels more aligned. While expanding her personal and professional networks globally, she's been able to create more varied and creative work opportunities while living closer to nature and studying landscape photography. "I felt like I'd been shoved from the nest," she said. "Like my life was saying to me, you're not in the city you're meant to be in, you're not in the right relationship, and you're not in a job that inspires you either. So, here you go–absolute freedom and groundlessness to create from." By pursuing a wider vision, she told me, her sense of adventure and exploration was sparked and, in turn, a drive and vision she'd been lacking while living out of alignment with her

authentic interests and talents was restored. "I wasn't able to see it that way without the expanse of possibility that came when everything familiar was cleared away. We live in a time where it's very possible to create your own freedom. Every person can be the entrepreneur or CEO of their own life if they expand their vision and consciousness to include multiple streams of opportunity. That's what I'm doing now."

This wider vision involves not only identifying all of the possibilities available to us, but also considering and reconsidering what matters to us with a willingness to reprioritize or remove things from consideration. Think of this like the climber entering base camp. As we discussed previously, the movement between times of climbing and times of recalibrating and resourcing at base camp are both critical parts of the climb. But base camp is about more than recalibrating the body to the right oxygen levels. It is also about considering what has changed on the last leg of the journey and what is needed for the next. This involves reflection: what items should we keep with us and what items should we leave behind and, perhaps, pick up on the way back? How is the weather on the mountain ahead? What do other climbers have to share that might be useful? That's why, if we recognize that disruptions—even painful ones—provide us with a prompt to take stock, we can consider not only the issue that caused the disruption, but also revisit every part of our lives to make sure we are properly resourced and as unburdened as we can be for the next leg of the journey. I think of this as putting everything on the altar with a willingness to let it go, no matter how precious and important it might seem.

Everything on the altar

Religions across the globe have traditions that involve sacrificing items on an altar as an act of trust, faith and commitment to that which is being honored in the rite or ritual. I view *placing*

everything on the altar as a helpful metaphor for *the practice of reconsidering whether the individual elements of the careers, lives and organizations we've created are aligned with what we value and what we hope to make present in the world.*

For Andrea, this meant shifting some firm ideas about money, stability, success and other things that she still values—but recognizing that she could create a container to prioritize exploration and possibility. For others, it means intentionally letting an aspirational dream go. This was the case for another woman I worked with for about six months. "Maybe I'm not ready to pursue this dream right now," she said, looking down at her coffee and avoiding eye contact. As she described her hesitation in more detail, it was clear that this was more than a What Now? Moment threat response. Opening the Pandora's box of deep introspection and intentional examination of the layered complexities of her own life proved to be more challenging than she had originally anticipated, and she wanted to understand more about the resistance she was feeling in herself and those around her before pressing forward toward a destination that she was beginning to question.

I watched her face relax and her shoulders drop as I told her, "We are so enamored with perpetual movement and big dreams delivered at scale that we sometimes miss real opportunities to serve where we are." This gave her space to share that the aspiration she was carrying around with her had become a burden rather than a motivation. When she put it on the altar, the big dream was supplanted by a deep desire to nurture her existing customers, her community and her family rather than take things to the next level. Somehow it had not occurred to her to give herself permission to bring her dream to life in a way that felt right-sized for her at the time.

Some people are surprised when I tell them I put my marriage and family on the altar in points of transitions and turning points. It is a particularly challenging notion for "family first" people who often struggle to make sense of a transition while

balancing personal commitments to partners, children, aging parents and others. I can see where they are coming from—especially since I've raised three children and been married for 25 years to my husband Martin, a man who I still view as not only a partner for life but my best friend. "How do you put that on the altar?"

I sometimes wonder if the fact that I *do* put them on the altar is what keeps things in place. So yes, at its most extreme, putting my husband on the altar means I could leave him if I chose to. While I have yet to make that choice (so far!), putting the marriage on the altar gives me the opportunity to recommit to the relationship over and over again with each point of transition. But in recommitting to the relationship, I also have the opportunity to recognize that our standing daily commitments to one another and our household might be unhelpful or problematic for my next leg of the journey. Putting something that seems immovable on the altar at a time of transition—whether relationships with family members, use of funds and savings, locations where we live, or any other variable—is a prompt to rethink that area of our lives and shift priorities intentionally to meet the moment, rather than juggle them as circumstances shift and change over time. This allows me to say to my husband, "I'm writing a book, so I need more support and will be unavailable for certain tasks—let's see how we can resource for it." It allows him to say, "I'm making this film, so I need space in the house or time out of it to devote myself to this task." Since we recognize that these reprioritizations are on a specific (and limited) time horizon and we are clear in our commitments within them, we don't have to renegotiate as we move through a project or priority. We can intentionally make the space and recalibrate as we go.

The same is true for organizations. If we normalize deploying resources in ways where we can reprioritize and adapt without making people feel threatened, we have a better chance of being the dynamic teams and organizations we say we want to be. If, instead, every shift makes people wonder who they are and if they have a

place in the organization, we create systems that spark What Now? Moments that can lead to fight, flight and freeze responses that many people are unlikely to share—or even identify in themselves. Making this explicit, before a disruption that calls to change open transitional learning space where even sacred cows are put on the altar, creates a more honest and open environment for inquiry. In doing so, we can mark the shift from execution to exploration and intentionally engage active resilience and gather the resources they need to navigate the uncertain transition ahead.

This kind of preparation and transparency helps to create psychological safety and engagement, and opens up people's ability to be more creative and innovative in the spaces they inhabit. It also makes space for people to share concerns and identify areas where change feels threatening, so they can move individually and in community from the fear loop and engage dispassionate curiosity in action through sensemaking and reprioritizing across domains, where necessary.

When we make sense of disparate items to explore new possibilities, it is our tendency (and our training) to separate, categorize and explore possibilities within particular domains. What are my possibilities at work? At home? In the community? Then, after we've categorized, we might prioritize or seek to create some "balance" between areas that invite us to 100 percent focus across four or five domains. But that means we find ourselves operating at 500 percent—and we wonder why so many people are feeling burned out, unsettled and lost.

That's why I invite you to take the risk and look at everything at once. Think of it like traversing the wilderness and climbing a tree or hiking to the top of a rise so you can get a more complete picture of the new environment. Then, rather than categorize, we can think about the entire terrain and consider how we might combine or consider things in new ways when operating across domains. Not to drive a quick decision, but to consider different ways when being and doing as an act of sensemaking.

Going back to the puzzle example, you already know how to do this. You try pieces that look like they might fit and try to put them

together. When it works, you put them together and grab another piece. When it doesn't, just try another piece or another area of the puzzle. Playing with possibilities *before* we decide raises new questions and offers new possibilities we might not otherwise consider. It also allows us to recalibrate our values or priorities to meet the needs of this What Now? Moment and removes the pressure of making a singular "right" choice in the midst of inquiry. This may mean intentionally putting aside one thing and over-focusing on another—not forever, but for a season. This involves a deeper, more interdimensional look at our work and our lives with a willingness to integrate across domains intentionally rather than waiting to have to do it when the s*&% hits the fan.

We can do this on our own, but there are benefits to collaborating with others. In my research, working together in small groups, in teams, or with a trusted partner can help us to see connections we might not otherwise consider because we are convinced (consciously or unconsciously) that those combinations are impossible for us in our situations. Getting someone with no horse in the race to ask new questions, we can encourage one another to consider new routes, not as advice or an assumption of knowing better, but in the spirit of identifying possibilities, raising new questions, and considering where we might explore further through experimentation.

TAKEAWAYS

- Gathering ideas, thoughts and information across professional and personal domains can help us to make sense of our lives in a holistic way.

- Considering the full locus of possibilities available to us at points of transition can help to identify surprising opportunities, but it takes time, attention and practice.

- Examining all of the information at our disposal and placing everything "on the altar" helps to identify sacred cows and creates space for us to examine our commitments as we discern possible routes forward.

PART THREE

Explore

A note to the reader as you begin to 'Explore'

As we begin to explore, it's helpful to pause and acknowledge all of the learning and work you've done to bring you to this point. You've paused your journey (or at least the forced forward momentum) to develop a better understanding of your relationship with *What Now?* Moments and how your reactions and responses might vary when interruptions or disruptions lead to incendiary emotions, disorientation or stuckness. You've recognized that resilience is more than "I am" or "I'm not" because we are all resilient in some circumstances, and less resilient in others. While identifying your own areas of resilience (or lack thereof) may still feel a bit overwhelming, please know that as you continue to craft a sustainable practice of rigorous self-awareness, you will gain a keener sense of the contours of your own strengths and vulnerabilities. Remember that this is a journey to gather resources for yourself, your family and friends, and your team across emotional, physical, material, social and other variables that are relevant to your unique circumstances.

Hopefully, as you've considered your relationship with change and transition, you've been able to identify one or more metaphors that help to illustrate how you perceive change in this moment. With this in mind, you've asked yourself if your metaphors are helpful or unhelpful, and perhaps have tweaked them or changed them outright. In the spirit of practicing rigorous self-awareness, you've probed questions about who you are, where you are and what might be possible if you gave yourself the time and the space

to consider change as a prompt to dispassionate curiosity and a hopeful willingness to consider paths forward that might not seem feasible or available on first blush.

If you're reading this book straight through for the first time, you've likely done more thinking about these things than doing these things. That's okay!

There is a reason this book's subtitle is "learn to" and not "how to." Learning is a process. The goal here is not to solve a particular problem by the end of the book. The goal is to view uncertainty and change as transitional learning space and to embrace the unknown as rich in possibilities when we approach it in new ways. We've teased out some great questions about where we are, what we need, what might be possible over the past several chapters—but that prompts another question: How do we translate the insights (or new questions) we've uncovered into action? One way is to move deeper into inquiry by moving from "ask" to "explore."

But what does that mean in practice? In this section, you're invited to move from gathering and considering questions to finding answers to those questions that can be applied in context.

Press on, explorer!

Joan

Learn by doing

The art and science of experimentation

When I met Jeneanne she was ready for a change. An educator, aspiring designer and single mother of a preteen daughter, she had big aspirations for her small family, and was ready to consider big moves to fulfill them. The particulars were still hazy at the time and involved a number of high-stakes moving parts. This fact and others made her a perfect fit for one of several year-long wayfinding research cohorts I launched that year. Working on her own and with a small group of diverse but like-minded women, her pursuit of rigorous self-awareness, sensemaking and reflection led to some concrete insights, interesting possibilities, and a lot of new questions. She established that she wanted to leave Chicago and that finding an intersection between her expertise as an educator, her love of design, and her deep commitment to social change was a priority. So was her daughter and the deep calling to find a vibrant, culturally enriching community where they both felt valued and nurtured.

When she thought about making a change in practice, however, every option she considered felt monumental—largely because they were. What if she took a job across the country that didn't work out? What if the schools were not a good fit for her daughter? Was it irresponsible to pursue her dreams at the risk of uprooting her child? Was it irresponsible not to? When she considered these questions as prompts for action, it was crystal clear that there was no simple framework or checklist she could follow to answer them. And she didn't want one. An educator and designer at heart, she had a sense of the life she wanted, and the capacity to carry it out. But, in practice, the liminal distance between the Chicago apartment where she and her daughter were living and a new reality living and working on the east coast felt like a chasm. She was ready to move beyond theoretical inquiry and explore how she might shift from identifying possibilities to bringing one of more of them to life, but was not yet ready to make a firm, committed decision. Rather than continue ruminating on "what if?" she engaged in a process of exploring how she might answer these questions in action.

Learning in action

There are many different ways to approach learning about the world around us. This simple fact applies to research scientists developing new theories and individuals as they try to make sense of the day-to-day in practice. In my role as a researcher, I favor ways of knowing that are grounded in learning by doing by co-creating solutions alongside the people who are facing them. That's why I embrace participatory action research (PAR) as a research methodology—and as a way of life. While I won't go deeply into the theory of it here (see Appendix G), the central tenets of action research involve learning about problems by engaging with others to solve them and helping people to strengthen the interconnections between self-awareness, the

unconscious, and life in society (Chevalier and Buckles, 2013). Unlike other methods that create distance between the researcher as observer and the research subject as observed, action research allows me to roll up my sleeves and get in the trenches with leaders, teams and individuals and address particular issues, in context, in real time. This can involve many different sorts of interactions, all grounded in learning by doing in community with others. Engagements are designed to shed light on the questions and challenges people face in their own domains and to help them to uncover culturally relevant ways to discover new possibilities that are built by and work for the communities in which they operate. I believe that all of us can benefit from learning to answer the big questions that get us stuck with experimentation.

Let me be clear: in the same way that navigation experts make a distinction between wandering and navigating, when I talk about learning in action, I make a distinction between "trying things" and experimenting. Of course, just like wandering has its place, so does trying things on to see if they fit. I fully support all forms of exploration as instrumental to the creative

In the same way that not all wilderness journeys lend themselves to wandering, some transitions require a more structured approach to exploration.

process and gathering insights that lead (eventually) to deeper learning. But, in the same way that not all wilderness journeys lend themselves to wandering, some transitions require a more structured approach.

This is especially true when resources are in short supply, time is a factor, the stakes are high, and we're stuck in transition. In fact, in my experience with people navigating uncertain transitions, randomly trying things can sometimes contribute to overwhelm and uncertainty. That's why it is critical to remember

that, while all experimentation involves exploration, not all exploration is experimentation, and it is important to clarify from the outset which you're are engaged in.

Contrasting Andrea's journey that we discussed previously with Jeneanne's situation provides a helpful illustration of this. In Andrea's case, she made an intentional decision to pack up her life in New York and make space for reflection and wandering with no particular outcome in mind. She chose to invest time and other resources in the opportunity to focus on rigorous self-awareness and replenishment—a sabbatical of sorts guided by some broad questions, but also designed for her to rest and consider possibilities over a longer stretch of time. Her recent move to Stockholm involves more of the same, with an eye on moving from exploration to execution in the coming months. Jeneanne, on the other hand, did not perceive herself to have that luxury.

Both stories are a call to action for organizational leaders—especially in times when an increasingly nomadic talent force seeking to reimagine how they work and live are eager to co-create mutually beneficial solutions to these problems with their employers. There is an opportunity embedded in all of these stories that is worth noting in the context of learning in action. Helping to create space for employees to explore and experiment as they navigate their particular career and life journey is the future of professional and personal development for smart, ambitious and purpose-driven people like Jeneanne, Andrea and others we've discussed. This principle also applies to educators experimenting in the classroom, and healthcare administrators co-creating solutions with their stakeholders. It may seem risky, but creating third spaces for people to explore options and test possibilities without needing to leave—like Ashley's company did for her (Chapter 1)—can have positive results. Unfortunately, not all companies have that kind of mechanism in place for their employees—and most individuals don't create it on their own.

Making space to explore

So, as we think about what it means to move from inquiry into exploration, it is important to acknowledge that what we hope to learn should dictate the way we approach learning it. The best way to learn to build a house is not to read a book, but to work alongside a builder. Psychotherapy or surgery, on the other hand, require some fundamental study of the human mind and body before learning by doing. That's why, when we think about learning by doing, it is not about choosing a right or wrong method of learning but understanding that we can be more creative about what we need to learn and how we want to learn it than simply choosing the latest popular online course or workshop or hoping a Google search that returns 40 million responses will lead us in the right direction.

So where do we begin?

Experiment design canvas

I came to the field of education and research from 17 years of practice in the communications field. Research was always part of that work, but it was predominantly related to very precise questions tied to gathering the particular information the team needed to accomplish a task, a goal or a specific objective. I'd encountered the scientific method in school, of course—but it wasn't until I decided to go to graduate school in my 40s that I learned what academic research was all about. And it was an eye opener! I respect theory building tremendously and publish papers in my field. But, as I mentioned previously, I've always been drawn to the intersection of rigorous inquiry and devoted practice. Through my work with wayfinding and liminal learning, I've come to believe that, in the information-saturated, highly dynamic world we now live in, we are all called upon to be citizen sensemakers and researchers in our own domains.

FIGURE 8.1 Experiment design canvas

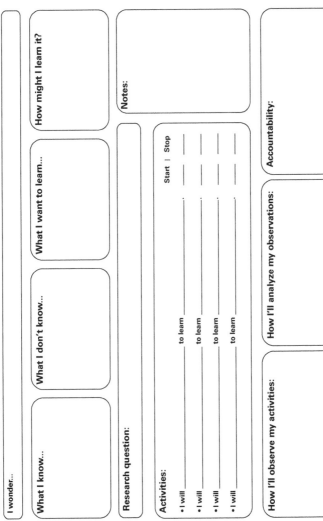

EXPERIMENT DESIGN CANVAS

I wonder...

What I know...

What I don't know...

What I want to learn...

How might I learn it?

Research question:

Activities:

- I will _____ to learn _____
- I will _____ to learn _____
- I will _____ to learn _____
- I will _____ to learn _____

Start | Stop

Notes:

How I'll observe my activities:

How I'll analyze my observations:

Accountability:

Yet, since this is an emerging phenomenon, we are not educated, equipped, or even focused on developing these new capacities and skills. Instead, we rely on thought leaders, social media influencers, and friends and family as our wayfinding tools and hope for the best. I created the experiment design canvas (see Figure 8.1) to help people think about experimentation at work or at home beyond throwing noodles on the wall to see if they stick. Instead, you can use this simple framework to develop a more deliberate way of structuring and launching time-boxed exploratory experiments that are designed to answer particular research questions.

Although it has its basis in the scientific method, the canvas is meant to bring some precision to the art of wayfinding when you have questions that you'd like to explore through experimentation. It is important to note that this does not promise quick, easy answers. Instead, like the resilience wheel, the hope compass, the sensemaking spaces and other approaches to inquiry we've discussed, it was created in the field as a tool to help wayfinders put the *learning* in learning by doing in their own ways. Launching experiments as a means to engage with relevant possibilities that emerge from the sensemaking process before making a concrete decision can be a helpful part of an active waiting practice. Experimentation provides a way to take time-boxed actions without committing to a particular course or decision in the long term. Many people find this liberating. For others it is too structured or not intuitive.

I invite you to play with it and see if it is for you. If it isn't, then put it down and move on. Design your own exploration tools that work for you. Better yet, send me a note and we'll design one together! The key here is not to create a massive tribe of experiment design canvas users. Instead, I hope for more people to recognize that, by choice or necessity, we are all increasingly in the wilderness more than we are on the path. As a result, identifying, creating, and playing with sensemaking and wayfinding tools is a fundamental skill for navigating modern life. In the spirit of the tool itself, the best way to know whether or not the experiment design canvas is for you is to experiment with using it. Like any

FIGURE 8.2 I wonder...

EXPERIMENT DESIGN CANVAS

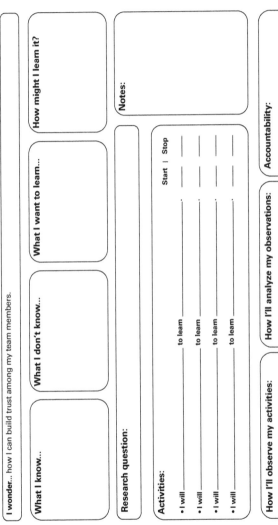

I wonder... how I can build trust among my team members.

What I know...

What I don't know...

What I want to learn...

How might I learn it?

Research question:

Activities:

- I will _____ to learn _____
- I will _____ to learn _____
- I will _____ to learn _____
- I will _____ to learn _____

Start | Stop

Notes:

How I'll observe my activities:

How I'll analyze my observations:

Accountability:

creative act of exploration, you need to develop your own practice. Let's take and example piece by piece to illustrate. In Figure 8.2 I offer a simple but common question that runs through many of the stories we've encountered in the previous chapters: I wonder how I can build trust among my team members?

I wonder...

"I wonder" questions are big picture, visionary questions that prompt consideration of many possibilities rather than a yes, no or maybe. They can point to who we are (I wonder who I will become if I stay in this job), where we hope to go (I wonder if I am meant to live in Spain), or how we hope to live, like in our example. In any case, these questions prompt secondary questions like: What do you mean by living a life that matters? What are your dreams? Are you prone to burning out? What's your time horizon for deciding your life matters? "I wonder" questions are an invitation to dig deeper and get to the questions behind the question. They are also the kinds of questions that can spark incendiary emotions when answers feel out of our grasp and we allow them to shift from creative prompts (I wonder how I might live a life that matters) to declarative statements (I will never have a life that matters, or I *know* I will live a life that matters) regardless of evidence in either direction. By creating a practice of defaulting to wonder, we are more prone to curiosity and can move naturally into inquiry to understand what we know, what we don't know, and how we might find out.

From "I wonder" to "let's find out"

Just below the "I wonder" question there are four spaces in the experiment design canvas that are designed to prompt reflection on what is and is not known and possible ways of finding out. This can involve traditional research: reading books, taking courses, observation. It can also include actions like connecting

FIGURE 8.3 What I do/don't know

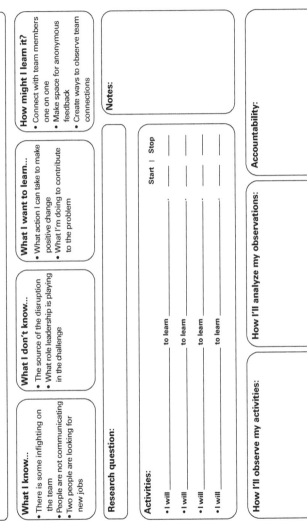

EXPERIMENT DESIGN CANVAS

I wonder... how I can build trust among my team members.

What I know...
- There is some infighting on the team
- People are not communicating
- Two people are looking for new jobs

What I don't know...
- The source of the disruption
- What role leadership is playing in the challenge

What I want to learn...
- What action I can take to make positive change
- What I'm doing to contribute to the problem

How might I learn it?
- Connect with team members one on one
- Make space for anonymous feedback
- Create ways to observe team connections

Notes:

Research question:

Activities:
- I will _____ to learn _____
- I will _____ to learn _____
- I will _____ to learn _____
- I will _____ to learn _____

Start | Stop

How I'll observe my activities:

How I'll analyze my observations:

Accountability:

FIGURE 8.4 Research question and activities

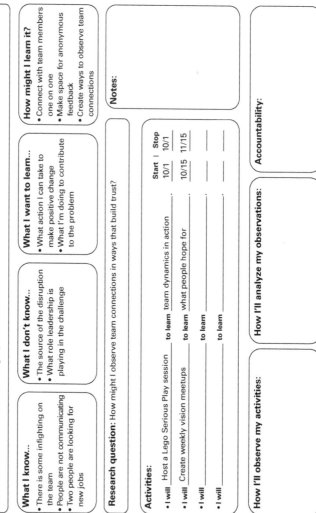

EXPERIMENT DESIGN CANVAS

I wonder... how I can build trust among my team members.

What I know...
- There is some infighting on the team
- People are not communicating
- Two people are looking for new jobs

What I don't know...
- The source of the disruption
- What role leadership is playing in the challenge

What I want to learn...
- What action I can take to make positive change
- What I'm doing to contribute to the problem

How might I learn it?
- Connect with team members one on one
- Make space for anonymous feedback
- Create ways to observe team connections

Research question: How might I observe team connections in ways that build trust?

Activities:

			Start	Stop
• I will Host a Lego Serious Play session	to learn team dynamics in action		10/1	10/1
• I will Create weekly vision meetups	to learn what people hope for		10/15	11/15
• I will _____	to learn _____		___	___
• I will _____	to learn _____		___	___

How I'll observe my activities:

How I'll analyze my observations:

Accountability:

Notes:

with people, launching a trial run, or testing a possibility in a low-stakes environment. Be as thorough as possible in this section because what you uncover here will help to identify the specific research question(s) that will guide your experiments. Figure 8.3 illustrates the gap between what the learner in our example knows and does not know in the first two sections and points to several things they want to learn about their "I wonder" question.

Research questions and time-boxed activities

There are at least three research questions that easily flow out of the "what I want to learn" and "how might I learn it" sections in Figure 8.3. The person in our example could choose to explore ways to connect one on one with team members, to make space for anonymous feedback, or to observe team connections. For our purposes, we'll engage with the third option with a set of time-boxed exploratory activities (see Figure 8.4). Creating the experiment with a set time horizon—whether that be three days or three months—is important, because it frees us up to take concrete actions without forcing an immediate decision.

Observations, analysis and accountability

Before you kick off your experiment, it is helpful to think about how you will capture your learning along the way so you can use it to make sense of the experience and gather insights that might inform your next steps. This can involve journaling, keeping voice notes, taking photographs, sending yourself notes or emails. Anything that fits in the rhythm of your day-to-day activities and prompts your thoughts, memories or imagination when the process is complete—including checking in with a partner or a friend. You might also think in advance about how you want to make sense of your observations, because it can help you to decide how to capture them. In our example

FIGURE 8.5 Observations and accountability

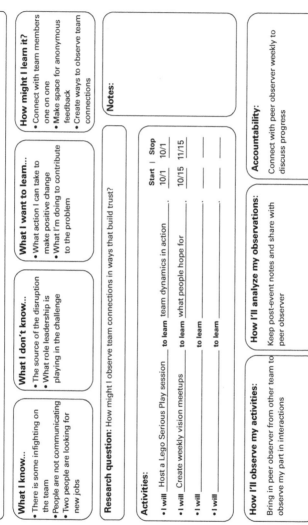

EXPERIMENT DESIGN CANVAS

I wonder... how I can build trust among my team members.

What I know...
- There is some infighting on the team
- People are not communicating
- Two people are looking for new jobs

What I don't know...
- The source of the disruption
- What role leadership is playing in the challenge

What I want to learn...
- What action I can take to make positive change
- What I'm doing to contribute to the problem

How might I learn it?
- Connect with team members one on one
- Make space for anonymous feedback
- Create ways to observe team connections

Notes:

Research question: How might I observe team connections in ways that build trust?

Activities:

			Start	Stop
• I will	Host a Lego Serious Play session	to learn team dynamics in action	10/1	10/1
• I will	Create weekly vision meetups	to learn what people hope for	10/15	11/15
• I will	_____	to learn _____	___	___
• I will	_____	to learn _____	___	___

How I'll observe my activities:
Bring in peer observer from other team to observe my part in interactions

How I'll analyze my observations:
Keep post-event notes and share with peer observer

Accountability:
Connect with peer observer weekly to discuss progress

(see Figure 8.5), the learner chose to bring in a peer observer as a second set of eyes, and to help the experiment designer to be part of the observation and have an objective view of the process.

Experiments are not decisions

If we choose the experimental approach to learning in action, it is important that we fully embrace the notion that *taking a step* in a certain direction is not a *decision to go* in that direction. This can seem counterintuitive for those of us who were raised in cultures that favor making a decision prior to action—preferably the "right" decision. Instead, by creating these experiments and exploring possible routes forward through action rather than speculation in a structured way, we can answer questions in practice rather than theory. "I don't think I would like coding" becomes "I wonder if I like coding? Perhaps I can code for 45 minutes a day for two months and see what I learn—about coding and about how I feel about coding." By taking steps in one direction or another, we can make sense of unfamiliar terrain and gain deeper understanding of the possibilities and choices in front of us.

This mimics a fascinating tactic that some trained wilderness experts use when they find themselves lost in the woods. First, they mark the spot where they first notice they are lost with a pile of rocks or another marker, so they are firm in their starting place. Then, using string or another marker (many backwoods explorers carry string for this very reason), they walk as far as they can in a direction of their choosing and tie a string on a tree or bush. Then, they walk further and do the same when the string is almost out of sight. They repeat the procedure until they either find a path or a landmark that is a better way forward, or they return to the pile of rocks and repeat the same procedure at 5 or 10 degrees in a different direction. They continue the process of moving out and back again until they've either found their way out or made a complete circle in all directions with the pile

of rocks at the center like a giant bicycle wheel with the rocks at the hub and lines of string as the spokes.

As you can imagine, this process will generally result in at least one of three things: 1) they find a way forward, 2) they have a much better understanding of a much larger area of territory so they can make a more educated next step, or 3) they create a much larger and more visible target for anyone who is out there looking for them.

This approach can be extended and translated to experimentation in our own professional and personal lives when we find ourselves at an impasse or point of transition. Taking steps in one direction or another as an experiment and not a decision frees us up to explore without the pressure of deciding which direction we are "meant" to go.

Taking steps in one direction or another as an experiment and not a decision frees us up to explore without the pressure of deciding which direction we are "meant" to go.

When we no longer feel burdened to choose which way to go before we begin, we are freed up to enter a process of exploration, where we are in active inquiry and discernment, rather than choosing a lane. This allows us to either discover a clear path forward or to learn more about ourselves, our circumstances and our options by doing. We can still gather new skills, make the money we need to pay our bills and live well while doing it. We're simply operating in the container of liminal learning—practicing active waiting through experimentation—before we make a firm choice. This approach also opens us up to new people, new experiences and, potentially, new opportunities that we might not have encountered (or had the courage to pursue) had we stayed still or required a firm comittment without first experimenting and gathering additional information.

Figuring it out or sussing it out

Language can be very helpful (or unhelpful) as we attempt to move from viewing uncertain transitions as a problem to solve to a more exploratory engagement with not knowing and an uncertain path forward. The phrase to "figure it out" is familiar to many of us and means *to solve*. It comes from mathematics and frames a problem as having right (or wrong) answer or solution. In uncertain transitions, the right or wrong binary is rarely the case, which can make "figuring it out" an unhelpful prompt for exploring uncharted territory. That's why I prefer to use a less frequently used phrase, to "suss it out." Many people who are familiar with both words view them as synonymous. But, to suss something out means *to discover*. Experimentation means suspending our impulse to figure it out and to approach the process of inquiry in the spirit of discovery. Rather than seek the most efficient solution in the shortest time possible (figure) we make time to ask great questions and seek surprising possibilities. Suss it out.

Experiment in practice

In Jeneanne's case, she knew that Chicago was no longer serving her needs, and Boston was calling her, despite not having lived there. She was looking to make a career change and believed there might be more opportunity for her on the East Coast. But she also knew there were some personal responsibilities and commitments that might make it difficult for her to make a big move—she had her daughter and her education, friends and wellbeing to think about. Much of it felt insurmountable, which led to stuckness. We discussed the possibility of setting up some low-fidelity experiments to see how she might learn by doing.

This led to two trips to Boston where she and her daughter explored what it might feel like to live in the neighborhood

where they were considering moving. During that time, they visited the local schools, connected with the school administrators, and her daughter spent a day there to see how she liked it. She attended local events and made some friends. Spending time in a place you're considering moving to probably doesn't seem like anything surprising or special. It wasn't *what* she did that was different; it was *how* she did it. Rather than trying it out, Jeneanne created small, time-boxed experiments that were designed to answer specific questions and used what she learned across these experiences to guide her way.

Instead of wondering if she would be able to get a job in Boston, could she create a portfolio and apply to jobs in Boston even before she decided to move there? In terms of her daughter, spending two weeks in Boston might answer some questions, but by delineating which questions she wanted to learn more about (How will my daughter feel in the school? How will I feel socially here? What is it like to date here?) she was able to do more than just take a vacation. She attended community events, had a few dates despite knowing she was only in town for two weeks, and arranged for her daughter to spend time in school. All of this provided a better snapshot of what the move would be in practice rather than speculation. It gave her concrete experiences and memories that she and her daughter could discuss in order to understand if this was potentially a right move for them. Two trips to Boston, a new portfolio and a new job later, Jeneanne moved to Boston with a new position—well-informed by action rather than speculation. Experience rather than projection. This is the heart of actively shifting from fear to curiosity rather than simply talking about it.

Of course, the story did not end there. After several months in Boston, yet another opportunity opened up for Jeneanne. She used the same process to consider that What Now? Moment, which she might not have considered otherwise, having just made a big change only months before. But she and her daughter now had an approach to think about the potential for this unexpected change and a language to use to discuss it. They are now

in the Pacific Northwest and Jeneanne is in a PhD program, thrilled to be solidifying her career change in this way.

The interesting part about this approach is that heading to Boston or even getting the PhD is not a concrete decision to make a career of it. On the contrary, it was an invitation to explore and gather additional information. This framing made entering new and unfamiliar territory an adventure—one that she is still on years later. When I asked her recently about her choices, she told me there are some elements of where she is and what she is doing that she likes better than others. For now, she is executing on the graduate degree and then will continue exploring when graduation poses the next What Now? Moment.

TAKEAWAYS

- Developing low-stakes, time-boxed experiments can help bring dispassionate curiosity into action as a means for developing a deeper understanding of options to help inform decisions.

- Identifying and testing multiple potential paths forward can help uncover next steps based upon experience rather than conjecture.

- Suspending our impulse to figure things out and making space for discovery before we make firm decisions can remove pressure to choose while opening space for new opportunities and insights to emerge.

CHAPTER NINE

Now pivot!

From exploration to execution

I know, I know. I said in Chapter 3 that we don't want to pivot. That opening a space for active waiting and a time horizon for inquiry and exploration is a fruitful way to move beyond being stuck in the pressure of making a premature decision when we are feeling threatened and lacking clarity about where we are and where we hope to go. And I meant it. When we face a What Now? Moment and cross the threshold into uncharted territory, the pivot metaphor can keep us from pausing to make sense of new terrain and identify the possibilities available to us if we make space to identify and coalesce them around our needs, wants, values and contextual cues. But, although some people are wanderers at heart, ambitions and the reality of day-to-day life mean eventually leaving base camp and heading up (or down) the mountain.

As a practical matter, most of us spend our time moving ourselves, our teams and our organizations between periods of

execution to exploration and back again. In the same way that stopping when we face a What Now? Moment and slowing the pace when we are executing to open space for inquiry can feel counterintuitive, it can be surprisingly difficult to make the transition from liminal space back into the world of timelines, plans and concrete decisions after we've made space for exploration.

This is not surprising for people who find their default in exploration. Artists, musicians and other creators sometimes feel like they are at their best when they are creating in a space without structure or boundaries. Liminal space is their sweet spot, since they can explore and experiment with new methods and approaches to their work. This kind of creativity is supercharged in the liminal—as long as it is pointed to creating a piece of art. Unfortunately, many of those same people find it difficult to apply that same creative thinking to business strategy or innovation outside of their creative domain.

Music artist, entrepreneur and tech innovator, Vérité, and her manager and business partner Vanessa Magos are the exceptions to this rule. Before I go too deeply into this example, it is important to mention that Vérité is my daughter, but she and Vanessa take their place among the wayfinders in this book for far more relevant reasons than her relationship to me. The two of them have spent the past seven years reimagining how music is created, distributed, valued and shared outside of traditional paths like music labels. From funding their project like a startup through angel investing, to engaging with cutting-edge music makers through podcasts, to experimenting with the blockchain, Vérité and Magos have mastered the art of moving from exploration to execution and back again as a way to carve a new way forward in an industry driven by well-worn pathways.

"This project was born in a What Now? Moment," Vérité told me, referring to a contract with a major label that fell through at the last minute. "It hadn't occurred to us to go independent at the time, but necessity inspired new questions about

how music gets made and what resources we needed to make a quality album." That reflection switched the inquiry from "How do I get signed to a label?" to "How can we access the funds we need to produce a quality album without one?" "That's when my identity shifted from music artist to creative entrepreneur. We've been experimenting and pivoting ever since."

Wait, I thought you said don't pivot

We've acknowledged that moving from the forward motion of a journey metaphor to creating a container for exploration territory can prove difficult given the cultural pressure to constantly move forward. What Now? Moments that disrupt or interrupt our journey provide us with the impetus to stop, engage in inquiry, and explore new options. But leaving the liminal container we created and returning to the journey, if that is the intention, is its own What Now? Moment that invites us to pivot from *exploration* to *execution*.

In Chapter 3, we challenged the pivot metaphor as unhelpful when a What Now? Moment invites us to slow the momentum, question perpetual motion, and allow ourselves to enter a transitional learning space. But how much learning is enough? What does it take to move from *divergent thinking*, which is what we're doing when we *explore many possible solutions in order to make new connections* to *convergent thinking*, which involves *organizing ideas in order to arrive at a particular choice* (Razumnikova, 2013)?

There are many models in design and other fields that discuss the importance of divergent and convergent thinking, but few of them talk about what it takes to move from one to the other. At what point have we learned what we need to learn from the experiment? How muddy do things have to be in order for us to characterize them as a What Now? Moment? How do we know when and how to pivot from wayfinding to waymaking?

Moving from wayfinding to waymaking

If you haven't gotten the memo yet, I am all about exploring, experimenting and learning. I have come to believe that it is a key part of working and living in liminal times. Opening up space to make sense of What Now? Moments and navigate through uncertainty is imperative—but at some point we can find ourselves with the desire (or the necessity) to choose a particular path forward or risk getting as stuck in exploration as we are in constant execution. So, how do we get out of base camp and back on the mountain? Asked another way, what does it take to discern between the locus of possibilities we've identified in our sensemaking activities and taking concrete steps forward—even small ones—while acknowledging that we don't know what will happen when we do?

Discernment at points of inflection

Figure 9.1 illustrates the experience of moving between exploration and execution and back again. By now you should be clear on how What Now? Moments catalyze inquiry and execution, but discerning between options and choosing how to press forward after we've gathered information and done our best to make sense is both an art and a science. A science because there are times that our inquiry and exploration lead to precise answers and firm decisions, like they would if someone lost in the woods climbed a tree to get a better view and saw a road close by. An art because sometimes we try multiple things, learn from them, and want or need to move forward, but have yet to identify a firm direction. This can be another kind of What Now? Moment that sparks a different sort of inquiry—the movement from divergent thinking to convergent thinking.

FIGURE 9.1   Discernment framework

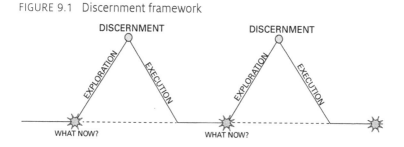

Just like the What Now? Moments that spark exploration, a What Now? Moment at a point of discernment can be viewed in the same way, just in a different direction. Rather than *stop, ask, and explore* how to open up liminal learning space, we can apply the same principles to learning how best to leave the liminal and pursue a course of action. This does not involve a set of particular steps—it is an approach. A set of practices. A way of being in the world that allows us to be interrupted and disrupted and constantly learning, discerning and choosing new ways forward—but always with an eye on interrogating those decisions to confirm that we are headed into the next leg of the journey in a direction that makes sense given what we've learned and is aligned with our aspirations, values and beliefs.

Sensemaking, discernment and moving into execution

In a perfect world, we would conduct our exploration and a single, well-lit, smooth and obvious path would open up ahead of us. And sometimes it does. Sometimes we get the call from our dream job, or the way is perfectly clear ahead of us. Unfortunately, sometimes the What Now? Moment out of inquiry is its own inquiry. Take the case of Erin Rech.

"Thank you so much for picking up the phone!"

Erin Rech, a high-energy communications executive I'd been working with for months, was knee deep in a job change and the process was down to two desirable executive positions. She needed to give an answer that afternoon and she found herself at an impasse. "The money and title are the same," she told me. "Same city and equal prestige." She went through a few other typical variables and was convinced that there was no difference between the two positions. By the time we connected, she just short of flipping a coin.

Erin had spent the previous several months developing a wayfinding practice driven by dispassionate curiosity, inquiry and experimentation. This contributed to her decision to leave her current role and transition to one that would give her the time and space she needed to concentrate on a book project that she was very passionate about. Shifting jobs would also be instrumental in her gathering the resources she would need to explore some other things that had the potential to change her professional and personal trajectory in profound ways. Erin was more than capable of making this decision without my input but had grown accustomed to opening up space for dispassionate curiosity and inquiry when she found herself at a point of uncertain transition. As a result, she wasn't looking for my advice. Instead, she was practicing active resilience by asking if I knew of any wayfinding tools that might help her to distinguish between two equally desirable paths forward. She'd done the work, and now needed to pivot from wayfinding to waymaking.

Thus, if stop, ask, explore *is the process of finding our way into and through uncharted territory,* learn, discern, choose, confirm *is the threshold to make our way out.*

When we think about making sense of where we've been after we've explored through inquiry and experimentation, we can begin the process of moving out of uncharted territory into a new path of our choosing. This may be an existing path that we

choose to follow—like taking one of the jobs Erin had at her disposal. Or it can be trying something completely new. Whatever the choice, moving out of exploration is a form of What Now? Moment that is informed by the information and experiences gleaned in the wilderness. Thus, if *stop, ask, explore* is the threshold to finding our way into and through uncharted territory, *learn, discern, choose, confirm* is the threshold to make our way out (see Figure 9.2).

Learn

By the time we consider moving from exploration to execution, we've learned a thing or two about what we like, what we don't like, what we value. We've also done some thinking about who we are and where we might hope to go—even if we haven't landed squarely on a precise destination. So, we've explored and experimented, which is great. But what did we learn from all of it? Just as we stopped at the beginning of this journey into uncharted territory, we also need to stop (briefly) on our way out. Without this pause, we might view things too simply or, once we hit the point of executing again, we may forget what we learned in the same way we do a few weeks after a motivational retreat or other reflective event. What we want to do here is

FIGURE 9.2   Learn, discern, choose, confirm

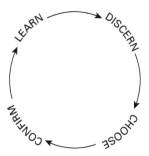

return to where we started. It's a time to pull out those Miro boards, Post-it notes and consider how we marked our entrance into the liminal learning space to really recall who we were and what direction we were headed in before and during our What Now? Moment. Go back to that X you created to mark the spot of entry into liminal space when you decided to enter inquiry and explore new possibilities. Then intentionally compare and contrast our perspectives on where we are now and where we started so we can identify what we've learned, how we've changed and our sense of direction.

QUESTIONS FOR REFLECTION

What insights have you gathered from your exploration so far?

What new questions have bubbled up?

What resistance is coming against you as you move from exploration to executing on your new knowledge?

What excited you about what you've learned?

What sparks fear or frustration?

Discern

Now, taking what we've learned, we can return to the locus of possibilities (Chapter 7) and see how they do or do not fit together. Do they remain distinct and separate items? Are there some that have morphed? Did what we took away from experimentation shift anything or point us to one or the other that becomes a clearer priority? Do we have new questions that need answering before we move forward, or can we begin to move toward a clearer path? These questions prompt reflection so we can more easily determine if we've gathered the information and insights we need to make sense of what we've uncovered (remember those puzzle pieces?) and discern how to proceed from here. Zoom out to collect thoughts and insights across all of the different domains to explore how the relative variables work together as a system.

Choose

In some cases, one choice will easily win out over the others. In others, as in Erin's situation, no clear choice will emerge. There are many ways to break a tie in this sort of situation. You can flip a coin, or you can resort to children's games like rock, paper, scissors. But these are effectively guessing games, and if you've taken the time to explore deeply what is possible, the decisions may come more easily. There are so many resources out there to help with choice making. In fact, as mentioned earlier, it is what most of our existing tools are designed to support. In Erin's case, she had considered her positions based upon typical variables: money, prestige, benefits. To break the tie, I invited her to consider some different domains, drawn from research my colleagues and I conducted to understand customer delight (Parasuraman et al, 2020) This exercise helped her to break the tie and see a clear distinction between two positions through the lens of six less common variables, all of which have been determined to drive delight.

EXERCISE

Designing for delight

Making sense of insights and information across domains invites us to consider what we need, want and value. The following items have been shown, individually and combined, to drive delight. Designing for delight involves considering these delight variables in addition to more concrete and specific factors like money, fame and happiness. It also makes space for delight to emerge in one domain when it is lacking in another.

1 Emotions

While what makes us happy is often used as an orientation tool, we know that it is a fleeting emotion that can be affected by uncertainty and exploring the unknown. There are a range of other positive emotions that can be more enduring in times of change and beyond such as contentment, gratitude, joy and peace that can be used instead of or in addition to happiness as a point of discernment. Consider how your locus of possibilities influences positive and negative emotions.

2 People

Our relationships with others and the communities in which we live and work are critically important to us as routes to delight. The aspects of who we will work with—or how work will affect our relationships outside of work—can be a useful tool to differentiate between options or to inform how we frame possibilities.

3 Getting the job done

This relates to goal setting. What problems do we want to solve for ourselves and others? What do we aspire to or hope for? Fulfilling our aspirations can be delightful and making choices that allow us to pursue a meaningful path can be crucial to wellbeing and flourishing. This might be a good time to return to the hope compass.

4 Beauty and environment

This refers to our environment and surroundings. It can relate to our office space or our homes. Aesthetics and beauty. How and where we are inspired in our spaces and places. Is it high on your list of needs or is living or working in uninspiring space a limiting factor for you? These questions can be helpful for discernment.

5 Timing

The timing of things being in alignment with our needs and expectations can be a source of delight or frustration. If we hope for things to move quickly, but others move slowly, that can cause distress. The opposite can be true when we want to take our time and feel rushed. Is the timing you're working with in alignment with your expectations and hopes? Do you have the flexibility to make things happen?

6 Freedom

The level of control or influence we have on outcomes and how we approach experiences and circumstances is another important variable. Do you prefer structured environments where you are given set tasks and timetables? If so, too much freedom to pave your own way might be unsettling. If you like having the freedom to schedule your activities, as long as the job gets done, too much structure can feel limiting. How much structure makes sense for you? What level of agency inspires you?

Allowing yourself to explore what's next based upon what will create delight for you and for those you hope to serve can be a useful tool for sensemaking and discernment.

Confirm

Moving forward from here — or on any journey— it is a good idea to create your own system or framework to help determine if the path you're on is one you actually want to be on. That confirmation can be based on a timetable, outcomes or on something else. The particulars are less important than committing to a practice of carrying forward into the execution all that you have learned in order to help to confirm whether you've chosen a path that makes sense to you or, if not, that you identify that quickly and acknowledge that you are facing another What Now? Moment. There is nothing wrong with this, of course, since all times of execution will eventually lead to another What Now? Moment. The key is to bring humility into our choices so we are able to recognize that we might have chosen poorly and that we should not persist if the evidence uncovers that we're moving in the wrong direction.

Execution to exploration and back again

The process of moving from execution to exploration and back again is the ebbing and flowing of life that we've all experienced, but we rarely consider the day-to-day. This is not about embracing a new process any more than naming and acknowledging the differences between spring, summer, winter and fall is. Instead, it is about acknowledging that our sense of (or lack of) clarity about our sense of direction waxes and wanes like the tides or the phases of the moon. We can survive perfectly well without identifying and acknowledging that—but it can also be helpful to see it for what it is and develop our own approaches to moving between them. If we do, it can help us to locate ourselves in both times of execution and times of exploration. It will provide us with the insight we need to access the right resources at the right time to navigate the part of the trail we find ourselves on and to have a better shot at finding and making our way through uncharted territory and back again.

TAKEAWAYS

- The move from wayfinding to waymaking is its own What Now? Moment.
- The transition from divergent and convergent thinking involves sensemaking and discernment.
- We can see where we are in this transition by understanding where we are on the *learn, discern, choose, confirm* spectrum.

CHAPTER TEN

Now follow your passion!

"I'm not a hero or a role model," Evan Dittig told me, "I'm just a skateboarder who loves it so much that I want to share that passion through education, service to others, here and across the globe." Evan is the founder and executive director of Shred.Co, an education company whose stated mission is to improve mental, physical, and social wellbeing on a local and global scale through skateboarding. A sponsored skateboarder since he was in his teens, Evan believes skateboarding can be a force for good, not just in his community, but around the world. In addition to running programs for children (and their parents!), he conducts therapeutic skateboarding engagements for mentally handicapped and addicted adults in the United States and is part of a global network of skateboard educators representing every continent who are committed to the sport as a means to build skills, capacity and confidence.

"The sickest part is that I'm actually able to make a living and support myself and my lifestyle just through skateboarding and sharing my passion and what I love to do with others, which is

the coolest thing." By applying the principles we've discussed in the previous chapters, Evan was able to identify a way to braid his love of skateboarding, his desire to be an educator/entrepreneur, and a deep desire to help others into a single entity that is as much a calling as a business. "Hopefully these kids will be doing awesome things when they grow up. That they are inspired to do even better work than I'm doing one day. We'll just all save the world through skateboarding."

This notion may sound strange or narrow to someone who does not share Evan's passion for his sport, but that is irrelevant. His trips to South Africa, Cuba and Nicaragua, and equipment drives to send new boards and skate shoes to young people in Zambia, Angola, Zimbabwe, Mozambique and South Africa are a testament to his drive and commitment. Born from passion, his initiative speaks for itself.

Yes, I said passion.

In the same way that the last chapter returned us to the concept of the pivot, we return to our passions and how they can motivate us to move from exploration to execution and persevere when we face resistance. As with the other practices we've explored together, I invite you to focus less on whether it is right or wrong to pivot or not pivot or follow your dispassion or passion, and think about liminal space as space we learn to move in and out of routinely. Passion, pivots, convergent and divergent thinking are all practices that are available to us and potentially helpful, if applied in ways that are appropriate to the situation and contexts in which we find ourselves. Following our passions when we are caught up in incendiary emotions—positive or negative—can create noise in the system, and drive us to make decisions that don't take into consideration all of the variables that might help us explore the entire locus of possibilities at our disposal when we face an uncertain transition. But, as we move out of exploration and into execution—from wayfinding to waymaking, as we discussed in Chapter 9—the very dispassion that helped us to pause and move into inquiry and exploration

can be a barrier to the motivation, perseverance and grit we need to stay the course and execute on our ideas and ambitions.

The key takeaway here is that we do not employ wayfinding practices to return to business as usual—even if the entire process results in recommitting to the course we were on before. The act of reorienting ourselves and engaging in liminal learning is meant to help us to reinvigorate, or identify for the first time, what matters to us and how we can engage our passions as a source of motivation. It's not just a matter of determining what *direction* I should go, but what it is that *motivates* me to go there? Both elements influence the bigger question we've been exploring here—how to get unstuck.

The very dispassion that helped us pause and move into inquiry and exploration can be a barrier to the motivation, perseverance and grit we need to stay the course and execute on our ideas and ambitions.

How much is enough?

This brings us back around to some of the challenges that get many people stuck in the first place—a lack of clarity about what they are passionate about and how to bring those passions to life in a way that is sustainable. The value of wayfinding is that, rather than finding ourselves stuck because we don't have an answer to these larger questions, we now have practices, principles and approaches we can draw upon to uncover what we find meaningful, and explore the varied routes we might take to get there, perhaps over a longer time horizon than we'd originally planned. Stuckness becomes an invitation to pause, ask new questions and explore, rather than view uncertainty as a threat.

This allows us to view following our passions as less of an incendiary response to an urgent call to win a race we may or may not have chosen to run, and more as a creative prompt that

inspires us to reflect on who we are and what matters to us—and to others. This is what Evan did as he reflected on what inspires him, and where his passions intersect with the impact he hopes to make. His efforts are both global and local by design—a networked structure that is small enough to let him engage with the individuals he serves at an intimate level. He does not seek to serve tens of millions, but to work at the grassroots level across the globe. This global/local approach

Stuckness becomes an invitation to pause, ask new questions and explore, rather than view uncertainty as a threat.

is aligned with the spirit of skateboarding culture and brings him great joy. This level of impact has given him a sense of personal and professional alignment at a scale that is both manageable and sustainable.

Pursuing your passions and making an impact

In a world where scale is favored, grassroots efforts like Evan's are sometimes perceived as less important than massive efforts that reach millions of people. Greater scale, more important, the thinking might go. And at some level, that makes sense. When it comes to deploying a vaccine for Covid-19 or developing a cure for cancer, scale is key. Like so many other things in this book, I take a both/and view on the matter of scale. There are many worthwhile things that are good for individuals and communities that happen at scale. That said, how or if we scale is an essential wayfinding question that we often overlook.

I cannot tell you how many times I've sat across a table or on the other side of a video call with someone whose What Now? Moment involves a decision about growing, changing, or something else related to bigger and more. I love that, and am happy

to help people reach really high-end goals at senior levels. I work with executives, thought leaders, and people who are trying to make big changes in ways that will have world-scale impact. Fantastic.

But that's not everyone.

We looked at the hope compass in Chapter 6 and considered the big questions: What do we hope for? What problems do we hope to solve? Whose problems? Why are we the right ones to solve them? What are the many possible ways we might solve them? What we didn't discuss is at what scale we should solve them—or the fact that the same aspiration can be deployed at many different levels of scale and still be profoundly meaningful. Unfortunately, we sometimes lose sight of this when we move fast and pivot forward without making time to consider if more, or bigger, or faster is always better. Let's think about this using a much-discussed current example: lifelong learning and skill building.

It is no secret that keeping our skills current and engaging in lifelong learning is a challenge we all face living in a rapidly changing world. Whether the focus is on equipping young people to be prepared for careers that don't yet exist, cross-training displaced mid-career workers for tech careers, or training emerging and established leaders to develop and employ new models to support the needs of a hybrid workforce, lifelong learning and helping people to equip themselves for the future is a fundamental challenge we face in the 2020s and beyond.

If we were to pose the question to a random room full of people in the education and learning sector across the globe, I am confident we would receive wildly different ideas about how best to address these very real challenges. One person (or more likely a large team) might suggest creating an online platform that can be accessed worldwide and provides a culturally relevant curriculum in multiple languages tied in with local offerings in ways that support what is happening on the ground. This sort of a project would necessitate global interaction and raising

millions of dollars to create the necessary infrastructure. If the leaders pull it off, they might reach millions of people and wind up on a 30 under 30 or 50 over 50 list and their efforts will garner press coverage. A large part of the day-to-day work for someone running an organization at that scale is executive-level oversight, relationship building, and gathering and connecting resources in support of a vision that goes way further than one community or neighborhood. This is the sort of grand vision many people have in mind (consciously or unconsciously) when they think about making a difference or doing something that has purpose or meaning. The people who set out to do these things and actually make it are the ones we view as successful. We look up to them and aspire to be them. They take a global view of life and address the systems and intersections we face across and between borders.

And we need them!

FIGURE 10.1 Impact funnel

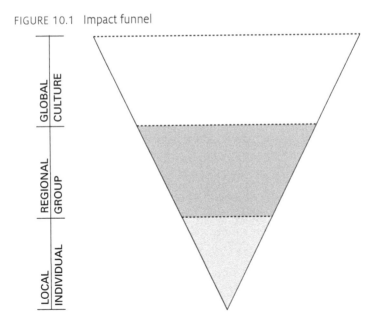

NOW FOLLOW YOUR PASSION!

But there are millions upon millions of people who are operating at other levels of attention in the education and learning domain. In fact, the vast majority of us have impact that is closer to the ground and less oriented toward solving global problems at scale. That's why understanding what level of impact we want to have, and at what scale, can both inform our wayfinding and help us to view our efforts at any scale as valuable and worthwhile, whether or not they will land us on a list in *Forbes* or *Fortune*. The impact funnel in Figure 10.1 provides a helpful visual reference for bringing our hopes for ourselves and others to life at whatever level of engagement makes sense to us.

Hope and impact

As we consider the prompt of the impact funnel, it is helpful to remember the hope compass, since these tools can work very well together. As you ask what problem you want to solve and whose problem you hope to solve, you can get a deeper understanding of your intentions if you also ask, where are those people? How many are there? Are they in my community or are they elsewhere? In doing so, you may uncover new opportunities—or give yourself a chance to rethink what particular impact you hope to have. In Evan's case, his hope is to bring confidence, connection and community to the people he serves, and it is at the center of all that he does. This passion can become a light that will help him to discern the shape Shred.Co will take over the coming years—and the impact it will have in doing so. If Evan expands beyond his passion for being on the skate board, connecting with other skaters, or creating community, he may build a bigger business, but not one that holds the same meaning to him or those he serves. If he remains smaller and more nimble, he may not spread worldwide. Neither path is better or worse than the other. Impact has many shapes and sizes. And needs

exist at every level of engagement. Does a person who devotes their life to caring for a single disabled child have a lesser impact than one who builds a global network?

That depends upon what you hope for, what problem you hope to solve, whose problem you want to solve, and how you want to solve it.

TAKEAWAYS

- A passionate response to moving from exploration to execution can motivate action and intention.

- Understanding where our passions help and where they hinder our wayfinding journey can help us to determine when to follow them and when they might lead us astray.

- The scale at which we choose to bring our passions to life can help to orient us on our wayfinding journey.

CHAPTER ELEVEN

What Now? Moments and life in uncharted territory

It is time now to explore the creative potential of interrupted and conflicted lives, where energies are not narrowly focused or permanently pointed toward a single ambition. These are not lives without commitments but lives in which commitments are continually refocused and redefined.

MARY CATHERINE BATESON

The uncertain transitions we face across the span of our interrupted and conflicted lives offer tremendous creative potential to reflect, refocus and redefine our commitments.

JOAN BALL

"It's strange," Sarah said, looking up from her camera to find the words as I watched across Zoom. "I know things are completely screwed up, but I feel surprisingly calm." It was mid-March 2020, and we were chatting about her response to the Covid-19 pandemic at work and in her personal life. I'd been

working with Sarah for about six months before the lockdown as part of a work-based training program. We hadn't spoken for two months before the pandemic hit, but she'd recognized it as a What Now? Moment, mapped some metaphors, and was curiously considering how she might experiment her way through an unprecedented time in modern history. "I still don't know exactly what to do next," she told me. "But I feel lighter. Like I know I this is uncharted territory, and I will find a way through."

I received many similar calls from people in early 2020. People who were adjusting more quickly and getting their bearings more easily because they had begun to understand their relationship with uncertainty and were developing their own unique practices with regard to a global What Now? Moment that led to so many different interruptions and disruptions for people in so many contexts. I spoke to leaders who were wrestling with what to do for their teams at the same time as determining what to do with, and for, their kids' education. I spoke to frontline workers sussing out ways to see their and families without exposing them to the virus. I spoke to hundreds of students navigating transitions at school and into the workforce. A grand and ubiquitous What Now? Moment experienced in so many particular ways by as many particular people.

As I've underscored in the preceding pages, these people were not pulling out a checklist and following a prescribed process. And thank goodness for that. Had that been the case, it is highly unlikely that anything I or anyone else might have suggested would have been relevant to so many people dealing with such different circumstances. Instead, by bringing the wayfinding principles they'd created for themselves to bear on their unique circumstances within the larger challenge, they were able to recognize their threat response and gather the resources they needed to have the best chance to respond rather than react.

While Covid-19 is a historic What Now? Moment, it confirmed how critical it is for us to prepare ourselves for the unimaginable by developing frameworks and approaches and built on a foundation of self-awareness and a recognition that understanding

who we are and where we hope to go is an evolving practice that unfolds across a lifetime. Keeping ourselves oriented and reoriented as we face what life brings is an invitation to dispassionate curiosity, inquiry and exploration, which requires attention, patience and humility, especially since we humans are prone to walk in circles.

Walking in circles

In his book *Finding Your Way Without a Map or a Compass* (1999), Harold Gatty describes why people tend to walk in circles—whether or not they are lost. His observations, which are based on research in a variety of contexts and with different communities of people across the globe, offer some insight into why navigation can be so challenging, regardless of our wayfinding skills and practices.

The challenge starts with who we are and how we're structured. Our right- or left-handedness creates strength differentials that impact direction in rowing, swimming or walking. Even a minimum difference in leg length can influence our direction over miles. "Practically everybody deviates," Gatty states. "Among the majority of people, the full blindfold deviation circle is formed in about half an hour. Others become displaced more slowly and may take from one to six hours to complete a circle. Practically nobody continues in a straight line." The degree of error is so consistent that he recommends that field training involve measuring the direction and extent of the general deviation so it can be accounted for when navigating without a map or compass. Dominance of one eye over the other, carrying a pack or even a rope in one hand can also have an impact in ways that are imperceptible in the moment but lead to walking off course and, eventually, in a circle. It's almost like we humans are not built to follow linear paths.

Our environment also influences our path when we, by choice or instinct, veer away from what Gatty calls an "irritant direction." Whether it is wind, rain, dust storms, or even sunshine, the conditions in the spaces we are trying to navigate can cause a person to lean their head away, which impacts direction. Even when a person takes on an irritant force head on, we carry, according to Gatty, a psychological preference to turn one way, usually right, when we face a barrier or a choice. So, he concludes, no matter our approach to navigating without a map or compass, we are being influenced by our physical bodies, our psychological predispositions, the territory in which we find ourselves, and the irritant forces we encounter along the way. Sounds a lot like finding our self-world fit.

Applying this lens to navigating change in uncertain times supports the notion that we wrestle with strengths, limitations, and the rhythms of our minds and bodies—and the "irritant forces" we encounter when changing environments can throw us off course. Perhaps we can learn to travel without walking in circles if we gather the emotional, physical, material, and social resources we toggle between in times of execution and exploration. Or, maybe, we accept that the world of work, life, community, and the systems they exist within might be more suited to our imperfections and peccadillos if they were designed to be less linear and more organic. Perhaps, as we explore what it means to develop a wayfinding mindset and practice our wayfinding skills, we can adapt our expectations to the very real fact that we are built to walk in circles—and the winds of change will not always be at our back. So, as you embark on your own journey, I leave you with the following thoughts and questions to ponder as we come to a close.

No matter our approach to navigating without a map or compass, we are being influenced by our physical bodies, our psychological predispositions, the territory in which we find ourselves, and the irritant forces we encounter along the way. Sounds a lot like finding our self-world fit.

What Now? Moments are inevitable—so prepare

We cannot prevent What Now? Moments from happening. In fact, if we become too obsessed with avoiding What Now? Moments, we can miss the creative opportunities that exist when we find ourselves at the edge of our understanding and comfort. So, as you consider who you are and where you hope to go, now is a good time to reflect:

How do I react to What Now? Moments in general?

Are those reactions different across different territories (home, work, community)?

Are those reactions different across different domains of the resilience wheel?

Are there certain people/circumstances that spark incendiary reactions, responses and behaviors in me and are they helpful or unhelpful?

Under what circumstances do I feel most resilient?

Under what circumstances do I feel least resilient?

When was the last time I reacted disproportionately to a What Now? Moment (i.e. treated it as life and death but later realized it was less incendiary than I thought)?

What is a way I might have dealt with that situation differently had I employed the *stop, ask, explore* framework?

Is there a time when I wish I had taken longer to reflect/consider the scenario and my options more carefully at a point of transition before responding/reacting?

If I had approached the situation dispassionately, might I have responded differently? Would the outcome have been different?

What resources might I gather now to be better prepared for my next What Now? Moment?

How can I help others or people in my team to navigate What Now? Moments?

What are some other questions I should be asking myself now?

Every What Now? Moment is novel—and similar

When a What Now? Moment hits and we are unsure what to do next, the brain responds—no matter how much training we give it. If the change feels like a threat, it can spark our incendiary emotions. Remember, there is nothing wrong with incendiary

emotions. We need the full range of emotions in our repertoire. No judgement for emotions, reactions and responses—just proper resourcing to help us learn to regulate and learn from them in ways that are helpful given our context. Some useful questions to reflect on here are:

Under what circumstances do I find it hard to *stop, ask or explore?*

What Now? Moments have I faced over the past five years? Did I fight? Flee? Freeze? Other?

How might I be more aware of future responses so I can detect patterns?

When I detect a negative pattern, what practice can I put into place to help me change my responses when I notice that the pattern may be surfacing?

Who can I ask to observe my behavior and give me honest (and kind!) feedback?

Approaching uncertainty takes confidence and humility

The firefighting metaphor we began with works so well here. Highly trained emergency services personnel bring all of that experience and training to the scene of a fire or other emergency but recognize that, while they know how to fight fires, they do not necessarily know how to fight THIS fire without gathering the best information they can and the appropriate resources they need

to respond. This means building skills and developing practices that give us the confidence we need to enter into liminal learning space, but also the humility to accept that we don't know how best to proceed unless we ask questions and are willing to learn from the answers. Here are some questions to reflect upon:

What is my relationship with confidence—and do I need to have more or less of it to be right-sized?

What is my relationship with humility—and do I need to have more or less of it to be right-sized?

Where does my confidence meet humility? How do they intersect?

Would my best friend agree with this assessment?

Would my partner agree?

Would my boss or business partner agree?

Would my subordinates agree?

Wayfinding is an art—no one size fits all

In the same way that any explorer has both tools of the trade and the art of their own approach, wayfinding is about developing

new capacities and practicing them in context. Not only will the tools you choose be different than those someone else chooses, but you will also likely have to adapt the tools you use to changing situations and circumstances. That is why this is about embracing a practice rather than implementing a preset framework or set of rules:

Which of the wayfinding practices presented here appeals to me instinctually?

Which of my existing practices might I adapt for wayfinding?

Do these tools suit me in practice as much as they do in theory? If I'm not sure yet, how might I find out?

How might I develop/fine-tune/tweak them further to better suit my own unique personality and needs?

How do I know if I am in a practice of execution (trekking up the mountain)?

How do I know if I am in a practice of exploration (active waiting in base camp)?

How can I practice moving from one to the other more easily?

Helping others to face What Now? Moments?

Learning to better navigate the liminal and create transitional learning spaces is a life skill that is under-discussed and under-practiced. If you're reading this book, you are ahead of the curve. But learning to *stop, ask, explore* is something we can not only utilize ourselves, but also help others to do. I'm not suggesting that you try to teach people while they are in incendiary emotions. That would be like trying to teach someone whose clothes are on fire about stop, drop and roll. Instead, when we get that call from a colleague or friend who is going through it, can we keep from matching their incendiary emotions or giving them advice with no context and encourage them to *stop, ask, explore*? Here are some questions for reflection:

When was a time one of my friends or colleagues asked for advice or called to vent when they were in a What Now? Moment?

Did I give advice? Listen? Console? Other?

If I received a call tomorrow from a person having a What Now? Moment, would it be helpful to do it differently?

How might I use *stop, ask, explore* with my team at work?

Could this be useful with my family?

Living in the liminal

Uncertain times call for new ways of being and doing. The paradox of living in a creative and generative way in uncharted territory is that we need to be at once incredibly humble and, at the same time, bold. We need to be willing to explore, but not get distracted and lost in searching. We need to be ready to have the rug pulled out from under us as the future of work, technology, cultural shifts, climate change, and social and economic challenges require us to adjust and adapt to a world that is constantly changing.

The name of this book was supposed to be *Flux*. I did the due diligence, bought the URL, and spent more than two years kneading the insights and approaches you've read about here into a proposal that captured the imagination of my editors and resulted in a book deal. We created graphics and wrote the blurbs. And, about a week before we were set to approve the cover design, I got a note from someone I encountered randomly online who said, "I noticed in your bio that you have a book coming out named *Flux*—so does my friend." She included a link to a book that was scheduled for release about four months before mine. Completely different content, but the same title.

This was, as you might imagine, a What Now? Moment for me. I was writing on a very aggressive and tight deadline and, taking my own medicine, I needed to stop writing to ask myself (and my editorial team) what the best path forward from there might be. There is something wonderful in the creative process when we get to use our research and theories in practice, which I do every day. To test it in our own spaces to see if what we observe in others comes to roost in our own lives. As I stopped for two weeks (which felt like an eternity if I had any shot at keeping to my writing deadlines) and considered how a title shift at that stage would affect the process, I was also able to see how other people processed my challenge.

I was able to see how my dispassionate curiosity landed with others—and they didn't like it. "You must be so upset," they told me. "Keep the name and fight it out... your book will be better than the other one, hold your ground."

All of that advice was delivered with just the sort of incendiary emotions I was tamping down in myself as I stopped, composed myself, gained my bearings, and reconsidered how I wanted to position the work and how what I knew about the other work (which wasn't much) might influence how I thought about the space between my own What Now? and what comes next. This got me thinking more about flux in general and the flux that is created in our own minds and in the minds of others who make our flux their own.

This What Now? Moment expanded and put a fine point on my aspiration for this work to be more than a "self-help" or "professional development" tool. Sure, it is my hope that people will use it to get much better at navigating their own What Now? Moments. But it also can support us in helping others when they engage us in their inflection points. Like the end result of so many What Now? Moments, the shift from "flux" to *Stop, Ask, Explore,* the new title I ultimately settled on, was a blessing in disguise. Times had changed drastically since those earlier drafts of the book. In 2021, nobody in the world needed to be convinced (or reminded!) that we are living in times of flux. Instead, *Stop, Ask, Explore* is meant to point toward potential solutions. Not in a prescriptive way, but as a clarion call for us to pay attention to our relationship with change and uncertainty and learn to embrace it as a route to growth and learning, even when it is frightening and uncomfortable. It invites us to think about who we are, where we are going, and how those two questions come together to help us in the simple, very human task of willfinding and wayfinding through life together.

Parting words

Whether we like it or not, we are living through uncertain times—and there's more to embracing it than training ourselves to respond to the unexpected. The approaches and practices we discuss in this book are an invitation for each and every one of us to become a trailblazer. An adventurer. An explorer with the willingness to ask new questions and experiment with new ways of being as we travel through life's calms and storms. A wayfinder.

So, even if external flux settles (which is unlikely any time soon), the natural rhythm of a life well lived invites us to learn, discern, choose, and confirm over and over again. If we can learn to choose the curiosity loop over the fear loop and proceed with an experimental mindset, this can become less and less challenging with each point of transition or change. The more we learn to trust our ability to suss things out—whether or not we know exactly where we're going—the more comfortable navigating transitions becomes. *Stop, Ask, Explore* is about embracing wayfinding as a way of life to learn to flourish even when the going gets tough. If we accept that change is inevitable, and we are up to the task of navigating it, we can create our own frameworks for future action that lead to success and personal wellbeing, however we choose to define them.

This book is not about motivation. It is not meant to give you a shot of dopamine and get you pumped up to make a change, only to get caught up in the day-to-day again and shift yourself back into whatever groove you were in before you picked it up. The kind of inquiry that I'm inviting you to (or, for those of you who were already at it, to pause and consider) is something different. In the same way that deciding to climb a mountain or start a business or run for elected office is the beginning of a much longer process, the premise of *Stop, Ask, Explore* is for it to spark possibility—and underscore that preparation, development, resourcing, and an inclination to dispassionate curiosity and learning in

practice are the skills and capacities we need to flourish in uncharted territory. And the 2020s are clearly uncharted territory.

So, as we close, I invite you to view this as the beginning, not the end. This is not about coming away from this with five easy steps, seven new ideals or ten superpowers to make all of your dreams come true. It is about a simple recognition that living in uncertain times—whether that be at the grassroots or global level of assessment—calls for a new set of skills and capacities.

And that will take more than simply learning to navigate change in uncertain times. It is the recognition that, as human beings navigating the world around us, we are exploring identities, getting our bearings and trying to flourish as we pursue our self-world fit. And so is everyone else.

So, What Now?

Conclusion

I came across Rob Freer's post on LinkedIn just a few days before I completed the manuscript for this book. I had notes in hand and a structure in place for what I thought would be the conclusion and decided to delete all of it when he agreed to allow me to share his heartfelt post in full here. I'll let Rob tell you who he is and where he is on his journey. He writes:

I resigned.

After nine and a half years at a large wine and spirits company, I have decided enough is enough. I intentionally gave up a successful career and steady paycheck because I need a break.

I resigned because I am burned out from a position that I feel is too much for one person to be successful, with a relentless volume of work.

I resigned because I felt undervalued, getting paid ~20% less than my counterparts.

I resigned because I hated that I would start to get annoyed at

my kids for procrastinating in the morning because I had to get to my computer to reply to emails.

I resigned because I need to slow down and take a break, not to wake up at 5 a.m. and have checking emails be the first thing I do.

This has been one of the biggest decisions of my career, leaving stability for the unknown.

This might be the best, or worst, decision for my career, however I am betting on myself, and I am curious about what a different future this will lead to.

I am going to miss the teams I worked with day in and day out, my friends and work family. Many have wished me the best. Many have said they would recommend me. Many have said it takes guts to what I'm doing. Some have said they might not be far behind.

I will miss the human connection, so if there are people out there that want to chat, reach out. I've got nothing but time. Whether it is about what I am doing, or you have a question about the spirits industry feel free to send me a message.

As for what is next? Who knows? I am going to take some time, reflect, recharge and rebuild. I will come out stronger and happier for doing this.

In choosing to stop, ask new questions, and explore new options for his work and life, Rob is embarking on a wayfinder's journey – whether or not he would use that language. And he is not alone. In the wake of a tumultuous start to the 2020s, millions of people around the globe have chosen, or been forced, to pause and reflect on who they are and what matters to them. Some believe that these moves are a knee-jerk reaction to pandemic shutdowns and a global forced pause we've not seen in modern history. While that may be true, this great resignation, or reshuffle, or reorientation in our tech-fueled world has been happening for more than a decade. It fueled the stuckness that catalyzed the research that laid the groundwork for this book, and it will continue to require us to stop, ask new questions and explore

new routes forward as we adapt to a changing landscape across the 2020s and beyond.

So how do we live in these tumultuous times? What resources do we need, individually and collectively, to create (and recreate) the systems we need to flourish rather than simply survive the world we are creating? How do we orient ourselves in this uncharted territory?

I've learned a lot about navigating change in uncertain times over the past decade, and there are many more questions that I will continue to pursue in the coming years. In fact, it is my deep hope that anyone reading this book who is interested in participating in this inquiry with me will engage with me in future research—as an individual or with your team. Whether you choose to join me on this quest, or you are more interested in continuing your inquiry in your own context, the most important thing is to view the end of this book as the beginning of a new relationship with change in uncertain times.

This is the exciting, and perhaps arduous, task facing every one of us in this early part of the of the 21st century. The new explorers who know and accept (maybe kicking and screaming) that the future lives in yet-to-be-imagined systems and processes for which there are no best practices and past successes to rely upon—or even rebel against. Reading these pages and engaging with the corresponding materials may have inspired you to slow down or speed up. You may be experimenting with some new things, or you may have made some concrete decisions. The work may inspire you to make a big change or to confirm that the path you're on is the one for you. There is no possible way that I could know the capacities you need to build, the resources you need to gather, or the changes you need to consider to get from where you are to where you hope to go. I have no idea what goals your organization and team are pursuing, or how you define success and what sacrifices you are willing to make to achieve it. You might not know that either. And it's into that unknown that we venture together.

These are the questions that drive my work in the world with people like Rob—and perhaps like you—who are choosing to see things differently and are willing to carve out new ways of working and being in the years to come. My dream is for the wayfinders of the world to find one another. To support one another. To share resources and ideas. What's worked and what hasn't. We can share what we are learning with one another. That is why this book is not about answers. Answers are too certain. Too absolute. Instead, let's raise questions together and create learning spaces that will uncover what it takes for companies to become places where people can do meaningful and productive work *and* flourish outside of it. Let's share insights and resources that will help light the way for those among us who are lost in the thick of the woods.

I invite you to join a growing community of wayfinders who are, by choice or circumstance, learning to navigate change in uncertain times by both exploring new ways to do things *and* using tried and true tools together to move from times of execution to exploration and back again. Whether you are a student transitioning from college to career, an early-career professional with an ambition to do work you love, or an established leader creating the future of work right now, recognizing the liminal space as a transitional—and potentially transformational—learning space is at the core of what I'm hoping to accomplish by sharing my work at this stage of my inquiry. If you choose to continue on this journey, I hope you've come away with some new perspectives to help guide you on your way. Some will resonate. Others will not. That is to be expected—and it is welcomed—since the wayfinding task we all face in this moment in history is to chart our own course and gather the relevant resources we need to follow it.

So please don't engage this work to add another checklist of activities to your already busy schedule. Instead, let's learn together what it takes enter the unknown with a sense of adventure. Let's find new ways to help one other to shape organizations,

communities and lives built for the pursuit of human flourishing. Let's commit to becoming willing and finding new ways to enter the unknown without a true north, compass or maps upon which to rely. And let's do it with an acknowledgement that despite the politics and the environment and the discord and the loans and the ageism and the economy, we are not doomed. Nor can we rely on the magic of positive thinking. Sure, the terrain might not feel very accommodating and change may be uncomfortable, but this is the straw we've pulled as human beings born in this time in this place. So, like so many others born before us to uncertain times, we need to examine ourselves and determine how we want to live, what meaning we hope to bring to bear on the circumstances we're facing and what it will mean to flourish in this new environment—in practice not just theory. That means asking ourselves new kinds of questions and creating spaces to answer them.

Questions like:

- If turning points inspire a threat response, how might we equip ourselves and our teams to face them?
- If perceptions of threat create unhelpful emotional and behavioral responses in ourselves and our teams, how might we reframe it?
- If fear leads to impulsive reactions and hopelessness in the face of uncertain transitions and change, how do we turn it around and engage uncertainty with an exploratory mindset (even when we feel under-resourced or find ourselves operating in unhelpful systems)?

I don't offer these questions as a matter of navel gazing or self-enlightenment. These are concrete and practical questions meant to prompt preparation for unrelenting change. A practice of active resilience that will equip future leaders working at every scale for the tasks they are called to—in service of others and on their own

wayfinding journeys. And we all need to be equipped. Whether you take on key issues and wicked problems at a global level, a regional level, or in your neighborhood or home, we need to recognize that, in addition to critical challenges like climate change, poverty, social unrest and inequality of every kind, there are new What Now? Moments on the horizon that are, as yet, beyond our imagining—and we need wayfinders with the resources, hope and experimental mindset to understand how to approach the opportunities and challenges we'll face in the 2020s and beyond with creativity, humility and care.

And the 2020s are going to be a wild ride.

Built on a foundation shaken by a global pandemic, political and social unrest, and mass adoption of technology for work and life, we stand together at a massive point of inflection. Ours is not the first What Now? Moment. Countless humans have stood at points of inflection throughout history asking the same questions that our ancestors across the globe have asked for millennia. Who are we? What does it mean to live a good life? Where do we go from here? These questions become even more poignant in the context of emerging massive changes we'll be dealing with over the coming decades.

Technology, science and virtual reality

We're on the brink of a massive shift in what we perceive to be real. I'm not just talking about gaming headsets. Artificial intelligence, machine learning, the blockchain, quantum computing, VR and AR, the Internet of Things, robotics—these technologies that are much discussed in blogging and podcast circles are already changing the fabric of fields as varied as healthcare, law, education, manufacturing, art and others. As we move closer to the convergence of these technologies on every aspect of our lives, the human toll remains unknown. How will we think about equity, access, and the distribution of resources and power that will come into question as these technologies become adopted more widely? What will

it mean for how we work and how we live together if we are inter-acting and engaging in multiple realities with our interactions mediated by machines? How will we address the gaps between those with access to these technologies and those without access?

Lifelong learning in an untrustworthy reality

The life cycle of skills and capacities to operate in these new reali-ties is shorter and shorter every year. This means that more people need to keep up with more information more frequently than ever before in human history. While we like to believe that having access to information means that we will be more educated, the way that information flows and is driven by algorithms means that we are increasingly receiving our information in echo cham-bers that can make even the most educated and interested people question whether the information they are receiving is accurate, trustworthy and complete. This means that it will become increas-ingly difficult for people to get and keep their bearings, even if we create global education systems. What does it mean to go to university if we no longer trust educators? How do we learn online if we don't trust platforms? How do we adapt to an evolv-ing understanding of history, power, diversity and inclusion and apply that understanding to bring about equality and justice in our systems, organizations and communities?

Healthcare, mental health and humanity

According to data collected by the UN, the average lifespan of human beings globally has increased by 20 years since the 1960s, and the trend is on the rise (Ruggeri, 2018). More people living longer, and healthier lives is a wonderful outcome of modern science. But what do our societies look like when living to 100+ is normal? How do our systems and societies deal with life spans that extend 30 or 40 years beyond traditional retirement? How

do we make space for one another and develop the systems we need to accommodate an older population, not only for physical health but for mental health? What are the implications for the planet, the economy, education systems? How will the technologies mentioned previously influence the way we live and die—especially if we become able to extend our minds into virtual spaces after our bodies are no longer able to sustain us? What does this mean for how we think about what it means to be human?

These things may seem like science fiction, but many are already in existence today—and they are just the tip of the iceberg. The further these technologies go, the further we (and the AIs) will take them. Keeping up with the pace of change is about more than creating new and better training programs at the local employment center. We stand on the brink of unimaginable uncharted territory—and the need for a global community of wayfinders to help make sense of it has never been greater.

I leave you with one final image (Figure 12.1) to guide your wayfinding journey and remind you that the curiosity loop and space for liminal learning is available to you. I hope I can count you among the fold.

FIGURE 12.1 Wayfinder's framework

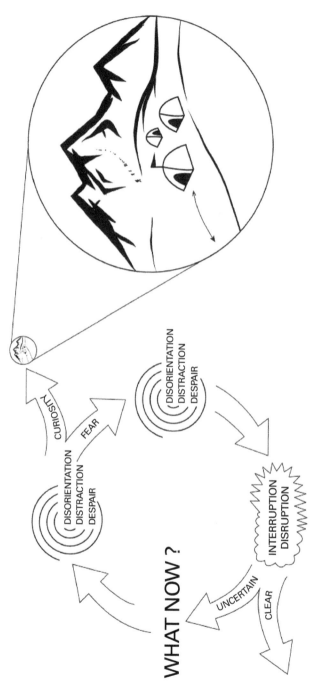

Appendices

Appendix A Emotion regulation

Appendix B Resilience

Appendix C Conceptual metaphor

Appendix D Transformative learning and threshold concepts

Appendix E Sensemaking

Appendix F Wayfinding and navigation

Appendix G Participatory action research

Appendix H Stop, ask and further exploration

Appendix A
Emotion regulation

Emotion regulation is a rich and diverse field of research that continues to evolve as we learn more about the psychological, physiological, philosophical, and cultural aspects of emotions and how they affect our thoughts, behaviour and self-concept. The following books and articles provide a stepping-off point for deeper exploration. This is not intended to be a complete list of relevant sources on this topic. It is, however, a representative sample of the resources that have helped to shape my thinking in the current research.

Books

How Emotions are Made: The secret life of the brain, Lisa Feldman Barrett

The Upside of Stress: Why stress is good for you, and how to get good at it, Kelly McGonigal, PhD

Emotional Agility: Get unstuck, embrace change, and thrive in work and life, Susan David, PhD

The Unapologetic Guide to Black Mental Health: Navigate an unequal system, learn tools for emotional wellness, and get the help you deserve, Rheeda Walker, PhD

The Gift of Fear: Survival signals that protect us from violence, Gavin de Becker

The Managed Heart: Commercialization of human feeling, Arlie Russell Hochschild

Handbook of Positive Emotions, Michele M Tugade, Michelle N Shiota and Leslie D Kirby

Handbook of Emotion Regulation, edited James J Gross

Unstuck: Your guide to the seven-stage journey out of depression,
James S Gordon, MD

Relevant academic articles

Aldao, A (2013) The future of emotion regulation research: Capturing context, *Perspectives on Psychological Science,* **8** (2) pp 155–72

Dewick, P, Hofstetter, JS and Schröder, P (2021) From panic to dispassionate rationality—Organizational responses in procurement after the initial COVID-19 pandemic peak, *IEEE Engineering Management Review,* **49** (2) pp 45–56

Feinberg, M, Ford, BQ and Flynn, FJ (2020) Rethinking reappraisal: The double-edged sword of regulating negative emotions in the workplace, *Organizational Behavior and Human Decision Processes,* **161,** pp 1–19

Ford, BQ and Troy, AS (2019) Reappraisal reconsidered: A closer look at the costs of an acclaimed emotion-regulation strategy, *Current Directions in Psychological Science,* **28** (2) pp 195–203

Ford, BQ Gross, JJ and Gruber, J (2019) Broadening our field of view: The role of emotion polyregulation, *Emotion Review,* **11** (3) pp 197–208

Ganesh, S (2014) Unraveling the confessional tale: Passion and dispassion in fieldwork, *Management Communication Quarterly,* **28** (3) pp 448–57

Gross, JJ (2001) Emotion regulation in adulthood: Timing is everything, *Current Directions in Psychological Science,* **10** (6) pp 214–19

Gross, JJ and Feldman Barrett, L (2011) Emotion generation and emotion regulation: One or two depends on your point of view, *Emotion review,* **3** (1) pp 8–16

Linton, JC, Kommor, MJ and Webb, CH (1993) Helping the helpers: The development of a critical incident stress management team

through university/community cooperation, *Annals of Emergency Medicine*, **22** (4) pp 663–68

Maroney, TA and Gross, JJ (2014) The ideal of the dispassionate judge: An emotion regulation perspective, *Emotion Review*, 6 (2) pp 142–51

Ren, S (2021) *Dispassion and the Good Life: A study of Stoicism and Zhuangism* (Doctoral dissertation, Duke University)

Sheppes, G, Scheibe, S, Suri, G, Radu, P, Blechert, J and Gross, JJ (2014) Emotion regulation choice: A conceptual framework and supporting evidence, *Journal of Experimental Psychology: General*, **143** (1) p. 163

Smith, AM, Willroth, EC, Gatchpazian, A, Shallcross, AJ, Feinberg, M and Ford, BQ (2021) Coping with health threats: The costs and benefits of managing emotions, *Psychological Science*, **32** (7) pp 1011–23

Vasilyev, P (2017) Beyond dispassion: Emotions and judicial decision-making in modern Europe, *Rechtsgeschichte-Legal History*, (25) pp 277–85

Webb, TL, Miles, E and Sheeran, P (2012) Dealing with feeling: A meta-analysis of the effectiveness of strategies derived from the process model of emotion regulation, *Psychological Bulletin*, **138** (4) p 775

Appendix B
Resilience

Resilience is a rich and diverse field of research that crosses disciplines and levels of analysis, from the individual to the community and ecosystem. The following books and articles provide a stepping-off point for deeper exploration. This is not intended to be a complete list of relevant sources on this topic. It is, however, a representative sample of the resources that have helped to shape my thinking in the current research.

Books

Change Your World: The science of resilience and the true path to success, Michael Ungar, PhD

Being Wrong: Adventures in the margin of error, Kathryn Schulz

Better by Mistake: The unexpected benefits of being wrong, Alina Tugend

Flourish: A visionary new understanding of happiness and well-being, Martin Seligman

Executive Resilience: Neuroscience for the business of disruption, Jurie G Rossouw with Pieter J Rossouw

Antifragile: Things that gain from disorder, Massim Nicholas Taleb

Psychological Capital and Beyond, Fred Luthans, Carolyn M. Youssef-Morgan and Bruce Avolio

Character Strengths and Virtues: A handbook and classification, Christopher Peterson and Martin EP Seligman

Relevant academic articles

Ayala, JC and Manzano, G (2014) The resilience of the entrepreneur: Influence on the success of the business, A longitudinal analysis, *Journal of Economic Psychology*, **42**, pp 126–35

Ball, J and Lamberton, C (2015) Rising every time they fall: The importance and determinants of consumer resilience, *ACR North American Advances*, pp 191–96

Bartone, PT (2006) Resilience under military operational stress: Can leaders influence hardiness?, *Military Psychology*, **18** (S) pp S131–48

Beutel, ME, Glaesmer, H, Decker, O, Fischbeck, S and Brähler, E (2009) Life satisfaction, distress, and resiliency across the life span of women, *Menopause*, **16** (6), pp 1132–38

Bonanno, GA (2004) Loss, trauma, and human resilience: Have we underestimated the human capacity to thrive after extremely aversive events?, *American Psychologist*, **59** (1), pp 20–28

Brougham, RR, Zail, CM, Mendoza, CM and Miller, JR (2009) Stress, sex differences, and coping strategies among college students, *Current Psychology*, **28** (2), pp 85–97

Fletcher, D and Sarkar, M (2013) Psychological resilience: a review and critique of definitions, concepts and theory, *European Psychologist*, **18** (1), pp 12–23

Luthar, SS, Cicchetti, D and Becker, B (2000) The construct of resilience: a critical evaluation and guidelines for future work, *Child Development*, **71** (3), pp 543–62

Masten, AS (2001) Ordinary magic: resilience processes in development, *American Psychologist*, **56** (3), pp 227–38

Masten, AS (2007) Resilience in developing systems: progress and promise as the fourth wave rises, *Development and Psychopathology*, **19** (3), pp 921–30

Morales, EE (2008) Exceptional female students of color: academic resilience and gender in higher education, *Innovative Higher Education*, **33** (3), pp 197–213

Morrison, GM and Allen, MR (2007) Promoting student resilience in school contexts, *Theory into Practice*, **46** (2), pp 162–69

Ong, AD, Bergeman, CS, Bisconti, TL and Wallace, KA (2006) Psychological resilience, positive emotions, and successful adaptation to stress in later life, *Journal of Personality and Social Psychology*, **91** (4), pp 730–49

Richardson, GE (2002) The metatheory of resilience and resiliency, *Journal of Clinical Psychology*, **58** (3), pp 307–321

Rutten, BPF et al (2013) Resilience in mental health: linking psychological and neurobiological perspectives, *Acta Psychiatrica Scandinavica*, **128** (1), pp 3–20

Tugade, MM and Fredrickson, BL (2004) Resilient individuals use positive emotions to bounce back from negative emotional experiences, *Journal of Personality and Social Psychology*, **86** (2), pp 320–33

Tugade, MM, Fredrickson, BL and Barrett, LF (2004) Psychological resilience and positive emotional granularity: examining the benefits of positive emotions on coping and health, *Journal of Personality*, **72** (6), pp 1161–90

Windle, G (2011) What is resilience? A review and concept analysis, *Reviews in Clinical Gerontology*, **21** (2), pp 152–69

Appendix C
Conceptual metaphor

The study of conceptual metaphor and the influence it has on the way we think, behave and frame our understanding of ourselves and the world around us is a well-established, but still evolving field of study. The following books and articles provide a stepping-off point for deeper exploration. This is not intended to be a complete list of relevant sources on this topic. It is, however, a representative sample of the resources that have helped to shape my thinking in the current research.

Books

Metaphors We Live By, George Lakoff and Mark Johnson
Marketing Metaphoria: What deep metaphors reveal about the minds of consumers, Gerald and Lindsay Zaltman
I Never Metaphor I Didn't Like: A comprehensive compilation of history's greatest analogies, metaphors and similes, Dr. Mardy Grothe
I is an Other, The Secret Life of Metaphor and How it Shapes the Way We See the World, James Geary

Relevant academic articles

Amin, TG (2009) Conceptual metaphor meets conceptual change, *Human Development*, 52 (3) pp 165–97
Amin, TG (2015) Conceptual metaphor and the study of conceptual change: Research synthesis and future directions, *International Journal of Science Education*, 37 (5–6) pp 966–91

Ball, J (2019) Ecosystems, Blueprints and Journeys–Oh My! Toward a practice-oriented typology of service design metaphors, *Touchpoint*, **11**, pp 70–76

Caballero, R and Ibarretxe-Antuñano, I (2009) Ways of perceiving, moving, and thinking: Revindicating culture in conceptual metaphor research, *Cognitive Semiotics*, **5** (1–2) pp 268–90

Casasanto, D (2009) When is a linguistic metaphor a conceptual metaphor? *New Directions in Cognitive Linguistics*, **24**, pp 127–45

Christensen, GL and Olson, JC (2002) Mapping consumers' mental models with ZMET, *Psychology & Marketing*, **19** (6) pp 477–501

Close, HG and Scherr, RE (2015) Enacting conceptual metaphor through blending: Learning activities embodying the substance metaphor for energy, *International Journal of Science Education*, **37** (5–6) pp 839–66

Danesi, M (2007) A conceptual metaphor framework for the teaching of mathematics, *Studies in Philosophy and Education*, **26** (3) pp 225–36

Daane, AR, Haglund, J, Robertson, AD, Close, HG and Scherr, RE (2018) The pedagogical value of conceptual metaphor for secondary science teachers, *Science Education*, **102** (5) pp 1051–76

Flensner, KK and Von der Lippe, M (2019) Being safe from what and safe for whom? A critical discussion of the conceptual metaphor of 'safe space', *Intercultural Education*, **30** (3) pp 275–288

Gibbs Jr, RW (2011) Evaluating conceptual metaphor theory, *Discourse Processes*, **48** (8) pp 529–62

Howie, P and Bagnall, R (2013) A beautiful metaphor: Transformative learning theory, *International Journal of Lifelong Education*, **32** (6) pp 816–36

Ibarretxe-Antuñano, I (2013) The relationship between conceptual metaphor and culture, *Intercultural Pragmatics*, **10** (2) pp 315–39

Kövecses, Z (2008) Conceptual metaphor theory: Some criticisms and alternative proposals, *Annual Review of Cognitive Linguistics*, **6** (1) pp 168–84

Kövecses, Z (2016) Conceptual metaphor theory. In *The Routledge Handbook of Metaphor and Language* (pp 31–45) Routledge

Kövecses, Z (2020) *Extended Conceptual Metaphor Theory*, Cambridge University Press

Lakoff, G and Johnson, M (1980) Conceptual metaphor in everyday language, *The Journal of Philosophy*, **77** (8) pp 453–86

Lakoff, G (1994) What is a conceptual system? *The Nature and Ontogenesis of Meaning*, pp 41–90

Lakoff, G (2008) Conceptual metaphor. In *Cognitive Linguistics: Basic readings* (pp 185–238) De Gruyter Mouton

Lakoff, G and Johnson, M (2020) Conceptual metaphor in everyday language. In *Shaping Entrepreneurship Research* (pp 475–504) Routledge

McGlone, MS (2007) What is the explanatory value of a conceptual metaphor? *Language & Communication*, **27** (2) pp 109–26

Shearer, RL, Aldemir, T, Hitchcock, J, Resig, J, Driver, J and Kohler, M (2020) What students want: A vision of a future online learning experience grounded in distance education theory, *American Journal of Distance Education*, **34** (1) pp 36–52

Slingerland, E (2004) Conceptions of the self in the Zhuangzi: Conceptual metaphor analysis and comparative thought, *Philosophy East and West*, pp 322–42

Soriano, C (2015) Emotion and conceptual metaphor. In *Methods of Exploring Emotions* (pp 226–34) Routledge

Stickles, E, David, O, Dodge, EK and Hong, J (2016) Formalizing contemporary conceptual metaphor theory: A structured

repository for metaphor analysis, *Constructions and Frames*, 8 (2) pp 166–213

Vervaeke, J and Kennedy, JM (2004) Conceptual metaphor and abstract thought, *Metaphor and Symbol*, **19** (3) pp 213–31

Wickman, SA, Daniels, MH, White, LJ and Fesmire, SA (1999) A "primer" in conceptual metaphor for counsellors, *Journal of Counseling & Development*, 77 (4) pp 389–94

Appendix D
Transformative learning and threshold concepts

The study of transformative learning and threshold concepts plumbs the depths of how we learn and what it takes to move into and through the learning process, even when it becomes troublesome. The following books and articles provide a stepping-off point for deeper exploration of this topic. This is not intended to be a complete list of relevant sources. It is, however, a representative sample of the resources that have helped to shape my thinking in the current research.

Books

Learning Spaces: Creating opportunities for knowledge creation in academic life, Maggi Savin-Baden

Transformations: Identity construction in contemporary culture, Grant McCracken

Threshold Concepts Within the Disciplines, Ray Land, Jan HF Meyer and Jan Smith (Eds)

The Handbook of Transformative Learning: Theory, research, and practice, Edward W Taylor and Patricia Cranton

The Fifth Discipline: The art and practice of the learning organization, Peter M Senge

A More Beautiful Question: The power of inquiry to spark breakthrough ideas, Warren Berger

Long-Life Learning: Preparing for jobs that don't even exist yet, Michelle R Weise

Curiosity The desire to know and why your future depends on it, Ian Leslie

The Creativity Leap: Unleash curiosity, improvisation, and intuition at work, Natalie Nixon

Insight: Why we're not as self-aware as we think and how seeing ourselves clearly helps us succeed in work and in life, Tasha Eurich

The Rites of Passage (2e), Arnold van Gennep

Relevant academic articles

Aboytes, JGR and Barth, M (2020) Transformative learning in the field of sustainability: A systematic literature review (1999–2019), *International Journal of Sustainability in Higher Education*, pp 993–1013

Alhadeff-Jones, M (2012) Transformative learning and the challenges of complexity, *The Handbook of Transformative Learning: Theory, research, and practice*, pp 178–94

Bishop, K and Etmanski, C (2021) Down the rabbit hole: Creating a transformative learning environment, *Studies in the Education of Adults*, pp 1–13

Bourn, D and Issler, S (2010) Transformative learning for a global society, *Education and Social Change: Connecting local and global perspectives*, pp 225–37

Buechner, B, Dirkx, J, Konvisser, ZD, Myers, D and Peleg-Baker, T (2020) From liminality to communitas: The collective dimensions of transformative learning, *Journal of Transformative Education*, **18** (2) pp 87–113

Christie, M, Carey, M, Robertson, A and Grainger, P (2015) Putting transformative learning theory into practice, *Australian Journal of Adult Learning*, **55** (1) pp 9–30

Elias, D (1997) It's time to change our minds: An introduction to transformative learning, *ReVision*, **20** (1) pp 2–7

Fleming, T (2018) Mezirow and the theory of transformative learning. In *Critical Theory and Transformative Learning* (pp 120–36) IGI Global

Gouthro, P (2018) Creativity, the arts, and transformative learning. In *The Palgrave International Handbook on Adult and Lifelong Education and Learning* (pp 1011–26) Palgrave Macmillan, London

Groen, J and Kawalilak, C (2016) Creating spaces for transformative learning in the workplace, *New Directions for Adult and Continuing Education*, 2016 (152) pp 61–71

Howie, P and Bagnall, R (2013) A beautiful metaphor: Transformative learning theory, *International Journal of Lifelong Education*, 32 (6) pp 816–36

Land, R, Rattray, J and Vivian, P (2014) Learning in the liminal space: A semiotic approach to threshold concepts, *Higher Education*, 67 (2) pp 199–217

Lange, E (2015) Transformative learning and concepts of the self: Insights from immigrant and intercultural journeys, *International Journal of Lifelong Education*, 34 (6) pp 623–42

Lee, N, Irving, C and Francuz, J (2014) Community-embedded learning and experimentation: Fostering spaces for transformative learning online. In A Nicolaides and D Holt (Eds), *Spaces of transformation and transformation of Space: Proceedings of XI International Transformative Learning Conference*, Teachers College, Columbia University, New York, October 24–26, 2014, (pp 499–506)

Mälkki, K and Green, L (2014) Navigational aids: The phenomenology of transformative learning, *Journal of Transformative Education*, 12 (1) pp 5–24

Martin, SD, Snow, JL and Franklin Torrez, CA (2011) Navigating the terrain of third space: Tensions with/in relationships in school-university partnerships, *Journal of Teacher Education*, 62 (3) pp 299–311

Morgan, AD (2010) Journeys into transformation: Travel to an "other" place as a vehicle for transformative learning, *Journal of Transformative Education*, 8 (4) pp 246–68

Nye, A and Clark, J (2016) "Being and becoming" a researcher: Building a reflective environment to create a transformative learning experience for undergraduate students, *Journal of Transformative Education*, 14 (4) pp 377–91

Savin-Baden, M, McFarland, L and Savin-Baden, J (2008) Learning spaces, agency and notions of improvement: What influences thinking and practices about teaching and learning in higher education? An interpretive meta-ethnography, *London Review of Education*, 6 (3) pp 211–27

Savin-Baden, M (2008) Liquid learning and troublesome spaces: Journeys from the threshold? In *Threshold Concepts Within the Disciplines* (pp 75–88) Brill Sense

Schnitzler, T (2019) The bridge between education for sustainable development and transformative learning: Towards new collaborative learning spaces, *Journal of Education for Sustainable Development*, 13 (2) pp 242–53

Selby, D, Selby, D and Kagawa, F (2015) Thoughts from a darkened corner: Transformative learning for the gathering storm, *Sustainability Frontiers: Critical and transformative voices from the borderlands of sustainability education*, pp 21–42

Simm, D and Marvell, A (2015) Gaining a "sense of place": Students' affective experiences of place leading to transformative learning on international fieldwork, *Journal of Geography in Higher Education*, 39 (4) pp 595–616

Taylor, PC (2013) Research as transformative learning for meaning-centred professional development, *Meaning-Centred Education: International perspectives and explorations in higher education*, pp 168–85

Ukpokodu, O (2009) The practice of transformative pedagogy, *Journal on Excellence in College Teaching*, 20 (2) pp 43–67

van Dellen, T and Cohen-Scali, V (2015) The transformative potential of workplace learning: Construction of identity in learning spaces, *International Review of Education*, **61**, pp 725–34

Watkins Jr, CE, Davis, EC and Callahan, JL (2018) On disruption, disorientation, and development in clinical supervision: A transformative learning perspective, *The Clinical Supervisor*, **37** (2) pp 257–77

Appendix E
Sensemaking

Sensemaking is a rich and varied field of study and practice that has several distinct streams of research and practice. The following books, articles and communities of learning and practice provide a stepping-off point for deeper exploration of sensemaking. This is not intended to be a complete list of relevant sources. It is, however, a representative sample of the resources that helped to shape my thinking in the current research.

Books

Cynefin: Weaving sense-making into the fabric of our world, Dave Snowden and friends

Rethinking Design Thinking: Making sense of the future that has already arrived, GK VanPatter

Managing the Unexpected (3e): Sustained performance in a complex world, Karl E Weick and Kathleen M Sutcliffe

Sensemaking in Organizations, Karl E Weick

Making Sense of the Organization, Karl E Weick

Transitions: Making sense of life's changes, William Bridges, PhD with Susan Bridges

Applied Imagination: Principles and procedures of creative problem solving, Alex Osborn

Range: Why generalists triumph in a specialized world, David Epstein

Small Data: The tiny clues that uncover huge trends, Martin Lindstrom

Relevant academic articles

Barry, D and Meisiek, S (2010) Seeing more and seeing differently: Sensemaking, mindfulness, and the workarts, *Organization Studies*, **31** (11) pp 1505–30

Böhler, D (2014) Order creation from a transactional perspective: Creating practices from sensemaking processes. In *On the Nature of Distributed Organizing* (pp 57–67) Springer Gabler, Wiesbaden

Brown, AD, Stacey, P and Nandhakumar, J (2008) Making sense of sensemaking narratives, *Human Relations*, **61** (8) pp 1035–62

Brown, AD (2000) Making sense of inquiry sensemaking, *Journal of Management Studies*, **37** (1) pp 45–75

Christianson, MK and Barton, MA (2020) Sensemaking in the time of COVID-19, *Journal of Management Studies*, **58** (2), pp 572–76

Colville, ID, Waterman, RH and Weick, KE (1999) Organizing and the search for excellence: Making sense of the times in theory and practice, *Organization*, **6** (1) pp 129–48

Craig-Lees, M (2001) Sense making: Trojan horse? Pandora's box? *Psychology & Marketing*, **18** (5) pp 513–26

Drazin, R, Glynn, MA and Kazanjian, RK (1999) Multilevel theorizing about creativity in organizations: A sensemaking perspective, *Academy of Management Review*, **24** (2) pp 286–307

Gioia, DA and Thomas, JB (1996) Identity, image, and issue interpretation: Sensemaking during strategic change in academia, *Administrative Science Quarterly*, pp 370–403

Gioia, DA and Chittipeddi, K (1991) Sensemaking and sensegiving in strategic change initiation, *Strategic Management Journal*, **12** (6) pp 433–48

Holt, R and Cornelissen, J (2014) Sensemaking revisited, *Management Learning*, **45** (5) pp 525–39

Kezar, A and Eckel, P (2002) Examining the institutional transformation process: The importance of sensemaking, interrelated strategies, and balance, *Research in Higher Education*, **43** (3) pp 295–328

Kurtz, CF and Snowden, DJ (2003) The new dynamics of strategy: Sense-making in a complex and complicated world, *IBM Systems Journal*, **42** (3) pp 462–83

Lüscher, LS and Lewis, MW (2008) Organizational change and managerial sensemaking: Working through paradox, *Academy of Management Journal*, **51** (2) pp 221–40

Lynam, T and Fletcher, C (2015) Sensemaking: A complexity perspective. *Ecology and Society*, **20** (1)

Maitlis, S, Vogus, TJ and Lawrence, TB (2013) Sensemaking and emotion in organizations, *Organizational Psychology Review*, **3** (3) pp 222–47

Mills, JH, Thurlow, A and Mills, AJ (2010) Making sense of sensemaking: The critical sensemaking approach, *Qualitative Research in Organizations and Management: An International Journal*, **5** (2) pp 182–95

Moore, DT and Hoffman, RR (2011) Sensemaking: A transformative paradigm, *American Intelligence Journal*, **29** (1) pp 26–36

Osland, JS and Bird, A (2000) Beyond sophisticated stereotyping: Cultural sensemaking in context, *Academy of Management Perspectives*, **14** (1) pp 65–77

Patriotta, G (2003) Sensemaking on the shop floor: Narratives of knowledge in organizations, *Journal of Management Studies*, **40** (2) pp 349–75

Pye, A (2005) Leadership and organizing: Sensemaking in action, *Leadership*, **1** (1) pp 31–49

Schildt, H, Mantere, S and Cornelissen, J (2020) Power in sensemaking processes, *Organization Studies*, **41** (2) pp 241–65

Schwandt, DR (2005) When managers become philosophers: Integrating learning with sensemaking, *Academy of Management Learning & Education*, **4** (2) pp 176–92

Seligman, L (2006) Sensemaking throughout adoption and the innovation-decision process, *European Journal of Innovation Management*, 9 (1), pp 108–20

Sharma, N (2006) Sensemaking: Bringing theories and tools together, *Proceedings of the American Society for Information Science and Technology*, 43 (1) pp 1–8

Snowden, D (2002) Complex acts of knowing: paradox and descriptive self-awareness, *Journal of Knowledge Management*, 6 (2) pp 100–111

Snowden, D (2005) Multi-ontology sense making: A new simplicity in decision making, *Journal of Innovation in Health Informatics*, 13 (1) pp 45–53

Snowden, D (2011) Naturalizing sensemaking. In *Informed by Knowledge* (pp 237–48) Psychology Press

Steigenberger, N (2015) Emotions in sensemaking: A change management perspective, *Journal of Organizational Change Management*, 28 (3) pp 432–51

Thomas, JB, Clark, SM and Gioia, DA (1993) Strategic sensemaking and organizational performance: Linkages among scanning, interpretation, action, and outcomes, *Academy of Management Journal*, 36 (2) pp 239–70

Thurlow, A and Mills, JH (2009) Change, talk and sensemaking, *Journal of Organizational Change Management*, 22 (5) pp 459–79

Weick, KE (2005) Managing the unexpected: Complexity as distributed sensemaking. In *Uncertainty and Surprise in Complex Systems* (pp 51–65) Springer, Berlin, Heidelberg

Weick, K, Sutcliffe, K and Obstfeld, D (2009) Organizing and the process of sensemaking, *Handbook of Decision Making*, 16 (4) p 83

Weick, KE (2012) Organized sensemaking: A commentary on processes of interpretive work, *Human Relations*, 65 (1) pp 141–53

Whiteman, G and Cooper, WH (2011) Ecological sensemaking, *Academy of Management Journal*, 54 (5) pp 889–911

Wright, CR, Manning, MR, Farmer, B and Gilbreath, B (2000) Resourceful sensemaking in product development teams, *Organization Studies*, **21** (4) pp 807–25

Wrzesniewski, A, Dutton, JE and Debebe, G (2003) Interpersonal sensemaking and the meaning of work, *Research in Organizational Behavior*, **25**, pp 93–135

Communities of learning and practice

Cognitive Edge: https://thecynefin.co/
The International Bateson Institute: https://batesoninstitute.org/
Humantific: https://www.humantific.com/
The Grey Swan Guild: https://www.greyswanguild.org/

Appendix F
Wayfinding and navigation

Wayfinding and navigation research crosses between two primary domains: the design of interior and exterior spaces, and spatial orientation in real and virtual environments. The following books and articles provide a stepping-off point for deeper exploration of wayfinding and navigation in both of those streams. This is not intended to be a complete list of relevant sources. It is, however, a representative sample of the resources that have helped to shape my thinking in the current research.

Books

Wayfinding: The science and mystery of how humans navigate the world, MR O'Connor
Discernment, Henri Nouwen
From Here to There: The art and science of finding and losing our way, Michael Bond
The Lost Art of Finding Our Way, John Edward Huth
Lead from the Outside: How to build your future and make real change, Stacey Abrams
Finding Your Way Without a Map or Compass, Harold Gatty
Pinpoint: How GPS is changing technology, culture, and our minds, Greg Milner
Design for the Real World: Human ecology and social change, Victor Papanek
Wayfinding: People, signs and architecture, Paul Arthur and Romedi Passini
Biomimicry: Innovation inspired by nature, Janine M Benyus
Entangled Life: How fungi make our worlds, change our minds and shape our futures, Merlin Sheldrake

Relevant academic articles

Allen, GL (1999) Cognitive abilities in the service of wayfinding: A functional approach, *The Professional Geographer*, 51 (4) pp 555–61

Ball, J and Barnes, DC (2017) Delight and the grateful customer: Beyond joy and surprise, *Journal of Service Theory and Practice*, 27 (1), pp 250–69

Blades, M (1991) Wayfinding theory and research: The need for a new approach. In *Cognitive and Linguistic Aspects of Geographic Space* (pp 137–65) Springer, Dordrecht

Cornell, EH, Heth, CD and Rowat, WL (1992) Wayfinding by children and adults: Response to instructions to use look-back and retrace strategies, *Developmental Psychology*, 28 (2) pp 328–36

Cornell, EH, Sorenson, A and Mio, T (2003) Human sense of direction and wayfinding, *Annals of the Association of American Geographers*, 93 (2) pp 399–425

Dalton, RC, Hölscher, C and Montello, DR (2019) Wayfinding as a social activity, *Frontiers in Psychology*, 10, p 142

Darken, RP and Peterson, B (2002) Spatial orientation, wayfinding, and representation. In *Handbook of Virtual Environments* (pp 533–58) CRC Press

Devlin, AS and Bernstein, J (1995) Interactive wayfinding: Use of cues by men and women, *Journal of Environmental Psychology*, 15 (1) pp 23–38

Farr, AC, Kleinschmidt, T, Yarlagadda, P and Mengersen, K (2012) Wayfinding: A simple concept, a complex process, *Transport Reviews*, 32 (6) pp 715–43

Giannopoulos, I, Kiefer, P, Raubal, M, Richter, KF and Thrash, T (2014) Wayfinding decision situations: A conceptual model and evaluation. In *International Conference on Geographic Information Science* (pp 221–34) Springer, Cham

Golledge, RG (1992) Place recognition and wayfinding: Making sense of space, *Geoforum*, **23** (2) pp 199–214

Golledge, RG, Klatzky, RL and Loomis, JM (1996) Cognitive mapping and wayfinding by adults without vision. In *The Construction of Cognitive Maps* (pp 215–46) Springer, Dordrecht

Hartley, T, Maguire, EA, Spiers, HJ and Burgess, N (2003) The well-worn route and the path less traveled: Distinct neural bases of route following and wayfinding in humans, *Neuron*, **37** (5) pp 877–88

Head, D and Isom, M (2010) Age effects on wayfinding and route learning skills, *Behavioural Brain Research*, **209** (1) pp 49–58

Hund, AM and Minarik, JL (2006) Getting from here to there: Spatial anxiety, wayfinding strategies, direction type, and wayfinding efficiency, *Spatial Cognition and Computation*, **6** (3) pp 179–201

Jamshidi, S and Pati, D (2021) A narrative review of theories of wayfinding within the interior environment, *HERD: Health Environments Research & Design Journal*, **14** (1) pp 290–303

Kato, Y and Takeuchi, Y (2003) Individual differences in wayfinding strategies, *Journal of Environmental Psychology*, **23** (2) pp 171–88

Klippel, A (2003) Wayfinding choremes. In *International Conference on Spatial Information Theory* (pp 301–15) Springer, Berlin, Heidelberg

Lawton, CA (1996) Strategies for indoor wayfinding: The role of orientation, *Journal of Environmental Psychology*, **16** (2) pp 137–45

Lawton, CA and Kallai, J (2002) Gender differences in wayfinding strategies and anxiety about wayfinding: A cross-cultural comparison, *Sex Roles*, **47** (9) pp 389–401

Lawton, CA (2010) Gender, spatial abilities, and wayfinding. In *Handbook of Gender Research in Psychology* (pp 317–41) Springer, New York, NY

Løvs, GG (1998) Models of wayfinding in emergency evacuations, *European Journal of Operational Research*, **105** (3) pp 371–89

Mackett, RL (2021) Mental health and wayfinding, *Transportation Research Part F: Traffic Psychology and Behaviour*, **81** pp 342–54

Myers, M (2010) 'Walk with me, talk with me': The art of conversive wayfinding, *Visual Studies*, **25** (1) pp 59–68

Parasuraman, A, Ball, J, Aksoy, L, Keiningham, TL and Zaki, M (2020) More than a feeling? Toward a theory of customer delight, *Journal of Service Management*, **32** (1) pp 1–26

Passini, R (1981) Wayfinding: A conceptual framework, *Urban Ecology*, **5** (1) pp 17–31

Passini, R (1996) Wayfinding design: Logic, application and some thoughts on universality, *Design Studies*, **17** (3) pp 319–31

Prestopnik, JL and Roskos–Ewoldsen, B (2000) The relations among wayfinding strategy use, sense of direction, sex, familiarity, and wayfinding ability, *Journal of Environmental Psychology*, **20** (2) pp 177–91

Raubal, M and Egenhofer, MJ (1998) Comparing the complexity of wayfinding tasks in built environments, *Environment and Planning B: Planning and Design*, **25** (6) pp 895–913

Schwering, A, Krukar, J, Li, R, Anacta, VJ and Fuest, S (2017) Wayfinding through orientation, *Spatial Cognition & Computation*, **17** (4) pp 273–303

Timpf, S, Volta, GS, Pollock, DW and Egenhofer, MJ (1992) A conceptual model of wayfinding using multiple levels of abstraction. In *Theories and Methods of Spatio-Temporal Reasoning in Geographic Space* (pp 348–67) Springer, Berlin, Heidelberg

Timpf, S (2002) Ontologies of Wayfinding: A traveler's perspective, *Networks and Spatial Economics*, **2** (1) pp 9–33

Wiener, JM, Büchner, SJ and Hölscher, C (2009) Taxonomy of human wayfinding tasks: A knowledge-based approach, *Spatial Cognition & Computation*, **9** (2) pp 152–65

Woollett, K and Maguire, EA (2010) The effect of navigational expertise on wayfinding in new environments, *Journal of Environmental Psychology*, **30** (4) pp 565–73

Appendix G
Participatory action research

P articipatory action research is a qualitative method of inquiry. The following resources provide a stepping-off point for deeper exploration of participatory action research. This is not intended to be a complete list of relevant sources. It is, however, a representative sample of the resources that have helped to shape my thinking in the current research.

Books

Participatory Research for Health and Social Well-Being, Tineke Abma, Sarah Banks, Tina Cook, Sonia Dias, Wendy Madsen, Jane Springett, Michael T Wright

Participatory Action Research: Theory and methods for engaged inquiry, Jacques M Chevalier and Daniel J Buckles

New Approaches to Qualitative Research: Wisdom and uncertainty, Maggie Savin-Baden and Claire Howell Major

How to Think Like an Anthropologist, Matthew Engelke

Ethnographic Thinking: From method to mindset, Jay Hasbrouck

Narrative Analysis: Qualitative research methods series 30, Catherine Kohler Riessman

Community-based Qualitative Research: Approaches for education and the social sciences, Laura Ruth Johnson

Relevant academic articles

Borda, OF, Reason, P and Bradbury, H (2006) Participatory (action) research in social theory: Origins and challenges. In *The Sage Handbook of Action Research: Participative inquiry and practice* , Sage, pp 27–37

Kemmis, S (2006) Participatory action research and the public sphere, *Educational Action Research*, **14** (4) pp 459–76

Khanlou, N and Peter, E (2005) Participatory action research: Considerations for ethical review, *Social Science & Medicine*, **60** (10) pp 2333–2340

Kidd, SA and Kral, MJ (2005) Practicing participatory action research, *Journal of Counseling Psychology*, **52** (2) p 187

Kindon, S, Pain, R and Kesby, M (2007) Participatory action research: Origins, approaches and methods. In *Participatory Action Research Approaches and Methods* (pp 35–44) Routledge

McTaggart, R (1991) Principles for participatory action research, *Adult Education Quarterly*, **41** (3) pp 168–87

McTaggart, R (1994) Participatory action research: Issues in theory and practice, *Educational Action Research*, **2** (3) pp 313–37

Ozanne, JL and Saatcioglu, B (2008) Participatory action research, *Journal of Consumer Research*, **35** (3) pp 423–39

Swantz, ML (2008) Participatory action research as practice. In *The Sage Handbook of Action Research: Participative inquiry and practice*, pp 31–48

Appendix H
Stop, ask and further exploration

I wrote this book as a means to share what I've learned so far about "stuckness" at points of uncertain transition. I also wanted to share the benefits of thinking about them before they happen as a means of preparing ourselves to have confidence in our ability to navigate them well when they come along—and they always come along. In some ways I view the contents of these chapters as a tribute to honor the amazing individuals, teams and organizations I've engaged with so far.

But this inquiry is far from over.

The work presented here barely scratches the surface of what we need to learn—in theory and in practice—about what it takes to navigate unrelenting change and how we best prepare ourselves and others to do it in a way that focuses on wellbeing and flourishing. For that reason, I view this as a work in progress. A conversation starter. A prompt to inspire, equip and encourage people to view top-of-mind issues like the future of work, the future of education, the future of culture, the future of the planet and where technology is taking us as a species and a planet through a creative problem-solving and wayfinding lens.

It is my hope that the work will inspire curiosity in you, the reader, and that some of you will join me on this journey of asking deeper questions and pursuing insights through empirical research and field engagements. You can find more information about ongoing projects and opportunities to connect on my website, www.stopaskexplore.com, or connect with me on LinkedIn, Twitter or other socials @joanpball.

References

Introduction

Arnett, J (2000) Emerging adulthood: A theory of development from the late teens through the twenties, *American Psychologist,* [55](5), pp 469–480

Black, P (2020) Retirement Or A 'Third Act': What Will You Choose? Forbes, 27 April, https://www.forbes.com/sites/forbescoachescoun cil/2020/04/27/retirement-or-a-third-act-what-will-you-choose/?sh= 35d2f929200e (archived at https://perma.cc/4WUR-LW5Q)

Carnevale, A, Hanson, A and Gulish, A (2013) Failure to Launch: Structural Shift and the New Lost Generation, https://1gyhoq479ufd3yna29x7ubjn-wpengine.netdna-ssl.com/ wp-content/uploads/2014/11/FTL_ExecSum.pdf (archived at https:// perma.cc/ASU5-6Y9Z)

Frost, R (1915) The Road Not Taken, *The Atlantic Monthly*, August

Fry, R (2013) A rising share of young adults live in their parents' home, https://www.pewresearch.org/ social-trends/2013/08/01/a-rising-share-of-young-adults-live-in-their- parents-home/ (archived at https://perma.cc/7VJB-TJFJ)

McKee, R (1999) *Story: Substance, structure, style and the principles of screenwriting*, Methuen Publishing, London

Robinson, O (2015) Emerging adulthood, early adulthood and quarter- life crisis: Updating Erikson for the twenty-first century, in Žukauskiene, R (Ed.) *Emerging Adulthood in a European Context,* Routledge, New York

Williams, C (2004) The sandwich generation, *Perspectives on Labour and Income*, **16** (4), pp 7–14

Chapter 1

Bateson, M (1989) *Composing a Life,* Grove Press, New York

Chapter 2

Hartley, C and Phelps, E (2010) Changing fear: The neurocircuitry of emotion regulation, *Neuropsychopharmacology*, **35** (1), pp 136–46

Taleb, N (2014) *Antifragile: Things that gain from disorder,* Random House, New York

Ungar, M (2019) *Change Your World: The science of resilience and the true path to success*, Sutherland House, Toronto

Chapter 3

Lakoff, G (2006) Conceptual metaphor, in Geeraerts, D (Ed), *Cognitive Linguistics: Basic readings,* pp 185–238, Mouton de Gruyter, Berlin

Lakoff, G and Johnson, M (1980) Conceptual metaphor in everyday language, *The Journal of Philosophy*, **77** (8), pp 453–86

Ries, E (2011) *The Lean Startup: how constant innovation creates radically successful businesses*, Portfolio Penguin, New York

Zaltman, G (2008) *Marketing Metaphoria: What deep metaphors reveal about the mind of consumers*, Harvard Business Press, Boston

Chapter 4

Hill, K (2011) Wayfinding and spatial reorientation by Nova Scotia deer hunters, *Environment and Behavior*, **45** (2), pp 267–82

Oldham, J (2015) The alternative DSM-5 model for personality disorders, *World Psychiatry*, **14** (2), pp 234–36

Savin-Baden, M (2008) *Learning Spaces: Creating opportunities for knowledge creation in academic life*, Open University Press, Maidenhead

Van Gennep, A (2019) *The Rites of Passage*, The University of Chicago Press, Chicago

Chapter 5

Eurich, T (2017) *Insight: Why we're not as self-aware as we think, and how seeing ourselves clearly helps us succeed at work and in life*, Penguin Random House, New York

Passini, R (1996) Wayfinding design: logic, application and some thoughts on universality, *Design Studies*, **17** (3), pp 319–31

Chapter 6

Luthans, F, Youssef, CM and Avolio, BJ (2015) *Psychological Capital and Beyond*, Oxford University Press, USA

Merril, R and McElhinny, M (1983) *The Earth's Magnetic Field: Its history, origin and planetary perspective*, Academic Press (International Geophysics Series, Volume 32), London and New York

Rand, K and Cheavens, J (2009) Hope Theory, in *The Oxford Handbook of Positive Psychology* (2nd ed), Oxford University Press, Oxford

Wiener, J, Schnee, A and Mallot, H (2004) Use and interaction of navigation strategies in regionalized environments, *Journal of Environmental Psychology*, **24** (4), pp 475–93

Chapter 8

Chevalier, J and Buckles, D (2013) *Participatory Action Research: Theory and methods for engaged inquiry*, Taylor and Francis, London

Chapter 9

Parasuraman, A, Ball, J, Aksoy, L, Keiningham, T and Zaki, M (2020) More than a feeling? Toward a theory of customer delight, *Journal of Service Management*, **32** (1), pp 1–26

Razumnikova, O (2013) Divergent Versus Convergent Thinking, in *Encyclopaedia of Creativity, Invention, Innovation and Entrepreneurship* (Ed Carayannis, E), Springer, New York

Chapter 11

Bateson, M (1989) *Composing a Life,* Grove Press, New York
Gatty, H (1999) *Finding Your Way Without Map or Compass,* Dover Publications, Mineola

Conclusion

Ruggeri, A (2018) Do we really live longer than our ancestors? BBC, 3 October, https://www.bbc.com/future/article/20181002-how-long-did-ancient-people-live-life-span-versus-longevity (archived at https://perma.cc/VMV2-F4T5)

Acknowledgments

This book would still be an ambition if it were not for the hundreds of people who allowed me to join them on their journeys into and through uncertain transitions and liminal spaces over the past 10 years. To the individuals, teams and organizations who I've worked with, thank you. The experiences you allowed me to share and the wisdom you uncovered inform the frameworks, approaches and tools in this book.

Many thanks to Aura Lehrer, Christine Anisko, Kim Gabelmann, Brittney Hiller, Stephanie Roth, Jody Weatherstone, Erika Simmons, Erica Buddington, Ashley Rigby, Tim Gilligan, Shireen Idroos, Tricia Douglas, Natalie Kuhn, Efrat Yardeni, Jamila Wallace, Erin Rech, Shikha Mittal, Matthew Politoski, Evan Dittig, Melissa Shaw Smith, Hannah Maxwell, Jordan Novak, Linda Mensch, Chelsea Simpson, Rebecca Pry, Elise Johansen, and Ava Burgos for all of the conversations and reflections. Your willingness to play in uncharted territory with me keeps me wondering and exploring.

I am so grateful to Kat Scimia (now Galbo!) for co-creating the earliest wayfinding workshops at St. John's University that eventually became the transition curriculum I use to support students transitioning from college to career. You, Winnie Li, Rachel Hoffman, Heidy Abdel Kerim, Kenzy Shetta, Ada Lee, Kristin Sluyk, Raquel Paul, Li Wanrong, Linyue Wang, and other former students helped me to see the need for this work and created the space for me to explore these questions at the earliest stages of this research.

On the editorial side, this book would not have been possible without writer, editor, teacher and creative coach Nancy Rawlinson. Nancy, your tireless reading, rereading and brilliant commentary on my proposal and manuscript helped me to make sense of what it was I hoped to say and to discern how best to

share this work and remain true to my own voice. This project would not have seen the light of day without you.

My sincere gratitude to consultant, speaker and author, Tom Goodwin. Tom, your willingness to share my work with Kogan Page helped to facilitate a wonderful working relationship with Commissioning Editor Géraldine Collard. Thanks Géraldine for your kindness, your counsel and for driving a hard bargain on a tight deadline. I could not ask for a better team than you and my other collaborators at Kogan Page. Many thanks one and all.

I am ever so grateful to my Clubhouse community and the members of the Wayfinders Club, whose stories, insights and questions allowed me to flush out my ideas and bring the work to life when Covid had us all at home.

Special thanks to my dear friend Rebecca Taylor for the long walks, generous edits and kind encouragement in the dog days of tight deadlines, and to a.m. Bhatt for social rooms and smart conversation. aJAR will be up and running by the time this book is published and I cannot wait to see where we take it.

Finally, and most importantly, I would like to thank my family. Kelsey—your input, edits and willingness to experiment with me made my research more fun than research should be. I am so glad to have you as a daughter and a friend. My dear Ian, your energy, joy and countless hours of transcription management helped keep me on track and gave me joy when I was in the weeds. To Andrew, our conversations and rides on the Peloton were a breath of fresh air in the writing process. And to my dearest Martin. Thank you for the stunning graphics, for listening to countless hours of me thinking out loud about this work for the better part of a decade. Whether sitting across a table, chatting from the car, or over Zoom from so many writing retreats, your willingness to listen and provide feedback was instrumental to this book becoming what it is. I love you and am so grateful for the space we make for one another to bring our dreams to life.

About the author

Joan Ball is an associate professor of Marketing at St. John's University in New York City and the founder of WOMBLab, a transition services firm. Her research, teaching and consulting focus on the design of systems and processes for lifelong learning, social impact and human flourishing. She is particularly interested in ways individuals and organizations in transition might engage service design strategies, tools and techniques to gather and distribute resources to support inquiry, exploration and wayfinding. She lives in the Hudson Valley of New York with her husband Martin.

Disclosures

Many of the examples, insights and models I use in these pages emerged from my work with individuals, groups and organizations. Some of them are referred to by name in these pages. Others chose to share their stories using a pseudonym or without a name to maintain their anonymity. In all cases, permissions were granted to share stories and insights derived from research and practice.

Index

Page numbers in *italic* indicate figures

action research 130–32
active resilience
  agency and 39
  building 38–40
  community building 39
  context dependence 46
  cultural context 39
  definition of resilience 39
  equipping your toolbox 40–45
  identifying where we perceive
    change as a threat 40–45
  preparing to be resilient 38–40
  resilience wheel 41–45
  resource dependence 46
  resource gathering 39–40
active waiting 68
  creating time for 56–57
  opening space for 54–56
adulting 6
agency
  feeling of 23
  role in resilience 39
aided wayfinding 101–02
anti-fragility concept 38
artificial intelligence 186–87, 188
Ask 79
  benefits of collaboration with
    others 126
  identify possibilities 115–26
  identify the locus of
    possibilities 120–22
  look at everything at once 125–26
  look at ideas without categorizing
    them 118–20
  making sense of new terrain 81–98
  making space for sensemaking
    116–18
  open a transitional learning
    space 23
  pause and gather your pieces
    116–18

  practice dispassionate curiosity 23
  putting everything on the
    altar 122–26
  role of rigorous self-awareness
    88–94
  self-inquiry 91–94
  sensemaking 94–98
  wayfinding 81–98
  wayfinding as sensemaking 96–98
  wayfinding from the outside
    in 99–114
  willingness to let things go 122–26
avoidance, response to disruptions 70

Bateson, Mary Catherine 11, 17, 167
beach scenario exercise 29–32
Bhatt, a.m. 9
bounce back from adversity 38, 39
brain
  metaphors for 52–53
  plasticity of 53
  reticular activating system
    (RAS) 119–20
build, measure, learn framework 50

career paths
  aided wayfinding 101–02
  directed wayfinding 103–04
  unaided wayfinding 101, 102–04
  undirected wayfinding *103*, 104
Carse, James P. vi
Centre for Social Innovation, New York
  beach scenario exercise 29–32
  transition workshops 6
change
  identifying where we perceive it as a
    threat 40–45
  navigating uncertain transitions
    12–14
  role of context in perception
    of 35–36

change management approaches
  applying what we learn 15–17
  gap between ideals and reality
    13–14
  identify the appropriate tools
    14–15
  range of tools 13–17
change myths 35–36
  change and uncertainty are scary 35
  I can't deal with uncertainty, so I'm
    not good at change 35
  some changes are good, and others
    are bad 35
commitments, willingness to let things
  go 122–26
community building, resilience and 39
confidence, approaching
  uncertainty 173–74
Consolidated Edison 20
container metaphor (base camp)
  54–56, 116
context
  role in how change is perceived
    35–36
  understanding 100–01
context-dependence of active
  resilience 46
convergent thinking 150–51
Covid-19 pandemic 5, 97
  global forced pause 182
  What Now? Moments 167–69
cultural context, role in resilience 39
curiosity loop 23, 45, 188, 189
current state mapping (exercise) 92–94

deadlines, time horizons 56–57
decision making
  limitations of the pivot-or-persevere
    choice 50–51
    pressure to make quick decisions 15
  use of solo retreat to help 15–17
deep metaphors 53–54
delight variables 155–57
designing for delight (exercise) 155–57
directed wayfinding 103–04
discernment 73
  at points of inflection 150–51
disjunctions 66–67
disorientation of being lost 67–68

disorienting dilemmas 66–67
dispassion
  concept 37–38
  motivational barrier 160–61
dispassionate curiosity 23, 39, 46,
  68, 95
disruptions
  cause of What Now? Moments
    18–21
  uncertainty caused by 13–14
divergent thinking 150–51

emergencies
  planning for 20–21
  responses to 20–21
emerging adulthood, theory
  of 4–5
emotional response see incendiary
  emotions
entrepreneurship, build, measure, learn
  framework 50
Eurich, Tasha 89
experiment design canvas 133–46
  experiment in practice
    (Jeneanne) 144–46
  experimental approach 142–43
  figuring it out or sussing it
    out 143–44
experimentation 129–46
expertise, role in understanding future
  challenges 33–35
exploration 103, 104
  moving from wayfinding to
    waymaking 150
Explore 127–28
  create opportunities for learning in
    action 23
  designing for delight
    (exercise) 155–57
  discernment at points of
    inflection 150–51
  execution to exploration and back
    again 158
  experiment design canvas 133–46
  from divergent thinking to
    convergent thinking 150–51
  from exploration to execution
    147–58
  learn by doing 129–46

learn, discern, choose, confirm framework 151, 153–57
learning in action 130–32
making space to explore 133

fear loop 23, 45, 66
financial crisis of 2008 4, 5
firefighters, response in high-threat environments 34–35
FOMO (fear of missing out) 7
Frost, Robert 7
future research on navigating change 183

Gatty, Harold 169–70
Gen A 2
Gen X 2
Gen Y see Millennials
getting our bearings, myth of true north 70–73
gig economy 65–66, 102
Gilligan, Tim 112
Google 84

Hill, Kenneth 67
hope 23
    as psychological capital 105
    as willfinding 106
    impact on performance 105
    role in getting your bearings 105–07
hope compass 106–13
    caution on the problem-solving orientation 108
    impact and 165–66
    in action (teamworking in uncertain circumstances) 112
    question for reflection 107
    route from problem to solution 109–12
    things to consider 113
hover-parenting 5
humility, approaching uncertainty 173–74

identity 86
    shift in 69–70
impact funnel 164, 165
incendiary emotions 36–38, 160

caused by shift in identity or role perception 69–70
feeling lost and 66
how you react to What Now? Moments 171–73
response to interruptions and disruptions 18–21
stop to self-regulate 22–23
information sources, questioning 187
inquiry
    intentionally entering into 23, 77, 95
    making space for 19–20
intentional inquiry 23, 77, 95
interruptions, cause of What Now? Moments 18–21

Jam Program 12
journey metaphor 54–56, 116

knee-jerk reactions 22, 33, 182

Langston League 65
learn, discern, choose, confirm framework 151, 153–57, 179–80
learning in action 130–32
    experiment design canvas 133–46
life cycle of skills and capacities 187
life goals
    expanding beyond old paradigms 70–73
    myth of true north 70–73
    pressure to pick a lane 70–71
life stages, stuckness at points of transition 4–7
lifelong learning, untrustworthiness of information 187
lifespan, impacts of living longer 187–88
liminal learning 69–70
liminal space 68–69
LinkedIn 181
locus of possibilities, identifying 120–22
lost
    psychology of being lost 67–68
    walking in circles 169–70
lost in transition, feeling of being 66–67

Magos, Vanessa 148
McKee, Robert 9
metaphors
    container metaphor (base
        camp) 54–56, 116
    cooks in the kitchen 60–61
    deep metaphors 53–54
    in practice 58–63
    influence on perceptions and
        actions 52–54
    journey metaphor 54–56, 116
    midwife metaphor 58–59
    mountain climbing metaphor
        54–56, 57
    personal metaphors to guide
        thoughts and actions
        58–63
    pivot metaphor 49–51
    playing with metaphor
        (exercise) 62–63
    puzzle metaphor 115–16,
        125–26
    reframing uncharted territory
        59–60
    reframing What Now?
        Moments 57–63
    step into the sunshine 61
    universal metaphor types 53–54
mid-life 'sandwich' or 'panini'
    generation 6
Millennials 2
    challenges faced by 4–7
    stereotype of 4–5
    stuckness caused by uncertainty
        and change 4–7
Miro 118
motivation 23
    passions as a source of
        159–61
mountain climbing metaphor
    54–56, 57
Muir, Owen 51, 86
multitasking 49–50
Mural 118, 119

neutral zone 68–69

online whiteboards 118
Owo, Yvette 119–20

participatory action research
    (PAR) 130–32
passion projects 12
passions
    as a source of motivation 159–61
    global/local impacts 162–66
    scale of impact you hope to
        make 162–66
    time to follow your passion 159–66
    see also dispassion
past experience, role in understanding
    future challenges 33–35
personal journeys, wayfinding 82–85
personal stories
    Andrea 87–88, 120–22, 123, 132
    Ashley 11–12, 15–17, 23–24, 71,
        77, 104, 132
    Erica 65–66, 67, 68, 70, 104
    Erin 151–53, 155
    Evan 159–60, 162, 165
    Jeneanne 129–30, 132, 144–46
    Rob 181–82
    Sarah 167–68
    Vérité 148–49
pivoting
    definition of 51
    from exploration to execution
        147–58
    from wayfinding to
        waymaking 151–53, 155
    limitations of the pivot metaphor
        50–51
    origin and meaning of 50
    pivot-or-persevere strategic
        view 50–51
    returning to the journey 149
    whether or not to pivot 49–50
points of inflection, discernment
    at 150–51
possibilities, identify the locus of
    possibilities 120–22
post-traumatic growth 38
preparing for uncertain
    transitions 167–69
preparing for What Now?
    Moments 171–73
problem solving, liminal learning 69–70
professional journeys, wayfinding
    82–85

psychological capital model 105
psychology of being lost 67–68
push back, response to disruptions 70
putting everything on the altar 122–26
puzzle metaphor 115–16, 125–26

quarter-life crisis 6
questions for reflection 154

relationships, putting everything on the
    altar 123–24
resilience *see* active resilience
Resilience Research Centre, Dalhousie
    University, Halifax, Canada 39
resilience wheel 41–45
resource-dependence of active
    resilience 46
resource gathering, role in
    resilience 39–40
Ries, Eric 50
rigorous self-awareness
    importance of 88–90
    in practice 90–94
The Road Not Taken (Frost) 7
role perception, shift in 69–70

Savin-Baden, Maggie 69
self-awareness 72, 88–94, 100–01
self-concept 67
    shift in 69–70
self-direction 67, 86
    skills 104
    threats to 70
self-inquiry 91–94
self-regulation 21–22
self-world fit 51, 86–88
sensemaking 73, 94–98
    look at ideas without categorizing
        them 118–20
    making space for 116–18
    making use of personal
        metaphors 58–63
    puzzle metaphor 115–16
sensemaking tools 118
sensemaking wayfinding 96–98
Shred.Co 159–60, 161, 165
skateboarding 159–60
solo retreat 15–17

Stop
    acknowledge feeling lost and how it
        affects us 66–67
    beach scenario exercise 29–32
    creating time for active waiting
        56–57
    creating transitional learning
        space 68–69
    developing your own approach
        70–73
    don't follow your passion 29–47
    getting our bearings 70–73
    influence of metaphors on perceptions
        and actions 52–54
    learning in liminal space 69–70
    limitations of the pivot-or-persevere
        choice 50–51
    lost in transition 65–78
    marking points of transition 74–77
    opening space for active
        waiting 54–56
    pausing in the face of
        uncertainty 27
    perils of reacting quickly in
        uncertain circumstances 29–32
    practicing stop in a world that
        wants go 32–36
    questions for reflection 75–76
    reactions to the call to stop 32–33
    settle incendiary emotions 22–23
    to self-regulate 21–22
    using metaphors to reframe What
        Now? Moments 57–63
    whether or not to pivot 49–50
Stop, Ask, Explore framework
    helping others with What Now?
        Moments 176
    living in the liminal 177–78
    ongoing process 179–80
    preparation for What Now?
        Moments 21–25
    purpose of the framework 8–9
    wayfinding as a way of life
        179–80
    see also Stop; Ask; Explore
stop, drop and roll, fire safety
    procedure 20, 21
Story (McKee) 9

stuckness
 caused by uncertain transitions
  12–13
 competing priorities and
  commitments 12
 consequence of uncertainty and
  change 4–7
 passions as a source of
  motivation 159–61
 reframing using personal
  metaphors 57–63
 resources for resilience in the face of
  change 38–40

Taylor, Rebecca 61
teachability 73
teams, creating a shared transitional
  learning space 68–69
technology, navigating the changes
  driven by 186–87, 188
third act 6–7
threat response 20–22, 46, 69, 70, 168
 discomfort prompted by threat
  perception 35
 identifying where we perceive
  change as a threat 40–45
thresholds to change, as important
  milestones 74–77
time horizons
 creating time for active waiting
  56–57
 definition of 56
transition, marking points of 74–77
transition workshops 6
transitional learning space 23
 creating 68–69
 marking entry into and exit
  from 74–77
trophy culture 5

unaided wayfinding 101, 102–04
uncertain circumstances
 limited relevance of past
  experience 33–35
 perils of reacting quickly without
  thinking 29–32
uncertain times
 determining how we want to
  live 185–88

end of the "job for life" 1–3
living in uncharted territory 167–80
navigating change 9
navigating the turmoil of the
  2020s 3–4
stuckness caused by 4–7
uncertain transitions
 approach to engaging with 46
 creating transitional learning
  space 68–69
 finding orientation points 86–88
 navigating 12–14
 pressure to make quick decisions 15
 space between What Now? and
  what comes next 17–18
undirected wayfinding 103, 104
Unger, Michael 39, 46

visual sensemaking tools 118

wayfinder's framework 188, 189
wayfinding 73
 aided wayfinding 101–02
 approach to using tools and
  tactics 104–05
 as a practice 104–05
 as a way of life 179–80
 as sensemaking 96–98
 community of wayfinders 184–85
 definition of 81
 determining how we want to
  live 185–88
 directed wayfinding 103–04
 embracing a practice 174–75
 experience of Rob Freer 181–82
 from the outside in 99–114
 fundamentals 101–02
 hidden influences 85
 hope compass 106–13
 impact of the Covid-19
  pandemic 182
 in a changing world 85–86
 more than just common sense
  85–86
 moving from ideals to action
  99–101
 moving to waymaking 150, 151–53
 professional and personal
  journeys 82–85

puzzle metaphor 115–16
rigorous self-awareness 100–01
role of hope in getting your
    bearings 105–07
self-world fit and 86–88
skills and tools for 83–85
types of wayfinders 81–82
unaided wayfinding 101, 102–04
understanding the context 100–01
undirected wayfinding 103, 104
walking in circles 169–70
zooming in and zooming out 97–98
wayfinding mindset 170
confidence and humility required to
    approach uncertainty 173–74
how you react to What Now?
    Moments 171–73
preparing for What Now?
    Moments 171–73
waymaking 150, 151–53
What Now? Moments
approach to facing 44–46
assessing your resources to respond
    to 40–45
beach scenario exercise 29–32
Covid-19 pandemic 167–69
definition of 18, 19
destabilizing effects of interruptions
    and disruptions 18–21
follow your dispassion 37–38
getting fired from work 36–38
helping others with 176
hope compass 106–13
incendiary emotional response
    to 18–21
life in uncharted territory 167–80

limitations of the pivot-or-persevere
    choice 50–51
making space for inquiry 19–20
pausing in the face of
    uncertainty 27
preparing for 171–73
reducing the sense of urgency and
    threat 54–56
reframing using metaphors
    57–63
resilience wheel 41–45
stop to self-regulate 21–22
using stop, ask, and explore to
    prepare for 21–25
your reactions to 171–73
willfinding, hope as 106
willingness to let things go
    122–26
WOMBLab 59
work
end of the 'job for life' 1–3
getting fired as a What Now?
    Moment 36–38
reorientation of priorities
    around 181–84

Zaltman, Gerald 53–54
ZMET™ technique 53
zooming in
rigorous self-awareness 88–94,
    100–01
wayfinding 97–98
zooming out
understanding the context
    100–01
wayfinding 97–98

CPSIA information can be obtained
at www.ICGtesting.com
Printed in the USA
JSHW011244100622
26897JS00015B/117